METAPHYSICAL

Some of the most eminent and enduring philosophical questions concern matters of priority: what is prior to what? What 'grounds' what? Is, for instance, matter prior to mind? Recently, a vivid debate has arisen about how such questions have to be understood. Can the relevant notion or notions of priority be spelled out? And how do they relate to other metaphysical notions, such as modality, truth-making, or essence? This volume of new essays, by leading figures in contemporary metaphysics, is the first to address and investigate the metaphysical idea that certain facts are grounded in other facts. An introduction introduces and surveys the debate, examining its history as well as its central systematic aspects. The volume will be of wide interest to students and scholars of metaphysics.

FABRICE CORREIA is Associate Professor at the Philosophy Department of the University of Geneva. He is the author of *Existential Dependence and Cognate Notions* (2005) and *As Time Goes By: Eternal Facts in an Ageing Universe* (with Sven Rosenkranz; 2011).

BENJAMIN SCHNIEDER is Professor of Philosophy at the University of Hamburg. He is the author of *Substanz und Adhärenz – Bolzanos Ontologie des Wirklichen* (2002) and *Substanzen und (ihre) Eigenschaften* (2004).

METAPHYSICAL GROUNDING

Understanding the Structure of Reality

EDITED BY

FABRICE CORREIA
University of Geneva

BENJAMIN SCHNIEDER
University of Hamburg

CAMBRIDGE
UNIVERSITY PRESS

CAMBRIDGE
UNIVERSITY PRESS

University Printing House, Cambridge CB2 8BS, United Kingdom

Cambridge University Press is part of the University of Cambridge.

It furthers the University's mission by disseminating knowledge in the pursuit of education, learning and research at the highest international levels of excellence.

www.cambridge.org
Information on this title: www.cambridge.org/9781107460287

© Cambridge University Press 2012

First published 2012
Reprinted 2013
First paperback edition 2014

A catalogue record for this publication is available from the British Library

Library of Congress Cataloguing in Publication data

Metaphysical grounding: understanding the structure of reality / [edited by] Fabrice Correia, Benjamin Schnieder.
pages cm
Includes bibliographical references and index.
ISBN 978-1-107-02289-8
1. A priori.   2. Knowledge, Theory of.   3. Metaphysics.
I. Correia, Fabrice.   II. Schnieder, Benjamin.
BD181.3.M48 2012
110–dc23
2012014618

ISBN 978-1-107-02289-8 Hardback
ISBN 978-1-107-46028-7 Paperback

Contents

Contributors

FABRICE CORREIA, Associate Professor of Philosophy at the University of Geneva.

BENJAMIN SCHNIEDER, Professor of Theoretical Philosophy at the University of Hamburg.

PAUL AUDI, Assistant Professor of Philosophy at the University of Nebraska at Omaha.

JODY AZZOUNI, Professor of Philosophy at Tufts University.

STEPHEN BARKER, Associate Professor and Reader in Philosophy at the University of Nottingham.

CHRIS DALY, Professor of Philosophy at the University of Manchester.

MICHAEL DELLA ROCCA, Andrew Downey Orrick Professor of Philosophy at Yale University.

KIT FINE, Silver Professor of Philosophy and Mathematics and Professor of Philosophy at New York University.

KATHRIN KOSLICKI, Associate Professor of Philosophy at the University of Colorado.

DAVID LIGGINS, Senior Lecturer in Philosophy at the University of Manchester.

E. J. LOWE, Professor of Philosophy at Durham University.

JONATHAN SCHAFFER, Professor of Philosophy at Rutgers University.

J. ROBERT G. WILLIAMS, Professor of Theoretical Philosophy at the University of Leeds.

Grounding: an opinionated introduction

Fabrice Correia and Benjamin Schnieder

I   GROUNDING INTRODUCED

Some of the most important questions in philosophy, we believe, concern
matters of priority. Here is a list of priority claims which have been held
in different areas of philosophy:

1. Mental facts obtain because of neurophysiological facts.
2. Legal facts are grounded in non-legal, e.g. social, facts.
3. Normative facts are based on natural facts.
4. Meaning is due to non-semantic facts.
5. Dispositional properties are possessed in virtue of categorical properties.
6. What accounts for the existence of a whole is the existence and
   arrangement of its parts.
7. A set of things is less fundamental than its members.
8. What makes something beautiful are certain facts about the reception
   of its beholders.
9. A substance is prior to its tropes or modes.
10. That snow is white is true because snow is white.

What concerns us here is not so much whether these specific claims are
true, but rather something they have in common topic-wise: it seems to us
that they all target a particular sort of non-causal priority which we would
like to call *grounding* and which we regard as a phenomenon of the highest
philosophical importance.

This volume collects papers in which this phenomenon is addressed
from various (both sympathetic and critical) sides. Summaries of those
papers are provided in Section 6 of this introduction. But first, we want to
walk you through an opinionated survey of pertinent issues, preparing the
field and putting the papers into perspective.

While the recent debate about grounding is not older than a decade,
the topic has been dealt with before. So, we start by briefly walking

I

through some important stages of the history of grounding. We then devote two sections on systematic issues, one on the theory of grounding proper, and one on its connections with other notions.[1]

2   A VERY SHORT HISTORY OF GROUNDING

For reasons of space, we are bound to comment on a highly selective choice of authors and issues here and we have to set aside many interesting sources. One important victim of this policy is Aristotle. His distinction between four different kinds of *aitiai* – or *becauses*, as Hocutt (1974) puts it – arguably involves the recognition of grounding in the formal and the material *aitiai*. If this is correct, then his theory of *aitiai*, as well as his related distinction between proofs which demonstrate that something is the case and proofs which demonstrate why something is the case, are important historical sources for treatments of grounding. But the interpretation of Aristotle's works is usually very controversial and we felt we lacked the space – and, frankly speaking, the confidence – to enter the discussion. Instead, for this historical excursion we focus on (a) the Euthyphro Argument, (b) the Principle of Sufficient Reason, and (c) Bernard Bolzano's theory of grounding.

2.1   The Euthyphro Argument

One of the earliest occasions on which the phenomenon of grounding has been dealt with is Plato's *Euthyphro* dialogue, in which Socrates inquires about the nature of piety. In response to the Socratic question – 'What is the pious?' – Euthyphro first announces that what he himself is doing is pious, namely to persecute the wrongdoer even if that means to persecute his own father. As Socrates explains, this is not the *kind* of answer he requested:

Call to mind that this is not what I asked you, to tell me one or two of the many pious acts, but to tell the essential aspect, in virtue of which all pious acts are pious; for you said that there is a single aspect by which all impious acts are impious and all pious ones pious. (*Euthyphro*, Stephanus page 6d)

Socrates here makes a demand which is typical for the early dialogues: he wants to be given a general answer, not an exemplary one. He wants to

---

[1] For further reading we recommend a survey article by Trogdon (forthcoming). While his paper naturally has some overlap with ours, he often has a different focus so that the two papers complement each other.

know conditions under which *any* given thing is pious. But he requires more; he does not want to know *any* sort of condition, he wants to be told the aspect *by* which, or *in virtue of* which, a pious thing is pious. The Socratic question, hence, aims at the *ground* of piety.

Socrates later uses considerations about grounding in his argument against Euthyphro's central proposal, i.e. that

EU   the pious is the god-beloved.

He and Euthyphro agree that

(1) If something is loved by the gods, it is loved by them because it is pious.

They conclude that the converse claim is false and agreed on:

(2) It is not because the gods love something that it is pious.

The inference from (1) to (2) is not commented on; apparently, Socrates and Euthyphro implicitly rely on the assumption that 'because' (or, as we would like to put it here, grounding) behaves asymmetrically.

They also agree that

(3) If something is god-beloved, it is so because the gods love it.

So they conclude that the converse claim fails, hence agreeing on:

(4) It is not because something is god-beloved that it is loved by the gods.

Why do Socrates and Euthyphro hold (3), though? Commentators have found it rather hard to make good sense of that claim. Of the many interpretations which have been suggested, one is noteworthy in the present context: with (3), Socrates wants to make the plausible grounding claim that something has a relational property (it is god-beloved) because it stands to something in a certain relation (it is loved by the gods).[2]

On the basis of claims (1) to (4), Socrates concludes that Euthyphro missed his goal and that EU must be rejected. For, Euthyphro produced EU as a reply to the question in virtue of what a pious thing is pious. Hence, it commits him to accept the claim that

(5) If something is pious, it is pious because it is god-beloved.

[2] See Allen 1970, 40.

In conjunction with (3), Socrates holds, it then follows that

(6) If something is pious, it is pious because the gods love it.

But how is this inference warranted? Answer: it implicitly relies on the assumption that 'because'-statements allow for chaining – put differently: on the assumption that grounding is transitive.

Now claim (6) contradicts claim (2) on which Euthyphro already agreed.[3] Socrates concludes that Euthyphro's proposal fails.

Construed this way, Socrates' argument makes essential use of principles about grounding. It involves one substantive grounding claim (relational properties are grounded in relations) and it implicitly draws on structural properties of grounding, namely asymmetry and transitivity, which are nowadays widely accepted among philosophers working on grounding.[4]

2.2 The Principle of Sufficient Reason

The *Principle of Sufficient Reason* (for short: *PSR*) says, in its simplest form, that everything has a reason. In the rationalist tradition the *PSR* was often regarded as one of the highest laws of thought. Initiated by Leibniz's works, there was a vivid debate about how to prove it and about its proper understanding and its applications (the debate petered out in the nineteenth century).

That debate is not easily accessible. Contributions to it are phrased in theoretical frameworks which are unfamiliar to modern readers, and they often employ concepts which seem insufficiently clear or sophisticated to us. But still, we deem it worthwhile to re-evaluate the discussion in light of the recent interest in grounding.[5]

Rationalists often distinguished different notions of a reason, some of which arguably aimed at the notion of a ground; and they distinguished different versions of the *PSR*, some of which accordingly aimed at principles about grounding. Two distinctions commonly appearing in the debate concerned

D.1   a. reasons of concrete things (substances and their modes)
versus
b. reasons of truths.

---

[3] For this take on the argument, see Sharvy 1972.
[4] Note that some introductions to philosophy boil the argument down to the requirement that we have to make a choice about which of the following is prior: that something is pious, or that it is loved by the gods. But Plato's own version is far more complex. Above we wanted to provide a brief reconstruction of the argument as it actually appears in Plato's dialogue.
[5] So does Della Rocca in his contribution to this volume.

(The former reasons were either equated with causes, or regarded as closely connected to them.)

D.2   a. objective reasons for a thing or fact *versus*
       b. reasons for knowing about it.

While the distinctions D.1 and D.2 were sometimes treated as if they were the same distinction put in different words, several philosophers argued that they must be kept apart. Against the identification of objective reasons with reasons of concrete things, Crusius and Schopenhauer both stressed that we must acknowledge objective reasons in the field of mathematics:[6] many mathematical entities and/or facts have reasons in being determined by others, while such things do not stand in causal relations to each other. And the young Kant complained that reasons for truth were sometimes regarded as mere reasons for knowledge.[7] Against that, he stressed the need to acknowledge reasons which *bring about* that something is true.[8] But those reasons do not coincide with reasons for knowing a truth, since the latter are only reasons of discovering a truth which must have been brought about independently. We can make sense of those claims in terms of grounding: Crusius and Schopenhauer drew attention to grounding relations between mathematical facts while Kant wanted to know what grounds the truth of a truth-bearer.

What is perhaps most puzzling about the rationalist tradition is the steadfast certainty with which the *PSR* was often accepted. For the *PSR* in effect denies that there are fundamental facts, i.e. facts that are not grounded by anything else. And most philosophers nowadays would agree that it is quite debatable whether or not there are such facts.

The rationalist stance may be even more surprising if we consider the arguments that were produced in favour of the *PSR*. Many of them look suspiciously like textbook examples of a fallacy (sometimes even of more than one). To cite but one example, a famous argument in the Wolffian school ran as follows:[9]

P.1   If the *PSR* fails, there must be some *x* which lacks a reason.
P.2   If *x* lacks a reason, then nothing is the reason of *x*.
P.3   However, nothing (that is, the void) cannot be the reason of anything.
C   Hence, the *PSR* holds.

---

[6] See Crusius 1743 and Schopenhauer 1813.   [7] See Kant 1755.
[8] Such a reason seems to be stated by sentence (10) from our list in Section 1.
[9] It is a slightly simplified version of Baumgarten 1757, §20.

The argument involves the very logical mistake for which Carnap later famously criticized Heidegger;[10] in premise P.3 it violates logical grammar and erroneously construes the quantifier 'nothing' as a singular term.

Of course, some rationalists soon realized the flaws of such fallacious arguments. But instead of consequently withholding assent from the principle, many of them rather sided with Leibniz, who famously claimed that the *PSR* is such an evident and fundamental truth that it would be a folly to ask for an argument in its favour.[11]

Perhaps we have to regard it as a genuine paradigm change that some hundred years ago, many prominent philosophers were so convinced of the *PSR* that they felt unable to understand how one could question it, while nowadays even friends of the *PSR* would hardly regard it as a principle beyond reasonable doubt.[12]

2.3   Bernard Bolzano's theory of grounding

Bolzano's work is a genuine milestone in the history of grounding. He developed a very rich and detailed theory of grounding, addressing numerous issues pertinent to the recent debate.[13] We will briefly describe some cornerstones of his account.

Bolzano conceived of propositions as abstract objects which are structured compounds of concepts and potential contents of judgements and assertions. He thought that we can make out an objective order among true propositions: some truths are the objective grounds of others (their consequences). The importance of discovering this order can, according to Bolzano, hardly be overestimated. He even argued that it is characteristic of a genuinely philosophical inquiry that it be concerned with the grounds of things, relying on an admittedly broad notion of philosophical inquiry, distinguished not so much by a particular subject matter but rather by a method or focus.[14] On his view, one can approach basically every subject matter (be it mathematics, politics, or physics) in a non-philosophical or a philosophical mood, depending on whether one only collects the facts of the matter or whether one also tries to understand their grounding structures. For instance, mathematical proofs are philosophical in method if they do not only demonstrate

---

[10] See Carnap 1931, 229f. Of course, the mistake had been recognized before; it is made fun of, for instance, in the dialogue between Alice and the King in *Through the Looking-Glass*.

[11] See Leibniz's fifth letter to Clarke, §§125ff. in Alexander 1956.

[12] For a recent attempt to defend the *PSR*, see Della Rocca 2010.

[13] For his mature theory of grounding, see Bolzano 1837, vol. II, §§168, 177, 198–222. All further references to sections are to 1837, vol. II. See also Tatzel 2002 for a reconstruction of its essentials.

[14] See Bolzano 1838.

that a certain mathematical truth holds but if they also disclose *why* it holds, that is, if they uncover its grounds. In fact, a major source for Bolzano's interest in grounding was his dissatisfaction with many available proofs in mathematics which often ran against the order of grounding.[15]

But let us turn to Bolzano's theory of grounding. He was inclined to think that the notion of 'groundhood', i.e. that property which makes something a ground, cannot be analysed in terms of other notions (§202),[16] even though he thought it can be illuminated by specifying its properties and by relating it to other notions.

First, some comparisons. On the negative side, Bolzano distinguished grounding from mere entailment, presenting pairs of propositions which stand in a mutual entailment relation, though not in a mutual grounding relation (e.g. that birds fly and that it is true that birds fly) (§§162, 198). He also distinguished objective grounds from reasons for knowing something; they may run in opposite directions, since sometimes we can discover a ground from observing its consequences (§198). On the positive side, he correlated talk about grounding to talk about dependence and talk about *making* something thus-and-so. And, most importantly, he took the sentential connective 'because' to introduce the notion of grounding: a sentence '*p* because *q*' is true iff the proposition expressed by '*q*' is a ground of the proposition expressed by '*p*' (§177). Note that Bolzano generally saw no problem in attributing a logical form to a sentence which strongly deviated from its surface form. So, since he conceived of grounding as a relation, he took the underlying logical form of grounding statements always to be a relational one, even if their surface form may look otherwise (e.g. involving a sentential connective instead of a relational predicate).

Second, some properties of grounding. Bolzano distinguished between complete and partial grounds and consequences (truths grounded in something): a complete ground of *x* can consist of several propositions, such that each of them then counts as a partial ground of *x* (the application of the distinction to the notion of a consequence is obvious). One might be tempted to think, Bolzano admitted, that a ground is always a single proposition, so that whenever several propositions *x*, *x'*, . . . seem to ground *y*, it is really the conjunction of *x*, *x'*, . . . that grounds *y*. However, the temptation should be resisted: a true conjunction is certainly itself a grounded truth, Bolzano argued, and it is grounded in its conjuncts. But a

---

[15] See Bolzano 1810.
[16] However, at one point (§221, note) he expresses sympathy with an analysis which approaches the notion in a somewhat holistic fashion; compare Mancosu 1999, 435f. and 451f.

conjunction cannot be grounded in the conjunction of its conjuncts, since then it would ground itself, which seems absurd (§205).

Bolzano furthermore distinguished between immediate and mediate grounds and consequences: a mediate ground of *x* is a ground of a ground of *x*, or a ground of a ground of a ground of *x*, etc. (again, the application of the distinction to the notion of a consequence is obvious) (§213).

The different notions of ground and consequence are clearly not independent of each other; Bolzano tentatively thought that the basic notion in that family is that of a complete and immediate ground, whereas the other notions are derivative of that basic one.

Bolzano attributed some crucial structural features to grounding (in all its varieties):

FACTIVITY   Grounding connects only true propositions. (§203)
IRREFLEXIVITY No proposition is a ground of itself. (§204)
ASYMMETRY   If *x* is a ground of *y*, then *y* is no ground of *x*. (§209)

(In fact, Irreflexivity is already entailed by Asymmetry.)

Bolzano finally considered the further structural property of

TRANSITIVITY   If *x* grounds *y*, and *y* grounds *z*, then *x* grounds *z*.

With respect to this property he held that mediate and immediate grounding come apart: the former is transitive while the latter is not (§213). Bolzano thought that the *PSR*, understood as a principle about grounding, fails and that there are fundamental, ungrounded truths. He based his belief mainly on some truths which seemed fundamental to him. At least the example he presents when making his claim is highly questionable from our perspective: it is the truth that something exists (§214). The example is on the wrong track if, what seems plausible to us, existential claims are grounded in their true instances.[17] Then far from being fundamental, Bolzano's example has numerous – arguably even an infinity – of grounds (e.g. that Bolzano exists, that Frege exists, etc.).[18]

Bolzano's views on grounding evolved over a long period of time. One crucial change in the way he thought about grounding concerns its relata: in his early works, he employed a multi-categorial notion of grounding.[19]

---

[17] See, e.g., Correia 2005, 59, Rosen 2010, Schnieder 2011, and Fine's contribution to this volume.
[18] In addition to such examples, Bolzano had one independent argument for the existence of fundamental truths (§221.3). It is based on substantial presuppositions, though, which we cannot discuss here for reasons of space.
[19] See Bolzano 1810–12.

Grounds could be of any ontological category, they could be substances, modes, propositions, or anything else. Relatedly, he then subsumed under the relation of grounding such relations as causation, dependence, and making something-thus-and-so (including truth-making), all of whose relata he called grounds and consequences. Later, though, he sharply distinguished grounding as a relation between truths from relations holding between things of other categories. But although he thus separated certain relations which he first threw together, he still took them to be intimately connected; in fact, he took the other relations to be definable in terms of grounding.

Take causation and grounding.[20] The mature Bolzano acknowledged that they are relations holding between different relata (grounding: truths, causation: concrete entities). But causation always goes together with true 'because'-statements (causal explanations) and Bolzano thought that 'because' always signifies the grounding relation. So he concluded that causation always corresponds to true grounding claims. This is a connection which needs to be accounted for, and Bolzano proposed to understand causation in terms of grounding: causes and effects are the objects featuring in grounding statements of a particular sort, in which the actual existence or occurrence of an entity explains that of another (e.g. the fire occurred because the collision did).

2.4 The decline of grounding

Bolzano's contribution looks very modern in many respects; in fact, it may seem as if the current debate took up where Bolzano left the issue more than 150 years ago. What happened in between? Bolzano's own work on the subject had been mostly ignored until recently. And indeed, after the debate on the *PSR* slowly petered out in the nineteenth century, engagement with the notion of grounding strongly decreased, until philosophy basically turned silent on the issue for decades. Several factors played a role in the decline of grounding. For one, due to the influence of the declaredly anti-metaphysical Vienna Circle, the metaphysical aspect of grounding must have seemed suspicious to many philosophers. Somewhat later, Quine's influence and his scepticism about non-extensional ideology probably scared off others from the notion. Another factor was that debates about reasons and 'because' were generally delegated to the theory of science, while that discipline strongly focused on scientific explanations and in particular on causal ones. Moreover, the

---

[20] On the following, see §201. For a detailed discussion of how Bolzano relates causation and grounding, see Schnieder forthcoming.

dominant approaches in the early analytic debate about explanation (in particular Hempel and Oppenheim's D-N model) were framed in decidedly non-metaphysical terms.

But even when metaphysics started to become respectable again, in particular due to the development of modal logic, it took time for the notion of grounding to resurface. For, in the heyday of modal logic, philosophers typically tried to account for any metaphysical notions in modal terms. But it is nowadays commonly acknowledged that this approach will not get us far with the notion of grounding (see Sections 3.2 and 4.1 below). In effect, a serious interest in grounding only arose again at the beginning of the twenty-first century.

3   SYSTEMATIC ISSUES I: ASPECTS OF THE PURE THEORY OF GROUNDING

Leaving the history of grounding behind, we now want to take a closer look at some systematic issues of a theory of grounding, a number of which were already touched upon in the historical walk-through. In the present section, we comment on four selected issues we take to be central for what could be called a pure theory of grounding. In the fourth section, we will turn to the connections between grounding and some related metaphysical notions of contemporary interest.

3.1   Formulation

As the list of claims of ground in Section 1 suggests, there are various grammatical forms such claims can take. While these claims might still share a common underlying or logical form, this seems somewhat unlikely to us.[21] But even if their logical forms differ, one of those forms may be taken to be 'canonical', in the sense of being the most faithful to the phenomenon described. The issue here is what we should assume such a canonical form to look like. Or, to use a different metaphor: by what grammatical form would grounding be expressed in a fundamental language that could be used to write the 'book of the world'?[22]

People have been mainly attracted towards two views, the *predicational* view and the *operational* view.[23] On the first view, claims of ground

---

[21] Pace Bolzano (see above).   [22] Cf. Sider 2011.

[23] There is a third, mixed view we do not discuss here, which takes seriously the form '*p* in virtue of the fact that *q*'.

should ultimately be formulated by means of a relational predicate, e.g. 'is grounded in', flanked by singular terms for entities of some sort. The most common view among predicationalists is that the relata of grounding are facts or propositions. A typical grounding claim would then look as follows:

(1) The fact that it is true that snow is white is grounded in the fact that snow is white.

On the second view, claims of ground should, on the ultimate level, rather be formulated by means of a sentential connective or operator, e.g. 'because' (taken in an appropriate sense), flanked by sentential expressions, as in:

(2) It is true that snow is white because snow is white.

Because it presupposes an ontology of facts or propositions, the predicational view is ontologically demanding and for some this is reason enough to opt for the operational view.[24]

However, it might be thought that predicationalists are in a better position than operationalists when it comes to formulating certain claims or defining certain notions. For consider the following definition of fundamentality:

(3) Fact f is fundamental iff$_{df.}$ there is no g such that f is grounded in g.

In the *definiens*, 'there is no g' is a standard quantifier which binds the nominal variable 'g'. The closest operationalists can get is something like:

(4) It is fundamental that p iff$_{df.}$ there is no q such that p because q,

where 'there is no q' is a quantified expression binding the sentential variable 'q'. Yet, some might say, such quantifiers are unintelligible. More generally, the thought is that only quantification into nominal position is legitimate, and that for this reason the operational language

---

[24] As we saw, Bolzano was a predicationalist (already on the level of logical form). Recent philosophers who also use the predicational idiom include Schaffer (2009b) and Rosen (2010), and philosophers who prefer the operational mode of expression include Fine (2001, this volume), Correia, and Schnieder. Notice that, like the early Bolzano and many philosophers in the traditional debate about the *PSR*, Schaffer imposes no restriction at all on the ontological category of the *relata* of his relation of grounding.

is less expressive than the predicational language. The operationalist may reply that the objection rests on a mistaken view about quantification, and argue that quantification into sentential position is perfectly legitimate.[25]

Another important issue about the formulation of claims of ground concerns their 'adicity'. Assuming the predicational mode of formulation, the issue is whether we should view all claims of ground as being of the form:

(5) f is grounded in g,

or whether we should allow the second position of the predicate for grounding to be filled in with plural terms, as in:

(6) f is grounded in g, g', and g''

and in:

(7) f is grounded in the facts which Φ.

A standard argument for the second option is that there can be cases where several facts *together* ground a further fact. For instance, the conjunctive fact that $2 + 2 = 4$ & Socrates was a philosopher seems to be grounded in the fact that $2 + 2 = 4$ *and* the fact that Socrates is a philosopher *taken jointly*.[26]

The issue also arises if we assume the operational mode of formulation. The question here is whether we should view all claims of ground as being of the form:

(8) p because q,

or whether we should allow the second position of the sentential operator to be filled in with sentential analogues of plural terms, for instance lists of sentential expressions as in:

(9) p because q, q', and q''.

It may be argued that the second option is preferable, for reasons similar to those invoked in the previous case. Notice that going for this option implies a departure from common ways of speaking, at least if it is granted that the English sentential operator 'because' is strictly binary.

---

[25] See, e.g., Prior 1971, 34–39, and Williamson 1999, §2.
[26] As we stressed above, Bolzano (1837, §205) already gave such an argument.

3.2 Primitive or analysable?

Can grounding be understood in different terms? It is perhaps tempting to believe that grounding can be analysed in modal terms, e.g. along the lines of:

(1) f is grounded in $g, g', \ldots$ iff$_{\mathrm{df.}}$ $g, g', \ldots$ all obtain, and necessarily (f obtains if $g, g', \ldots$ do)

or of:

(2) p because $q, q', \ldots$ iff$_{\mathrm{df.}}$ q & q' & $\ldots$, and necessarily (p if q & q' & $\ldots$),

where 'necessarily' is appropriately understood. Yet, as has often been noted, these accounts fail. One standard objection against (2) is that it predicts the truth of all instances of 'p because q' where 'p' is necessarily true and 'q' is true. But some such instances are clearly false, like for instance '$2 + 2 = 4$ because Socrates was a philosopher' or '(if Socrates was a philosopher, then he was a philosopher) because dodos are extinct'.

This objection invokes cases where 'p' holds of necessity and the relationship between the truth of 'p' and the truth of 'q' is immaterial. Another standard objection, different on these two counts, is to the effect that (2) predicts the truth of all instances of 'p because (p & q)' where 'p & q' is true, whereas it is plausible to hold that some (indeed, *all*) of these instances are false. Of course, similar objections can be mounted against (1).

(1) and (2) are only two particular accounts of grounding framed in terms of (some notion of) necessity and the truth-functional connectives (plus, in the case of the first account, the notion of obtainment). Yet there is a general consensus to the effect that no account of this type can be satisfactory. As Bolzano did, most contemporary philosophers even rest content with the view that the concept of grounding cannot be analysed in other terms.[27]

---

[27] See, e.g., Bolzano 1837, Schaffer 2009b, Rosen 2010, and Fine's contribution to this volume. (on Bolzano, see however also footnote 16). Correia (forthcoming b) argues that the prospects of an account of grounding in terms of the concept of essence are not as bad as Fine thinks, but without taking a definitive stand on the issue.

3.3   Granularity

There appears to be a consensus to the effect that grounding is *hyperintensional*,[28] in the sense that the following two schemas have false instances:

(1) If the fact that p is grounded in $g, g', \ldots$ and as a matter of logical necessity, p iff r, then the fact that r is grounded in $g, g', \ldots$

(2) If f is grounded in the fact that $q, g', \ldots$ and as a matter of logical necessity, q iff r, then f is grounded in the fact that $r, g', \ldots$

– or, if we assume the operational instead of the predicational mode of formulation, in the sense that the following two schemas have false instances:

(3) If p because $q, q', \ldots$ and as a matter of logical necessity, p iff r, then r because $q, q', \ldots$

(4) If p because $q, q', \ldots$ and as a matter of logical necessity, q iff r, then p because $r, q', \ldots$

As an illustration, although it is plausible to hold that the fact that {Socrates} exists is grounded in the fact that Socrates exists, one may deny that the first fact is grounded in the fact that (Socrates exists or some tree is not a tree) and that the second fact grounds the fact that ({Socrates} exists and every tree is a tree).

Holding that grounding is hyperintensional is not to deny that grounding is subject to closure principles other than (1)–(4). One may still wish to hold, for instance, that all the instances of the following two schemas, where 'a' and 'b' are to be replaced by directly referring singular terms, are true:

(5) If the fact that $F(a)$ is grounded in $g, g', \ldots$ and $a = b$, then the fact that $F(b)$ is grounded in $g, g', \ldots$

(6) If f is grounded in the fact that $F(a), g', \ldots$ and $a = b$, then f is grounded in the fact that $F(b), g', \ldots$

– or again, that all the instances of the following schemas are true:

(7) If the fact that $\neg(p \lor q)$ is grounded in $g, g', \ldots$, then the fact that $(\neg p \land \neg q)$ is grounded in $g, g', \ldots$

(8) If f is grounded in the fact that $\neg(p \lor q), g', \ldots$, then f is grounded in the fact that $(\neg p \land \neg q), g', \ldots$

---

[28] Our current use of 'hyperintensional' is non-standard, since the adjective is usually reserved for linguistic expressions rather than for notions or concepts.

One important question is: Exactly which closure principles should be accepted?

By the Indiscernibility of Identicals, predicationalists are bound to accept (all instances of) the following two principles:[29]

(9) If f is grounded in $g, g', \ldots$ and $f = h$, then h is grounded in $g, g', \ldots$

(10) If f is grounded in $g, g', \ldots$ and $g = h$, then f is grounded in $h, g', \ldots$.

Taking (9) and (10) for granted, one may ask when statements of identity between facts hold. In particular, there is the important question: Under which conditions is a statement of type 'the fact that $p =$ the fact that q' true?

There is disagreement on this issue of factual identity. The disagreement concerns the "granularity" of facts, the question of how fine-grained they are.[30] To illustrate, consider the following identities:

(11) The fact that Sam is a bachelor = the fact that Sam is an unmarried man.

(12) The fact that a is a water molecule = the fact that a is an H_2O molecule.

Are they true or not? There are several coherent ways to go. Consider the following two views about the facts referred to in (11) and (12):

View I. These facts are complexes composed of two items, an individual and a *property*. Their components are as follows:

	Individual	Property
The fact that Sam is a bachelor	Sam	Being a bachelor
The fact that Sam is an unmarried man	Sam	Being an unmarried man
The fact that a is a water molecule	a	Being a water molecule
The fact that a is an H_2O molecule	a	Being an H_2O molecule

[29] At least if the application conditions of the predicate 'ground' depend only on what objects are denoted by its argument terms – which may seem a desirable feature for a predicate used in metaphysics. However, one should be aware that natural language expressions that are used to talk about grounding might fail to meet this standard. They might sometimes be sensitive not only to what is denoted by their argument terms, but also to features of those terms themselves; cf. Schnieder 2010. The above discussion should be understood as operating with an idealized vocabulary which is sensitive only to the referents of the argument terms.

[30] For instance, Correia (2010) puts forward a view on which the *relata* of the relation of grounding are significantly less fine-grained than on the views advocated by Rosen (2010) and Fine (this volume).

View II. These facts are complexes composed of two items, an individual and a *concept*. Their components are as follows:

	Individual	Concept
The fact that Sam is a bachelor	Sam	BACHELOR
The fact that Sam is an unmarried man	Sam	UNMARRIED MAN
The fact that a is a water molecule	a	WATER MOLECULE
The fact that a is an H_2O molecule	a	H_2O MOLECULE

It is natural, on these views, to hold that any two of these facts are identical iff they share their individual components and their other component (property or concept, as the case may be). We guess that a number of philosophers are attracted to the view that the property of being a water molecule and the property of being an H_2O molecule are identical, whereas the concept WATER MOLECULE and the concept H_2O MOLECULE are distinct. If this is taken for granted, then on View I (12) is true while on View II it is not. We also guess that, in contrast, a number of philosophers believe that the property of being a bachelor and the property of being an unmarried man are identical, and that the same goes for the corresponding concepts. If this is taken for granted, then (11) is true on both View I and View II. Yet there is room for conceptions of properties or concepts as more fine-grained, on which some of the properties or concepts deemed identical above are in fact distinct.

Similar questions arise on the operational view. In this case, though, questions regarding factual *identity* are replaced by questions regarding factual *equivalence*. Thus, instead of principles (9) and (10), operationalists will accept certain principles of the following form:

(13) If p because $q, q', \ldots$ and $p \approx r$, then r because $q, q', \ldots$
(14) If p because $q, q', \ldots$ and $q \approx r$, then p because $r, q', \ldots$,

where the sentential operator '$\approx$' expresses factual equivalence. They then face the task of characterizing the relevant notion of factual equivalence. Here issues of granularity arise in the same way as before, this time about factual equivalence rather than facts.

Although some work on closure principles for grounding already exists,[31] much remains to be done – in particular on the varieties of views which may be put forward, and on which approach, if any, is preferable.

---

[31] See Correia 2010, Schnieder 2010, Fine 2012a, and Fine's contribution to this volume.

3.4 Logic

Another field where much remains to be done is the logic of grounding. We can distinguish between the pure and the impure logic of grounding.[32] Principles of the *pure* logic of grounding concern the question of which grounding claims follow from which, without considering the logical structure of what is said to ground or to be grounded. What belongs to this part of the logic of grounding are, for instance, the structural principles of asymmetry, transitivity, and factivity mentioned earlier in this introduction. In fact, these principles form part of all existing systematic approaches to the pure (but also to the impure) logic of grounding.[33]

The *impure* logic of grounding extends the pure logic by taking into account the logical complexity of the sentences that are used to state what grounds and what is grounded. For instance, it may investigate how sentences involving truth-functors, quantifiers, or modal operators behave in the scope of a grounding operator. Let us briefly comment on existing approaches to the connections between grounding and classical truth-functors, as well as grounding and classical quantifiers.

The guiding idea of the existing approaches to the first connection is that truth-functional compounds are connected to their component parts by grounding ties. Thus, a true disjunction is grounded in its true disjunct(s), a true conjunction in its conjuncts, etc.

There are variations, however, with respect to how this guiding idea is elaborated. In particular, the issue of granularity plays a role here. For illustration, let us focus on the predicationalist view of grounding and assume that grounding relates facts. Now consider double negation. The described guiding idea initially suggests that we should accept the schematic principle

DN   If p, then the fact that p grounds the fact that $\neg\neg p$.

However, on a not too fine-grained conception of facts, the fact that $\neg\neg p$ just is the fact that p. On that conception, the sentences 'p' and '$\neg\neg p$' differ conceptually, but they pick out the same fact in the world. Working with such a conception of facts may then be a reason to reject the otherwise plausible principle DN. A detailed discussion of how the

---

[32] See Fine's chapter in this volume.
[33] Nevertheless, the principles are not beyond doubt. For a discussion of transitivity, see Schaffer's contribution to this volume. For doubts about irreflexivity, see Jenkins 2011.

guiding idea should be implemented in a deductive system depending on how the system individuates facts can be found in Correia 2010.

The relation between grounding and the classical quantifiers has been discussed less extensively so far. A promising idea is to build on the connection between existential quantifications and disjunctions on the one hand, and universal quantifications and conjunctions on the other hand. Given the above approach to the link between grounding and truth-functors, the idea would be that true existential statements are individually grounded in their true instances (just as disjunctions are individually in their true disjuncts), and that true universal quantifications are jointly grounded in their instances (just as conjunctions are jointly grounded in their conjuncts).[34]

While the above issues have been treated in some papers, the logic of grounding definitely deserves further exploration, especially at the level of semantic characterization. The systematic studies on the logic of grounding are few: there is Correia 2010, Schnieder 2011, Fine 2012a, and Fine's contribution to this volume. Proof theories for languages for the logic of grounding have been put forward, but to date no fully satisfactory semantic characterization has been proposed. Let us briefly comment upon the papers just mentioned.

Correia 2010 proposes a logic of grounding and factual equivalence. He provides a partly algebraic semantics for the logic, which interprets the sentential expressions flanking the operator for grounding as standing for facts, and establishes completeness. Yet the study is not fully satisfactory for the following reason: completeness is achieved thanks to an axiom (schema), the 'reduction axiom', which has both plausible and implausible instances, and accordingly the whole system is conceptually adequate only in a limited range of applications. The question of the semantic characterization of the system without the reduction axiom remains open.

Schnieder 2011 introduces a deductive system for the natural language connective 'because', focusing on occurrences of the connective in which it is used to state non-causal explanations. The connective can then be seen as expressing a strictly binary notion of grounding where the grounding links expressed can be 'incomplete', in so far as the explanans need not be sufficient to that which is explained. The deductive system is shown to be a conservative extension of the classical propositional calculus, and some applications (in particular explanations of logical truths) and variations of it are discussed.

---

[34] See Schnieder 2011, Fine 2010b, and Fine's contribution to this volume.

Fine 2012a is a study of the pure logic of grounding. Fine actually presents a system which concerns *four* notions of grounding, which he calls 'strict-full', 'weak-full', 'strict-partial', and 'weak-partial', respectively. He provides a semantic characterization of the system inspired by the idea of a fact making a statement true, establishes soundness and completeness, and then studies fragments of the system. Although this study is of great interest, it leaves untouched the question of the impure logic of ground, in particular the question of the interaction of grounding with the truth-functions (which Correia 2010 and Schnieder 2011 tackle).

Fine's contribution to this volume, in contrast, does raise these questions. It contains in particular an axiomatic characterization of the interaction of grounding with the truth-functions and first-order quantification, as well as a semantics for the corresponding language, of the same sort as in the paper on the pure logic of ground. Yet, as Fine admits, the semantics is not adequate for the system. For instance, the semantics validates the schema '$p \vee p \leq p$' (which says that $p \vee p$ is a weak full ground for p), whereas this schema is intended by Fine to be invalid (and indeed it is inconsistent with other principles of the system).

4   SYSTEMATIC ISSUES II: CONNECTIONS WITH OTHER NOTIONS

Even granted that grounding cannot be understood in other terms, it is plausible to hold that grounding is strongly connected with other notions of central importance to philosophy. In this section we focus on some of these notions: the (alethic) modalities, explanation, existential dependence, truth-making, and reduction.

There are other notions whose relationships to grounding deserve attention, but for reasons of space we chose to concentrate on those listed above. Two notions which we would otherwise have liked to include in our discussion are those of supervenience and essence. Let us at least spend a few words on each: the idea that properties or facts of a certain type supervene on properties or facts of another type has often been taken to involve the idea that the supervenient items are exemplified or obtain *in virtue of* the subvenient items. The phrase 'in virtue of' indicates a sort of priority, and it is reasonable to think that, in at least some cases of interest, the relevant notion of supervenience should be cashed out in terms of the concept of grounding rather than in purely modal terms, as so often has been

the case.[35] The discussions of the connections between grounding
and essence are much more recent, and accordingly largely underdevel-
oped. Those we have in mind concern (i) the view that connections of
ground hold in virtue of the essence of suitable items,[36] (ii) the view
that metaphysical necessity is grounded in the essence of things,[37] and
(iii) the view that grounding reduces to essence.[38]

4.1   Grounding and modality

A number of writers hold that grounding induces necessary connections,[39]
more precisely that the following principle holds (for the sake of simplicity we assume a predicational mode of formulation, but the subsequent
discussion applies *mutatis mutandis* if we assume the operational mode
instead):

> (1) For all facts f, g, g', $\ldots$, if f is grounded in g, g', $\ldots$, then as a
> matter of metaphysical necessity, f obtains if g, g', $\ldots$ do.

Following accepted terminology in truth-making theory, we may call this
principle 'Necessitarianism'.

When faced with certain putative counterexamples, friends of Necessitarianism often reply that the putative grounds are only *partial* grounds,
whereas the principle is intended to involve the concept of *full* grounding.
Thus, consider the following objection to (1):

> The fact f that the set {Socrates, Plato} exists is grounded in the fact g
> that Socrates exists. But given that it is metaphysically possible
> that Socrates exists without Plato, and hence without {Socrates,
> Plato}, it is *not* metaphysically necessary that f obtains if g does.
> Therefore, (1) fails.

Most friends of the principle would reply by saying that f is only partly,
not fully, grounded in g; what fully grounds f is not g alone, but g
together with the fact that Plato exists (and maybe other facts as well).

Granted that there are these two notions of grounding, there arises
the question of how they are related, and in particular whether one is to
be understood in terms of the other. On one plausible view, partial

---

[35] See Kim 1993, 131–60, Fine 2001, and Correia 2005, ch. 6.
[36] See Rosen 2010 and Fine's contribution to this volume.
[37] See the references in the foregoing footnote, and also Koslicki 2012.
[38] See Fine's contribution to this volume and Correia forthcoming 2.
[39] E.g. Correia 2005 and Rosen 2010.

grounding is to be understood in terms of full grounding in the obvious way: f is partly grounded in g iff$_{df.}$ f is fully grounded in g and other facts. On another, perhaps less plausible view, there is a third notion of grounding in terms of which both full and partial grounding are to be understood. On such a view, f is fully grounded in $g, g', \ldots$ iff$_{df.}$ f is grounded in $g, g', \ldots$ & as a matter of metaphysical necessity, f obtains if $g, g', \ldots$ do; and f is partly grounded in $g, g', \ldots$ iff$_{df.}$ f is grounded in $g, g', \ldots$ & it is metaphysically possible that f fails to obtain even if $g, g', \ldots$ do obtain.

One may hold a stronger view than (1) which involves *conceptual* necessity instead of the weaker notion of metaphysical necessity:[40]

(2) For all facts $f, g, g', \ldots$, if f is grounded in $g, g', \ldots$, then as a matter of conceptual necessity, f obtains if $g, g', \ldots$ do.

Still another view is that, just as we can distinguish between varieties of necessity, e.g. logical, conceptual, and metaphysical necessity, we can distinguish between various kinds of notions of grounding, e.g. between logical, conceptual, and metaphysical grounding.[41] On one such view, all cases of logical grounding are cases of conceptual grounding, all cases of conceptual grounding are cases of metaphysical grounding, but the converses fail, i.e. there are cases of conceptual grounding which are not cases of logical grounding and cases of metaphysical grounding which are not cases of conceptual grounding. The following list may serve to illustrate:

(3) The fact that $2 + 2 = 4$ or $2 + 3 = 4$ is grounded$_{logical}$ in the fact that $2 + 2 = 4$

(4) The fact that it is true that $2 + 2 = 4$ is grounded$_{conceptual}$ in the fact that $2 + 2 = 4$

(5) The fact that {Socrates, Plato} exists is grounded$_{metaphysical}$ in the fact that Socrates exists and the fact that Plato exists.

(4) is plausibly a case of conceptual yet not logical grounding, and it can be argued that (5) is a case of metaphysical yet not conceptual grounding.

Another plausible principle connecting grounding and metaphysical necessity, which we may call 'Non-Contingency', goes as follows:[42]

---

[40] Schnieder (2006c) seems sympathetic to this view.
[41] See Correia 2005, 59 and Correia 2008, and also Fine's contribution to this volume.
[42] Correia 2005, 65.

(6) For all facts $f, g, g', \ldots$, if f is grounded in $g, g', \ldots$, then as a matter of metaphysical necessity, f is grounded in $g, g', \ldots$, if $g, g', \ldots$ obtain.

Necessitarianism indeed follows from Non-Contingency and the plausible principle that grounding is factive, in the sense that as a matter of metaphysical necessity, if a fact is grounded in other facts, then all these facts (the grounded fact and the grounders) obtain. Friends of the view put forward in the last paragraph are likely to accept the three versions of (6) corresponding to the three notions of grounding.

4.2   Grounding, 'because', and explanation

As can be seen from the list of examples from the beginning of this introduction, we think that the natural language connective 'because' can convey the notion of grounding; many philosophers in the debate would agree. However, this raises the question how exactly grounding is related to the semantics of 'because'.

Let us explore some options. In a particularly strong interpretation, saying that 'because' can convey the notion of grounding means that 'because' at least sometimes semantically expresses grounding (or has the notion as its semantic value).[43] Then we would have to explain how this relates to the fact that some 'because'-sentences convey a causal affair. Three options are:

AMBIGUITY. 'because' is semantically ambiguous; it has different senses in which it expresses different notions. In one sense it expresses grounding (metaphysical priority), in another it expresses causal priority.

CONTEXTUALITY. 'because' is univocal but context-sensitive and the context settles what notion it expresses.

INVARIANCE. 'because' always expresses the same notion of grounding, even when it is used to give a causal explanation.

The second option seems to be van Fraassen's (1980) view, while the third option was held by Bolzano who took causal explanation to be a

---

[43] Since we intend the formulation to be neutral with respect to the controversy between operationalists and predicationalists, we are talking about the *notion* of grounding instead of the *relation* of grounding. Predicationalists could indeed always substitute 'relation' for 'notion' in this section. Operationalists may treat our talk about the notion of grounding as a placeholder for their preferred way of talking about grounding.

particular sort of grounding claim. Although we do not know anyone who seriously defended the first option, it may be a popular initial stance and presumably it has its proponents. One could perhaps read Aristotle as hinting towards the option when he says that 'ground' – 'aitia' – can be predicated of something in different senses, by which he may mean it is ambiguous (but the textual evidence is somewhat indecisive).[44] If he does, and if 'because' means as much as 'on the ground of', then he should think that 'because' inherits the ambiguity. However, we think that as a methodological rule of thumb the postulation of ambiguities requires strong linguistic evidence which has yet to be adduced in this case.

There are also weaker interpretations of the claim that 'because' can convey grounding which might be considered. In a particularly weak but, we think, uninteresting interpretation it makes a merely pragmatic point without any semantic impact. But between the strong and the weak interpretation there is a middle ground:

> QUANTIFICATION. 'because' never expresses a *particular* notion of priority (or have it as its semantic value). Instead, it always expresses an existential quantification over (certain) notions of priority, among them causation and grounding.

A related and last possibility would be the following:

> DISJUNCTION. 'because' always expresses a disjunctive connection of certain notions of priority (e.g. causal priority and grounding, but perhaps also some other notion of priority).

This disjunctive view is closely related to the quantificational view. On both views, 'because' always expresses the same sense; it is univocal and context-invariant. However, on both views a sentence of the form '*p* because *q*' can be true on different grounds, e.g. because the fact that *p* is causally posterior to the fact that *q*, or because it is grounded in it, etc. (We are assuming here that a true disjunction of the sort under consideration is grounded in its true disjuncts, and likewise that a true existential quantification of the relevant kind is grounded in its true instances.) One difference is, however, that on the disjunctive view the relevant priority notions are a direct part of the meaning of 'because' and would have to be mentioned in its semantic clause. On the quantificational view, no particular notion of priority would have to be mentioned.

---

[44] See Aristotle's *Physics* II.3, 195.

Lacking the space for an extensive discussion, we must leave the matter unresolved. There is a further, related issue we would like to mention briefly: grounding is often called an *explanatory* notion. Since 'explanation' is a highly flexible term, this can mean different things. In one (perhaps its central) sense, 'explanation' means communicative acts with particular epistemic qualities; the acts must be potentially illuminating with respect to some cognitive predicament. In other senses, 'explanation' may denote the contents of explanatory acts, or perhaps also the linguistic vehicles used to perform them. We assume that many philosophers who call grounding explanatory employ a weak and vague sense of 'explanation' and mean not much more than what has been discussed above, i.e. that 'because'-sentences, typical devices for explanations, can convey grounding (in one of the ways indicated). But some may have a full-blooded notion of explanation in mind, with all its pragmatic and epistemic connotations. If grounding was intimately tied to explanation in that sense, it might inherit all sorts of context-dependence and interest-relativity that go along with such a notion of explanation. To us it seems advisable, however, to separate the objective notion of grounding, which belongs to the field of metaphysics, from an epistemically loaded notion of explanation. In particular communicative situations, grounding claims may well have the epistemic qualities required to call them 'explanations'; but whether they have them or not is a different issue from the question of whether the claims are true, that is, of whether the facts talked about stand in the grounding relation or not.

4.3   Grounding and existential dependence

Notions of dependence play an important role in describing how different entities can be related from an ontological point of view. Following standard usage, we will mean by existential dependence a relation which can hold between entities of any category, and which is informally introduced by saying that one entity needs another in order to exist.[45]

On one traditional take on dependence, arguably going back to Aristotle, it should moreover be the converse of a *priority* relation: if a thing x depends on a thing y, then y is ontologically prior or more fundamental than x.[46] But there is also a weaker, purely modal understanding of dependence, on

---

[45] We here focus on a specific concept of individual existential dependence; the family of existential dependence concepts is much broader – see, e.g., Simons 1987, Correia 2005, and Correia 2008.

[46] On Aristotle's views see, e.g., Corkum forthcoming.

which cases of dependence do not always involve priorities (see Simons 1987). One need not regard modal notions of dependence and priority notions of dependence as rivals; one can be a pluralist about the issue instead.

A priority notion of dependence obviously seems to be connected to grounding. But how exactly? Some authors proposed an equivalence of the following sort (presented in its predicational and its operational variant):

Pred x existentially depends on y iff some fact about y grounds the fact that x exists

Op x existentially depends on y iff $\exists F$ (x exists because y is F)

Variations of the right-hand side (which may, e.g., have a modal force or involve relativizations to times) can be formulated for different members of the family of concepts of dependence.

If such an equivalence is accepted, one might go a step further and use it to define the notion of dependence in terms of that of grounding.[47] This has the advantage of ideological parsimony; we would work with the basic notion of grounding and get dependence for free. However, the step is not mandatory. The question is itself one of priority: if we accept the definition, we take existential dependence to be a relation induced by certain cases of grounding. But one may also think that facts about existential dependence are prior to corresponding grounding claims, and in fact ground those claims (even if the ideology of the latter need not be definable in terms of the ideology of the former).[48]

4.4   *Grounding and truth-making*

From the 1980s onwards, the notion of truth-making has attracted constantly growing attention from philosophers. Truth-making seems to induce some sort of priority relationship: the priority of a thing's existence over the truth of a truth-bearer. How is it connected to grounding?

Again, an equivalence has been proposed:[49]

---

[47] See Schnieder 2006a. Correia (2005) defines his notion of 'simple dependence' by modalizing the right-hand side of the equivalence: x simply depends on y iff$_{df.}$ necessarily, if x exists, then for some F, x exists because, or partly because, Fy.

[48] Cf. Orilia (2009, note 334), Koslicki (forthcoming).

[49] Cf. Correia 2005, §3.2, Schnieder 2006c, Caputo 2007.

Pred   *x* makes proposition *y* true iff the fact that *x* exists grounds the fact that *y* is true

Op   *x* makes proposition *y* true iff (*y* is true because *x* exists)

As in the case of existential dependence, parsimony may suggest to use the equivalence for definitional purposes. Truth-making would then be defined in terms of grounding: it would, in effect, come down to the grounding relation holding between particular sorts of facts, namely facts about existence and facts about truth. (We formulated the point from the predicationalist perspective; the operationalist would have to put the issue differently and he might well have problems finding an elegant formulation.)

Acceptance of the above connection between truth-making and grounding (be it as a definition or not) will have implications for theories of grounding and truth-making which deserve to be explored in detail. Here, we can only mention one resulting issue.[50]

Aristotle famously drew attention to a contrast concerning attributions of truth: 'It is not because we think truly that you are white, that you are white, but because you are white we who say this have the truth.'[51] Many philosophers think that the remark generalizes and expresses an important insight on truth: truth is a derivative property whose possession by a truth-bearer is grounded in what the truth-bearer is about. Schematically put:

Aristotelian Insight   If *p*, then: that *p* is true because *p*.

(The other half of Aristotle's quotation then follows from the above schema by the asymmetry of 'because' or grounding.)

If the proposed equivalence between grounding and truth-making is combined with the Aristotelian Insight on truth, a serious constraint on truth-maker theories results. Since snow is white, the Aristotelian schema gives us the following grounding claim which seems to be a case of immediate grounding (here expressed in the operationalist variant; what will be said can easily be applied to the predicationalist variant):

AI   That snow is white is true because snow is white.

Now let *SNOW* name the entity which is supposed to make it true that snow is white (typical truth-maker theories would take *SNOW* to be

---

[50] But see Correia 2011 for further thoughts. On the following issue compare Schnieder 2006c and Liggins's contribution to this volume.

[51] *Metaphysics*, 1051b6–8 (the translation follows Ross 1954). Sentence (10) in our opening list is an obvious reminiscence to Aristotle's point.

either the whiteness of snow, or the fact that snow is white). A truth-maker theorist should then defend the following grounding claim:

TM   That snow is white is true because *SNOW* exists.

Since AI and TM deliver a different ground for the same truth, the truth-maker theorist should account for their relation. One natural possibility is the *mediation view* which says that AI states an immediate ground, whereas TM only states a mediate ground, mediated by the following grounding claim:

TM*   Snow is white because *SNOW* exists.

On this view, TM results from AI and TM* by the transitivity of grounding. If the truth-maker theorist wants to pursue this option, s/he should defend TM*. At least to some authors, it would seem that the direction of grounding runs in the opposite direction:[52]

TM*-Con   *SNOW* exists because snow is white.

But the asymmetry of grounding allows only for one direction.

Moreover, there is a battery of grounding claims structurally similar to TM*-Con which may all seem equally plausible:

(1) It is true that snow is white because snow is white.
(2) It is a fact that snow is white because snow is white.
(3) The whiteness of snow exists because snow is white.
(4) Snow is a member of the set of white things because snow is white.
(5) Snow has the property of being white because snow is white.
(6) Snow falls under the concept WHITE because snow is white.
(7) Snow belongs to the mereological sum of all white things because snow is white.

A proponent of the mediation view will probably opt for a mediation claim whose converse has an entry on the list above. So, s/he will reject at least one entry on that list. But assume s/he finds at least some entries on the list acceptable; then s/he should explain what distinguishes those entries from the reverse of their favoured mediating claim.

As an alternative to the mediation view, a truth-maker theorist could hold that AI and TM both state an immediate ground for the same truth. There are two possible views then: on the *partiality* view, AI and TM only

---

[52] See, e.g., Schnieder 2006c and Section 1.3 of Fine's contribution to this volume.

state partial immediate grounds for the same truth, which jointly provide a complete immediate ground of it. But this seems rather implausible to us. An alternative is the *overdetermination view*, on which AI and TM state independent complete grounds for the same truth.[53] That it is true that snow is white would then be ground-theoretically overdetermined. This sort of overdetermination need not in general be objectionable, since a disjunction with two true disjuncts may seem to be a plausible example of it. Still, one might expect a proponent of the overdetermination view to say more on the case in question.

The above issue should be addressed by any truth-maker theorist who accepts the strong connection between truth-making and grounding we proposed.

4.5   *Grounding and reduction*

The issue of granularity, discussed in Section 3.3, has a direct bearing on a certain view about the relationships between grounding and statements like the following, which are sometimes called statements of 'reduction' or 'analysis':

(1) Its being the case that $\neg\neg(2+2=4)$ consists in its being the case that $2+2=4$.

(2) Its being the case that Sam is a bachelor consists in its being the case that Sam is an unmarried man.

(3) Its being the case that this is a water molecule consists in its being the case that this is an H_2O molecule.

Some may find it plausible to hold that there is a systematic connection between such statements and statements of ground, to the effect that if any of (1)–(3) is true, then the corresponding statement below is true as well (we here focus on the predicational mode of formulation only for the sake of brevity):

(4) The fact that $\neg\neg(2+2=4)$ is grounded in the fact that $2+2=4$.

(5) The fact that Sam is a bachelor consists in its being the case that Sam is an unmarried man.

(6) The fact that this is a water molecule is grounded in the fact that this is an H_2O molecule.

---

[53] See Mulligan 2006.

Yet even if it is granted that there is no such systematic connection, it still remains plausible to hold that *some* statements of reduction and the corresponding statements of ground are true – e.g. (2) and (5), or (3) and (6).

We face here a situation which is reminiscent of the so-called 'paradox of analysis'. For suppose that, say, both (2) and (5) hold. Given that (2) holds, it is then plausible to say that the fact that Sam is a bachelor and the fact that Sam is an unmarried man are just one and the same fact. But if they are the same fact, then (5) cannot hold since grounding is irreflexive. This contradicts our assumption, and so we must admit that (2) and (5) are jointly inconsistent. Generalizing from the particular example, we must conclude that – contrary to what seemed plausible – *no* pair of statements consisting of a statement of reduction and of the corresponding statement of ground can be a pair of true statements.

This is where considerations of granularity enter the picture. For the sake of illustration, focus on the argument about (2) and (5). A crucial assumption was that if (2) holds, then the fact that Sam is a bachelor and the fact that Sam is an unmarried man *are just one and the same fact*. But are they? As we stressed in Section 3.3 there are several coherent ways one might want to go on this issue, and it may be argued that there are several coherent ways to go even on the assumption that (2) is true.[54]

5   CONCLUDING REMARKS

It is time to take stock. As we said in the beginning, we believe that there is a sort of non-causal priority which features in a whole number of central philosophical debates. We have called this priority 'grounding' and tried to illuminate it in different ways. On the one hand, we tried to give a survey of pertinent issues and notions. On the other hand, we also presented a number of claims about grounding which we find defensible. Of course, not everyone will agree on what we said; sceptics surely abound, raising their voices in protest.

What do they say? Local sceptical worries take issue with particular claims about grounding. For instance, they might opt for completely different views about the logic of grounding, or think that some of the examples employed are just misconceived. Of course, such worries can be legitimate and should be addressed in the debate. Global sceptical worries

[54] See Schnieder 2010 and Rosen 2010.

are more dangerous since they concern the whole project we have described. They do not aim to contribute to the debate; they want the debate to come to an end. Such worries can take several forms and concern the intelligibility, the unity, the instantiation, or the epistemic accessibility of grounding. Let us briefly go through these global sceptical options.

The most radical sceptic calls into doubt the very intelligibility of talk about grounding.[55] She claims not to understand what the discussion is about, asserting that the proponents of grounding have failed to provide the terms they use with any specific conceptual content. To claim that something grounds something else is to claim nothing at all; instead, it is to inadvertently toy with empty signs.

A somewhat less radical sceptic admits to some understanding of the debate but holds that several very diverse phenomena and notions are inadequately garbled together under the title 'grounding'. There may be *some* truth, then, in saying that some things ground some other things. But what truth there is to such a claim varies crucially with the things in questions; there is no unified phenomenon to be systematically discussed.[56]

The third kind of sceptic does not take issue with the *notion* of grounding. She admits that the proponents of grounding have succeeded in delineating a particular concept, but she also holds that this concept is empty. Nothing grounds anything.

The fourth and final sort of sceptic is more modest. She just claims that we do not, and could not, know whether anything grounds anything. The notion of grounding, she thinks, makes grounding facts epistemically inaccessible to us.

While such sceptical charges certainly deserve to be taken seriously, we are confident that those worries can be met. But to show this is the task for another day.[57]

6   ON THE PAPERS IN THIS VOLUME

Having presented a survey on the topic of grounding, we would like to complete our introduction by giving an overview of the chapters of this volume. They can, roughly, be grouped into four categories:

---

[55] Compare Daly's contribution to this volume.   [56] Compare Hofweber 2009.

[57] For responses to some sceptical challenges, see Audi's contribution to this volume or Raven forthcoming.

1. General discussions of grounding (understood along the lines in which the notion has been treated in the foregoing survey) (see the papers by Kit Fine, Chris Daly, and Paul Audi);
2. Discussions of more specific aspects of a theory of grounding (see the papers by Jonathan Schaffer and Michael Della Rocca);
3. Alternative approaches to the phenomenon that theories of grounding are designed to deal with (see the papers by J. Robert G. Williams and Stephen Barker);
4. Discussions of notions of priority which are related to grounding, in particular dependence and truth-making (see the papers by Kathrin Koslicki, E. J. Lowe, Jody Azzouni, David Liggins, and – again – Stephen Barker).

Let us briefly introduce the chapters one by one.

Chapter 1 – 'Guide to ground'. The volume starts with Fine drawing a grand picture of grounding. His rich paper addresses numerous aspects of a theory of grounding. For a start, he introduces and illuminates the notion of ground and discusses its general importance for metaphysics and philosophy at large (Sections 1.1, 1.2). He then goes on to argue that the notion of ground is better suited for its job than the notion of truth-making (Section 1.3), and he discusses the logical form of statements of ground (Section 1.4). After having introduced a number of important distinctions between different kinds of ground (Section 1.5), Fine enters into a penetrating discussion of the logic of ground (Sections 1.6–1.10), starting with the pure logic of ground and moving on to the relation of grounding to the truth-functional connectives, the quantifiers, and lambda abstraction. He closes the chapter (Section 1.11) with a discussion of the relation between ground and essence, arguing that they are distinct fundamental notions both necessary for metaphysics.

Chapter 2 – 'Scepticism about grounding'. Impressive as Fine's picture is, Daly remains unconvinced. In the second chapter of this volume, he presents himself as a radical sceptic about grounding: he defends the thesis that talk of grounding is unintelligible. His arguments directly attack those who – like Fine or Schaffer – hold that 'ground' is a primitive yet comprehensible term, the understanding of which can be fostered through (i) a specification of its logical properties, (ii) its connections to other philosophical terms, and/or (iii) examples of its applications. Daly goes through a number of attempts to clarify talk of grounding by those means and argues that each of them fails. In particular, he holds that (i) the formal properties ascribed to 'ground' do not suffice to identify its content; that (ii) the term indeed belongs to a family of metaphysical notions, all of which are equally unintelligible; and that (iii) difficulties in understanding 'ground' carry over to understanding any supposedly true applications of the term.

Chapter 3 – 'A Clarification and defense of the notion of grounding'. Audi's essay contains a direct response to Daly's worries. Audi argues that the notion of grounding is intelligible through our understanding of kindred notions such as causality and explanation, and that fairly ordinary explanations serve both to make grounding facts known and to show the indispensability of grounding. Audi also addresses the worries of a less radical sceptic who holds that expressions introducing grounding, such as 'in virtue of', are used in too wide a variety of ways. While he partly acknowledges the worry, he retorts that the proper reaction is not to ban the phrases – instead, we should regiment our use of them. Apart from replying to the sceptics, Audi pursues three goals of a more positive nature. First, he argues that there is a relation of grounding (a relation of non-causal determination) on the basis of realism about explanation. Second, he argues for a worldly – as opposed to conceptual – view of grounding. And third, he ties grounding to the natures of properties; relations of grounding manifest the essences of the properties involved.

Chapter 4 – 'Grounding, transitivity, and contrastivity'. Grounding – at least when understood as a binary relation between facts – is generally taken to be transitive: if the fact that φ grounds the fact that ψ, and if in turn the fact that ψ grounds the fact that ρ, then the fact that φ grounds the fact that ρ. Schaffer challenges the received view by offering three counterexamples to transitivity (Section 4.2). He then (Section 4.3) puts forward a contrastive treatment of grounding, akin to a now popular contrastive treatment of causation, according to which the logical form of basic claims of ground should be taken to be 'the fact that φ rather than φ^* grounds the fact that ψ rather than ψ^*' rather than 'the fact that φ grounds the fact that ψ'. Contrastive grounding, Schaffer argues, obeys a simple transitivity principle, which is not threatened by the previously proposed counterexamples.

Chapter 5 – 'Violations of the Principle of Sufficient Reason (in Leibniz and Spinoza)'. Some important versions of the Principle of Sufficient Reason (PSR) state that everything (literally everything; or every fact; or every truth; . . .) is grounded. The PSR, in one form or another, notoriously played an important role in the philosophies of Spinoza and Leibniz. Leibniz, for instance, endorsed the PSR friendly principle that whenever some objects stand in a relation, the relation must be grounded in some thing(s). Della Rocca argues (Section 5.1) that this principle led Leibniz to the idealist conclusion that relations are grounded in a mind (ultimately, in God's mind). Yet this conclusion is in conflict with Leibniz's own view that certain relations are real and not merely ideal, e.g. creation and the causal relation that links a substance and its states (Section 5.2). Leibniz is caught in a dilemma: either deny that there are pluralities of objects standing in relations, or deny the PSR friendly principle mentioned above. Della Rocca defends the view (Section 5.3) that Spinoza is able to avoid the dilemma by taking both horns, holding that multiplicities and relational states do not exist fully but still enjoy existence to a lesser degree, and holding that some relations do violate the PSR friendly principle, these violations being nevertheless less than fully existent. Della Rocca finally argues (Section 5.4) that Leibniz cannot adopt Spinoza's strategy, which ultimately relies on his monism, i.e. the view that there (fully) exists only one substance – a view which Della Rocca himself tentatively endorses.

Chapter 6 – 'Requirements on Reality'. How is it possible to endorse a minimal metaphysics – say, one according to which there are no abstracta like numbers or pure sets, or no macro material objects like planets and tables – without there by being committed to the view that common sense and science are massively mistaken? One strategy, as Williams stresses (Section 6.1), involves distinguishing between what is *derivatively* the case from what is *fundamentally* the case – a distinction which is itself often characterized in terms of the notion of grounding. What the minimal metaphysics purports to describe, so the view goes, is what is fundamentally the case; if the metaphysics rejects the existence of numbers and heavenly bodies, it remains compatible with the view that it is the case, albeit derivatively, that $2 + 2 = 4$ and that there are eight planets in orbit around the Sun. Williams contrasts this metaphysical strategy with representational strategies, which focus on the relationships between linguistic representations and reality and purport to tell a story about what reality must be like for representations to be correct. Williams discusses some strategies he takes to be representational, the Quinean paraphrase strategy and certain contemporary fictionalist views (Section 6.2), and develops his own representational account (Section 6.3).

Chapter 7 – 'Varieties of Ontological Dependence'. Koslicki focuses on an important relation of ontological posteriority often labelled 'ontological dependence', a relation which is plausibly taken to hold between e.g. smiles and the corresponding smiling mouths, fights and the people involved, or again non-empty sets and their members (Section 7.2).

She concentrates on what she takes to be a promising account of onto-logical dependence in terms of a non-modal and sufficiently constrained conception of essence developed by Fine in the mid 1990s. She argues that even this essentialist account is, as it stands, not fine-grained enough to recognise different varieties of dependence which ought to be distin-guished even within the realm of ontology (Section 7.3). In some cases, an entity (e.g. a non-empty set) may be ontologically dependent on the essential constituents out of which it is constructed; but in other cases, an entity (e.g. a trope) may be ontologically dependent on another (e.g. its 'bearer') for a different reason (e.g. because the former is a feature of the latter). A framework which glosses over these differences, Koslicki argues, does not offer a proper diagnosis of why one entity ontologically depends on another, and she puts forward an account which is meant to do justice to the differences in question (Sections 7.4 and 7.5).

Chapter 8 – 'Asymmetrical Dependence in Individuation'. According to a prominent idea, an ontologically dependent entity is an entity which is individuated by other entities. Lowe clarifies the relevant notion of individuation and points out that it is not an epistemic but an ontological one. Corresponding to those two notions of individuation, he holds, we must distinguish between two principles of identity: mere criteria of identity serve *us* to individuate or distinguish entities, while genuine principles of individuation state from where the entities themselves receive their identity, that is, what makes them the very things they are. Individu-ation in the ontological sense is plausibly an anti-symmetric affair: if one entity individuates another, the latter cannot also individuate the former. However, Lowe notes, this idea seems in conflict with certain structuralist ontologies, in which all entities in a given system are taken to be indivi-duators of each other. Lowe challenges such ontologies and makes a case for the claim that in any coherent system of ontology, some entities must be self-individuating, with these entities ultimately accounting for the identities of all other entities in the system.

Chapter 9 – 'Simple Metaphysics and "Ontological Dependence"'. While Azzouni's essay is also concerned with the notion of ontological dependence, it looks at it from a rather critical point of view. Ideas about ontological dependence are typically motivated, Azzouni holds, as a reac-tion to an important observation; the truth of statements about certain kinds of objects (e.g. holes) is grounded in (or is to be non-causally explained by) the ways that certain other objects are. But he takes this observation to be a poor motivation of the distinction between dependent and more fundamental existents. For, as part of his *Simple Metaphysics,* he claims that what we actually use as a criterion for what exists is independence from linguistic and psychological processes – and he argues that the application of this criterion to candidate cases of ontologically dependent entities proves the supposed entities to be non-existent. Azzouni's position on ontology can fruitfully be contrasted with Schaffer's (2009): both could agree that our important ontological commitments are to the fundamental, non-dependent entities. But unlike Schaffer, Azzouni can be seen as taking the fundamental entities to be in fact the only ones that exist. Where Schaffer would countenance additional, derivative existents, Azzouni takes them to be ruled out of existence by just those intuitions which make Schaffer categorize them as derivative.

Chapter 10 – 'Truth-makers and Dependence'. Liggins's paper addresses the connection between the notions of truth-making, non-causal dependence, and grounding. He argues that the phenomenon of grounding should be acknowledged, by appeal to non-causal explanation (cf. Audi's essay), and he links the (established) debate over truth-maker theory to the newer debate about grounding, arguing that truth-maker theory makes unattractive commitments regarding the metaphysics of grounding. In the first part of the chapter, Liggins gives examples of explanations (concerning realization, constitution, and value) which seem to be underpinned by non-causal dependence. He uses them to reply to a recent challenge to truth-maker theory. But he does want to let truth-maker theory of the hook. Instead, he uses the notion of non-causal dependence in the second part of the chapter to mount his own challenge to truth-maker theory. He takes truth-maker theory to be motivated by truth's dependence on reality: truth-maker theorists try to account for this dependence by positing a relation of non-causal dependence which truth-makers bear to the propositions they make true. Liggins sets out alternative accounts of the metaphysics of non-causal dependence in general and argues that they are superior to the theory formed by extending truth-maker theory to cover other cases of non-causal dependence.

Chapter 11 – 'Expressivism about truth-making'. Barker advocates the view that truth-making, like all other kinds of non-causal making, reduce to 'making-the case', a relation between facts which others would prefer to call 'grounding' (Section 11.1). He devises an expressivist theory of making-true and making-the case: in claiming that some facts make-the case another fact *f*, or make-true a proposition *p*, one expresses a commitment to a derivation – a derivation of *f* or of the truth of *p* using certain rules of inference in certain ways (Sections 11.2–11.4). While the account is expressivist and hence does not purport to give truth-conditions for claims of making-true or making-the case, Barker emphasizes, it is nevertheless compatible with the view that these claims are truth-apt and about the world (Section 11.5).[58]

---

[58] Acknowledgements: Thanks to Lisa Grunenberg, Stephan Krämer, Robert Schwartzkopff, Alex Steinberg, Maik Sühr, and Nathan Wildman for comments on the introduction, and Christian Folde as well as Yannic Kappes for their help with the manuscript and the index. We would also express our gratitude for financial funding which made our research possible. Correia's research leading to these results has received funding from the European Community's Seventh Framework Programme under grant agreement PITN-GA-2009–238128, and was also partially funded by the Consolider-Ingenio project CSD2009–0056 (Spanish Ministry of Science and Innovation) and by the projects PP001–114758, PP00P1–135262, and CRSI11–127488 (Swiss National Science Foundation). Schnieder's research has received funding from the Emmy Noether programme of the DFG.

CHAPTER I

Guide to ground

Kit Fine

A number of philosophers have recently become receptive to the idea that, in addition to scientific or causal explanation, there may be a distinctive kind of metaphysical explanation, in which explanans and explanandum are connected, not through some sort of causal mechanism, but through some constitutive form of determination. I myself have long been sympathetic to this idea of constitutive determination or "ontological ground"; and it is the aim of the present chapter to help put the idea on a firmer footing – to explain how it is to be understood, how it relates to other ideas, and how it might be of use in philosophy.[1]

I.I THE NOTION OF GROUND

There is an intuitive notion of one thing holding in virtue of another. Here are some examples:

(1) The fact that the ball is red and round obtains in virtue of the fact that it is red and the fact that it is round;
(2) The fact that the particle is accelerating obtains in virtue of the fact that it is being acted upon by some net positive force;
(3) The fact that his action is wrong obtains in virtue of the fact that it was done with the sole intention of causing harm.

There are some alternative – more or less equivalent – ways of saying the same thing. Thus instead of (2), we might say that the particle was accelerating *because* it was acted upon by a positive force or that the

---

[1] A number of other philosophers (they include Audi [forthcoming], Batchelor [2010], Schaffer [2009b], Correia [2005, 2010], Raven [2009], Rosen [2010], Schnieder [2011]) have done related work in defense of the notion; and I have not attempted to make a detailed comparison between their ideas and my own. I am grateful to the participants at the Boulder conference on dependence and to Neil Tennant for many helpful comments on an earlier draft of the chapter. I should add that, for reasons of space, some of the material in the chapter originally submitted to the volume had been abridged.

particle's being acted upon by a positive force *made it true* that the particle was accelerating; and similarly for (1) and (3).

In each of the above cases, there would appear to be some sort of modal connection between explanandum and explanans. Thus from (1)–(3), it would appear to follow that:

(1) Necessarily, if the ball is red and it is round then it is red and round;

(2) Necessarily, if the particle is acted upon by some positive force then it is accelerating;

(3) Necessarily, if the action was done with the intention of causing harm then it is wrong.

However, it is arguable that the "force" or "strength" of the modal operator is different in each case. The first conditional ('if the ball is red . . . ') holds of *metaphysical* necessity, the second of *natural* necessity, and the third of *normative* necessity.[2]

Whether or not this is so, there would appear to be something more than a modal connection in each case. For the modal connection can hold without the connection signified by 'in virtue of' or 'because'. It is necessary, for example, that if it is snowing then $2 + 2 = 4$ (simply because it is necessary that $2 + 2 = 4$), but the fact that $2 + 2 = 4$ does not obtain in virtue of the fact that it is snowing; and it is necessary that if the ball is red and round then it is red but the fact that the ball is red does not obtain in virtue of its being red and round. In addition to the modal connection, there would also appear to be an *explanatory* or *determinative* connection – a movement, so to speak, from antecedent to consequent; and what is most distinctive about the in-virtue-of claims is this element of movement or determination.

We may call an in-virtue claim a statement of *ontological* or *metaphysical ground* when the conditional holds of metaphysical necessity and I shall talk, in such cases, of the antecedent fact or facts *grounding* or being a *ground for* the consequent fact. Thus we may say, in the first of the cases above, that the fact that the ball is red and round is grounded in the fact that it is red and the fact that it is round. Just as metaphysical necessity is the strictest form of necessity (at least as compared to natural and normative necessity), so it is natural to suppose that statements of metaphysical ground are the strictest form of in-virtue-of claim. In the other cases, we may sensibly ask for a stricter or fuller account of that in virtue of

[2] I have attempted to argue in Fine 2005a, Chapter 7, that these are the basic forms of necessity, with no one of them reducible to the others.

which a given fact holds. So in the case of the particle, for example, we may agree that the particle is accelerating in virtue of being acted upon by a positive force but think that there is some kind of gap between the explanans and explanandum which could – at least in principle – be filled by a stricter account of that in virtue of which the explanandum holds. But if we were to claim that the particle is accelerating in virtue of increasing its velocity over time (which is presumably a statement of metaphysical ground), then we have the sense that there is – and could be – no stricter account of that in virtue of which the explanandum holds. We have as strict an account of the explanandum as we might hope to have.

It is for this reason that it is natural in such cases to say that the explanans or explanantia are *constitutive of* the explanandum, or that the explanandum's holding *consists in nothing more* than the obtaining of the explanans or explanantia. But these phrases have to be properly understood. It is not implied that the explanandum just *is* the explanans (indeed, in the case that there are a number of explanantia, it is clear that this requirement cannot be met). Nor need it be implied that the explanandum is unreal and must somehow give way to the explanantia. In certain cases, one might wish to draw these further conclusions. But all that is properly implied by the statement of (metaphysical) ground itself is that there is no stricter or fuller account of that in virtue of which the explandandum holds. If there is a gap between the grounds and what is grounded, then it is not an explanatory gap.[3]

I have remarked that to each modality – be it metaphysical, natural, or normative – there corresponds a distinct relation of one thing holding in virtue of another. It is plausible to suppose that the natural in-virtue-of relation will be of special interest to science, the normative relation of special interest to ethics, and the metaphysical relation of special interest to metaphysics. Each of these disciplines will be involved in its own explanatory task, that will be distinguished, not merely by the kinds of things that explain or are explained, but also by the explanatory relationship that is taken to hold between them.

It is an interesting question whether each of these explanatory relations should be defined in terms of a single generic relation. Thus it might be thought that "metaphysical ground" should be defined by:

the fact that A grounds the fact that B iff the fact that B obtains in virtue of the fact that A (in the generic sense) and it is a metaphysical necessity that if A then B,

---

[3] My remarks on this point in Fine 2001, p. 16, have been over-interpreted by a number of authors.

and similarly for the other cases, but with another modality in place of metaphysical necessity. It might, on the contrary, be thought that each basic modality should be associated with its "own" explanatory relation and that, rather than understanding the special explanatory relations in terms of the generic relation, we should understand the generic relation as some kind of "disjunction" of the special relations. If there is a generic notion here, it is that which *connects* the modality to the corresponding explanatory relationship and that has no status as an explanatory notion in its own right.

I myself am inclined to favor the latter view. For consider the fact that a given act was right or not right ($R \lor \neg R$). This is grounded, we may suppose, in the fact that it is right (R). The fact that it is right, we may suppose, is (normatively) explained by the fact that it maximizes happiness (R'). So the fact that the given act is right or not right is explained in the generic sense by the fact that it maximizes happiness. But it is a metaphysical necessity that if the act maximizes happiness then the act is right or not right ($\Box(R' \supset R \lor \neg R)$), since it is a metaphysical necessity that the act is right or not right ($\Box(R \lor \neg R)$). However, the fact that the act maximizes happiness does not metaphysically ground the fact that it is right or not right, contrary to the proposed definition. Nor is it altogether clear how the definition might be modified so as to avoid counterexamples of this sort.

I.2   THE IMPORTANCE OF GROUND

Once the notion of ground is acknowledged, then I believe that it will be seen to be of general application throughout the whole of philosophy. For philosophy is often interested in questions of explanation – of what accounts for what – and it is largely through the employment of the notion of ontological ground that such questions are to be pursued. Ground, if you like, stands to philosophy as cause stands to science.

But the principal importance of the notion is to the question of reality. We may distinguish, in a broad way, between two main branches of metaphysics. The first, which I call *realist* or *critical*, is concerned with the question of what is real. Is tense real? Is there genuinely tense in the world and not merely in language? Are values real? Are there genuinely values out there in the world and not merely in our minds? Are numbers real? Are numbers out there in the world waiting to be discovered or merely something that we have invented? The second branch of metaphysics, which I call *naive* or *pre-critical*, is concerned with the nature of things without regard to whether they are real. We might ask, for example, whether material things exist in time in the same way as they exist in space (with the four-dimensionalists thinking they do and the three-dimensionalists thinking they do not) or we might ask whether fictional characters are genuinely created by their authors; and these are questions that we can properly consider even if we decide at the end of the day to adopt a position in which the reality of the external world is rejected in favor of the reality of a purely phenomenal world or in which fictional characters are dismissed in favor of the literary works or acts by which they are introduced.

Questions of ground are not without interest to naive metaphysics, but they are *central* to realist metaphysics. Indeed, if considerations of ground were abolished, then very little of the subject would remain. For the anti-realist faces an explanatory challenge. If he wishes to deny the reality of the mental, for example, then he must explain or explain away the appearance of the mental. It is likewise incumbent upon the realist, if he wishes to argue against his opponent, to show that this explanatory challenge cannot be met.

The question now is: how is this explanatory challenge to be construed? What is it to explain the appearance of a world with minds in terms of a mindless world or the appearance of a world with value in terms of a purely naturalistic world? My own view is that what is required is that we somehow *ground* all of the facts which appear to presuppose the reality of the mental or of value in terms of facts which do not presuppose their reality.[4] Nothing less and nothing else will do.

It will not do, for example, to say that the physical is *causally* determinative of the mental, since that leaves open the possibility that the mental has a distinct reality over and above that of the physical. Nor will it do to require that there should be an analytic definition of the mental in terms of the physical, since that imposes far too great a burden on the anti-realist. Nor is it enough to require that the mental should modally supervene on the physical, since that still leaves open the possibility that the physical is itself ultimately to be understood in terms of the mental.

The history of analytic philosophy is littered with attempts to explain the special way in which one might attempt to "reduce" the reality of one

---

[4] The above account of *ground* and of its role in realist metaphysics is further discussed in Fine 2001. I do not presuppose that the one set of facts must ground-theoretically supervene on the other set of facts.

thing to another. But I believe that it is only by embracing the concept of a ground as a metaphysical form of explanation in its own right that one can adequately explain how such a reduction should be understood. For we need a connection as strong as that of metaphysical necessity to exclude the possibility of a "gap" between the one thing and the other; and we need to impose a form of determination upon the modal connection if we are to have any general assurance that the reduction should go in one direction rather than another.

The explanatory challenge constitutes the core of realist metaphysics. An anti-realist position stands or falls according as to whether or not it can be met. And so given that the challenge is to be construed in terms of ground, the subject of realist metaphysics will be largely constituted by considerations of ground. We must attempt to determine what grounds what; and it will be largely on this basis that we will be in a position to determine the viability of a realist or anti-realist stand on any given issue.

In addition to this grand role, the notion of ground has a humbler role to play in clarifying the concepts and claims of interest to other branches of philosophy. Let me give one of my favorite examples. How are we to distinguish between a three- and four-dimensionalist view of the nature of material things? The distinction is often put in terms of the existence of temporal parts, with the three-dimensionalist denying that material things have temporal parts (or a suitable range of temporal parts) and the four-dimensionalist insisting that they have such parts. But even the three-dimensionalist might be willing to admit that material things have temporal parts. For given any persisting object, he might suppose that "in thought," so to speak, we could mark out its temporal segments or parts. But his difference from the four-dimensionalist will then be over a question of ground. For he will take the existence of a temporal part at a given time to be grounded in the existence of the persisting object at that time, while his opponent will take the existence of the persisting object at the time to be grounded in the existence of the temporal part. Thus it is only by introducing the notion of ground that this account of the difference between the two positions can be made at all plausible.[5]

---

[5] Cf. Hawthorne 2006, p. 100. Rosen (2010, fn 1) has another example concerning the analysis of *intrinsic property* and Correia (2005, Chapters 4 and 5) provides various accounts of dependence in terms of ground.

I.3 GROUND AND TRUTH-MAKING

The notion of ground is a close cousin of the notion of truth-making. Both are bound up with the general phenomenon of what accounts for what, but there are some significant differences in how they structure the phenomenon.[6]

The relation of truth-making relates an entity in the world, such as a fact or state of affairs, to something, such as a statement or proposition, that represents how the world is; and the intended understanding of the relation is that the *existence* of the worldly entity should guarantee the *truth* of the representing entity. Ground, on the other hand, is perhaps best regarded as an operation (signified by an operator on sentences) rather than as a relation (signified by a predicate). But insofar as it is regarded as a relation, it should be seen to hold between entities of the same type and, insofar as a choice needs to be made, these entities should probably be taken to be worldly entities, such as facts, rather than representational entities, such as propositions. Thus it is that the ball is red and that the ball is round that makes it the case that the ball is red and round, and not the existence of the *facts* that the ball is red and that the ball is round that make the *proposition* that it is red and round true.

From the perspective of the theory of ground, truth-maker theory has an unduly restricted conception of what is grounded. One might of course be interested in the ground for the truth or correctness of our representations of the world (in which case, it is presumably not merely the truth of one class of representations that will be of interest, but the class of all representations – be they linguistic, mental, or abstract). But these are by no means the only questions of ground or "making" that will arise. For whenever we consider the question of what makes the representation that P true, there will also arise the question of what, if anything, makes it the case that P. Indeed, it might well be thought that the question concerning the representation will always divide into two parts, one concerning the ground for what it is for the representation that P to represent P and the other having nothing to do with representations as such, but concerning the ground for P.

From the perspective of the theory of ground, truth-maker theory is also unduly restrictive in its conception of what grounds. For it insists that grounds should take the form of existential attributions; it is always the

---

[6] Truth-making has been widely discussed (see, for example, Mulligan, Simons, and Smith 1984, Fox 1987, and Armstrong 1997, 2004) and a number of authors (most notably Schnieder 2006b and Horwich 2008) have made some related criticisms concerning the connection between truth-making and ground. Cameron forthcoming provides a recent survey of the literature.

existence of something that properly accounts for the truth of the representation. But there is no reason in principle why the ultimate source of what is true should always lie in what exists. Perhaps it can lie in something relational, *a* standing in the relation R to *b*, or the negation of something relational, *a* not standing in the relation R to *b*, or in something of some other form.

Indeed, the existential view of ground is somewhat suspect in itself. For it is much more natural to suppose that it is because P (e.g. it is raining) that the fact that P exists, rather than the other way round. One can only conjecture as to why truth-maker theorists might have built such an implausible view into their conception of truth-making. One possible reason is that they wanted something that would clearly indicate that the grounds were in the world and, just as truth indicates that what is grounded lies on the side of representation, so existence indicates that what grounds lies on the side of the world. Be that as it may, it is clearly preferable if our conception of what accounts for what should remain neutral over the form of the relata.

The lack of uniformity between what grounds and what is grounded gives rise to another limitation in truth-maker theory. For the attempt to determine what grounds what naturally proceeds in stages – one first determines the relatively immediate grounds for the truths in question, then the relatively immediate grounds of those grounds, and so on until one reaches the ultimate grounds. So one might first ground the normative in the natural, for example, then the natural in the physical, and then the physical in the micro-physical, thereby establishing that the normative was grounded in the micro-physical.

But the existence/truth dichotomy that is built into the notion of truth-making makes it ill-suited to this step-by-step procedure. For what is grounded is a truth and what grounds is the existence of something, which is not of the right form for itself to be grounded. Thus the truth of the normative will be grounded in the existence of the natural, which is not of the right truth-theoretic form to be grounded in the existence of the physical.

It might of course be suggested that whenever:

(i)   the existence of the fact that q makes true the proposition that r

and

(ii)   the existence of the fact that p makes true the proposition that q,

then:

(iii)   the existence of the fact that p will make true the proposition that r.

The legitimacy of "chaining" is thereby preserved. But why think this chaining principle holds, given the shift in the middle term from the existence of the fact that q in (i) to the truth of the proposition that q in (ii)? Presumably, this can only be because the truth of q is some kind of ground for the existence of the fact that q. But this goes against the whole tenor of truth-making theory, which takes the existence of the fact to ground the truth of the proposition, rather than the other way round.

Perhaps there is some other, more ingenious, way to establish the legitimacy of chaining on the truth-maker approach. But why go through these contortions when there is a simple and natural alternative under which the grounds are already suited to have grounds? The truth-maker theorist is like someone who, faced with the problem of fitting a round peg into a round hole, first makes the round peg square and then attempts to solve the problem of fitting a square peg into a round hole.

The difficulties over the relation of truth-making do not merely concern the relata; they also concern the relation itself. For the relation is usually explicated in modal terms: f will be a truth-maker for p if the existence of f necessitates the truth of p ($\Box(E(f) \supset T(p))$). But as has often been pointed out, this lets in far too much. Any necessary truth, for example, will be grounded by anything and, not only will the fact that Socrates exists be a truth-maker for the proposition that singleton Socrates exists, the fact that singleton Socrates exists will be a truth-maker for the proposition that Socrates exists. Thus whereas the form of the relata makes truth-making too restrictive, the nature of the relation makes it too liberal.

It is conceivable that the restrictions on the relata were a way for compensating for the deficiencies in the relation. For if P were taken to be a truth-maker for Q whenever P necessitated Q, then every truth would trivially be a truth-maker for itself. By insisting that the grounds should take the form of something that exists and that what is grounded should take the form of something that is true, we avoid trivializations of this sort; and we can even ensure that the relation be irreflexive and anti-symmetric, since the objects to the right and left of the relation will be of different type.

But we have here a mere chimera of substantiality. Indeed, on certain quite plausible metaphysical views, there will still exist wholesale trivializations of the truth-making project. One might well think, for example, that for any truth p, the fact that p will exist and will require the truth of p for its existence. The fact that p will then be a truth-maker for any true proposition p. Or one might think that the world exists and could not exist without being the way it is. The world would then be a truth-maker for any true proposition. But such innocuous metaphysical views cannot legitimately be regarded as enabling us to find a truth-maker for every truth.

The notion of truth-making is thoroughly ill-suited to the task for which it was intended: it arbitrarily restricts the relata between which the relation should be capable of holding; it does not allow truth-making connections to be chained; and it trivializes the project of finding truth-makers. Perhaps the best that can be said in its favor is that it provides a necessary condition for the intended relation: if P genuinely grounds Q then the fact that P will be a truth-maker for the proposition that Q. It is therefore possible that, by looking for truth-makers while guided by a sense of what is really in question, we will alight on genuine grounds. But it should not be pretended that the relation of truth-making is anything but a pale and distorted shadow of the notion of genuine interest to us.

1.4   THE GRAMMAR OF GROUND

How should we formulate statements of ground? My preferred view is that the notion of ground should be expressed by means of a sentential operator, connecting the sentences that state the ground to the sentence that states what is grounded. If we use '<' for this connective, then (1) above might be formulated as:

The ball is red, The ball is round < The ball is red and round.[7]

Perhaps the closest we come to an ordinary language formulation is with "because." Thus we might say 'the ball is red and round because the ball is red and the ball is round'. But, of course, 'because' does not convey the distinctive sense of *ground* and is not able to distinguish between a single conjunctive antecedent and a plurality of non-conjunctive antecedents.

Corresponding to the notion of ground as a sentential operator is a notion of ground as a sentential predicate. If we use '◁' for the predicate, then 'A, B < C,' say, will be true just in case 'A,' 'B' ◁ 'C'. Likewise, corresponding to the notion of ground as a sentential operator is a notion of ground as a propositional predicate (or as a predicate of facts). If we use '◀' for this predicate, then 'A, B < C' will be true just in case that-A, that-B ◀ that-C.

---

[7] Different authors have used different symbols for this notion. Audi (forthcoming) uses '→$_g$,' Correia (2005) uses '▷,' and Rosen (2010) uses '←.' My own notation derives partly from the need to distinguish between a strict (<) and weak (≤) notion of ground and partly from the metaphor in which the ground is "lower" than what it grounds.

But it is important here that the notion of proposition be properly understood. For the truth of 'A, B < C' might be taken to depend not merely upon the propositions expressed by 'A,' 'B,' and 'C' but also upon *how* these propositions are expressed; and, in this case, the clauses 'that-A', 'that-B,' and 'that-C' should also be taken to indicate the manner in which the proposition is expressed in addition to the proposition itself. One might think, for example, that this is water in virtue of its being H_2O. But if the proposition that this is water is the same as the proposition that it is H_2O then we would have here an unacceptable case of a proposition being a ground for itself. So if we are to use the propositional mode to express this statement of ground, we must adopt a richer conception of what propositions are in question. One of the advantages of the operator approach is that it enables us to remain neutral on such matters.

The grounding operator '<' is variably polyadic; although it must take exactly one argument to its "right," it may take any number of arguments to its "left" – be they of zero, finite, or infinite number. This means that there is both a conjunctive and a disjunctive sense in which a given statement C may be multiply grounded. It will be *conjunctively* grounded in $A_1, A_2, A_3, \ldots$ insofar as $A_1, A_2, A_3, \ldots$ collectively ground C; and it will be *disjunctively* grounded in $A_1, A_2, A_3, \ldots$ (or, more generally, in $A_{11}, A_{12}, \ldots$ and $A_{21}, A_{22}, \ldots$ and $A_{31}, A_{32}, \ldots, \ldots$) insofar as it is grounded in A_1 and in A_2 and in $A_3, \ldots$ (or in $A_{11}, A_{12}, \ldots$ and in $A_{21}, A_{22}, \ldots$ and in $A_{31}, A_{32}, \ldots, \ldots$).

The case in which a given statement is *zero*-grounded, i.e. grounded in zero antecedents, must be sharply distinguished from the case in which it is *un*grounded, i.e. in which there is no number of statements – not even a zero number – by which it is grounded. We may bring out the difference by means of an analogy with sets. Any non-empty set {a, b,...} is generated (via the "set-builder") from its members a, b,.... The empty set { } is also generated from its members, though in this case there is a zero number of members from which it is generated.

An urelement such as Socrates, on the other hand, is ungenerated; there is no number of objects – not even a zero number – from which it may be generated. Thus "generated from nothing" is ambiguous between being generated from a zero number of objects and there being nothing – not even a zero plurality of objects – from which it is generated; and the empty set will be generated from nothing in the one sense and an urelement from nothing in the other sense.

We might imagine that we have a machine that manufactures sets. One feeds some objects into one end of the machine and turns it on; and the set of those objects then emerges from the other end of the machine. The empty set is the object that emerges from the machine when no objects are fed into it, while the urelements are those objects that never emerge from the machine.

There is a similar distinction to be drawn between being zero-grounded and ungrounded. In the one case, the truth in question simply disappears from the world, so to speak. What generates it, just as what generates the empty set, is its zero-ground. But in the case of an ungrounded truth, just as in the case of an urelement, the truth is not even generated and simply stays in place.

Of course, in any putative case of a zero-grounded statement, we should provide some explanation as to how it might be zero-grounded. But this may not be impossible. Suppose we thought that there was a operator of conjunction '∧' that could apply to any number of sentences A, B, . . . It might then be maintained, as a general principle, that the conjunction ∧(A, B, . . .) was grounded in its conjuncts A, B, . . . So in the special case in which the operator ∧ was applied to zero statements, the resulting conjunction T = ∧( ) would be grounded in its zero conjuncts.

Indeed, the case of zero-grounding may be more than an exotic possibility. For suppose that one held the view that any necessary truth was ultimately to be grounded in contingent truths. Now, in the case of some necessary truths, it may be clear how they are to be grounded in contingent truths. It might be thought, for example, that the statement A ∨ ¬A was always to be grounded in either A or ¬A. But in other cases – as with Socrates being identical to Socrates or with Socrates belonging to singleton Socrates – it is not so clear what the contingent truths might be; and a plausible alternative is to suppose that they are somehow grounded in nothing at all.[8]

1.5   CONCEPTIONS OF GROUND

The general notion of ground comes in different "strengths" – normative, natural, and metaphysical. But it also comes in different "flavors." There will be different ways of conceiving of the notion, even when its strength has been fixed. I begin with some familiar distinctions in how the notion is to be conceived, and then turn to some less familiar distinctions.

Factive/Non-factive

There is a familiar distinction between the factive and a non-factive conception of ground. On the factive conception, we can only correctly

---

[8] A similar strategy may be on the cards when what is to be explained is not a necessary truth but the necessity of a truth, as with the dilemma posed by Blackburn 1987.

talk of something factive – such as a true statement or a fact – being grounded; and what grounds must likewise be factive. But on the non-factive conception, we can also correctly talk of something non-factive – such as a false statement or a merely possible fact – being grounded; and what grounds may likewise be non-factive. Thus on the factive conception, A ∧ B can only be grounded in A and B if A ∧ B (and hence A and B) are indeed the case while, on the non-factive conception, A ∧ B can be grounded in A and B even if A or B (and hence A ∧ B) is not the case.

We may define the factive notion ($<$) in terms of the non-factive notion ($<_\circ$) as follows:

(F-N) $\Delta < A$ iff $\Delta <_\circ A$ and Δ (i.e. each statement of Δ is the case).

Some statements Δ factively ground another statement A iff they non-factively ground the other statement and are the case. This equivalence (and even its necessary truth) would appear to be relatively unproblematic.

We also appear to be able to define the non-factive notion in terms of the factive notion:

(N-F) $\Delta <_\circ A$ iff $\Diamond(\Delta < A)$.

Some statements non-factively ground another if they possibly factively ground the other. In this way, we may extend the "field" of the relation from the actual facts, so to speak, to the possible facts.

However, this definition is subject to a difficulty. For presumably a statement of the form A can non-factively ground A ∨ B (i.e. it is possible that A factively grounds A ∨ B, viz. when A is the case) and A ∨ B and ¬A together can non-factively ground (A ∨ B) ∧ ¬A (i.e. it is possible that A ∨ B and ¬A factively ground (A ∨ B) ∧ ¬A, i.e. when ¬A and B are the case). It should then follow (upon replacing (A ∨ B) in the previous statement of ground with A) that A and ¬A can non-factively ground (A ∨ B) ∧ ¬A. But this is not possible according to the definition given that it is impossible that A and ¬A should both be the case.

The difficulty arises from the fact that the antecedents Δ must be jointly possible if they are non-factively to ground A and this is too restrictive. But it does not help to allow the antecedents Δ to non-factively ground A whenever they are jointly impossible. For then A would non-factively ground A whenever A is impossible and, presumably, we do not want any statement to ground itself. The difficulties in coming up with a straightforward account of non-factive ground, in addition to the more intuitive considerations, strongly suggest that the factive notion is the more fundamental notion;

the difficulties of the non-factive notion are a product, so to speak, of its artificiality. But that is not to say that we should give up on the non-factive notion. For we can think of it as being obtained from the factive notion by a process of "rounding out," in which the possible cases of factive grounding are extended to cases of grounding from impossible antecedents in such a way that the basic principles governing the behavior of ground are preserved (it is in much the same way that we extend the number system). However, this is not the place to consider how this might be done.

Full/Partial ground

Another familiar distinction is between full and partial ground. Ground in the previous sense is *full* ground. A is a *partial* (or what we shall later call a *partial strict*) ground for C if A, on its own or with some other truths, is a ground of C (i.e. A, Γ < B, where Γ is a possibly empty set of "other truths"). Thus given that A, B is a full ground for A $\wedge$ B, each of A and B will be a partial ground for A $\wedge$ B. Each will be relevant to the grounding of A $\wedge$ B, even though neither may be sufficient on its own.

Partial ground has been defined in terms of full ground, but it would not appear to be possible to define full ground in terms of partial ground. For the partial grounds of A $\vee$ B and A $\wedge$ B are the same, i.e. A and B when A and B are the case. But each of A and B is a full ground of A $\vee$ B though not, in general, of A $\wedge$ B. And so how are we to distinguish between the full grounds of A $\vee$ B and A $\wedge$ B if appeal is only made to their partial grounds? It is for this reason that pride of place should be given to the full notion in developing an account of ground.[9]

Mediate/Immediate ground

The third distinction, between mediate and immediate ground, is not so familiar. Ground in the previous sense is *mediate*. An *immediate* ground, by contrast, is one that need not be seen to be mediated. The statement that A $\wedge$ (B $\wedge$ C) is mediately grounded in the statements that A, B, C, since the grounding must be seen to be mediated through B, C grounding (B $\wedge$ C) and A, (B $\wedge$ C) grounding A $\wedge$ (B$\wedge$ C). The statements B, C, by contrast, immediately ground B $\wedge$ C, since the grounding in this case is not mediated through other relationships of ground.[10]

[9] In contrast to the approach of Schnieder 2011.
[10] I have proposed drawing a similar distinction in the case of essence (Fine 1995b, 61–2).

I say that an immediate ground is one that "need not be seen to be mediated" rather than "is not mediated" because there are cases of immediate ground that are in fact mediated even though they need not be seen to be mediated. The truth that A, for example, is a ground for A ∨ (A ∨ A). It is furthermore an immediate ground for A ∨ (A ∨ A) since A in its capacity as a left disjunct, so to speak, is not a mediated ground for A ∨ (A ∨ A). However, A is an immediate ground for (A ∨ A) and (A ∨ A) is an immediate ground for A ∨ (A ∨ A); and so A also stands in a mediated relationship of ground to A ∨ (A ∨ A).

Mediate ground can be defined in terms of immediate grounds. For all relationships of mediate ground can be obtained by appropriately chaining relationships of immediate ground. Thus each relationship of immediate ground can be taken to be a degenerate case of a mediate ground; and given that Δ is an immediate ground for A and Γ_1, A, Γ_2 a mediate ground for B, we can take Γ_1, Δ, Γ_2 to be a mediate ground for B. But a definition in the other direction would not appear to be possible. For, in the example above, the truth that A is an immediate ground for A ∨ (A ∨ A). But, as we have seen, the ground is also mediated, with A being an immediate ground for (A ∨ A) and (A ∨ A) for A ∨ (A ∨ A). We wanted to say that the ground A for A ∨ (A ∨ A) need not be *seen* to be mediated, but it is hard to see how to convert this idea into a definition from mediate ground.

The notion of immediate ground would appear to be give us something genuinely new; and I find it remarkable how strong our intuitions are about when it does and does not hold. It surely is the case, for example, that A ∧ B is *immediately* grounded in A and B and that statements about cities are, at best, *mediately* grounded in statements about atoms. It is the notion of immediate ground that provides us with our sense of a ground-theoretic hierarchy. For given any truth, we can take its immediate grounds to be at the next lower level. Thus as long as mediate grounds are always mediated through immediate grounds, any partial ground for the truth will always be at some finite level below the level of the truth.

Weak/Strict ground

The fourth distinction, between weak and strict ground, is less familiar still. Ground in the previous sense is *strict* and does not allow a truth to ground itself, while ground in the weak sense allows – and, indeed, requires – that a truth should ground itself.

We might perhaps express weak ground by means of the locution 'for – and for – and ... is for –', where the last 'for' specifies the statement to be grounded and the first 'for's specify its grounds. Thus for John to marry Mary is for John to marry Mary, for John to marry Mary is for Mary to marry John, and for John to marry Mary and for Mary to marry John is for John to marry Mary. Or to take a somewhat different example, for Hesperus to be identical to Phosphorus and for Phosphorus to be a planet is for Hesperus to be a planet (in this case, it might be argued that, in contrast to the others, the grounded truth does not weakly ground any of its grounds).

What is characteristic of these cases is that any explanatory role that can be played by the given truth can also be played by their grounds. Thus if John's marrying Mary accounts for the existence of the married couple John and Mary, then Mary's marrying John also accounts for the existence of the married couple. Or if John's marrying Mary accounts for John's marrying Mary or Bill's marrying Sue then Mary's marrying John will also account for John's marrying Mary or Bill's marrying Sue.

We might think of strict ground as moving us down in the explanatory hierarchy. It always takes us to a lower level of explanation and, for this reason, a truth can never be strict ground for itself. Weak ground, on the other hand, may also move us sideways in the explanatory hierarchy. It may take us to a truth at the same level as what is grounded and, for this reason, we may always allow a given truth to be a weak ground for itself.[11]

Given the notion of weak ground, it would appear to be possible to define strict ground. For we may say that Δ strictly grounds C if (i) Δ weakly grounds C and (ii) C, on its own or with some other statements, does not weakly ground any member B of Δ – i.e. for no Γ does Γ, C weakly ground B. Thus a strict ground is a weak ground which cannot be "reversed," with the explanandum C helping to explain one of the explanantia.

It would also appear to be possible to define the weak notion of ground in terms of the strict notion. For we may say that Δ weakly grounds C if Δ subsumes the explanatory role of C, i.e. if Δ, Γ strictly grounds B whenever C, Γ strictly grounds B.

There is an interesting question as to which of the notions, if either, is more fundamental than the other. We naturally gravitate towards the strict notion and think of the weak notion as an artificial offshoot. But my own inclination is to think of the weak notion as more fundamental (just as one might see the notion of proper-or-improper part as more fundamental than the notion of proper part). As we shall see, it has a

---

[11] We might compare truths which are weak grounds for one another with "equations" in systems of term rewriting (Terese 2003). Term rewriting, in general, enjoys deep analogies with the calculus of ground.

simpler semantics; and it seems to provide a simpler and more natural starting point in developing a general theory of ground.

Varieties of strict/partial ground

Once we introduce the notion of weak ground, it is possible to make further distinctions in the notion of strict/partial ground. There is first of all the partial notion that is the natural counterpart of strict full ground and that we might naturally think of as *the* notion of partial ground. P will be a partial ground of Q in this sense if P, on its own or with some other truths, is a strict full ground for Q. We have called this notion *partial strict* ground and might symbolize it by $\prec^*$.

There is then the notion of strict/partial ground that is the natural counterpart to the notion of weak partial ground. P is weak partial ground for Q if P, possibly with some other truths, is a weak full ground for Q; and P will be a corresponding strict/partial ground for Q if P is a weak partial ground for Q but Q is not a weak partial ground for P. We call this notion *strict partial* ground and symbolize it by $\prec$ and it is this notion, rather than the previous notion of partial strict ground, that we shall later use in formulating the principles of ground.

Finally, there is the result of chaining partial strict ground with weak partial ground. P will be a partial/strict ground for Q in this sense if, for some truth R, P is a partial strict ground for R and R is a weak partial ground for Q. We call this notion *part strict* ground and symbolize it by $\prec'$. There is also a corresponding notion that results from chaining weak partial ground with partial strict ground. But it gives nothing new – the result is coincident with partial strict ground.

It is readily shown, under plausible assumptions, that if P is a partially strict ground for Q then P is a part strict ground for Q and that if P is a part strict ground for Q then P is a strictly partial ground for Q. However, there is no obvious way to establish the reverse implications and it may plausibly be argued – either by reference to the semantics or by appeal to counterexamples – that they fail to hold.

The notion of strict partial ground provides us with a natural partial notion of ground for which a partial ground need not always be part of a full ground. One might wish to say, for example, that the truth that P is a partial ground for knowledge that P, even though there is nothing one might add to P to obtain a strict full ground for knowledge that P (as in the view of Williamson 2000). But let it be granted that P and the knowledge that P is a weak full ground for knowledge that P. Then knowledge that P is presumably no part of a weak full ground for P and so P will be a strict partial ground, in the intended sense, for knowledge that P.[12]

Distributive/non-distributive ground

Finally, let us note that although we have taken ground to be a many–one connection, allowing any number of antecedents on the left but requiring a single consequent on the right, there are natural ways in which we may interpret it as a many–many connection, i.e. as a connection between any number of statements on either the left or the right. The obvious way to do this is to understand $\Delta < \Gamma$ to mean that Δ *simultaneously* grounds each statement of Γ, i.e. that $\Delta < C$ for each C in Γ. However, for a number of purposes, it is more natural to understand $\Delta < \Gamma$ to mean that Δ *distributively* grounds Γ, i.e. there is a decomposition of Δ into subsets $\Delta_1, \Delta_2, \ldots$ (with $\Delta = \Delta_1 \cup \Delta_2 \cup \ldots$) and a corresponding decomposition of Γ into members $C_1, C_2, \ldots$ (with $\Gamma = \{C_1, C_2, \ldots\}$) such that $\Delta_1 < C_1$, $\Delta_2 < C_2, \ldots$ (and similarly when weak full ground is in question).[13]

This understanding of ground is naturally involved in statements of supervenience. It might be thought, for example, that the psychological supervenes (in the sense of *ground*) upon the physical. Let Γ be the set of all psychological truths $C_1, C_2, \ldots$ Then for an appropriate set Δ of physical truths (one containing a physical ground Δ_i for each psychological truth C_i) Δ will be a distributive ground for Γ. We shall see that the notion of distributive ground is also naturally involved in formulating ground-theoretic principles for the logical connectives.

1.6 THE PURE LOGIC OF GROUND

We might divide the logic of ground into two parts: "pure" or structural; and "impure" or applied. The pure logic of ground is simply concerned with what follows from statements of ground without regard to the internal structure of the truths that ground or are grounded. Thus the pure logic of ground might state that if A grounds B and B grounds C then A grounds C. The impure logic of ground, on the other hand, also takes into account the internal logical structure of the truths. Thus the impure logic of ground might state that A is a ground for A ∨ B (given that A is the case).

---

[12] See Fine 2012a for further discussion.
[13] The many-many notion of ground introduced here is to be sharply distinguished from the many-many notion discussed by Shamik Dasgupta in his unpublished paper "The Status of Ground".

In developing the pure logic of ground, there are a number of choices of the ground-theoretic primitives that one might make, but it turns out to be convenient to adopt the following four operators as primitive:[14]

$\leq$ weak full
$\preceq$ weak partial
$<$ strict full
$\prec$ strict partial

We may set these out in a chart as follows:

	Strict	Weak
Full	$<$	$\leq$
Partial	$\prec$	$\preceq$

There are four corresponding statements of ground:

$\Delta \leq C$ weak full
$A \preceq C$ weak partial
$\Delta < C$ strict full
$A \prec C$ strict partial,

where Δ in the statements of full ground is used to indicate an arbitrary number of antecedent truths $A_1, A_2, \ldots$

Let us place the premisses of a valid rule of inference above a horizontal line and the conclusion below the line. The pure theory of ground, with these primitives, may then be taken to be constituted by the following rules:

Subsumption

$$(</\leq): \quad \frac{\Delta < C}{\Delta \leq C} \qquad\qquad (\prec/\preceq): \quad \frac{A \prec C}{A \preceq C}$$

$$(</\prec): \quad \frac{\Delta, A < C}{A \prec C} \qquad\qquad (\leq/\preceq): \quad \frac{\Delta, A \leq C}{A \preceq C}$$

---

[14] The pure logic of ground is developed in much greater detail in Fine 2012a. Jon Litland in two recent unpublished papers – "Grounding Ground" and "Natural Deduction for Logics of Ground" – has developed natural deduction systems for the logic of ground in which one ground-theoretic statement may be embedded within another.

$$\underline{\text{Cut}} \ (\leq / \leq): \quad \frac{\Delta_1 \leq A_1 \ \ \Delta_2 \leq A_2 \ldots A_1, A_2, \ldots \leq C}{\Delta_1, \Delta_2, \ldots \leq C}$$

$$\text{Transitivity} \ (\preceq/\preceq): \ \frac{A \preceq B \ B \preceq C}{A \preceq C} \quad (\preceq/\prec): \ \frac{A \preceq B \ B \prec C}{A \prec C} \quad (\prec/\preceq): \ \frac{A \prec B \ B \preceq C}{A \prec C}$$

$$\text{Identity} \ (\leq): \quad \frac{}{A \leq A} \qquad\qquad \text{Non-Circularity} \ (\prec): \quad \frac{A \prec A}{\perp}$$

$$\text{Reverse Subsumption} \ (\leq / \prec): \quad \frac{A_1, A_2, \ldots \leq C : A_1 \prec C \ A_2 \prec C \ldots}{A_1, A_2, \ldots < C}$$

The Subsumption Rules tell us how to weaken a statement of ground. They enable us to go from strict ground (either full or partial) to weak and from full ground (either strict or weak) to partial. The Cut Rule allows us to chain statements of ground; the antecedents in a weak statement of ground may be replaced by their grounds. The Transitivity Rules allow us to chain two partial statements of ground, and the resulting statement will be strict as long as one of the given statements is strict. According to Identity, we may infer (from zero premises) that any truth is a weak ground for itself; and according to Non-Circularity, no truth is a strict partial ground for another. Reverse Subsumption permits us to go from a weak statement $A_1, A_2, \ldots \leq C$ of ground to the corresponding strict statement $A_1, A_2, \ldots < C$ as long as all of the antecedents $A_1, A_2, \ldots$ are strict partial grounds for the consequent C.

A couple of comments are in order:

(1) The most striking difference from the structural rules for classical consequence is the absence of Weakening. Even though Δ is a strict (or weak) ground for C, we cannot infer that Δ together with an arbitrary truth A is a strict (or weak) ground for C. This is because all of the grounds must be relevant to conclusion. Indeed, if Weakening held, then Non-Circularity could no longer be maintained. For surely at least one strict statement of ground $\Delta < C$ is true. But given Weakening, Δ, $C < C$ should then hold and so C would be a strict partial ground for C ($C \prec C$) – contrary to Non-Circularity.

(2) From the above rules, we can derive the following Amalgamation Rule for strict ground:

$$\frac{\Delta_1 < C \; \Delta_2 < C \ldots}{\Delta_1, \Delta_2, \ldots < C}$$

In other words, the strict grounds for a given truth can be amalgamated, or combined, into a single ground. It is not usual to include this rule (or anything from which it might be derived) among the rules for ground. But the plausibility of the rules from which it can be derived provides a strong argument for its adoption; and I doubt that there is simple and natural account of the logic of ground that can do without it.

We may also argue more directly in favor of the rule without appeal to the weak notion of ground. For consider the case in which $\Delta < C$ and $\Gamma < C$ (the case in which there are more than two premises to the rule is similar). Now C, C is a ground for $C \wedge C$ (this is an instance of the general truth that A, B is a ground for $A \wedge B$). So by the application of Cut for $<$, $\Delta, \Gamma < C \wedge C$, i.e. Δ, Γ is a strict ground for $C \wedge C$. But then how can Δ, Γ fail to be a strict ground for C? What difference in the relationship of ground could be marked by such a distinction?

It follows from Amalgamation that there will always be a maximum ground for a grounded truth. In other words, if $\Delta < A$ then there will be a Δ^+ such that (i) $\Delta^+ < A$ and (ii) $\Gamma \subseteq \Delta^+$ whenever $\Gamma < A$. For we may simply let Δ^+ be the union of all the Γ for which $\Gamma < A$. On the other hand, there may be no minimum ground for a grounded truth A, i.e. a Δ^- for which (i) $\Delta^- < A$ and (ii) $\Delta^- \subseteq \Gamma$ whenever $\Gamma < A$. For suppose A is a truth of the form $(p_1 \wedge p_2 \wedge p_3 \wedge \ldots) \vee (p_2 \wedge p_3 \wedge p_4 \wedge \ldots) \vee (p_3 \wedge p_4 \wedge p_5 \wedge \ldots) \vee \ldots$ Then for each $k = 1, 2, \ldots$, $p_k, p_{k+1}, p_{k+2}, \ldots < A$ and so, if there were to be a minimum ground for A it would have to be empty.

This example also puts paid to the idea that we might get at the idea of relevance through minimality. In other words, starting with a notion of ground $<^+$ that is subject to Weakening one might hope to define a "relevant" notion of ground $<$ that is not subject to Weakening via the definition:

$\Delta < C$ if $\Delta <^+ C$ and for no proper subset Δ' of Δ does $\Delta' <^+ C$.

But this would then prevent there from being any relevant ground for $A = (p_1 \wedge p_2 \wedge p_3 \wedge \ldots) \vee (p_2 \wedge p_3 \wedge p_4 \wedge \ldots) \vee (p_3 \wedge p_4 \wedge p_5 \wedge \ldots) \vee \ldots$ in the example above.

1.7 THE GROUND OF LOGIC (INTRODUCTION RULES)

We turn to the "impure" logic of ground. The central question concerns the ground for truth-functional and quantificational truths; and, for this reason, we may think of this part of the logic of ground as constituting an account of the ground of logic.

There are two kinds of ground-theoretic rules that we might provide for logically complex truths, loosely corresponding to the introduction and elimination rules of classical logic. The first provides sufficient conditions for something to ground a logically complex truth of a specified form; the second provides necessary conditions. We consider the first kind of rule here and the second in the next section.[15]

What are the grounds for a logically complex truth – be it a conjunctive truth $A \wedge B$, a disjunctive truth $A \vee B$, a universal truth $\forall xFx$, an existential truth $\exists xFx$, or a negative truth $\neg A$? Let us begin with conjunction and disjunction, then turn to the quantifiers, and finally deal with the case of negation. I shall only concern myself with the question of strict ground, although there is a parallel question of weak ground that might also be considered.

It has usually been supposed that conjunction and disjunction should be subject to the following "introduction" rules:

$\wedge$I. $A, B < A \wedge B$

$\vee$I-L. $A < A \vee B$ $\vee$I-R. $B < A \vee B$

Thus A and B, together, are a ground for $A \wedge B$, while A or B, separately, is a ground for $A \vee B$. These rules are fine as far as they go, but there is a way in which the rule for disjunction may be inadequate. For, as we have already argued, ground should be subject to Amalgamation. This means that if A and B are separate grounds for $A \vee B$ then A, B should be a collective ground for $A \vee B$. Thus in addition to $\vee$I-L and $\vee$I-R, we should also have:

$\vee$I$^+$. $A, B < A \vee B$

(under the assumption, of course, that A and B are both true).

We may argue for the plausibility of this further rule in the same way as before. For suppose that A and B is each a ground for $A \vee B$, according to the original rules. Then A, B is a ground for $(A \vee B) \wedge (A \vee B)$ by the rule for conjunction. But do we then want to deny that A, B is a ground

---

[15] I hope to give a more detailed account of the impure logic elsewhere.

for (A ∨ B), thereby creating what appears to be an invidious distinction in the grounds for (A ∨ B) and (A ∨ B) ∧ (A ∨ B)?

Of course, if the original rules are stated within a context in which the Amalgamation Rule can be derived, then there is no need for the additional rule. But the contexts within which these rules are stated are not usually taken to be of this sort; and the additional rule is then required.[16]

We turn to the quantifiers. The obvious rules, in analogy to rules for ∧ and ∨, are:

∀I. $B(a_1), B(a_2), \ldots < \forall x B(x)$

∃I. $B(a) < \exists x B(x)$

where $a_1, a_2, a_3, \ldots$ are names for all of the objects of the domain and a is the name for one such object.[17] As with the rule for disjunction, we should also allow (through either stipulation or derivation) for the application of Amalgamation ∃I:

∃I$^+$. $B(a), B(b), B(c), \ldots < \exists x B(x)$

But there is another difficulty with ∃I. For take the case in which B(x) is x = x (a similar difficulty also arises when B(x) is of the form ¬(Fx ∧ ¬Fx) for some predicate F). Then Socrates being identical to Socrates (a = a) will ground the truth that something exists (in the sense $\exists x(x = x)$). But then necessarily, if Socrates is identical to Socrates, Socrates being identical to Socrates will ground the truth that something exists and hence will imply that something exists. But necessarily, Socrates is identical to Socrates. And so necessarily, something exists – which is not so (at least on most views of the matter).

The standard solution to this difficulty is to take the ground for $\exists x B(x)$ to be not simply B(a) but B(a) along with the truth that a exists (Ea). Thus the rule now takes the form:

$B(a), Ea < \exists x B(x)$

However, this proposal is often coupled with the suggestion that the relevant existential claim Ea should be understood as the existential $\exists x(x = a)$. But let

---

[16] There are some extraordinary logical circumstances, related to the paradoxes, that may lead one to question some of these rules and some of the associated rules for the quantifiers. They are discussed in Fine 2010b but will not be considered here. I should note that, since writing the paper, I have had reservations about insisting upon the rule of Amalgamation and its various consequences.

[17] I assume for simplicity that the quantifiers are unrestricted although an analogous account could be given for restricted quantification.

B(x) be x = a. According to the revised version of $\exists$I, a = a, $\exists$x(x = a) will then ground $\exists$x(x = a) – contrary to the non-circularity of ground.

One could try to circumvent this difficulty by placing restrictions on the B for which B(a), Ea grounds $\exists$xB(x), but I doubt that there is any reasonable way in which this might be done and it would be desirable, in any case, to have uniform rules of ground for the logical constants. The proposal also has other counter-intuitive consequences. For if allowed, $\exists$x(x = a) would in general be a partial ground for $\exists$xB(x) and, since a = a partially grounds $\exists$x(x = a), a = a would in general be a partial ground for $\exists$xB(x). But surely the truth that a = a is in general irrelevant to the truth of $\exists$xB(x) – Socrates being identical to Socrates, for example, is irrelevant to someone being a philosopher.

Rather than give up the idea that the existence claim is irrelevant to the ground of the existential truth, I should like to suggest that it is relevant but should not itself be understood in terms of existential quantification. This is not to deny that there is a necessary equivalence between Socrates existing and there being something that is Socrates. But once we are sensitive to ground we will be sensitive to differences between necessarily equivalent statements that turn on differences in their ground. A $\vee$ ¬A and B $\vee$ ¬B, for example, are necessarily equivalent (since each is neces-sarily true) but will generally differ with regard to their ground, with the grounds for A, should it be true, being a ground for A $\vee$ ¬A though not in general a ground for B $\vee$ ¬B. And similarly, or so it might be thought, in the present case.

We can get at the relevant notion of existence by asking what grounds $\exists$x(x = a). Intuitively, it is not just a = a (which is the only relevant instance) but also something about a, what we might call its existence. But then the existence of a in this sense, if it is to serve as a partial ground for $\exists$x(x = a), cannot itself be understood as $\exists$x(x = a). Indeed, it would not normally be supposed that the identity of an object with itself is a ground – or even a partial ground – for the existence of the object. What grounds Socrates' existence might turn on whether he was born of such and such parents, for example, but it is hard to see how it could turn, even indirectly, on the identity of Socrates to himself.

There is a dual difficulty for the universal quantifier. Suppose that a_1, a_2, a_3, ... are (names for) all the individuals that there are. Let B(x) be the condition that x is identical to one of the individuals that there are, something we may write as:

$$x = a_1 \vee x = a_2 \vee x = a_3 \vee \ldots$$

Then given the rule $\forall$I above, the truths:

$$a_1 = a_1 \lor a_1 = a_2 \lor a_1 = a_3 \lor \ldots,$$
$$a_2 = a_1 \lor a_2 = a_2 \lor a_2 = a_3 \lor \ldots,$$
$$a_3 = a_1 \lor a_3 = a_2 \lor a_3 = a_3 \lor \ldots,$$
$$\ldots$$

will ground $\forall x(x = a_1 \lor x = a_2 \lor x = a_3 \lor \ldots)$. And since:

$$a_1 = a_1 \text{ grounds } a_1 = a_1 \lor a_1 = a_2 \lor a_1 = a_3 \lor \ldots,$$
$$a_2 = a_2 \text{ grounds } a_2 = a_1 \lor a_2 = a_2 \lor a_2 = a_3 \lor \ldots,$$
$$a_3 = a_3 \text{ grounds } a_3 = a_1 \lor a_3 = a_2 \lor a_3 = a_3 \lor \ldots,$$
$$\ldots$$

it follows that $a_1 = a_1, a_2 = a_2, a_3 = a_3, \ldots$ grounds $\forall x(x = a_1 \lor x = a_2 \lor x = a_3 \lor \ldots)$. But each of $a_1 = a_1, a_2 = a_2, a_3 = a_3, \ldots$ is necessary; and so it should be necessary that $\forall x(x = a_1 \lor x = a_2 \lor x = a_3 \lor \ldots)$, i.e. necessary that $a_1, a_2, \ldots$ are all of the objects that there are – which is not so (at least on most views of the matter).

This difficulty is usually solved by appeal to the "totality" claim that a_1, $a_2, \ldots$ are all of the individuals that there are. Let us signify this truth by $T(a_1, a_2, \ldots)$. Then the ground for $\forall x B(x)$ should be taken to be not simply $B(a_1), B(a_2), B(a_3), \ldots$ but $B(a_1), B(a_2), B(a_3), \ldots$ along with $T(a_1, a_2, \ldots)$.

However, this proposal is usually coupled with the suggestion that the totality claim $T(a_1, a_2, \ldots)$ should itself be understood as the universal claim: $\forall x(x = a_1 \lor x = a_2 \lor x = a_3 \lor \ldots)$. But let $B(x)$ be the condition $(x = a_1 \lor x = a_2 \lor x = a_3 \lor \ldots)$. Then the ground for $\forall x B(x)$, i.e. for $\forall x(x = a_1 \lor x = a_2 \lor x = a_3 \lor \ldots)$, will be the truths:

$$a_1 = a_1 \lor a_1 = a_2 \lor a_1 = a_3 \lor \ldots,$$
$$a_2 = a_1 \lor a_2 = a_2 \lor a_2 = a_3 \lor \ldots,$$
$$a_3 = a_1 \lor a_3 = a_2 \lor a_3 = a_3 \lor \ldots,$$
$$\ldots$$

along with $\forall x(x = a_1 \lor x = a_2 \lor x = a_3 \lor \ldots)$ – contrary to the non-circularity of ground.

One could try to circumvent this difficulty by placing restrictions on the $B(x)$ for which $B(a_1), B(a_2), B(a_3), \ldots$ in conjunction with $T(a_1, a_2, \ldots)$ grounds $\forall x B(x)$, but, again, I doubt that there is any reasonable way in which this might be done, and it would be desirable, in any case, to have uniform rules of ground for the logical constants. The proposal also has other counter-intuitive consequences. For the totality claim $T(a_1, a_2, \ldots)$ will in general be a partial ground for $\forall x B(x)$ and each of $a_1 = a_1, a_2 = a_2,$

$a_3 = a_3$, . . .will partially ground $T(a_1, a_2, \ldots)$ under the proposed account of $T(a_1, a_2, \ldots)$; and so the identities $a_1 = a_1, a_2 = a_2, a_3 = a_3, \ldots$ will in general be a partial ground for the universal truth $\forall x B(x)$. But surely the truth of $a = a$ is in general irrelevant to the truth of $\forall x B(x)$ – Socrates being identical to Socrates, for example, is irrelevant to the truth that everything is either not a man or is mortal.

What I would like to suggest, in the same way as before, is that $T(a_1, a_2, \ldots)$ should indeed be taken to be part of the ground of any universal truth $\forall x B(x)$ but that it should not itself be understood as a universal truth. Thus even though $\forall x(x = a_1 \lor x = a_2 \lor x = a_3 \lor \ldots)$ and $T(a_1, a_2, \ldots)$ are necessarily equivalent, they differ with respect to their grounds. The identities $a_1 = a_1, a_2 = a_2, a_3 = a_3, \ldots$ are directly relevant to the grounds of $\forall x(x = a_1 \lor x = a_2 \lor x = a_3 \lor \ldots)$ but are neither directly nor indirectly relevant to the grounds of $T(a_1, a_2, \ldots)$.

There is a variant on the above position which I am inclined to prefer on general theoretical grounds. We have taken the totality claim $T(a_1, a_2, \ldots)$ in the weak sense that $a_1, a_2, \ldots$ are *at most* the objects that there are, but we might also take it in the strong sense that $a_1, a_2, \ldots$ are *just* the objects that there are (something which is equivalent to $\forall x(x = a_1 \lor x = a_1 \lor \ldots) \land Ea_1 \land Ea_2 \land \ldots$). We may then take the ground for an existential truth $\exists x B(x)$ to consist of some true instances and the appropriate totality claim. Thus it will be part of the grounds for a quantificational truth, whether it be universal or existential, that the objects of the domain are what they are; and a separate category of existence facts will not be required.

The issue of the ground for universal truths has caused a great deal of puzzlement in the philosophical literature, going back to Russell (1918) and continuing to this day (Armstrong 2004). But if I am right, there is a purely logical aspect to the problem which is readily solved once one draws a distinction between the totality claim and the corresponding universal claim. Of course, this still leaves open the question of the grounds, if any, for the totality claim. But this is a question that lies on the side of metaphysics, so to speak, rather than of logic; and it should not be supposed that there is anything in our general understanding of the quantifiers or of the concept of ground that might indicate how it should be answered.

We turn finally to negation. In this case, it is hard to see how one might state the grounds for $\neg A$ in terms of A, since if $\neg A$ is a truth then A is a falsehood. What we might do instead is to take the case in which A is logically complex and then state grounds for $\neg A$ in terms of the components of A. There are five cases in all:

¬∧I.   ¬A < ¬(A ∧ B)   ¬B < ¬(A ∧ B)

¬∨I.   ¬A, ¬B < ¬(A ∨ B)

¬¬I.   A < ¬¬A

¬∀I.   ¬Fa₁, Ea < ¬∀xFx

¬∃I.   ¬Fa₁, ¬Fa₂, ..., T(a₁, a₂, ...) < ¬∃xFx

Given these rules, the grounds for negations can be driven inwards until we reach atomic truths and their negations.

1.8 THE GROUND OF LOGIC (ELIMINATION RULES)

We have provided sufficient conditions for a logically complex truth to be grounded by simpler truths. But we would also like to know something about the necessary conditions under which a logically complex truth will be grounded. We know, for example, that the truths A and B will ground A ∧ B. But when in general will an arbitrary set of truths Δ ground A ∧ B? For all that we have said, any set of truths could ground A ∧ B; and so clearly, something more should be said on the question if such unpalatable possibilities are to be excluded.

This further question, to my knowledge, has been almost completely ignored; and the little that has been said has not been accurate. It turns out that, in order to provide an adequate formulation of the necessary conditions, we need to appeal to the weak notion of ground (≤), even when it is only the strict grounds for a given truth that are in question. This is therefore another case in which appeal to the weak notion is critical in developing an adequate theory of ground.

For consider again the question of when a set of truths Δ is a (strict full) ground for A ∧ B. We naturally want to say that any grounds for A ∧ B should be mediated through A and B; the conjuncts are the conduit, so to speak, through which truth to the conjunction should flow. But we cannot express this as the thought that Δ must divide into two parts Δ₁ and Δ₂ (with Δ = Δ₁ ∪ Δ₂) which are respectively strict grounds for A and B. For A and B ground A ∧ B and so, when Δ = {A, B}, the required division of Δ into strict grounds for A and B will not exist. Nor can we say that either Δ must divide into two such parts Δ₁ and Δ₂ or should be identical to {A, B}, since the same difficulty will arise when Δ consists of ground-theoretic equivalents A′ and B′ of A and B.

What we should say instead is: if Δ is a strict full ground for A ∧ B (Δ < A ∧ B), then, for some division of Δ into the parts Δ₁ and Δ₂, Δ₁ and Δ_2 are weak full grounds for A and B respectively ($\Delta_1 \leq$ A and $\Delta_2 \leq$ B), using the notion of weak ground on the right in place of the notion of strict ground. An alternative way to express the consequent is that Δ should be a (weak) distributive ground for {A, B}, given our previous notion of distributive ground. Let us use "$\Delta \leq \Gamma$," with set-symbols to the left and right, to indicate that Δ is a weak distributive ground for Γ. The "elimination" rule for $\wedge$ will then take the form:[18]

$\wedge$E.
$$\frac{\Delta < A \wedge B}{\Delta \leq \{A, B\}}$$

There is a corresponding rule for disjunction. What we would like to say is that the grounds for a disjunction A ∨ B should be mediated through its disjuncts. But when the grounds for the disjunction are strict, we should allow the grounds for the disjuncts to be weak; and given the possibility of amalgamation, we should also allow that the ground for the disjunction may be a distributive ground for its disjuncts. We are therefore led to the following principle:

If Δ is a strict full ground for A ∨ B, then either Δ is a weak full ground for A or a weak full ground for B or a weak distributive ground for A and B. Or more formally:

$\vee$E.
$$\frac{\Delta < A \vee B}{\Delta \leq A; \Delta \leq B; \Delta \leq \{A, B\}}$$

(where the semicolons are used to indicate the disjunctive character of the conclusion).

For the universal quantifier, we wish to say that a set of truths will be a strict full ground for $\forall x B(x)$ if it distributively grounds the totality claim and all of its instances. That is:

---

[18] The formulation calls for a further extension of our framework. For once we spell out the notion of distributive ground, we see that $\Delta \leq$ {A, B} is equivalent to: ($\Delta_{11} \leq$ A ∧ $\Delta_{12} \leq$ B) ∨ ($\Delta_{21} \leq$ A ∧ $\Delta_{22} \leq$ B) ∨..., where {Δ_{11}, Δ_{12}}, {Δ_{21}, Δ_{22}},... run through all the divisions of Δ into pairs. But we may wish to express the same conclusion without embedding the statements of ground within the truth-functional connectives. To this end, note that this disjunction of conjunctions is equivalent to a conjunction of disjunctions. Thus we can state that $\Delta \leq$ {A, B} is a consequence of $\Delta < A \wedge B$ by stating that each of the conjoined disjunctions $D_1 \vee D_2 \vee ...$ is a consequence; and this may then be expressed as a multiple-conclusion inference:

$$\frac{\Delta < A \wedge B}{D_1, D_2, ...}.$$

∀E.
$$\frac{\Delta < \forall x B(x)}{\Delta \leq \{T(a_1, a_2, \ldots), B(a_1), B(a_2), \ldots\}}$$

where a_1, a_2, ... are names, as before, for all of the individuals of the domain.

For the existential quantifier (under the variant approach I suggested), we shall wish to say that a set of truths will be a strict full ground for $\exists x B(x)$ if it distributively grounds the totality claim and some of its true instances. That is:

∃E.
$$\frac{\Delta < \exists x B(x)}{\Delta \leq \{T(a_1, a_2, \ldots), B(a_{11}), B(a_{12}), \ldots\}; \Delta \leq \{T(a_1, a_2, \ldots), B(a_{21}), B(a_{22}), \ldots\}; \ldots}$$

where the a_{k1}, a_{k2}, ... run through all of the non-empty subsets of the a for which $B(a)$ is true.

For the different kinds of negative statement, we have the following elimination rules:

¬∧E.
$$\frac{\Delta < \neg(A \wedge B)}{\Delta \leq \neg A; \Delta \leq \neg B; \Delta \leq \{\neg A, \neg B\}}$$

¬∨E.
$$\frac{\Delta < \neg(A \vee B)}{\Delta \leq \{\neg A, \neg B\}}$$

¬¬E.
$$\frac{\Delta < \neg\neg A}{\Delta \leq A}$$

¬∀E.
$$\frac{\Delta < \neg\forall x F x}{\Delta \leq \{T(a_1, a_2, \ldots), \neg F a_{11}, \neg F a_{12}, \ldots\}; \Delta \leq \{T(a_1, a_2, \ldots), \neg F a_{21}, \neg F a_{22}, \ldots\}; \ldots}$$

¬∃E.
$$\frac{\Delta < \neg\exists x F x}{\Delta \leq T(a_1, a_2, \ldots), \neg F a_1, \neg F a_2, \ldots}$$

From the introduction and elimination rules together, we can establish inferential counterparts of the following biconditionals, which relate the strict ground for a logically complex truth on the left to the weak grounds for its simpler constituents on the right (in the biconditionals for the quantifiers, we use a_1, a_2, ... as names for all of the individuals in the domain and b_1, b_2, ... as names for some of the individuals in the domain):

$\wedge$IE. $\Delta < A \wedge B$ iff there are Δ_1 and Δ_2 for which $\Delta_1 \cup \Delta_2 = \Delta$, $\Delta_1 \leq A$ and $\Delta_2 \leq B$;

$\neg\wedge$IE. $\Delta < \neg(A \wedge B)$ iff $\Delta \leq \neg A$ or $\Delta < \neg B$ or there are Δ_1 and Δ_2 for which $\Delta_1 \cup \Delta_2 = \Delta$, $\Delta_1 \leq A$ and $\Delta_2 \leq B$;

$\vee$IE. $\Delta < A \vee B$ iff $\Delta \leq A$ or $\Delta \leq B$ or there are Δ_1 and Δ_2 for which $\Delta_1 \cup \Delta_2 = \Delta$, $\Delta_1 \leq A$ and $\Delta_2 \leq B$;

$\neg\vee$IE. $\Delta < \neg(A \vee B)$ iff there are Δ_1 and Δ_2 for which $\Delta_1 \cup \Delta_2 = \Delta$, $\Delta_1 \leq \neg A$ and $\Delta_2 \leq \neg B$;

$\neg\neg$IE. $\Delta < \neg\neg A$ iff $\Delta \leq A$;

$\forall$IE. $\Delta < \forall x B(x)$ iff there are $\Delta_0, \Delta_1, \Delta_2, \ldots$ for which $\Delta = \Delta_0 \cup \Delta_1 \cup \Delta_2 \cup \ldots$ and $\Delta_0 \leq T(a_1, a_2, \ldots)$, $\Delta_1 \leq B(a_1)$, $\Delta_2 \leq B(a_2)$, $\ldots$;

$\neg\forall$IE. $\Delta < \neg\forall x B(x)$ iff there are $\Delta_0, \Delta_1, \Delta_2, \ldots$ for which $\Delta = \Delta_0 \cup \Delta_1 \cup \Delta_2 \cup \ldots$ and $\Delta_0 \leq T(a_1, a_2, \ldots)$, $\Delta_1 \leq \neg B(b_1)$, $\Delta_2 \leq \neg B(b_2)$, $\ldots$;

$\exists$IE. $\Delta < \exists x B(x)$ iff there are $\Delta_0, \Delta_1, \Delta_2, \ldots$ for which $\Delta = \Delta_0 \cup \Delta_1 \cup \Delta_2 \cup \ldots$ and $\Delta_0 \leq T(a_1, a_2, \ldots)$, $\Delta_1 \leq B(b_1)$, $\Delta_2 \leq B(b_2)$, $\ldots$;

$\neg\exists$IE. $\Delta < \neg\exists x B(x)$ iff there are $\Delta_0, \Delta_1, \Delta_2, \ldots$ for which $\Delta = \Delta_0 \cup \Delta_1 \cup \Delta_2 \cup \ldots$ and $\Delta_0 \leq T(a_1, a_2, \ldots)$, $\Delta_1 \leq \neg B(a_1)$, $\Delta_2 \leq B(a_2)$, $\ldots$

Suppose that Δ in the IE rules above is confined to "simple" truths – those that are of the form $Fa_1 a_2, \ldots a_n$ or $\neg Fa_1 a_2, \ldots a_n$ for some atomic predicate F or are of the form Ea or $T(a_1, a_2, \ldots)$. Then by using the introduction and elimination rules for weak grounding, it can be shown that the strict grounding statement on the left can be replaced with a weak grounding statement, since the only way some simple truths can be a weak ground for a complex truth is by being a strict ground for the complex truth. Thus in place of $\wedge$IE, we have:

$\wedge$IE* $\Delta \leq A \wedge B$ iff there are Δ_1 and Δ_2 for which $\Delta_1 \cup \Delta_2 = \Delta$, $\Delta_1 \leq A$ and $\Delta_2 \leq B$,

with weak grounding on both left and right; and similarly for the other cases. This reformulation is significant because of its recursive character:

the weak grounding of a complex truth (via simple truths) will successively reduce to the weak grounding of simpler truths.

There is one lacuna in the above account. For it might be hoped that one could say more about when two truths are ground-theoretic equivalents. Two very plausible principles of this sort concern alphabetic variance:

$$\forall x B(x) \leq \forall y B(y) \qquad \exists x B(x) \leq \exists y B(y).$$

The ground-theoretic import of a quantified truth is not affected by a change in variables. Some other principles, though less obvious, might also be adopted. For example:

$A \wedge B \leq B \wedge A$

$A \wedge (B \wedge C) \leq (A \wedge B) \wedge C$

There are, however, definite limits on how far one can go in laying down such principles compatibly with the other rules. One cannot adopt:

$A \wedge A \leq A,$

for example, given $A < A \wedge A$, since then $A < A$. I do not pretend to have a full understanding of how much leeway actually exists.

Given a stock of rules for weak grounding, one might then hope to provide elimination rules for weak grounding. Suppose, for example, that we wish to provide necessary conditions for when Δ is a weak full ground for the conjunction $A \wedge B$. One case, already covered by the rules, is when Δ is a strict full ground for $A \wedge B$. So let us suppose that Δ is a weak but not a strict full ground for $A \wedge B$. Then even though Δ is not itself a strict full ground for $A \wedge B$, it may contain subsets Γ that are strict full grounds for $A \wedge B$. By Amalgamation, the union Γ^* of all such subsets will also be a strict full ground for $A \wedge B$. Let Δ' be the result of removing Γ^* from Δ. Then in this case it may be maintained that Δ' must consist of ground-theoretic equivalents of $A \wedge B$. And so, once we know what these are, we will be done.

1.9 LAMBDA-ABSTRACTION

The lambda operator may be used in two different ways, which are not normally distinguished. Given an open sentence $A(x)$ (such as 'x is unmarried and x is a man'), we may use a lambda operator, call it 'λx,' to form the predicate expression $\lambda x A(x)$ ('is an x such that x is unmarried and x is a man') or we may use a lambda operator, call it 'Λx,' to form the property expression ΛxA(x) ('the property of being an x such that x is unmarried and x is a man'). The resulting expressions will differ syntactically; for the first will be an expression that occupies predicate position while the second will be one that occupies nominal position. They will also, plausibly, differ semantically; for the first will play a descriptive role, enabling us to say how things are, while the second will play a designative role, enabling us to pick out things to be described.[19]

Given a monadic predicate expression P (say 'is wise') and a nominal expression t (say 'Socrates'), let us use P(t) for the result of predicating P of t ('Socrates is wise'); and given a property term Π (say 'the property of being wise') and a nominal expression t (say 'Socrates'), let us use Π[t] to indicate that the object designated by t has the property designated by Π ('Socrates has the property of being wise'). The natural view is that Π[t] itself is the result H(t, Π) of predicating the 'has' predicate H of t and Π.

The two forms of abstraction (we might call them *predicate* and *property* abstraction, respectively) are plausibly taken to conform to the following introduction rules:

ΛI. $\lambda x A(x)(c) < \Lambda x A(x)[c]$ ¬ΛI. $\neg \lambda x A(x)(c) < \neg \Lambda x A(x)[c]$

λI. $A(c) < \lambda x A(x)(c)$ ¬λI. $\neg A(c) < \neg \lambda x A(x)(c)$

According to ΛI (¬ΛI is analogous) John's having the property of being an unmarried man, say, is grounded in the fact that Charles is an unmarried man; and according to λI (again, ¬λI is analogous), John's being an unmarried man is grounded in the fact that Charles is unmarried and Charles is a man.

The two rules are very different. ΛI effects a reduction in ontological complexity; properties are eliminated in favor of predicates. λI, by contrast, effects a reduction in logical complexity; complex predication is eliminated in favor of simple predication. ΛI and λI are often merged:

$$A(c) < \Lambda x A(x)[c].$$

But we see the merger as the product of two separate ground-theoretic connections.

---

[19] An analogous distinction may be drawn for the functional reading of the λ-notation. For λxt(x) may be understood either as a functional expression or as a term for a function.

There are corresponding rules of elimination:

ΛE. $$\frac{\Delta < \Lambda xA(x)[c]}{\Delta \le \lambda xA(x)(c)}$$ ¬ΛE. $$\frac{\Delta < \neg\Lambda xA(x)[c]}{\Delta \le \neg\lambda xA(x)(c)}$$

λE. $$\frac{\Delta < \lambda xA(x)(c)}{\Delta \le A(c)}$$ ¬λE. $$\frac{\Delta < \neg\lambda xA(x)(c)}{\Delta \le \neg A(c)}$$

Thus, according to λE, any strict ground for λxA(x)(c) must be mediated through a weak ground for A(c).

There are also some rules for weak ground-theoretic implication (or equivalence) that one may wish to lay down. Thus corresponding to the rule of alphabetic variance for the quantifiers, we have:

$$\Lambda xA(x)[c] \le \Lambda yA(y)[c] \qquad \lambda xA(x)(c) \le \lambda yA(y)(c).$$

One might, in addition, adopt the following rule of equivalence for λ:

$$P(c) \le \lambda xP(x)(c) \qquad \lambda xP(x)(c) \le P(c)$$

The predicate λxP(x), where what follows λx is a simple predication P(x), is to be treated the same as P. The second of the two principles is, of course, incompatible with λI above, since this requires that $P(c) < \lambda xP(x)(c)$; and so, if we adopt the equivalence, we must restrict λI to the case in which A(x) is not a simple predication.

The original introduction principles, ΛI and λI, raise some troubling issues, related to the paradox of analysis. For according to λI, $A(c) < \lambda xA(x)(c)$. But there surely must then be a sense of "proposition," in which the proposition expressed by A(c) can be taken to stand in a relation of ground to the proposition expressed by λxA(x)(c). Using <A> to signify the proposition expressed by A, we therefore have that <A(c)> grounds <λxA(x)(c)>. In the case in which c is 'Charles,' for example, and A(x) is the open sentence 'x is unmarried & x is a man,' we will have the proposition that Charles is an unmarried man will ground the proposition that he is a bachelor.

But how can that be? For both propositions are predicatively composed of the subject Charles and the property of being a bachelor; the property is predicated of the subject to form the proposition. And so how can the propositions be different, as would be required for the one to ground the other?

Likewise, according to ΛI, $\lambda xA(x)(c) < \Lambda xA(x)[c]$. So $<\lambda xA(x)(c)>$ grounds $<\Lambda xA(x)[c]>$ – the proposition that Charles is bachelor, for example, will ground the proposition that Charles has the property of being a bachelor. But again, how can that be, given that both propositions are predicatively composed of Charles and the property of being a bachelor?

I suggest that we solve this puzzle by distinguishing between different ways in which a proposition may be predicatively composed of a subject and a property. It can be *straight* predication. Thus if the subject is Charles and the property is the property of being an unmarried man ($\Lambda x(x$ is unmarried $\&$ x is a man$)$), then the resulting proposition is the one expressed by the sentence 'Charles is an unmarried man' ('$\lambda x(x$ is a man $\&$ x is unmarried$)$(Charles)'). Thus the property occurs as a property (or predicatively) in the resulting proposition.

The predication can also be *upward*. Thus if the subject is Charles and the property is the property of being an unmarried man ($\Lambda x(x$ is unmarried $\&$ x is a man$)$), then the resulting proposition is the one expressed by the sentence 'Charles has the property of being an unmarried man' ('$\Lambda x(x$ is a man $\&$ x is unmarried$)$[Charles]'). Here the property occurs as an object (or nominally) in the resulting proposition. As I have mentioned, a plausible view is that the upward predication of P of x is the same as the straight predication of the relation of having of P and x; and if this is so, then upward predication is directly reducible to straight predication.

Finally, the predication can be *downward*. If the subject is Charles and the property is the property of being an unmarried man ($\Lambda x(x$ is unmarried $\&$ x is a man$)$), then the resulting proposition is the one expressed by the sentence 'Charles is a man $\&$ Charles is unmarried.' Here the property occurs as an abstract (or as the result of abstraction) in the resulting proposition. It is seen to be present in the proposition through a process of abstraction whereby the subject (Charles) is removed and the property remains. We cannot give a direct definition of downward predication in terms of straight predication but the result of downward predication can always be seen to be the result of straight predication. The proposition that Charles is unmarried $\&$ Charles is a man, for example, can also be seen to be the result of conjoining the straight predication of the property of being unmarried of Charles with the straight predication of the property of being a man of Charles.

So even though the propositions expressed by '$\Lambda x(x$ is unmarried $\&$ x is a man$)$[Charles],' '$\lambda x(x$ is unmarried $\&$ x is a man$)$(Charles),' and 'Charles is unmarried $\&$ Charles is a man' are each the result of predicating the property of being an unmarried man of the subject Charles, they are each this result by means of a different manner of predication; and there is therefore no difficulty in distinguishing between the propositions or in allowing the various grounding relations between them to obtain.[20]

1.10 THE SEMANTICS OF GROUND

There is a standard "possible worlds" semantics for logical consequence or entailment. Under this semantics, each sentence A of the language under consideration is associated with the "truth-set" |A| of possible worlds in which it is true, and it is then supposed that:

C is a consequence of A_1, A_2, ... iff a world w verifies C (i.e. is a member of the truth-set |A|) whenever it verifies each of A_1, A_2, ... (i.e. whenever it belongs to each of the truth-sets $|A_1|$, $|A_2|$, ...).

This semantics is not suited to the notion of ground since it yields Weakening. If C is a consequence of A_1, A_2, ... then it is a consequence of A_1, A_2, ... along with any other sentences B_1, B_2, ... But is there any alternative account of the semantics of sentences and of the connection of ground that might be made to work?

It turns out that one can provide a very natural semantics of this sort in terms of the idea of truth-making. I have said some harsh things about truth-maker theory. But even though it might not amount to much as an approach to ontology, it provides an ideal framework within which to set up a semantics for ground. For in setting up such a semantics, we would like to be able to appeal to something analogous to the relationship between a sentence and the worlds within which it is true; and it turns out that the relationship between a sentence and the facts that make it true will exactly fit the bill.

---

[20] Rosen (2010, p. 125) is of the view that the proposition that *a* is grue (where to be grue is to be red or green) and the proposition that *a* is red or green will differ in that (i) the former but not the latter will contain *grue* and (ii) the latter but not the former will contain *green*. Thus where I see a difference in the manner of composition (or predication), he sees a difference in the constituents. The first of his two claims is much more plausible than the second, but only the first is required to distinguish between the two propositions. I could perhaps agree with him on the first claim (even if not on the second) under a construal of composition in which composition through abstraction is not allowed. However, I believe that the downward form of composition should not simply be ignored but should be recognized as a genuine form of composition in its own right. For more on the underlying conception of composition, see Fine 2010a.

Just as we previously supposed that each sentence A was associated with a truth-set |A|, the set of possible worlds in which it is true, we may now suppose that each (true) sentence is associated with a verification-set [A], the set of facts which make it true. Facts differ from worlds in two respects. First, they are actual and not also possible. Second, they need not be complete, i.e. they need not settle the truth-value of every proposition. Facts, on this conception, are *parts* of the actual world.

There is a natural sense in which facts may be *fused*. So, for example, given the fact *f* that this ball is red and the fact *g* that it is round, there will be a *fused* fact *f.g* to the effect that the ball is both red and round; and in general, given any facts *f, g, h*, . . ., there will exist a fusion *f.g.h*. . . . of those facts. It will be supposed that the verification set [A] for each true sentence is closed under fusion. In other words, the fusion of facts that verify a sentence also verifies the sentence (this is a kind of semantic counterpart of Amalgamation).

We may now adopt the following semantical clause for weak ground:

(i) $A_1, A_2, \ldots$ is a weak full ground for C ($A_1, A_2, \ldots \le$ C is true) iff $f_1.f_2.f_3.\ldots$ verifies C (i.e. $f_1.f_2.f_3.\ldots$ is a member of the verification-set [C]) whenever f_1 verifies A_1, f_2 verifies A_2, f_3 verifies A_3 . . . (i.e. whenever each of $f_1, f_2, f_3,\ldots$ is a member of the respective verification-sets $[A_1], [A_2], [A_3],\ldots$).

Note that the fact $f_1.f_2.f_3.\ldots$ that is to verify C is the fusion of the facts f_1, $f_2, f_3\ldots$ that verify the antecedents $A_1, A_2, A_3,\ldots$; they cooperate, so to speak, in verifying the consequent C. It is because of this difference in the clause for consequence that Weakening no longer holds. For suppose that A is a weak full ground for C, so that any fact that verifies A will verify C. There is then no guarantee that A, B is also a weak full ground for C. For given that *f* verifies A and that *g* verifies B, we will know that *f* verifies C but not that the fusion *f.g* will verify C.

Similar clauses can be given for the other notions of ground:

(ii) A is a weak partial ground for C (A $\le$ C is true) iff for some sentences $A_1, A_2, \ldots$ (and assignment of verification-sets to them) A, $A_1, A_2, \ldots$ is a weak full ground for C;

(iii) $A_1, A_2, \ldots$ is a strict full ground for C ($A_1, A_2, \ldots <$ C) iff A_1, $A_2, \ldots$ is a weak full ground for C and C is not a weak partial ground for any of $A_1, A_2, \ldots$;

(iv) A is a strict partial ground for C (A $\prec$ C is true) iff A is a weak partial ground for C but C is not a weak partial ground for A.

Using these clauses, we can then establish soundness and completeness for the pure logic of ground, as set out above. This provides some kind of vindication both for the system and for the semantics.

There is a natural extension of the above semantics to the connectives and the quantifiers. To allow for the presence of negation in the language, we now associate with each sentence C both a set $[C]^+$ of verifiers and a set $[C]^-$ of falsifiers. One of these sets is non-empty, depending upon whether the sentence is true or false, while the other is empty.[21] Let us use τ for the totality fact. Then using the recursive rules at the end of Section 1.10 as our guide, we are led to adopt the following semantical clauses for when a fact will verify or falsify a logically complex sentence:

(i) $\wedge$T f verifies A $\wedge$ B iff there are f_1 and f_2 such that $f_1.f_2 = f$, f_1 verifies A and f_2 verifies B;

        $\wedge$F f falsifies A $\wedge$ B iff f falsifies A or f falsifies B or there are f_1 and f_2 such that $f = f_1.f_2$, f_1 falsifies A and f_2 falsifies B;

(ii) $\vee$T f verifies A $\vee$ B iff f verifies A or f verifies B or there are f_1 and f_2 such that $f = f_1.f_2$, f_1 verifies A and f_2 verifies B;

        $\vee$F f falsifies A $\vee$ B iff there are f_1 and f_2 such that $f = f_1.f_2$, f_1 falsifies A and f_2 falsifies B;

(iii) $\neg$T f verifies $\neg$A iff f falsifies A;

        $\neg$F f falsifies $\neg$A iff f verifies A;

(iv) $\forall$T f verifies $\forall$xB(x) iff there are $f_1, f_2, \ldots$ such that $f = \tau. f_1. f_2. \ldots$, and f_1 verifies B(a_1), f_2 verifies B(a_2), $\ldots$ (with $a_1, a_2, \ldots$ running through all of the individuals);

        $\forall$F f falsifies $\forall$xFx iff there are $f_1, f_2, \ldots$ such that $f = \tau. f_1. f_2. \ldots$, and f_1 falsifies B(b_1), f_2 falsifies B(b_2), $\ldots$ (with $b_1, b_2, \ldots$ running through some of the individuals);

(v) $\exists$T f verifies $\exists$xFx iff there are $f_1, f_2, \ldots$ such that $f = \tau. f_1. f_2. \ldots$, and f_1 verifies B(b_1), f_2 verifies B(b_2), $\ldots$;

        $\exists$F f falsifies $\exists$xFx iff there are $f_1, f_2, \ldots$ such that $f = \tau. f_1. f_2. \ldots$, and f_1 falsifies B(a_1), f_2 falsifies B(a_2), $\ldots$

The clause for $\wedge$T, for example, corresponds to rule $\wedge$IE* above, but with the facts f, f_1, and f_2 in place of the grounding sets Δ, Δ_1, and Δ_2 and with the fusion $f_1. f_2$ of the facts f_1 and f_2 in place of the union $\Delta_1 \cup \Delta_2$ of the grounding sets Δ_1

---

[21] Bas van Fraassen (1969) has developed some related ideas but his semantical clauses and the logic he gets out of them are somewhat different from my own.

and Δ_2. It should be noted that, under this semantics, the "factual content" of A ∨ ¬A and of B ∨ ¬B will not in general be the same, since the verifiers for A ∨ ¬A will be the facts that either verify or falsify A while the verifiers for B ∨ ¬B will be the facts that either verify or falsify B; and similarly for A and (A ∧ B) ∨ (A ∧ ¬B) and many other truth-functionally equivalent formulas.

I believe that the factualist semantics has numerous other applications – to the semantics of counterfactuals, for example, to confirmation theory and the theory of verisimilitude, to the frame problem in AI, and to a number of problems in linguistics; and I find it remarkable that the semantics should have an independent "purely metaphysical" motivation in terms of the inferential behavior of ground.[22]

I.II   ESSENCE AND GROUND

Given an object or some objects, we may say that it lies in the nature of those objects that such and such should hold – that it lies in the nature of singleton Socrates, for example, that it should have Socrates as a member. But what then is the connection between statements of nature or essence and statements of ground?[23]

A natural view is this. Given that the fact F is grounded in the facts G_1, G_2, ..., then it lies in the nature of the fact F (or of the items that it involves) that it should be so grounded given that the facts G_1, G_2, ... do indeed obtain. So, for example, given that the fact that the ball is red and round is grounded in the fact that it is red and the fact that it is round, it will lie in the nature of the fact that the ball is red and round that this fact will be grounded in the fact that the ball is red and the fact that the ball is round (given that the ball is in fact red and is in fact round).[24]

Unfortunately, this view will not quite do as it stands. The fact that someone is a philosopher, we may suppose, is grounded in the fact that Socrates is a philosopher (and perhaps also that he exists and is a person).

---

[22] An application to counterfactuals is developed in Fine 2012b. It should be made clear, however, that the factualist semantics in its current form is not adequate as a semantics for the previous logic of ground. The semantics does not distinguish between A and A ∨ A, for example, the verifying and the falsifying facts being the same in each case. But we shall need to distinguish between them within the logic, since A will be a strict ground for A ∨ A while A ∨ A is not a strict ground for A.

[23] The concept of essence is further discussed in Fine 1994.

[24] I say that it lies in the nature of the *fact* that the ball is red and round and thereby treat the fact as an object (perhaps identical to the *proposition* that the ball is red and round). But there is something to be said for allowing it to lie in the nature of what it is for the ball to be red and round, where this is represented by a sentential rather than by a nominal complement to the essentialist operator.

But it does not lie in the nature of the fact that someone is a philosopher that the fact is so grounded given that Socrates is indeed a philosopher. The fact, so to speak, knows nothing of Socrates. Or again, the fact that the ball is colored is grounded, we may suppose, in the fact that it is red. But it does not lie in the nature of the fact that the ball is colored that it is so grounded given that the ball is indeed red. The fact and *color*, in particular, know nothing of the specific colors.

The difficulty in these cases arises from the grounds G_1, G_2, ... being merely an instance of the grounds that the given fact F is capable of possessing. Thus the fact that someone is a philosopher could equally well be grounded in the fact that Plato is a philosopher and the fact that the ball is colored could equally well be grounded in the fact that it is blue. But suppose that we generalize the statement of ground. We say that the fact that someone is a philosopher is, for any person x, grounded in the fact that x is a philosopher given that x is indeed a philosopher and that the fact that the ball is colored is, for any color c, grounded in the fact that the ball is of color c given that the ball is indeed of color c. It does then seem plausible to say that these generalized statements of ground will hold in virtue of the nature of the grounded fact – that it lies in the nature of the fact that someone is a philosopher, for example, that this fact will, for any person x, be grounded in the fact that x is a philosopher given that x is indeed a philosopher.

Let us state the point more generally. Suppose that the truth C is grounded in B_1, B_2, ... Then the grounds B_1, B_2, ... will concern certain existing items a_1, a_2, ... and so may be stated in the form $B_1(a_1, a_2, ...)$, $B_2(a_1, a_2, ...)$, ... A generalization of this particular connection of ground will therefore take the form:

$$B_1(x_1, x_2, ...), B_2(x_1, x_2, ...), ... \text{ is a ground for C whenever } A(x_1, x_2, ...),$$

where $A(x_1, x_2, ...)$ is a condition that in fact holds of a_1, a_2, ...[25] Thus given that $A(x_1, x_2, ...)$ in fact holds of the existing items a_1, a_2, ..., the particular connection of ground will logically follow from the general connection.

What we may now claim is that whenever a given truth C is grounded in other truths, then there is a generalization of the particular connection of ground that will hold in virtue of the nature of C (or of the items it

---

[25] Strictly speaking, we should also require that it is a *necessary* truth that $B_1(x_1, x_2, ...)$, $B_2(x_1, x_2, ...)$, ... is a ground for C whenever $A(x_1, x_2, ...)$ and $B_1(x_1, x_2, ...)$, $B_2(x_1, x_2, ...)$, ... are the case.

involves). Thus the particular explanatory connection between the fact C and its grounds may itself be explained in terms of the nature of C.

It should be noted that what explains the ground-theoretic connection is something concerning the nature of the fact that C (or of what it is for C to be the case) and not of the grounding facts themselves. Thus what explains the ball's being red or green in virtue of its being red is something about the nature of what it is for the ball to be red or green (and about the nature of disjunction in particular) and not something about the nature of what it is for the ball to be red. It is the fact to be grounded that "points" to its grounds and not the grounds that point to what they may ground.

One might hold that the ground-theoretic connection holds in virtue of the nature of its grounds and the general nature of ground in addition to the nature of the fact to be grounded. But this is a far weaker and far less interesting claim. For it might be held as a general thesis that every necessary truth is grounded in the nature of certain items (Fine 1994); and, as a rule, these will be the items involved in the necessary truth itself. But given that C is grounded in B_1, B_2,..., it will be necessary that C is grounded in B_1, B_2, ... if B_1, B_2, ... are the case; and so it will follow from the general thesis that it lies in the nature of certain items – presumably those involved in C and B_1, B_2,... and *ground* itself – that this is so. Claiming that the fact to be grounded bears full responsibility, so to speak, for the ground-theoretic connection is to make an essentialist claim that goes far beyond the assertion of a general link between necessity and nature.

Part of the interest of the stronger thesis lies in its bearing upon the methodology of metaphysics. For investigation into ground is part of the investigation into nature; and if the essentialist locus of ground-theoretic connections lies in the fact to be grounded and not in the grounds, then it is by investigating the nature of the items involved in the facts to be grounded rather than in the grounds that we will discover what grounds what. Thus the asymmetry supports a top-down approach in which we start with the facts to be grounded and work our way down to their grounds, rather than the other way round.

Part of the interest of the stronger thesis also lies in its bearing upon the general nature of objects. If we were merely given a general link between necessity and nature, then this would be perfectly compatible with ground-theoretic connections always holding partly in virtue of the nature of *ground*. Thus the nature of *being colored* might have nothing to do with *ground*; and so whereas it might lie in the nature of *being colored* that anything colored was of a particular color, it would not lie in the nature of *being colored* that anything colored was colored *in virtue of* being a particular color. What then accounted for the fact that anything colored was colored *in virtue of* being a particular color would be something about the nature of *being colored* and something about the nature of *ground*. The nature of *ground* would somehow "feed off" the nature of *being colored* to give us this particular ground-theoretic connection.

But what is being claimed is that this is not so and that ground-theoretic connections will be inextricably involved in the nature of certain things. It is not just that they must, by their very nature, behave in a certain way but that there must, by their very nature, be a certain ground-theoretic basis for their behavior. Thus it may well be thought to be essential to the nature of being colored not merely that anything colored is of a specific color but that anything colored is colored *in virtue of* being a specific color; the ground-theoretic basis for being colored is built into the very identity of what it is to be colored.

Rosen (2010, pp. 132–3) has suggested some counterexamples to the proposed link between ground and essence (and even to weaker versions of the link). Suppose, for example, that something's being right or good is grounded in certain naturalistic features of the object. Then on a non-reductive view of normativity, it will not lie in the nature of *right* or *good* that it is grounded in these particular features. And similarly for the case of a non-reductive materialist, who thinks that facts about pain are grounded in facts about our brain or the like and yet does not think that it lies in the nature of pain that it should be so grounded.

My own view is that the apparent plausibility of these counterexamples depends upon conflating different conceptions of ground. Corresponding to the concepts of normative and natural necessity will be normative and natural conceptions of ground, which are to be distinguished from the purely metaphysical conception. The view that the normative is grounded in the natural is only plausible for the normative conception of ground and the view that the mental is grounded in the physical is only plausible for the natural conception. Since the grounding relation in these cases is not metaphysical, there is no need for there to be an explanation of its holding in terms of the essentialist nature of the items involved. What may be plausible, though, is that it should lie in the nature of *goodness*, say, that it should have *some* ground in what is natural and that it should lie in the nature of *pain* that it should have *some* ground in what is physical; and if the respective conceptions of ground here are normative and natural, then we see that these other conceptions of ground may have an important role to play in delineating the nature of certain essentially "realized" properties or features.[26]

Given the proposed connection between essence and ground, it might be wondered whether it might somehow be converted into a definition of ground.[27] For given that B_1, B_2, ... is a ground for C, there will be some generalization of this statement of ground that will hold in virtue of the nature of C. Now this generalization will be a general statement of what grounds what. But corresponding to this ground-theoretic generalization will be a ground-free generalization in which the notion of material implication replaces the notion of ground. Thus instead of saying 'C is grounded in B_1, B_2, ... (or the like) if B_1, B_2, ... (or the like) hold,' we simply say 'C if B_1, B_2, ...' It may now be suggested that we define B_1, B_2, ... to ground C just in case some ground-free generalization of the statement of ground holds in virtue of the nature of C.

However, there are a number of things wrong with this definition. One is that it does not enable us to distinguish between the plural ground B_1, B_2, ... and the single conjunctive ground $B_1 \wedge B_2 \wedge ...$, since the ground-free generalization will be the same in each case. Another is that it will predict the result that $A \wedge A$ grounds A, since it will be true in virtue of the nature of A that A if $A \wedge A$. Thus the proposed definition will not even provide a sufficient condition for weak ground.

To this last objection, it may be responded that it will only be true in virtue of the nature of A that A if $A \wedge A$ under a "consequentialist" conception of essence, one in which the essentialist truths are taken to be closed under some notion of logical consequence. But it might be thought that underlying any consequentialist conception of essence is a "constitutive" conception, which will not be automatically closed

[26] I have benefitted from Rosen's (2010, §13) discussion of these issues and our views are somewhat alike. But note that whereas I have one thesis, that any ground-theoretic connection can be generalized to one that flows from the nature of the items involved in the given fact, he has two theses: that any ground-theoretic connection can be generalized; and that any general ground-theoretic connection will flow from the nature of the items involved in the given fact and its grounds. Thus my view traces the source of the ground-theoretic connection to the nature of the items involved in the given fact while his also appeals to the nature of the items involved in its grounds. I should add that there are problems with his formulation of *Formality* (p. 131). Merely saying that a statement of ground has a generalization is not enough. The ball is perhaps red or round because it is red. But the required level of generality is not achieved by saying that anything will be red or round because it is red. Moreover, the appropriate generalization cannot in general be stated simply through appeal to propositional forms. One might think, for example, that the species Dog exists because there are dogs. But how are we to generalize this without appealing to the connection between Dog and being a dog? Our own formulation avoids these problems.

[27] E. J. Lowe considers and points out some difficulties in providing an essentialist account of truth-making in Chapter 11 of Lowe and Rami 2008.

under logical consequence and for which it will not be true in virtue of the nature of A that A if A ∧ A.[28]

There is no doubt that appeal to a constitutive conception of essence will enable us to approximate more closely to the notion of ground. But how are we to understand the relationship between constitutive and consequentialist essence? One view is that we understand the latter in terms of the former. Roughly, to belong to the consequentialist essence of something is to be a logical consequence of what belongs to the constitutive essence. But another view, to which I am more inclined, is that we understand the former in terms of the latter. One statement of consequentialist essence may be partly grounded in others. The fact that it lies in the nature of a given set to be a set or a set, for example, is partly grounded in the fact that it lies in the nature of the set to be a set. The *constitutive* claims of essence can then be taken to be those consequentialist statements of essence that are not partly grounded in other such claims. This way of conceiving the distinction enables us to "factor out" the purely essentialist aspect of the concept of essence from the partly explanatory aspect. But it means that the constitutive concept of essence is then of no help to us in understanding the concept of ground.

But there is perhaps a more serious objection to the proposed definition, which may arise even when we make use of the constitutive conception of essence. For certain statements of essence appear to be symmetric between ground and what is grounded. It might be thought, for example, that there is a distinction between existing *at a time* and existing *simpliciter* and that it is essential to any object that exists in time that it exists simpliciter iff it exists at a time. But the definition will then give us an equal right to say that the object exists simpliciter in virtue of existing at a time and that it exists at a time in virtue of existing simpliciter. But compatibly with the essentialist claim, we might want to make the first of these ground-theoretic statements to the exclusion of the other and we would certainly not want to make both statements under a strict conception of ground or even under a weak conception of ground, given that existing at a time essentially involves the notion of time while existing simpliciter does not.

I think it should be recognized that there are two fundamentally different types of explanation. One is of identity, or of what something is; and the other is of truth, or of how things are. It is natural to want to reduce them to a common denominator – to see explanations of identity

---

[28] The distinction between the two conceptions of essence is further discussed in Fine 1995b.

as a special kind of explanation of the truth or to see explanations of truth as a special kind of explanation of identity or to see them in some other way as instances of a single form of explanation. But this strikes me as a mistake.

Carnap distinguished some time ago between formation and transformation rules. The former were for the construction of formulas and the latter for the construction of proofs. The formation rules provide an explanation of identity, of what the formulas are, while the transformation rules help provide an explanation of truth, of when a formula is true (or valid). It would clearly be an error to think of the one kind of rule as an instance of the other or to see them as falling under a common rubric. And it seems to me that there is a similar error – but writ large over the whole metaphysical landscape – in attempting to assimilate or unify the concepts of essence and ground. The two concepts work together in holding up the edifice of metaphysics; and it is only by keeping them separate that we can properly appreciate what each is on its own and what they are capable of doing together.

CHAPTER 2

Scepticism about grounding

Chris Daly

2.1 INTRODUCTION

A minimal claim that any theory of grounding will make is that talk of grounding is intelligible. Yet it is controversial whether such talk *is* intelligible. Two (mutually exclusive) strategies to support that minimal claim are available. One is to define 'grounding' using terms that are already well understood. The other is to take 'grounding' as a primitive term but to use various ways to convey its meaning. This chapter will offer sceptical responses to both strategies whilst paying special attention to the second. The chief contention of the chapter is that, if treated as a primitive, 'grounding' is unintelligible. Grounding theorists are alive to this sceptical response and have tried to counter it. The chapter will seek to show that their attempts to date fail.

2.2 THE TARGET CLAIMS

Jonathan Schaffer, Gideon Rosen, and Paul Audi share the following view: Hume was mistaken. Causation is not the cement of the universe. There are other equally important metaphysical relations that structure the universe. Causation is just one species of the generic relation of determination. Besides causal determination, there are various species of non-causal determination, including necessitation. In addition to those two categories of relations, there are relations of supervenience (which itself has species), ontological dependence, and grounding. Furthermore, grounding cannot be understood in other terms although it is ubiquitous and invaluable in understanding many philosophical issues (see Audi this volume, manuscript c, Rosen 2010, and Schaffer 2009b).

Two points of clarification: First, Schaffer, Rosen, and Audi do not speak with one voice. They disagree, for example, about what the relata of the grounding relation are. For the purposes of this discussion, we will follow Rosen and Audi in taking facts to be the relata of the grounding relation. The fact that *a* is F will be represented as: [F*a*]. Nothing of substance will turn on this construal of the relata of the grounding relation. Second, the view to be attributed to Schaffer, Rosen, and Audi is a *collective view* in the following sense. We will be considering claims that one or other of these three philosophers make, provided that none of the others have stated a contrary claim. The purpose of considering a collective view is that we have before us the most articulated and defensible statement of Schaffer, Rosen, and Audi's theories.

The collective view involves three claims of particular interest:

(1) The term 'grounding' is intelligible.
(2) The term is primitive.
(3) The term is useful.

It is perhaps natural to seek to understand 'grounding' by defining it in terms that are (supposedly) better understood. To this end, we might try to define '[Fa] is grounded by [Gb]' as: [Fa] is necessitated by [Gb], or as: [Fa] is a constituent of an essential property of [Gb], or as: [Gb] supervenes on [Fa]. The case which grounding theorists such as Schaffer, Rosen, and Audi provide against these definitions (e.g. Schaffer 2009b, pp. 363–4) cumulatively provide a case for claim (2).

If 'grounding' cannot be defined, it has to be taken as primitive. How can we then understand it? Indeed, how can the term be shown even to be intelligible? Claim (1) involves a three-point response.

First, Schaffer, Rosen, and Audi state what they take to be the formal properties of 'grounding'. Here is a summary of their findings. Grounding is irreflexive, asymmetric, and transitive. It is factive (so that if [Fa] grounds [Gb], it follows that both of those facts exist). It is non-monotonic (so that if [Fa] is grounded by [Gb], it does not follow that [Fa] is grounded by [Gb] and any other fact). It is relative (it is consistent with [Gb] grounding [Fa] that there is some other fact, [Hc], that grounds [Gb]). It is partial (it is consistent with [Gb] grounding [Fa] that there is some other fact, [Id], that also grounds [Fa]). It is hyperintensional (so that even if [Fa] grounds [Gb], and the proposition that [Fa] exists is logically equivalent to the proposition that [Hc] exists, it does not follow that [Hc] grounds [Gb]). Expansion and contraction inferences are not valid for it. It is category-neutral. Lastly, it is governed by metaphysical laws (if [Fa] is grounded by [Gb], this is because of metaphysical laws governing facts about F's and G's).

Second, Schaffer, Rosen, and Audi specify some important terms that 'grounding' is analytically related to, including 'fundamental', 'existent', and 'reduction', and which we supposedly have some antecedent understanding of.

Third, they use familiar examples as illustrations of grounding. By appreciating the examples, we can come to understand 'grounding' better.

Having been given some explanation about how to understand 'grounding', it remains to be seen how useful the term is. To support claim (3), Schaffer, Rosen, and Audi cite a range of philosophical issues that involve grounding. They include issues about, for example, property identity, the mind–body problem, and the debate between moral particularism and moral generalism (Audi this volume). Work by other philosophers, such as Fine, Lowe, Kim, and Ruben, further supports this claim. (See Fine 1994, 1995a, Lowe 2005b, 2009, Kim 1974, and Ruben 1990, chapter VII.) We will return to Fine and Lowe's work briefly in Section 2.7.

2.3 SELECTING THE SCEPTICAL STRATEGY

If one were to challenge any of claims (1)–(3), it might seem that the least promising strategy would be to deny claim (1). In fact, that strategy turns out to be the most promising.

First of all, it promises the greatest dividends. If a term *t* is unintelligible, it lacks even a primitive meaning. So any case against claim (1) would automatically be a case against claim (2). The converse, however, does not hold: a term that does not have a primitive meaning may be definable and so not be unintelligible. Again, if *t* is unintelligible, then it cannot do any genuinely useful work. So any case against claim (1) would automatically be a case against claim (3). The converse, however, does not hold: a term that does not be have a primitive meaning may be both definable and able to do useful work. Still, the strategy promises the greatest dividends only since it is the most ambitious. Yet why think it is the most promising *to succeed*? This takes us to the second and third points.

Consider the rival sceptical strategies. Suppose that claim (1) is conceded. Arguing against claim (2) would require meeting Schaffer and others' arguments in support of that claim. More importantly, to concede claim (1) and to argue against claim (2) would *ipso facto* lend support to the claim that 'grounding' is definable. Doing that would only help rehabilitate talk of grounding in the philosophical community. Far from advancing the case of the sceptic about grounding, conceding (1) and arguing against (2) would only play into the hands of a grounding theorist who made that selection and then further claimed that talk of grounding is philosophically useful.

For the third point, suppose that (1) and (2) are conceded but (3) is denied. As noted, Schaffer, Rosen, and Audi draw up a series of philosophical issues that can be formulated in terms of grounding. The sceptic's task would then be to show that all of these issues can be equally well formulated without talk of grounding and so that such talk does not have special utility. How might the sceptic argue for that? If the sceptic had argued that talk of grounding is unintelligible, such an argument would be available. But we have supposed that the sceptic has conceded that such talk is intelligible. The sceptic's eliminating just a few issues by showing that talk of grounding does not add anything of explanatory value to them is of limited value. Although it would proportionately weaken the grounding theorists' overall case for their view, it would fail to overturn it. Instead, what the sceptic would need to argue is that, although talk of grounding is intelligible, it is explanatorily empty.

How might the sceptic's argument for denying claim (3) proceed? There seem to be three ways in which it can be argued that a given hypothesis is explanatorily vacuous. The hypothesis either (a) merely re-labels the phenomena, or (b) passes the buck, or (c) is obscure. Take these in turn.

(a) A hypothesis can be explanatorily vacuous because it merely re-labels the phenomena it purports to explain. There are two ways in which this can happen. One way involves the supposed *explanans* having the same content as the *explanandum*; the other way involves the supposed *explanans* having more content than the *explanandum*.

On the first way, the hypothesis's supposed *explanans* has the same content as the *explanandum*. Given that explanation is an irreflexive relation, the hypothesis fails to give an explanation. Now the grounding hypothesis purports to explain certain modal phenomena by saying what makes it the case that some fact obtains (Audi this volume, p. 102). Examples of these modal phenomena include the following. Objects that are indiscernible with respect to their natural properties are indiscernible with respect to their normative properties. Objects that are indiscernible with respect to their functional properties and their environments are indiscernible with respect to their propositional attitudes. And complex objects that are indiscernible with respect to their parts are indiscernible. (Following Kim 1984, 'indiscernibility' is here defined as follows: x in world w is indiscernible with respect to some set of properties A from y in world $w' =_{df}$ for every property ϕ in A, x in w has ϕ if and only if y in w' has ϕ.) Suppose it is claimed that the grounding hypothesis has the same content as its *explananda*. The *explananda* can be described without using such terms as 'grounding' or 'in virtue of' or any of their cognates. For example, we have just seen how the indiscernibility of objects can be described using possible worlds semantics and quantification over properties. Given the assumed sameness of content, is this kind of talk to be explained in terms of talk of grounding, or vice versa? The first option seems unpromising: it is hard to see how alethic necessity and possibility, for example, can be explained in terms of grounding. This leaves only the second option: that talk of grounding is to be explained in other terms. It would follow that talk of grounding is not primitive. Yet that is a questionable consequence for the reasons that Schaffer and others have given. Therefore, there are reasons to reject the supposition that the grounding hypothesis has the same content as its *explananda*.

On the second way, the hypothesis has more content than the *explanans* but only re-labels the *explanans* without explaining it. For example, the hypothesis that events are fated is explanatorily vacuous in this sense. According to that hypothesis, an event occurs if and only if it is fated to occur. Stating that event *e* was fated to occur has more content than stating that *e* occurred. But the hypothesis is explanatorily vacuous because it rules nothing in and rules nothing out and there is no independent way of determining just what is fated. In general, it has been claimed that a hypothesis is explanatorily vacuous if it is not independently testable (Hempel 1965, p. 433, Salmon 1984, p. 114, and 1989, p. 179).

This criterion of independent testability is very restrictive. According to it, the only explanations of empirical phenomena are hypotheses that can pass empirical tests:

The laws invoked in a proposed scientific explanation are of course capable of test; and adverse test results may lead to their rejection ... An account that has no implications concerning empirical phenomena cannot serve this purpose [i.e. arriving at 'an objectively testable and empirically well-supported body of empirical knowledge'], however strong its intuitive appeal: from the point of view of science, it is a *pseudo-explanation*, an explanation in appearance only. (Hempel 1965, p. 433)

It is sufficient to require that statements of alleged explanatory 'facts' be reasonably well confirmed before they are asserted in explanatory contexts – or at the very least, that they be open to scientific confirmation or disconfirmation. (Salmon 1984, p. 114)

Hempel and Salmon's criterion is non-obvious and this chapter does not endorse it. What will now be shown, however, is that the grounding hypothesis does not violate the criterion.

What the criterion's implications for the grounding hypothesis are depends on whether the hypothesis is supposed to explain some empirical phenomenon. Either the hypothesis is concerned with at least one empirical phenomenon, or it is not concerned with any empirical phenomena.

The grounding hypothesis is concerned both with non-empirical phenomena, such as facts about non-empty sets and their members, and empirical phenomena, such as dispositional and categorical facts. More carefully, it is concerned with a relation (grounding) that is supposed to hold between ordered pairs of these facts, and the issue is whether it is an empirical matter whether this relation holds between some of these ordered pairs.

Suppose it is an empirical matter. Then the issue arises as to whether the grounding hypothesis is open to scientific confirmation or disconfirmation. The matter is unclear. Here is a consideration that might be used to argue that the hypothesis *is* open to scientific confirmation. The grounding theorist might run a parallel argument to the indispensability argument for the existence of mathematical objects (Quine 1951a, §6, and Putnam 1971). The grounding theorist might argue that the grounding hypothesis is a high-level hypothesis about how the empirical (and non-empirical) world is structured and that it can receive indirect evidential support from successful predictions made by our total theory. This suggestion cannot be pursued further here. The relevant point is that if it is an empirical matter that the grounding relation holds between certain ordered pairs of facts, the grounding theorist would have at least a good initial case for claiming that his hypothesis is *not* explanatorily vacuous because it merely redescribed the phenomena.

Alternatively, suppose it is not an empirical matter whether the grounding relation holds between various ordered pairs of facts. Then Hempel and Salmon's criterion of independent testability has no bearing, because that criterion concerns only hypotheses that seek to explain empirical phenomena. That criterion underpinned the second way in which a hypothesis could be explanatorily vacuous because it merely redescribed the *explanans*. It follows that there would be no basis for claiming that the grounding hypothesis was explanatorily vacuous for that reason.

To sum up, there are two ways of construing the claim that a hypothesis can be explanatorily vacuous because it merely re-labels the phenomena that it purports to explain. The grounding hypothesis does not seem to be explanatorily vacuous in either of those ways.

(b) A hypothesis can be explanatorily vacuous because it 'passes the buck'. This means that the hypothesis purports to explain certain phenomena but its explanation involves only another instance of the same phenomena. For example, the sense datum theory seems to have this failing. Perception represents how the world is: the experience of there looking to be something red in front of you represents there being something red in front of you. The sense datum theory purports to explain how perception does this. The theory says that the experience of there looking to be something red in front of you consists in your being aware of a red mental object (a sense datum). Your being aware of a red mental object, however, is an experience of its looking that there is something red in front of you. So it too involves your representing there being something red in front of you. The sense datum theory defers, and fails to accomplish, the task of explaining how perception represents the world (Jackson manuscript, §1).

The hypothesis that talk of grounding is explanatory does not seem to be guilty of 'passing the buck'. As noted in (a) above, talk of grounding is supposed to explain certain phenomena. For example, it is supposed to explain why objects indiscernible with respect to natural properties are indiscernible with respect to normative properties in terms of natural facts grounding normative facts. That explanation does not seem to involve buck-passing. Facts of one kind (facts about indiscernibility in one respect being necessarily accompanied by indiscernibility in another respect) are explained in terms of facts of another kind (facts about what grounds what). There is no attempt to explain facts of one kind in terms of more facts of the same kind.

(c) A hypothesis can be explanatorily vacuous because it is highly obscure. In general, the more obscure a hypothesis is, the less explanatory it is. But notice too that the more obscure a hypothesis is, the less intelligible it is – that is, the less sense we can make of the hypothesis's content. For example, Heidegger's claim that the Nothing itself nothings ('das Nichts selbst nichtet') fails to explain anything just because it fails to be intelligible (cf. Carnap 1932, p. 69). This link between obscurity and intelligibility entails that maintaining that talk of grounding is explanatorily vacuous on the grounds of obscurity is inconsistent with the concession that 'grounding' is an intelligible term. So we cannot concede claim (1) and maintain that talk of grounding is explanatorily vacuous because of its deep obscurity.

To sum up, we have been seeking the most promising sceptical strategy in response to talk of grounding. Conceding claim (1) but denying claim (2) only lends support to a grounding theorist who claims that 'grounding' is definable. Conceding claim (1) but denying claim (3) requires justifying the charge that talk of grounding is explanatorily vacuous. We have canvassed various reasons why a hypothesis may be explanatorily vacuous. We have found that those reasons *either* fail to show that grounding hypothesis is explanatorily vacuous, *or*, if they succeed in showing that, are inconsistent with claim (1). By elimination, then, the best strategy for the sceptic about grounding is to deny that talk of grounding is intelligible.

2.4   IMPLEMENTING THE SCEPTICAL STRATEGY

The sceptic about the intelligibility of 'grounding' is not a straw man. Alex Oliver warns that 'we know we are in the realm of murky metaphysics by the presence of the weasel words "in virtue of"' (Oliver 1996, p. 48). He calls for the phrase to be 'banned' (Oliver 1996, p. 69, note 56). In similar vein, Thomas Hofweber decries esoteric practices in metaphysics and remarks that

The most common way to be an esoteric metaphysician in practice is . . . [to] rely on a notion of metaphysical priority: some notion that claims that certain facts or things are metaphysically more basic than other facts or things. (Hofweber 2009, p. 268)

It seems fair to assume that Nelson Goodman would have had similar reservations about talk of grounding or the *in virtue of* relation. Goodman wrote that

some of the things that seems to me inacceptable [*sic*] without explanation are powers or dispositions, counterfactual assertions, entities or experiences that are possible but not actual, neutrinos, angels, devils, and classes . . . My sample list of suspect notions is of course far from complete. (Goodman 1954, p. 33)

David Lewis eschews talk of ontological priority when he advocates an account of supervenience 'unencumbered by dubious denials of existence, claims of ontological priority, or claims of translatability' (Lewis 1999b, p. 29). It is not clear from this quotation whether Lewis finds talk of ontological priority unintelligible or whether he thinks that it is intelligible but has some other serious failing. In the same quotation Lewis eschews taking supervenience to involve denials of existence or claims of translatability. But presumably the reason for Lewis's eschewal is not that he finds such talk unintelligible but that he finds it gratuitous. Perhaps that was also Lewis's attitude to talk of ontological priority.

A point of clarification: scepticism about talk of grounding need not carry over to scepticism about all forms of non-causal determination. Talk of the part–whole relation, supervenience, and counterfactual dependence, for example, is intelligible and useful. It is only the case of grounding that raises special problems. This point strengthens the sceptic's case because he can show that he already has an adequate tool kit for understanding talk of (say) metaphysical explanation or of physicalism, and so that such talk need not be understood in terms of talk of grounding. For example, the concept of grounding seems to be at work in contemporary discussions of physicalism. Barry Loewer characterizes physicalism as the view that 'the fundamental properties and facts are physical and everything else obtains *in virtue of* them' (Loewer 2001, p. 39). But the sceptic about grounding can formulate physicalism along familiar lines in terms of supervenience (following, for example, Lewis 1986, pp. 15–16, and 1999b, pp. 33–8, and Jackson 1998, pp. 6–27; but see also Leuenberger 2008, §§2.2 and 2.3, for doubts about the adequacy of this approach). Insofar as the sceptic can make sense of talk of 'in virtue of' at all, he will explicate it using talk of all facts supervening on fundamental physical facts. ('Explication' is here understood in Quine's sense of the replacement of a vague and unclear term by a more precise and clear term: Quine 1960, p. 258.) And the sense in which certain physical entities are fundamental is that the behaviour of all other entities can be scientifically explained in terms of them, and not vice versa. (We return to the issues raised in this paragraph in Section 2.7.)

How might the sceptic's strategy be implemented? The sceptic can make a two-fold case. The first part involves reporting what his philosophical conscience tells him. The second part consists in a rebuttal of the opposition's charge that talk of grounding is intelligible.

2.5 THE PHILOSOPHIC CONSCIENCE

In the section entitled 'On the philosophic conscience' in his *Fact, Fiction and Forecast*, Goodman makes three points relevant to the first part of the sceptical strategy (Goodman 1954, Chapter 2, §1). First, we lack a sound general principle for distinguishing what is intelligible from what is not. Second, the lack of such a principle does not collapse or discredit that distinction: a 'lack of a general theory of significance does not turn empty verbiage into illuminating discourse' (Goodman 1954, p. 32, note 1). Third, without a principle of that sort, 'the individual can only search his philosophic conscience' (Goodman 1954, p. 32). As Goodman goes on to explain, this talk of philosophic conscience is only a figurative way of putting the point that one's judgements about what does or does not make sense cannot be further supported. Accordingly, the sceptic about the intelligibility of 'grounding' is not obliged to provide additional evidence for his view.

Of course, the grounding theorist might make a parallel move. He might echo what Lewis says about 'singleton', and state that he somehow understands the primitive term 'grounding' although he has no idea how he could understand it (Lewis 1991, pp. 36, 59). He might then seek a stalemate with the sceptic. How satisfying such a result would be partly depends on what one expects exchanges of philosophical views to achieve. Lewis wrote elsewhere that the purpose of philosophical argument 'is to help expound a position, not to coerce agreement' (Lewis 1999c, p. 304). That looks like a false dilemma. We want our arguments to be persuasive, and, if you find that the arguments for your position do not persuade anyone else, that gives you some reason to reconsider whether it should remain your position. Unless you have reason to question your audience's intellectual credentials, it seems likely that you are missing something that others have spotted. Lewis thinks that he understands 'singleton' although he does not know how. Grounding theorists think that they can defend their claim to understand 'grounding' more robustly. As we saw in Section 2.2, they offer reasons in support of their claim. The second part of the sceptic's case consists in rebutting those reasons.

2.6   WHY WE DON'T UNDERSTAND 'GROUNDING'

A distinction can be drawn between a theory-relative primitive term and an absolute primitive term (Goodman 1951, pp. 45–6). A term t is primitive relative to a theory T if t is not definable in the (other) vocabulary of T (in conjunction with whichever logical resources are being used). That is not quite what the grounding theorist wants. He wants to talk both of absolutely primitive terms and absolutely primitive non-linguistic entities. We can define a notion of an absolute primitive term using the notion of a theory-relative primitive term, where the theory in question is privileged in some respect. For example, we might take the theory in question to be the conjunction of all true theories. Or we might take the theory to be one's total theory (the conjunction of the theories that one holds) (Nolan 2002, p. 34).

To talk of primitive non-linguistic entities, we might say that e is a primitive entity if it is designated by a term t such that t is an absolute primitive. This, however, will not serve the grounding theorist's purposes. He wants to allow that a term can be primitive although the entity, or kind of entity, that it picks out is not primitive. It might be, for example, that the terms 'whole' and 'parts' cannot be defined, but that facts about wholes are grounded by facts about their parts, and so wholes are not primitive kinds of entity. The grounding theorist might then seek to explain what it is for an entity to be primitive in terms of grounding. On this approach, *e* is a primitive entity iff nothing grounds *e*. (This is the approach taken by Schaffer 2009b, pp. 373–4; he uses 'fundamental' instead of 'primitive'.)

Any term selected as primitive by a given theory needs to be clarified by means of an informal explanation (Goodman 1951, p. 46). As we saw in Section 2.2, grounding theorists seek to explain 'grounding' (a) by specifying its logical properties, (b) by citing its connections with other terms, and (c) by giving examples. How much does this help?

(a) A specification of the logical properties of 'grounding' will constrain whatever content it has without determining that content. Consider the use of the term 'explains' that is involved in sentences of the form '[F*x*] explains [G*y*]'. In this use, 'explains' has each of the formal features listed in Section 2.2. Yet 'explains' (as so used) and 'grounds' differ in their supposed extensions: causes do not ground their effects, but they do explain them. Rosen and Audi are explicit that causes do not ground their effects. Where [F*a*] grounds [G*b*], the proposition that G*b* entails the proposition that F*a* (Rosen 2010, §7). But where *c* causes *e*, the proposition that *c* occurs does not entail the proposition that *e* occurs. Audi states an equivalent claim to Rosen's: if [F*a*] grounds [G*b*], it is essential to [F*a*] that it grounds [G*b*]. Yet if *c* causes *e*, it is not essential to *c* that it causes *e* (Audi this volume, pp. 112–113).

On these views, then, causes do not ground their effects. Yet since causes explain their effects, it follows that 'explains' and 'grounds' have different contents. It follows in turn that, unsurprisingly, the logical properties of 'grounding' do not fix its content.

(b) One way to understand a term is to trace its analytic connections with terms that are already understood. The difficulties facing grounding theorists' attempts to use this measure is that *either* the terms appealed to are such close cognates to 'grounding' that they are as obscure as it is, *or* the terms appealed to have are sufficiently and independently clear but their connection to 'grounding' is questionable.

Take the connecting links offered by Schaffer and Rosen. We will consider a selection of what are hopefully representative cases. It should be a straightforward matter to see how the points made here apply to the remaining cases. To start with, 'grounding' is supposed to have links to 'fundamentality' and to 'degrees of reality'. An entity is fundamental if and only if it terminates a grounding chain (Schaffer 2009b, p. 375):

x is fundamental $=_{df.}$ nothing grounds *x*

Since the above definition defines 'fundamental' in terms of 'grounding', any understanding we have of 'fundamental' has to be given to us through understanding 'grounding'. What we wanted, however, was to gain an understanding of 'grounding'.

The comparative term 'greater degree of reality' might be defined simply as follows:

x has a greater degree of reality than $y =_{df} x$ grounds y

Like talk of fundamentalness, talk of degrees of reality is quasi-technical philosophical talk. And, as before, whatever understanding we have of it will be by means of the above definition. Our understanding is parasitic on our understanding of 'grounding'. This comes out in the fact that it seems that the only possible way in which to tell whether fact [Fa] has a greater degree of reality than fact [Gb] is to establish whether [Fa] grounds [Gb].

These points about 'fundamental' and 'has a greater degree of reality than' are representative. It is easy to see how they carry over to other terms such as 'existent' or 'mere aggregate'. Schaffer defines these as follows (Schaffer 2009b, p. 374):

x is an existent $=_{df} x$ is fundamental or x is derivative.

x is a mere aggregate $=_{df}$ each of x's proper parts ground x.

The sceptic will take these and related definitions to show that, of these many terms, the grounding hypothesis needs to take only 'grounding' as a primitive term. The definitions themselves, however, do nothing to advance our understanding of 'grounding'. Instead, they require that we already understand 'grounding' and the complaint here is that nothing has been done to provide the requisite understanding.

This complaint is not an illustration of the following devious tactic that Lewis exposed:

any competent philosopher who does not understand something will take care not to understand anything else whereby it might be explained. (Lewis 1986, p. 203, note 5)

We can come to understand one term when it is explained by using another term provided that we understand the other term. But if the other term has to be explained by using the original term, we have run in a small circle and have not increased in understanding. Yet this is exactly the situation with 'grounding', 'fundamental', 'has a greater degree of reality than', and the other terms mentioned.

Instead of definitions a grounding theorist might offer only equivalences between sentences containing 'grounding' and sentences containing antecedently understood terms. But that approach is open to the same difficulty that faces the definitional project. As we have seen, the sceptic denies that terms such as 'fundamental' or 'has a greater degree of reality than' are already understood. They are no better understood than 'grounding'. You cannot bootstrap yourself into understanding a term by connecting it in any fashion with other terms that you do not understand either.

By way of contrast to the above cases, consider the term 'reduction'. Rosen says this about the 'grounding-reduction link':

If p's being the case consists in q's being the case, then p is true in virtue of the fact that q. (Rosen 2010, p. 123)

The difficulty here is quite different. In the literature on (non-eliminative) reduction in the philosophy of science, it is standard to take a reduction of X's to Y's to be the discovery that X's are identical to Y's. Reducing light waves to electromagnetic radiation is to discover that light waves are identical to electromagnetic radiation. Reducing genes to strands of DNA is to discover that genes are identical to strands of DNA. (See Sklar 1967, p. 120, and Schaffner 1976, pp. 614–15, for representative statements of this view of reduction.) Now identity is reflexive and symmetric whereas we are told that grounding is irreflexive and asymmetric. There cannot be pairs of facts that stand both in the identity relation and in the grounding relation. It follows that, if 'reduction' is understood in the above way, the alleged connective links do not hold between it and 'grounding'. Consequently, our prior understanding of 'reduction' cannot be exploited to further our understanding of 'grounding'.

Perhaps Rosen understands 'reduction' in some other way. What might it be? Reduction is supposed to be a non-eliminative relation between non-linguistic entities, and that rules out an understanding of 'reduction' as *meaning translation* or *meaning analysis*. Perhaps it is an understanding drawn from the tradition of pre-Kantian metaphysics, whereby (for example) X's are reducible to Y's if and only if X's are less fundamental than Y's, and where 'fundamental' is defined in terms of 'grounding'. The obvious problem facing this manoeuvre is that it returns us to the first limb of the dilemma and our impoverished understanding of terms such as 'fundamental' and 'has a greater degree of reality than'.

Another example to be put alongside reduction would be the idea of metaphysical explanation. Talk of grounding might be taken to provide definitions such as the following:

x partly metaphysically explains $y =_{df} x$ grounds y

Xs wholly metaphysically explain $y =_{df} X$s are all and only the grounds of y

It should be noted, however, that talk of metaphysical explanation would only be talk of grounding by another name. It would not be talk of different concepts. So introducing this new way of talking achieves nothing. It would not advance our understanding of talk of grounding, and it would not integrate that talk further with talk which we already understand. All that has been done is to pin another label on grounding – the label 'metaphysical explanation' – and then to declare that the concept of grounding has been connected to various explanatory concepts. Yet the concept of grounding cannot be connected to these other concepts just by being re-labelled 'metaphysical explanation'. Lewis complained about this tactic in another context:

But I say that [the relation] N deserves the name of 'necessitation' only if, somehow, it really can enter into the requisite necessary connections. It can't enter into them just by bearing a name, any more than one can have mighty biceps just by being called 'Armstrong'. (Lewis 1999b, p. 40)

Moreover, if we chose to talk of metaphysical explanation, it is open to the sceptic to understand such talk in other ways, such as in terms of supervenience or metaphysical necessitation, thereby creating a fissure between talk of grounding and talk of metaphysical explanation.

We can understand a term such as 'natural necessity' on the basis of understanding 'necessity' together with a restriction to the laws of the actual world. 'It is naturally necessary that p' can then be understood as: the actual laws of nature necessitate that p. Could we understand 'grounding' on the basis of understanding 'explains' together with some suitable restrictions or modifications? This depends of course on the intelligibility or otherwise of the restrictions put in place. Kim and Ruben have the intuition that it is never a brute fact that one thing explains another thing (Kim 1974 and Ruben 1990, Chapter VII). For every explanation, there is an underlying determinative relation. As Audi puts it, 'an important kind of explanation explains by citing what makes it the case that some fact obtains. Any such explanation requires an underlying relation of determination between what is explained and what explains it'

(Audi this volume, p. 102). Presumably in order to communicate the content of 'grounding', the kind of restriction to be placed on 'explains' is a metaphysical determinative relation as opposed to, say, a causal one. As we saw in the collective view outlined in Section 2.1, grounding was supposed to be just such a metaphysical determinative relation and one that could not be supplanted by other non-causal determinative relations such as supervenience or metaphysical necessitation. Yet the project here is to understand 'grounding' in terms of 'explains' plus a suitable restriction. There seems nothing to be gained from seeking to understand 'grounding' in terms of 'explains' plus a restriction in terms of 'grounding'.

To sum up, grounding theorists' appeal to connective links between 'grounding' and other terms seems to be supposed to serve as an implicit definition of 'grounding'. Our recognition and understanding of the other terms used in the definition helps us to understand 'grounds'. The problem here was that either we lack independent understanding of the terms, or, insofar as we do, it is doubtful whether they bear connective links to 'grounding'.

(c) Lastly, grounding theorists give examples to which 'grounding' has been applied (Audi this volume, pp. 103–104, Rosen 2010, §2, and Schaffer 2009b, p. 375). A selection from their wider sample will hopefully suffice here. We are told that mental facts are grounded by physical facts, that dispositional facts are grounded by categorical facts, that normative facts are grounded by non-normative facts, that ethical facts are grounded by natural facts, that facts about holes are grounded by facts about their hosts, and that facts about wholes are grounded by facts about their parts.

Appealing to examples may seem the strongest card the grounding theorist has to play in conveying the content of 'grounding'. In fact, it is indecisive. Anyone who does not understand 'grounding' will not understand any example that uses it. How could compiling examples from the literature be expected to change the situation? Sceptics such as Oliver and Hofweber already know the literature and are conversant with the stock examples. Like most of us, they probably first came across 'in virtue of' talk and 'ontological priority' talk in the context of certain claims and debates in philosophy. They did not understand that talk wherever they came across it, and what they have said in print about it simply summarizes their incomprehension about the whole class of claims and examples. Not understanding talk of 'grounding' in the abstract is of a piece with not understanding any examples that use it. Certainly all the examples are familiar and in widespread circulation, but whether they are comprehensible is another issue altogether.

Some terms can be learned (and perhaps can only be learned) by means of ostending exemplars and foils. Be that as it may, the sceptic denies that 'grounding' can be learnt in such a way. As noted, the sceptic is familiar with the (alleged) examples of grounding and he can follow a 'divide and conquer' strategy. *Either* he finds that he does not understand the claims being made, and so the examples offered are as baffling as the general claim that some facts ground others. *Or* he finds that the examples are best construed as examples of relations of supervenience or identity, relations that are supposedly distinct from the relation of grounding.

The appeal to examples is allied to claim (3), the claim that talk of grounding is useful. As Rosen puts it (Rosen 2010, p. 111):

it would be very good if these notions [of grounding and ontological dependence] were in fact intelligible, for we would then be in a position to frame a range of hypotheses and analyses that might otherwise be unavailable, and which may turn out to be worth discussing.

In addition to the examples in which grounding is supposedly at work, grounding theorists will invoke grounding to explain certain modal phenomena that the sceptic about grounding does admit. It is natural, for example, to want to know why no possible objects indiscernible with respect to natural facts are indiscernible with normative facts. The grounding hypothesis presents itself as a candidate explanation of such phenomena.

The degree of utility of a term provides a corresponding degree of reason to admit that term into our ideology (i.e. into our stock of primitive terms: see Quine 1951b). But only a term that is intelligible has utility. That is, only a term that is intelligible can genuinely contribute to our theorizing. As Goodman put it, 'the utility of a notion testifies not to its clarity but to the philosophical importance of clarifying it' (Goodman 1954, p. 32). So the utility of 'grounding' has to wait upon, and cannot prejudge, the verdict on whether 'grounding' is an intelligible term.

2.7   CONCLUSION

Goodman described talk of classes as 'essentially incomprehensible' (Goodman 1951, p. 25). His claim seems ill advised since talk of classes is ubiquitous in mathematics and science. Is the sceptic about the intelligibility of 'grounding' on better ground? We have to decide these issues on the merits of each case. Lewis comments that 'philosophers who repudiate all that they cannot understand have very often gone astray' (Lewis 1991, p. *ix*). As a salutary reminder, Lewis's comment seems fair enough, but it can hardly justify any philosopher's retaining anything that they cannot understand! Philosophers who have *not* repudiated all that they cannot understand have very often gone astray too – and very likely have gone further astray.

Since some philosophers set such store by talk of grounding, they ought to have a good reply to the sceptic. These philosophers may have a range of responses. Here we will consider two sharply contrasting responses.

One response would be that if the best sceptical strategy is to query the intelligibility of talk about grounding, then the sceptical threat is not unduly worrying. The sceptical challenge to the purported intelligibility of talk of grounding is no more pressing than the sceptical challenge to the purported intelligibility of talk of metaphysical modality. Talk of grounding is then in good company (cf. Rosen 2010, §14). Let's consider this appeal to metaphysical modality first as a general tactic, and then specifically the parallel with grounding.

As a general tactic, it invites both a '*no news*' and a '*no carte blanche*' response. The tactic provides no news. We already know that some terms are primitive and that we can understand them. The issue is whether 'grounding' can and should be added to them. The tactic is also indiscriminate. It provides as much (or as little) licence for admitting Heidegger's term 'nothings' as a primitive as it does for admitting 'grounding'. But there is no carte blanche for admitting primitive terms and it is good methodology to minimize our stock of them.

The sceptic will further doubt whether drawing a parallel between metaphysical modality and grounding is treating like with like. We have an understanding of talk of metaphysical modality that is independent of philosophical theorizing. We display our understanding of this talk by how we describe humdrum examples in ordinary (i.e. non-technical) language. For example, the opening pages of an introductory work on modality can introduce talk of metaphysical modality by drawing a distinction between accidental and essential properties of a thing. That distinction is in turn introduced by deploying ordinary non-philosophical examples such as 'Joe is tall' and 'Joe is human' and claiming that, whereas Joe might not have been tall, Joe could not have failed to be human. These examples of *de re* modality are then contrasted with equally ordinary examples of *de dicto* modality. (For such an approach, see Melia 2003, pp. 2–4, and Divers 2002, pp. 305–6, note 2.) The provision of such examples by no means settles all issues about the *de re/de dicto* distinction, but nor are they intended to. It is enough if they make the distinction 'serviceable' (in Divers's phrase) and so convey the concept of metaphysical modality. The upshot is that there is reason independent of philosophical claims for taking us to have some understanding of talk of metaphysical modality and that this understanding can be conveyed to us by ordinary descriptions of everyday examples.

By contrast, talk of grounding seems to be entirely a philosopher's invention. It seems to be used exclusively in philosophical theorizing and does not have a role in non-philosophers' thinking. The comparison between grounding and metaphysical modality is then specious. It may be that talk of (say) the categorical grounds of dispositions comes naturally to us. But although grounding theorists seek to treat such a case as illustrative of their hypothesis, it is unclear that this use of 'grounds' should be understood in this way. To say that a disposition D has a categorical ground can be understood as meaning only that there is some non-dispositional property, P, such that it is a law of nature that anything with P has D. Again, as we saw in Section 2.4, scientists' talk of fundamental particles and forces need not be understood in terms of the grounding hypothesis. It can be understood as saying only that certain types of particles and forces can be used to explain all other types of particles and forces but not vice versa. Similar accounts can be given of scientists' use of cognate terms such as 'basic' and 'based on'. Section 2.4 also showed how scientists' talk of reduction can be construed in a way that had no connection with the grounding hypothesis.

It might be suggested that outside of philosophy, people invoke the concept of grounding when they say such things as:

If this stone were to be dropped, it would fall, owing to the direction of the gravitational field.

Anand and Topolov cannot both win, owing to the laws of chess.

Publishing your story is illegal in virtue of the gagging order.

Birds are able to fly, thanks to their having wings.

Without seeking to offer a uniform account of the use of all the natural language idioms that the grounding theorist might appeal to, the sceptic might offer the following suggestions. These examples are cases of restricted necessities. It follows from the laws of nature that if the stone were dropped, and the gravitational field has a certain gradient, then the stone would fall. It follows from the laws of chess that competing players cannot both win a game. It follows from the laws of the land that if your story is published, and the gagging order obtains, then your story is illegal.

Lastly, from the laws of nature it follows that if birds have wings, they can fly. The sceptic's tactic here is to maintain that commonly understood non-philosophical idioms can be understood without invoking the concept of grounding but instead by invoking restricted modalities and other concepts that he understands.

The other extreme response to the sceptical challenge is to take a leaf from the early Wittgenstein and say that talk of grounding is 'illuminating nonsense' (cf. Sorensen 2009, §12). But it is questionable whether the supposed distinction between illuminating and unilluminating nonsense is itself intelligible. So this response faces a challenge of the same kind as the challenge it seeks to allay. That aside, the response is ad hoc since there is no independent reason to think there is a category of illuminating nonsense, and it is special pleading to claim that talk of grounding falls in that category rather than in the category of unilluminating nonsense.

This chapter has concentrated exclusively on the sceptical case against those philosophers who take 'grounding' to be primitive. Fine uses a cluster of terms. He talks of ontological dependence (in his 1994 and 1995a) and also of grounding (in his 2001). 'Grounds' is taken to be a primitive designating the 'tightest [explanatory] connection' (Fine 2001, pp. 15–16). Where it is the case that *S* consists in nothing more than its being the case that *T, U, . . .* , then 'the propositions on the right (*collectively*) *ground* the proposition on the left and . . . each of them *partly grounds* that proposition' (Fine 2001, p. 15). Given its assumed primitive status, the sceptical case against grounding in this paper applies to Fine's talk of grounding as well.

Fine and Lowe's use of the term 'ontological dependence' assigns it some of the theoretical role that 'grounding' has in the hands of Schaffer, Rosen, and Audi (Fine 1994, 1995a, and Lowe 2005b, 2009). Fine and Lowe also seek to define 'ontological dependence' in other terms. Two sceptical responses to their approach are available.

First, the sceptic might claim that the terms appealed to in the *definiens* offered by Fine and Lowe – of one thing depending on its identity on another thing, and the like – are as dubiously intelligible as talk of grounding.

Second, criticisms of Fine and Lowe's definitions (e.g. by Schaffer 2009b, p. 364) can be simply co-opted by the sceptic and put into service for his own ends. It might be wondered whether the sceptic can endorse criticisms of attempts to define 'grounding' (or equally of 'ontological dependence') unless he has some grasp of this term. (A parallel query has been raised about Quine's scepticism about 'synonymy': see Taylor 1955, p. 522.) The reply to this is as follows. The sceptic does not understand 'grounding' at all. It is consistent with this that he also knows something about (a) how 'grounding' is used by grounding theorists and (b) what philosophical roles they want it to occupy. Regarding (a), the sceptic knows, for example, that users of the term apply it to such ordered pairs as dispositional facts and categorical facts, facts about holes and facts about hosts, facts about non-empty sets and facts about members, and facts about brains and facts about minds. Regarding (b), the sceptic knows that grounding theorists want to explain, for example, the formation of wholes from their parts and the formation of sets from their members by appeal to grounding. This combined knowledge makes the sceptic sufficiently well placed to reject attempts to convey the content of 'grounding'. In addition, the sceptic's criticism can be construed as an *ad hominem*. When presented with an attempt to convey the content of 'grounding', the sceptic can use the method of counterexample against it without himself endorsing the counterexample. All that is necessary for his purposes is that, by the lights of his opponent, the sceptic has provided a counter-example (Lepore 1995, p. 477, note 7).[1]

[1] I am very grateful to Rina Arya, Paul Audi, Michael Clark, Fabrice Correia, Julian Dodd, Eve Garrard, Harry Lesser, David Liggins, and Benjamin Schnieder for comments on earlier drafts of this paper. My thanks also to Jonathan Schaffer for very helpful correspondence.

CHAPTER 3

A clarification and defense of the notion of grounding

Paul Audi

3.1 INTRODUCTION

This paper defends a particular version of the idea that there is a non-causal relation of determination, *grounding*, often expressed by the phrase "in virtue of." This relation corresponds to certain non-causal explanations, including those philosophers give, e.g., in saying that a statue has its aesthetic properties in virtue of its physical properties, or that a thing has its dispositional features in virtue of its categorical features, or that a person has a reason to believe that *p* in virtue of her perceptual experiences. Indeed, it is the fact that there are such explanations, together with the fact that their correctness cannot be underwritten by any causal relation, that makes it incumbent on us to recognize grounding.

The claim that there is a grounding relation has been attacked from various quarters. There are those who consider the very idea of grounding incoherent. And there are those who try to undermine it by arguing that it cannot do the philosophical work its advocates want it to do. I will answer the most serious such objections below. But first, I want to sketch my own conception of grounding, and show how it differs from some of the other conceptions on the table. I believe my conception evades certain objections that the other views must tackle head-on (in part because I deny that certain cases to which some authors appeal are genuine cases of grounding).

On my view, grounding is not a bridge between two degrees of reality, and it does not allow us to take for granted the existence of disputed entities (like numbers, norms, or complex objects), trading questions of their existence for questions of their fundamentality.[1] On my view, grounded facts and ungrounded facts are equally real, and grounded facts are an "addition of being" over and above the facts in which they are

---

[1] Here I differ from Fine 2001, and Schaffer 2009b.

grounded. The mere fact that some entity is grounded does not make it any more (or less) ontologically innocent. The grounded is every bit as real – and real in precisely the same sense – as that which grounds it.

My approach here will be to elucidate grounding within the boundaries set by some of my other metaphysical positions. For example, I will largely assume a substance-attribute ontology in which properties and particulars represent mutually irreducible ontological categories. I will assume that facts must involve the instantiation of genuine properties. And I will assume that existence is not a property, and that there are no disjunctive properties.[2] The cost of working within these assumptions is that the resulting theory will not serve to adjudicate certain metaphysical disputes that one might have thought grounding was supposed to help settle.[3] The benefit is that those who agree with me about other areas of metaphysics will see how grounding can be rendered compatible with our shared metaphysical beliefs. One reason it is important to me to show that grounding can be posited within these constraints is that I have genuinely worried at times that it could not be.[4]

3.2   A ROUGH SKETCH OF GROUNDING

Grounding is the relation expressed by certain uses of the phrase "in virtue of," as in "the act is wrong in virtue of its non-moral properties." I do not claim that every felicitous use of "in virtue of" should be taken to express grounding. Rather, we should begin to regiment our use of "in virtue of" to fall in line with the philosophical theory of grounding. Below I will discuss certain uses of the term that, though they are perfectly good English, ought to be avoided on metaphysical grounds. We should not use "in virtue of" where it might express a reflexive relation, such as identity. Since grounding is a relation of determination, and closely linked to the concept of explanation, it is irreflexive and asymmetric. So it would be a mistake, for example, to say that someone is a bachelor *in virtue of* being an unmarried eligible man, if to be a bachelor *just is* to be an unmarried eligible man.[5]

---

[2] I argue that there are no disjunctive properties in Audi manuscript b.
[3] Thanks in particular to Kit Fine for pointing out the costs of my approach.
[4] Discussions with John Heil have been especially helpful in this regard by providing very sensible challenges to the idea of grounding.
[5] Here I differ from Fine 2001 and Rosen 2010. They agree on irreflexivity and asymmetry, but hold that the fact that someone is a bachelor can be distinguished from the fact that he is an unmarried man.

On my view, grounding is a singular relation between facts, understood as things having properties and standing in relations. Facts, on this conception, are not true propositions, but obtaining states of affairs. They are individuated by their constituents and the manner in which those constituents are combined. Call this the *worldly* conception of facts. It is opposed to the *conceptual* view of facts, according to which facts will differ if they pick out an object or property via different concepts. It is not part of my theory that facts are a fundamental category of entity. Properties, particulars, and instantiation are fundamental. A fact is just a thing's instantiating a property (or some things' instantiating a relation).[6]

If grounding is a relation between facts so understood, then grounding is not a relation between *objects* or *substances*.[7] On my view, it would be a mistake to say, e.g., that the statue is grounded in the clay. We could try to render this in fact-talk as "the fact that the statue exists is grounded in the fact that the clay exists," but this move fits poorly with the worldly conception of facts, because (I shall assume) existence is not a genuine property. So there really are no such facts, and so this case is not a candidate to be an example of grounding.[8] Of course, grounding may not be the only relation of ontological priority, and so this is consistent with holding that things like statues depend ontologically on their constituent matter.

On my view, grounding relations depend on the natures of the properties involved in them. Take a normative case. Let us suppose that you have a (defeasible) reason to believe that *p* in virtue of a certain sensory experience. It is of the essence of that experience to yield this reason (and of the essence of this reason that one way it can come about is through that experience). It is not peculiar to you that when *you* have this experience, it grounds a reason of the relevant sort. Anyone with an experience of precisely the same kind will have a reason of precisely the same kind.[9]

---

[6] If properties are tropes, then facts might just be identical with tropes, assuming that a given trope is essentially tied to the particular that possesses it.

[7] Here I differ from Schaffer 2009b.

[8] Chris Daly suggested to me that we might instead say the statue is grounded in the clay – in a derivative sense – when some genuine facts about the statue are grounded in genuine facts about the clay. I will not here give this idea the attention it deserves.

[9] Content externalists should disagree not with my claim that grounding is invariant in this way, but rather with the assumption that the sensory experience – understood as a purely internal conscious experience – is sufficient to ground the relevant reason. They should claim instead that one has the relevant reason in virtue of having the sensory experience caused in the right way and in the right circumstances, etc.

This illustrates the general fact that grounding relations do not vary from instance to instance of the properties involved in the facts in question.[10] Similarly, they do not vary from world to world. (I will return to the relation between grounding and the natures of properties below.)

3.3   THE ARGUMENT FOR GROUNDING

Now, why should we accept that there is any relation answering to these descriptions? The reason we must countenance grounding is that it is indispensible to certain important explanations. Starting with the idea that explanations must answer why-questions, such as "why is *a F*?," note that one way to answer such a question is to say what makes it the case that *a* is *F* – what, that is, determines *a*'s being *F*. This is a particularly important way to answer the why-question, since presumably the way the world is – as opposed to our concepts or interests – settles what determines what. An explanation whose correctness is underwritten by a determination relation, then, is an explanation that tells us something about the nature of our world. The interesting point, for our purposes, is that not all such explanations can be causal. For example, if we ask why a given act was obligatory, one clearly correct answer might be that its agent had promised it. But promising to φ does not *cause* φ to be obligatory. It seems overwhelmingly plausible to say that having been promised and being obligatory are properties of the same event (certainly of the same action), and so simply not candidates to be causally related.[11] Or, to take a non-normative example, it seems that there is an explanation of why a sphere has the disposition to roll in terms of its shape. But being spherical does not *cause* things to have the power to roll. Nor is being spherical identical with the power to roll, since the power to roll is a power also of cylinders, which are not spherical.[12] So the fact that a given thing is spherical non-causally determines the fact that it has the power to roll.

---

[10] Applied to moral properties, this implies a strong metaphysical version of moral generalism, opposed to the views of Dancy 1993. I discuss this further in Audi forthcoming.

[11] Even defenders of fine-grained conceptions of events, who claim that we have two events here, must concede that they are awfully intimately related events. It is at best a strain to claim that events so closely related are cause and effect.

[12] I argue at length that dispositional properties are grounded in categorical ones in Audi manuscript a. For the view that dispositions are identical with the categorical properties that apparently ground them, see Heil 2004.

It is worth making the argument explicit:

(1) If one fact explains another, then the one plays some role in determining the other.
(2) There are explanations in which the explaining fact plays no causal role with respect to the explained fact.
(3) Therefore, there is a non-causal relation of determination.

The argument is valid, but the premises are controversial. Some will object to (1) on the ground that it makes explanation too ontologically robust, when in fact explanation is a merely pragmatic and heavily interest-relative affair.[13] Here, I will assume that this is false. The correctness or incorrectness of an explanation, I assume, is at least in part a matter of its matching up with the structure of the world, structure that is conferred by the determination relations that hold among the world's inhabitants.

But (1) might be doubted for a different reason, namely, that *determination* is not the only relation suited to underwrite the correctness of an explanation. In particular, one might think that *identity* can do so. For example, suppose one thinks that the kind water just is the kind H_2O. One might think that, for this very reason, the fact that there is water in the glass is explained by the fact that there is H_2O in it. I believe this is mistaken. Either this is not a genuine explanation, or the claim of identity is false.[14] For if there is truly identity here, we have neither the asymmetry nor the irreflexivity that explanations require.

One who agrees that identity cannot serve to make explanations correct might still think some other, appropriately asymmetric, non-causal relation is available. One might appeal here to the relation of *constitution*. (Note that I am assuming that constitution is not a determination relation, so that if it can do the required work, it is premise (1) that fails.) For example, one might think that items like statues are not identical with the matter of which they are constituted (even assuming that matter to be in a statue-like condition), and that the asymmetrical relation of constitution is what underlies the explanation of the statue in terms of its constituting matter and the properties of that matter. Whether or not this is a genuine explanation, it is clear that not every putative case of non-causal explanation can be supported by the constitution relation. For example, suppose the wrongness of a given act is explained by its natural properties. This is clearly not an analogous case; the natural properties do not constitute the

---

[13] See, e.g., van Fraassen 1980, Chapter 5.   [14] For a denial that water $= H_2O$, see Johnston 1997.

wrongness in anything like the way an appropriately shaped lump of clay might constitute a statue.[15] So even if we allow some explanations to be underwritten by the constitution relation, we still need a non-causal relation of determination to account for the correctness of certain other explanations.[16]

Moving on to premise (2), its chief support is from examples. There are a number of putative examples of explanations in which it seems quite clear that causation is not involved at all. The plausibility of (2) hangs on the plausibility of treating these as genuine examples of explanation. Among the most compelling examples are:

> Normative facts are grounded non-normative facts.
> Dispositional facts are grounded in categorical facts.
> Aesthetic facts are grounded in non-aesthetic facts.
> Semantic facts are grounded in social and psychological facts.[17]

Why think these are cases of explanation? First, they are not cases of identity. Take a particular example of the first kind of case: a given act is wrong in virtue of being a lie (let us assume). Not all wrong acts are lies, and so the property of wrongness cannot be the property of being a lie.[18] Now, might the property *instances* be identical? Might it be the case that we have one trope here that is at once a wrongness trope and a lie trope? I think this makes sense only if we deny that there is truly a property of wrongness. One could claim, for example, that "wrongness" does not pick out a genuine property, but can pick out any of a number of different properties that are loosely grouped by some imperfect similarity among them. I do not find this view very plausible, however. Take, say, a promise-breaking and a stabbing. Considered just in terms of their non-normative characteristics, do they seem imperfectly similar in any respect

---

[15] In fact, I do not think it is correct to say that the natural properties of an act *constitute* its wrongness at all (though we do sometimes speak this way). Wrongness isn't *made up of* natural properties.

[16] If one takes constitution to be a case of grounding, then one will agree that constitution does not obviate the need for grounding, but disagree that we need grounding as an alternative to constitution. Jonathan Schaffer, for instance, would take constitution to be a case of grounding – provided constitution is not understood as identity (personal communication). One reason I resist treating constitution as grounding is that if what is being explained is the *existence* of the statue, then on my view we fail to have a genuine *fact*, the instantiation of a genuine property by something. The relation I am interested in is a relation intimately linked to the natures of properties. It seems to me that a relation of which material constitution is a case cannot be assimilated to this framework.

[17] Or, if externalism is true, semantic facts are grounded in social and psychological facts together with certain causal facts.

[18] Wrongness also is not the disjunction of all particular wrong-making features. See Audi manuscript b for why I reject disjunctive properties.

relevant to their prima facie wrongness? They are imperfectly similar, surely, in irrelevant respects, such as occurring in space and time, involving the expenditure of energy, and so forth, but these similarities are shared with many permissible things as well. (A consequentialist, which I am not, may hold that the relevant similarities are extrinsic; both cause pain.)[19] There is in any case strong pre-theoretical support for the view that there is a property of wrongness.

This discussion illustrates one of the most important general convictions involved in my approach to grounding: it requires us to accept certain kinds of property (normative, dispositional, aesthetic, semantic) that are recognized in pre-theoretical thought, but that seem never to be instantiated brutely.[20] What we want from our philosophical theories of these properties is a non-circular account of the conditions under which they are instantiated. Critics of grounding, then, may wish simply to deny that there are any such properties. I will not argue at any length here that they would be wrong. But we see immediately one cost of this move; a great deal of common-sense thought must be abandoned.

I have now established a positive case for recognizing grounding. I do not claim that it is conclusive. But it puts us in a fairly good position vis-à-vis the critics of grounding. In a moment, I will begin discussing specific challenges to the belief in grounding. In some cases, it will be appropriate to fall back on the positive argument. "I have given an argument," I can now say, "that there must be some such relation. If I am mistaken, one of these premises must be false." I think the critics' best hope is to attack the examples (as Chris Daly argues).[21] But for the reasons just given, I think there is strong reason to accept them as bona fide cases of non-causal

---

[19] This rejection of wrongness is a special case of the view that determinable predicates simply collect determinate properties under relations of imperfect similarity. What I find implausible about this view is the denial that these imperfect similarities between determinates correspond to perfect similarities between determinables. It seems to me that *what it is* for two things to be similar is for there to be a property that both have. If this is right, then since being scarlet ≠ being maroon, either scarlet things do not resemble maroon things in respect of their color, or their resemblance consists in the fact that there is another property, redness, that both things have. In other words, denying that redness (or any other determinable or "multiply realizable" property) exists severs the link between similarity and property-sharing.

[20] Fine's theory of grounding, by contrast, can sidestep the question of whether *any* properties exist, given his view that grounding is best expressed by a sentential operator, rather than (as on my view) a predicate applied to certain facts. See Fine this volume, Section 1.4. Fine is motivated in part by a wish to stay neutral on certain questions about the ontology of grounding while laying out the most general theoretical framework. One such question is precisely what the relata of grounding are. My answer to that question – facts – is responsible for much of what I say here, and for many of my disagreements with Fine and Schaffer.

[21] See Daly this volume.

explanation. Once again, given the idea that explanations cannot hold brutely, these examples provide strong reason to believe in non-causal determination.

3.4   GROUNDING AND THE NATURES OF PROPERTIES

Before defending grounding against its detractors, I want to return to the relation between grounding and the natures of properties. Let's begin with what are on my view the relata of grounding, facts, understood to be things' having properties and standing in relations. Taking these to be the relata of grounding has an interesting consequence: grounding does not relate ordinary particulars, objects, considered apart from their properties. A composite object, for example, is not grounded in its simple parts. How could it be, if grounding is a relation between facts? Neither the composite nor any of its simple parts is a fact. Furthermore, while it might seem fine at a glance to speak of the fact that the composite exists, and take that to be grounded in the fact that its simple parts do (and are arranged in such-and-such a way, say), this will not do. For existence is not a genuine property. So there is no genuine fact that the composite exists. This is not to deny that it exists, but only to deny that its existing is properly speaking a fact. Assuming that there are composite objects, there is little doubt that they are in some fashion ontologically dependent on their parts. But that dependence cannot be grounding, if grounding is a relation between facts.[22]

Treating grounding as a relation between facts suggests another important point about the nature of grounding. Grounding is importantly tied to the natures of properties. Whether two facts are suited to stand in a grounding relation depends heavily upon what properties are involved in those facts. Facts involving redness and loudness, for example, never stand in grounding relations with one another. Nothing could be red in virtue of being loud, or loud in virtue of being red (and no range of intermediaries could ever link them together in a chain of grounding). These properties are simply too disparate. Compare maroonness. The fact that a thing is maroon is *bound* to ground its being red (assuming, for the moment, that a given thing's redness is not identical with its maroonness). To label this relationship, let us say that facts are suited to stand in a relation of grounding only if their constituent properties are *essentially connected.*

---

[22] See, e.g., Lowe 2009 for discussion of this kind of ontological dependence.

Now, the reason for this label is that it seems to be of the essence of maroonness that its instances ground instances of redness (in the same particular). And likewise, it is of the essence of redness that an instance of it can be grounded in an instance of maroonness. Equally, we can say that these relations depend on the *intrinsic natures* of these properties. But note that this does not entail that these properties have complex essences, or any kind of internal complexity that might allow us to say more specifically why it is that they stand in that relation. For the sake of example, let's assume that the determinate colors are simple, phenomenal properties. On this account, the fact that maroonness is a determinate of the determinable redness is no doubt relevant. But even so, that relation between the properties does not itself hold in virtue of anything about their natures that we could specify except to repeat that they are so related. There is nothing intrinsic to maroonness that explains why it is a determinate of redness, *except* that it is *this color*, i.e., maroonness.[23]

This is important because the terms "essence" and "intrinsic nature" can cause confusion. It may be that there is nothing illuminating we can say about the essence of a property because it is a *simple* property. But it would be a mistake to say that therefore it has no intrinsic nature. It is just that there is nothing to say about its intrinsic nature except what property it is. (I thereby embrace *quidditism* about properties, the view that every property is identical with some non-relational entity.) Perhaps one cannot have exhaustive knowledge of such a property unless one is *acquainted* with it.[24] Fortunately, we are acquainted with at least some of these properties. And that acquaintance makes it quite obvious that nothing can be maroon without being red. (I do not say it is obvious that a thing's being maroon *grounds* its being red.)

Because grounding holds only between facts whose constituent properties are essentially connected, what grounding relations obtain at a world depends on the intrinsic natures of the properties instantiated at that world. And this amounts just to saying that what grounding relations obtain

---

[23] Compare Rosen 2010 on Formality, Mediation, and Moorean Connections, and Fine this volume, Section 1.10. Interestingly, Fine takes the essence of the grounded fact to explain the connection, and holds that the nature of the grounding fact, so to speak, knows nothing of the fact it grounds (at least in many cases).

[24] See Schaffer 2004 on knowledge of quiddities. It seems to me that one could know, say, that a given quiddity exists without being acquainted with it (perhaps this is our situation with respect to unit negative charge), but knowledge of the *intrinsic nature* of such a property, if it is simple, requires acquaintance with it.

depends on what properties are instantiated. Now, since the nature of a property does not vary from world to world, what is *appropriate* to ground what does not vary from world to world at all. But, on my view, since grounding is a relation between facts, a grounding relation actually obtains only when the relevant properties are instantiated.

3.5   GROUNDING AND REDUCTION

Before shifting to a defensive stance, let me discuss briefly one last thing that sets my account of grounding apart from the views of others. I deny that when p grounds q, q thereby *reduces to p* (or is *nothing over and above p*). Also, I deny what Rosen calls the *grounding-reduction link*:

(GRL) If q reduces to p, then p grounds q.[25]

I reject (GRL) because it is incompatible with the following principles which I do accept:

Irreflexivity of Grounding: If p grounds q, then $p \neq q$.

Reduction as Identity: If p reduces to q, then $p = q$.

Worldly Conception of Facts: Facts are individuated by their worldly constituents and the manner of their combination.

To take an example of Rosen's, let's suppose that the fact that a certain thing, a, is a square reduces to the fact that it is an equilateral right quadrilateral (ERQ). Let's use the notation "$[p]$" to stand for "the fact that p." On my view, reduction (in this metaphysical sense) is nothing other than identity. So $[a$ is a square$]$ is the same fact as $[a$ is an ERQ$]$. Given the worldly conception of facts, it follows that $[a$ is a square$]$ and $[a$ is an ERQ$]$ have the same constituents (a and a certain property) and the same manner of combination (a instantiates the property in question). So the property of being a square just is the property of being an ERQ (and any appearance of asymmetry is owed to a difference between the concepts we used to pick out this property). But if this is right, it had better not be the case that $[a$ is a square$]$ is grounded in $[a$ is an ERQ$]$, or we have a violation irreflexivity. So, to keep these three principles, (GRL) must be rejected.

---

[25] See Rosen 2010, pp. 124–5. Cf. Schaffer 2009b, p. 378.

Rosen rejects instead the worldly conception of facts.[26] This seems to me to yield a very different picture of grounding from the one that I am after, one on which what grounds what is determined at least as much by our concepts as it is by the antecedent structure of the world. What we get from grounds is, at least in cases of reduction, not something *responsible for* the grounded fact, but rather a more accurate conceptual rendering of the very same worldly state-of-affairs. There is of course more to be said, but this should indicate why I reject (GRL). I address the matter at length elsewhere.[27]

3.6   THE THEORY AT WORK: SOME PUTATIVE CASES REJECTED

The idea that there might be a grounding relation has been the subject of a number of skeptical attacks. Alex Oliver charges that the phrase "in virtue of" should be banned.[28] Thomas Hofweber accuses the friends of grounding of "esoteric metaphysics," metaphysics that is so detached from ordinary concepts that its theories are immune from the facts – that is (I gather), not susceptible of being either supported or falsified by what the world is like.[29] And Chris Daly argues that there is in fact no intelligible notion of grounding.[30] As it happens, I agree with much of what Oliver, Hofweber, and Daly say, but their criticisms show only that there are important constraints on any plausible theory of grounding, not that the notion of grounding should be abandoned. Furthermore, none of these critics' attacks addresses the positive argument for grounding that I have given above.

Let us begin with Oliver, who, in a discussion of Keith Campbell on properties, expresses stern skepticism about a relation corresponding to "in virtue of."[31] He discusses two questions raised by Campbell:

In virtue of what is a given red thing red?
In virtue of what are a given pair of red things both red?[32]

He then comments:

We know we are in the realm of murky metaphysics by the presence of the weasel words "in virtue of." Campbell seems to be asking for some sort of non-causal metaphysical explanation of the facts mentioned in his questions.[33]

---

[26] Rosen 2010, pp. 124–5.   [27] Audi forthcoming.   [28] Oliver 1996.   [29] Hofweber 2009.
[30] Daly this volume.   [31] Oliver 1996.   [32] Campbell 1990.   [33] Oliver 1996, p. 48.

Oliver suggests that there are only three possible interpretations of the words "in virtue of" that would give them any sense. According to him, the question "in virtue of what is *p* the case" could be interpreted as the demand for a *conceptual analysis* of *p*, for the *ontological commitments* of *p*, or for the *truth-makers* of *p*.[34] In the same vein, he writes "the question 'in virtue of what is this sentence true?' can be interpreted as a demand for a truth-maker for the sentence." Then, in a note to this sentence, he continues:

> It can also be understood as a demand for the ontological commitments of the sentence. Hence a confusion between truth-makers and ontological commitments. "In virtue of" really ought to be banned.[35]

Banning the phrase "in virtue of" might well have prevented these confusions, but a precise account of what its correct use requires prevents confusion at least as well. As it happens, I agree with Oliver that there are serious mistakes in the cases he discusses, though I blame not the mere use of the phrase "in virtue of" but the misuse of it. Oliver interprets Campbell as asking for a non-causal explanation of why some individuals are red, and why some pairs of individuals are alike in being red, and then dismisses this notion of explanation as too vague.

Against this, first, here is a good place to refer to my positive argument for grounding. If I am right, we must recognize some such relation, and so it cannot be so lightly dismissed. Second, it is precisely because at least certain aspects of the notion of explanation can be made precise that we can see Oliver to be right in rejecting Campbell's proposed cases. Notice that Campbell's question is supposed to be fully general, so that an answer would fill in the schema:

For any property, *F*, and any individual *x*, *x* is *F* in virtue of _____.

But should we think this schema can always be filled in? I think not. Presumably, the candidates to fill it in that Campbell has in mind are things like "*x*'s possessing an *F*-ness trope" and "*x*'s standing in the relation of instantiation to the universal *F*-ness." But, familiarly, this merely pushes the problem back. For we might as well ask, now, in virtue of what a thing possesses a trope, or in virtue of what a thing is related by instantiation to a universal. We can avoid the regress only by insisting that fundamental properties are just instantiated by things, or not.[36] There will probably be

---

[34] Oliver 1996, p. 50.   [35] Oliver 1996, p. 69.

[36] For all I have said, a fundamental property may be something like instantiation, or it may be something like negative charge.

causal explanations of why they are instantiated, but there must be – on pain of regress – some properties whose instantiation is ungrounded. Property instantiation seems to be a very plausible stopping-point for metaphysical theories. Very little, if anything, can be explained except by appeal to what properties are instantiated. And on my own theory of grounding, it is clear that we would get a regress if we demanded that every property instantiation have a ground, since on my view only property instantiations – facts – are candidates to be grounds. Campbell should have asked *what it is* for x to be F. Is it for x to possess an F-ness trope, or for x to stand in some relation to an abstract universal of F-ness? This is not a demand for an *explanation* of a property's instantiation, but a theory of it. It is, in other words, simply the demand for a theory of properties.

As for similarity, can we say that a and b are similar in being F in virtue of the fact that a is F and b is F? Only if those are different facts. But I doubt they are. I think what it is for two things to be similar *just is* for there to be some property that both have. Given that this is a case of identity, it is not one of grounding. Here again, the matter is settled not by abandoning talk of grounding but by clarifying it. Grounding is irreflexive and asymmetric, identity reflexive and symmetric. Where there is identity, there is no grounding.

I believe that what I have said about similarity is also true of truth-making. What it is for a given proposition to be true is (a) for it to correspond to a certain state of affairs, and (b) for that state of affairs to obtain, i.e., to be a fact. Note that the nature of the proposition – it's declaring that a certain state of affairs obtains – is a crucial part of truth-making, just as the obtaining of the state of affairs is. Now, I see no reason to think that the truth of the proposition is anything other than the holding of these conditions, and so I see no need to posit a grounding relation here. The real definition of truth as the holding of these conditions gives us the ontic requirement on truth – truth is constrained by how the world is – that the truth-maker principle seeks to capture. But it does not bring the idea of grounding into the understanding of truth-making. In particular, it does not *explain* truth in terms of the conditions that bring it about. It *defines* truth as the obtaining of these conditions.

Now, all of this can be said while taking "in virtue of" on board. For, of course, those of us who think that phrase (or something with the same significance) is indispensible think there are good and bad ways to use it. No one thinks that we should help ourselves to the locution without demanding any rigor in its application.

3.7 WHY GROUNDING IS NOT "IMMUNE FROM THE FACTS"

Another critic of grounding is Thomas Hofweber, who writes:

The most common way to be an esoteric metaphysician ... [is to] rely on a notion of metaphysical priority: some notion that claims that certain facts or things are metaphysically more basic than other facts or things.[37]

This is supposed to make metaphysics esoteric because one has to under-stand the relevant notion of metaphysical priority in order to make any sense of what is being claimed. As I read him, Hofweber doubts that any of us really understands this notion. Now, he is aware of various attempts to render the notion intelligible, especially by providing examples, but he claims that the examples are never strictly relevant. The examples used to tie down the idea will be of some ordinary notion of priority – causal priority or conceptual priority – not of the kind of metaphysical priority that holds especially between necessary truths or objects.

Hofweber's work suggests a dilemma: either the example is one of some acceptable sort of priority – some ordinary sort of priority, that is, that harbors no commitment to grounding – or there is no pressure at all to accept it as any kind of priority at all. The reason behind the second horn, I take it, is that since the relata of the alleged priority relation are both necessary, nothing hangs on whether or not we accept the proposed priority. The same facts will obtain in either case, which shows that these claims of priority are immune from the facts. I want to consider this dilemma as Hofweber deploys it against the work of Kit Fine.[38] I agree with some of his criticisms. But, as with Oliver's, I think the criticisms are motivated by a basic grasp of what grounding is. In defense of that claim, I will argue against Hofweber's contention that grounding is not tied to any relatively ordinary, non-esoteric concept – and in particular, I will argue that it is tied to the concept of explanation.

Hofweber discusses two of Fine's cases. The first is disjunction, about which Fine claims that the fact that a disjunct holds is more basic than the fact that the disjunction holds.[39] This is supposed to give us a handle on the notion of priority in play. But Hofweber charges that while this is indeed a plausible example of priority, it is mere logical priority, just in the sense of asymmetric implication. For any propositions p and q, p implies $p \lor q$, though $p \lor q$ does not imply p. Now, I join Hofweber in denying that we have a case of grounding here, but only because I think

---

[37] Hofweber 2009, p. 268.   [38] Fine 2001.   [39] Rosen 2010 accords with Fine on disjunction.

we should say that on the relevant conception of fact – the worldly conception according to which a fact consists in something's having a property – there really is no disjunctive fact distinct from the fact that one disjunct is instantiated (or, if both disjuncts are instantiated, from the fact that they both are). There is not, for example, a fact that consists in the instantiation of some disjunctive property (I think there is no such thing). And there is no *worldly* fact that has a disjunctive nature. The truth-maker for the disjunctive truth-bearer is just the truth-maker for the true disjunct (or for both of them, if both are true). Still, it should be said in Fine's defense that if one allows the disjunctive fact, there is no question that it will be posterior to the fact that at least one of its disjuncts holds. And this will not be mere logical priority because the facts in question are not propositions, and not suited to stand in logical consequence relations.

A more interesting case Hofweber discusses is Fine's case of the marriage of Jack and Jill:

Its being the case that the couple Jack and Jill is married [is grounded in] its being the case that Jack is married to Jill.[40]

Hofweber remarks on this as follows:

And this [grounding] relationship is supposed to be an explanatory one. But I have to admit not to follow this. It is a conceptual truth, I take it, that

(6) A and B are a married couple iff A and B are married to each other.

But how is it an explanatory relationship? Even if conceptual connections can be explanatory ... this doesn't seem to be a case of it ... It certainly would not be a good answer to the ordinary question why Jack and Jill are a married couple to reply because they are married to each other.[41]

Now, again, I want to join Hofweber in rejecting the case, but, again, for different reasons. First, the case should be understood so that the existence of a certain thing, a couple, is grounded in the relevant relation (or that a certain property of a complex object, the couple, is grounded in a relation between its parts).[42] I have some sympathy for the view that there is no such thing as the couple. But even if there is, since I restrict grounding relations to facts, and deny existential facts, I am committed to rejecting this case. But I agree with Hofweber that if p and q look to be the same fact in different linguistic or conceptual guises, then it is implausible to think of "them" as standing in any metaphysical priority relation.

---

[40] Fine 2001, p. 15.   [41] Hofweber 2009, p. 270.   [42] Thanks to Kit Fine for pointing this out.

Now I want to address Hofweber's objection that grounding does not correspond to, and cannot be illuminated by, any ordinary notion of priority. Why think grounding is so extraordinary? If we return to a case in which the facts are plausibly considered non-identical, it is not hard to imagine perfectly ordinary people implicitly grasping that one explains the other. "Don't do that!" "Why ever not?" It's wrong!" "Why is it wrong?" "It's *unfair!*" Compare the case in which the final reply is "Because it's just wrong." I think the ordinary person is apt to *dismiss* that reply, whereas if one thinks the action is not wrong, one will feel some pressure to *deny* the charge of unfairness. Since there is good reason to doubt that this is a causal explanation, it is a good reason to think that ordinary folk can grasp non-causal explanations. Such explanations are *metaphysical,* insofar as they concern matters metaphysical, but, being accessible to the folk, they are not *esoteric.*[43]

What is more, similar points seem to show that grounding is not, contrary to Hofweber's objection, immune from ordinary facts. His thought seems to be that the ordinary facts are compatible with grounding relations holding in either direction, so that the ordinary facts cannot settle what grounds what. But the order of explanation, in many cases (such as the normative case above), seems to me to be a perfectly ordinary fact. And grounding, far from being immune from such facts, is our only hope of capturing them. Perhaps not all cases are so ordinary, and of course Hofweber is right that two parties can agree that *p* and *q* obtain and disagree about which grounds which. But if the objection that this renders grounding immune from the facts amounts to anything other than the worry that it is esoteric, then it is question-begging. For according to those of us who accept grounding, the facts about the world include the facts about what grounds what.

Furthermore, it is not clear that claims about grounding are insulated from empirical confirmation or disconfirmation. As Daly points out, facts about grounding might be indirectly empirically confirmable by having a place in a well-confirmed theory, a theory confirmed through its empirical consequences.[44] It might also be that claims about grounding are justified

---

[43] Indeed, I have reservations about the distinction between the ordinary folk and the metaphysician or the philosopher. Philosophers are folk who've spent a great deal of time thinking about these matters, and are well-informed regarding what others have thought about them. Also, to claim that some concept is a pure artifact of philosophy *and thereby illegitimate* presupposes that the concepts applied in everyday pre-philosophical thought are adequate to express everything we need to say about the world. But that is hard to believe.

[44] Daly this volume.

in a process of reflective equilibrium. We have beliefs about particular explanatory connections and we have general beliefs about the rules of explanation. Neither is indefeasible, but they can be mutually reinforcing.

Let me sketch an account of how we might, in several stages, come to be justified in believing a grounding claim, say, that something's being an electron grounds its having a certain causal power, negative charge.

1. We have contact with electrons in a way that enables us to refer to the property of *being an electron*, the quiddity, the intrinsic nature of electrons.

2. We discover a disposition associated with being an electron, the power to repel certain things, and we call this power *negative charge*.

3. We discover that this disposition is associated with other things besides electrons, such as down quarks.

4. We may conclude from this that being an electron is not the very same thing as having negative charge.[45]

5. We find reason to think that things' having negative charge is explained in terms of other facts about them (not the same fact in the case of electrons as in the case of down quarks).

6. These cannot be causal explanations.

7. We conclude that being an electron *grounds* having negative charge.

Now, this account is epistemically hybrid. At least steps 2 and 3, and maybe also 5, involve empirical discoveries. But steps 4 and 6 seem to be a priori. All these steps are crucial evidence for 7, the claim about grounding. So it would be oversimple to say only that grounding claims are a priori, or for that matter to say only that they are empirical. Like most substantive philosophical claims, their support derives in part from experience and in part from reflection on the information that experience provides.

3.8   THE INTELLIGIBILITY OF GROUNDING

I want now to consider some skeptical worries about grounding due to Chris Daly.[46] He points out, quite rightly, that logical principles about grounding (including irreflexivity, asymmetry,

---

[45] I think this is true, but the matter is complicated. See Audi manuscript a.
[46] Daly this volume.

transitivity, non-monotonicity, and so forth) set limits on what grounding could be, but fall short of fixing precisely what the content of "grounding" is. A more promising approach is to attempt to elucidate grounding by noting its connections with more familiar notions. Daly considers a number of putative connections, and finds them lacking.

For example, consider the following definition:

x has a *greater degree of reality* than $y =_{df.} x$ grounds y.[47]

This definition connects the notion of grounding with the notion of having a greater degree of reality. Daly worries that this is a strange notion. Ordinarily, we do not recognize degrees of reality; things are real or they are not. But, as Daly notes, this could be construed as a technical notion of metaphysical priority. (Compare Hofweber on this point.) But while that may protect the notion from doubts we have about degrees of reality in the ordinary sense of reality, it prevents this definition from serving as a means of connecting grounding with an ordinary and well-understood notion.

Now, I would not want to explicate grounding in terms of degrees of reality, but it is worth noting that this approach is not a non-starter. Suppose we take the relevant notion of reality to be connected with the notion of a substance: to be real, in the relevant sense, is just to be a substance. So we can get a handle on this notion of degrees of reality, perhaps, through our antecedent understanding of substance. (This will presumably require that we have some grip on the notion of a substance other than as the kind of thing that serves as an ultimate ground.) One might think, for instance, that grounding is essentially tied to the Aristotelian idea that all entities ultimately depend on substances. Grounding is the relation of dependence doing the work in this hierarchical structure.

I think this goes some way toward answering Daly's worry, but it is not a path open to me, since I do not think substances are candidates to stand in grounding relations (at least, not taken en bloc, considered apart from what properties they instantiate). Furthermore, I join Daly's skepticism about any salvageable notion of degrees of reality in any ordinary sense of that term. On my view, a grounded fact is every bit as real – and real in precisely the same sense – as the fact that grounds it. But note that someone who espouses the above treatment of

---

[47] This approach, and its elaboration in terms of substance, was floated by Jonathan Schaffer (in personal communication).

"degrees of reality" in terms of substance can nevertheless deny that there are degrees of reality in the ordinary sense in which to be real is simply to exist.

Consider now another connection between grounding and a more familiar notion, namely, that of explanation. It seems we can safely say that

x (at least partly) *metaphysically explains y* just in case x grounds y.

Might this connection help to explicate grounding? Daly worries that we really have a single concept here, that this move amounts to mere re-labeling, and so fails to shed any light on grounding. Now, the best response to this objection is to insist that grounding is not a form of explanation, even though it is intimately connected with explanation.[48] (Here it is important that the "just in case" be read as a mere biconditional, not as definitional.) But even on the view that grounding should be cashed out as a kind of explanatory relation, a plausible response to Daly is possible. To be sure, stipulating that grounding may be called "metaphysical explanation" does no work at all. But one might insist that grounding *deserves* this name because of an antecedent connection it bears to the idea of explanation. If we already understand explanation, then to some extent at least we already understand grounding.[49]

The intimate connection between grounding and explanation comes through in my own positive argument for grounding. I take "explanation" to be a generic term, with the specific forms of explanation differentiated by the relations of determination that underlie the correctness of the relevant token explanatory claims. Causal explanation is familiar, and a fortiori explanation as a generic concept is familiar. We have only to consider that certain particular explanations cannot be causal to see that there must be a non-causal relation of determination. It is that relation by which non-causal explanations are differentiated, and which accounts for their correctness.

Now, my understanding requires explanation to be different from grounding and there are powerful reasons to think that it is. For all I have said, it may be only a necessary condition of an explanation's holding between two facts that a relation of determination hold between them. More might be required to fill out a sufficient condition (such as

---

[48] On the difference between grounding and explanation, see Audi forthcoming (Section 2, ii) and Schaffer this volume (Section 4.1.1).

[49] Thanks to Jonathan Schaffer for discussion of this section.

pragmatic or epistemic factors). And even if there are no requirements of that sort – even if, necessarily, p non-causally explains q if and only if p grounds q – we should say that the explanation is not grounding itself, but a proposition expressing the grounding relation. An explanation, then, is something you can literally *know*; a grounding relation is merely something you can know *about.* The obtaining of the grounding relation, on this account, differs from the explanation in the same way any truth-maker differs from the truth it makes true.

So I believe that the concept of explanation does a great deal to tie down our notion of grounding. And, what is more, philosophical work on grounding helps clarify the notion of explanation, in particular those explanations philosophers are wont to give using the phrase "in virtue of." Can we now claim to have a precise account of grounding, one that captures the exact content of the term "grounding"? Probably not, but we are getting closer. Of course, to a great extent, the content of any term is determined by usage. But usage does not merely create content out of nothing, because usage is often sensitive to antecedent constraints (in this case, those that apply thanks to the connection between grounding and explanation), and to new constraints that arise as we go along. A case in point may be, if I am correct, the relation between grounding and reduction. Grounding may not have been well enough understood initially for it to be obvious that grounding and reduction are incompatible. But by considering what would have to be the case for reduction to imply grounding we find new constraints on what grounding can be. As Rosen points out, perhaps we should cut our losses if we find that incoherencies or insurmountable difficulties with grounding arise early on.[50] But if there are coherent solutions to the difficulties that do arise, this is a reason to continue our attempt to elucidate the notion of grounding and see what work it can do for us.

3.9   CONCLUSION

I agree with a number of the points raised by the skeptics about grounding, and I agree that we cannot afford to be facile about grounding's coherence or its ultimate defensibility. But I see no reason yet to abandon the notion. As Daly says, the most promising strategy for pinning down the notion of grounding is the appeal to examples, but (and I agree) this strategy is inconclusive; more work is required to show definitively that the cases to which I have appealed are truly

[50] Rosen 2010.

cases involving non-causal explanation.[51] I have indicated why it is plausible to think they are.

I think the most promising skeptical strategy is to insist on either identity or elimination wherever grounding is alleged to hold. For example, the skeptic might charge that the fact that one has a reason to avoid a given pain *just is* the fact that one is in pain. The pain is the reason. Or the skeptic could insist that categorical properties just *are* dispositional properties.[52] Or the skeptic could argue that there really are no aesthetic properties. If, however, these properties are admitted, and are not identical with the properties that we very naturally claim contribute to explaining their instantiation, then the case for grounding is very strong. Only the notion of non-causal determination can account for the correctness of the relevant explanations. None of the skeptical arguments we have seen gives us reason to doubt that the properties in question – normative properties, dispositions, beauty, meaning, and the like – are instantiated, or to doubt that there are explanations of their instantiation. If philosophy can vindicate the common-sense picture of the world as containing these properties, then we must recognize that there is a relation of grounding underlying the explanations of why they are instantiated.[53]

---

[51] I have attempted some of this work in Audi forthcoming and manuscript a.

[52] See, e.g., Heil 2004. I argue against this view in Audi manuscript a.

[53] I received extensive comments on an earlier draft from Michael J. Clark, Chris Daly, Kit Fine, Jonathan Lowe, Jonathan Schaffer, and Dennis Whitcomb. I am very grateful to them for their help and advice, though I have not yet been able to address all of the issues they raised. I also thank Fabrice Correia and Benjamin Schnieder for inviting me to present at the Because II conference, sponsored by the Phlox Research Group, at the Humboldt-Universität, Berlin, August 2010. There I received very helpful feedback from the organizers and participants. I learned more than I can express through this chapter. In particular, I thank Elizabeth Barnes, Ross Cameron, Shamik Dasgupta, Louis deRosset, Geoff Ferrari, Mark Jago, Carrie Jenkins, Stephan Leuenberger, Thomas Sattig, Kelly Trogdon, and Steve Yablo.

CHAPTER 4

Grounding, transitivity, and contrastivity

Jonathan Schaffer

Grounding is something like metaphysical causation. Roughly speaking, just as causation links the world across time, grounding links the world across levels. Grounding connects the more fundamental to the less fundamental, and thereby backs a certain form of explanation. Thus the right sort of physical system can support a biological organism such as a cat, and one way to answer the question of *why there is a cat afoot* is to describe the underlying physical system.

Grounding is generally assumed to be transitive. The assumption of transitivity is natural. For instance, if the physical system grounds the chemical arrangement, and the chemical arrangement grounds the biological organism, then it is natural to thereby infer that the physical system must ground the biological organism. Moreover the assumption of transitivity is useful. By treating grounding as transitive (and irreflexive), one generates a strict partial ordering that induces metaphysical structure.

Yet I will offer counterexamples to the transitivity of grounding. Such counterexamples should not be so surprising given that grounding is akin to causation, and that there are known counterexamples to the transitivity of causation. I will conclude by explaining how a contrastive approach can resolve the counterexamples while retaining metaphysical structure.

4.1 BACKGROUND

4.1.1 Grounding

Here is a natural picture, with roots tracing back at least to Democritus:

Atomism: Fundamentally there are just atoms in the void. But there are also derivative composites like pebbles, persons, and planets, which are grounded in their fundamental atomic parts.

No sooner is *Atomism* sketched then a relation of grounding comes into view, connecting the fundamental atoms to their derivative composites.

Of course, *Atomism* is hardly mandatory. For instance, one might revise the picture of what is fundamental in various ways. Indeed I myself would prefer to speak of what is fundamental in terms of the whole spatiotemporal manifold and the fields that permeate it, with parts counting as derivative from the whole.[1] But grounding remains integral. Such a revision only affects what grounds what.

One might also revise *Atomism* to excise grounding from the picture altogether. For instance, one might deny that there are any derivative entities at all: no pebbles, persons, or planets, but only the fundamentals (e.g. only atoms in the void).[2] Or one might allow that there are particles, pebbles, persons, and planets, but refuse any distinction in fundamentality between them.[3] But on any sort of picture which is neither radically eliminative nor radically egalitarian – that is, on any sort of picture which distinguishes more from less fundamental entities – grounding relations remain connecting the more fundamental to the less.

Given that grounding is an integral aspect of such a natural sort of picture, it is perhaps unsurprising that there has been a surge of interest in grounding,[4] though there remains disagreement over the details. Some of these disagreements affect the proper formulation of grounding claims, and thus affect the form in which a transitivity schema must be phrased, and to which the counterexamples must be fitted. For the sake of simplicity and definiteness, I will speak in terms of a singular–singular relation between facts,[5] with the following schematic form:

The fact that ϕ grounds the fact that ψ

---

[1] See Schaffer 2009a, 2010a, and 2010b (inter alia) for elaboration of this monistic view, and Sider 2007, 2008, and Morganti 2009 for some critical discussion.

[2] See Sider 2011 for a defense of such a radically eliminative view. See Horgan and Potrč 2008 for a defense of the radically eliminative monist counterpart view on which only the whole cosmos is real.

[3] This is the "flatworlder" view that Bennett (forthcoming) labels "crazypants."

[4] See for instance Fine 2001, Correia 2005, Schaffer 2009b, Rosen 2010, Bennett 2011, Skiles manuscript, and Trogdon forthcoming. For some criticism, see Hofweber 2009, deRosset 2010, and Wilson manuscript.

[5] This way of speaking is controversial in at least three respects. First, it involves speaking of grounding as a *relation*. Correia (2010) argues that grounding is better regimented via an operator. Second, it involves treating grounding as a relation *between facts*. Rosen (2010) restricts grounding to a relation between facts, while Schaffer (2009b) allows grounding between entities of arbitrary ontological category. Third, it involves treating grounding as singular–singular. Schaffer (2009b) treats grounding as a singular–singular relation, Correia (2010), Fine (2012a), and Rosen (2010) treat grounding as irreducibly plural on the side of the more fundamental, and Dasgupta (manuscript) advocates treating grounding as irreducibly plural on both sides. See Trogdon forthcoming for a useful overview of these and other controversies.

I myself would prefer to speak of grounding as holding between things. (One should distinguish the worldly relation of grounding from the metaphysical explanations between facts that it backs, just as one should distinguish the worldly relation of causation from the causal explanations between facts that it backs.) But I need not quibble over these details. The counterexamples I offer are robust. The reader who would prefer to regiment grounding claims differently should be able to re-phrase the discussion as she prefers.

But one point should be explicitly clarified. It is useful to distinguish between a *partial ground* for the occurrence of a given fact, and its *whole grounds*.[6] I am here concerned solely with relations of partial ground, and the occurrence of "grounds" in the above schema should be read accordingly. (The reader may substitute "helps ground" for "grounds" if that helps fix the intended meaning for her.)

4.1.2   Transitivity

It is natural to assume that grounding is transitive. That is, it is natural to assume the validity of the following inference schema:

The fact that φ grounds the fact that ψ
The fact that ψ grounds the fact that ρ
_____

Thus: the fact that φ grounds the fact that ρ

Indeed, the assumption of transitivity is so natural that it is widely incorporated into accounts of grounding without any further discussion. For instance, Schaffer (2009b, p. 376) baldly asserts that grounding is transitive, Fine (2010, p. 100; also Correia 2010) includes a transitivity axiom as one of his general ground-theoretic assumptions, and Whitcomb (2011, §2) says that transitivity and irreflexivity are both "*obviously* true, in the way that it is obviously true that the *better than* relation is transitive and irreflexive." The exception proves the rule: Rosen (2010, p. 116) strikes a note of caution with "[t]he grounding relation is not obviously transitive," but then immediately takes up transitivity as an assumption.

---

[6] Indeed, Fine 2012a also distinguishes between a *strict ground* that is prior in the grounding order, and a *weak ground* that is merely not posterior. In the main text I am working with the notion of a strict partial ground.

This assumption is moreover very plausible in many of its instances. Thus the following instance of the transitivity schema looks solid:

1. The fact that there are particles arranged in this way grounds the fact that there are chemicals arranged in that way
2. The fact that there are chemicals arranged in that way grounds the fact that there is a cat afoot
3. Thus the fact that there are particles arranged in this way grounds the fact that there is a cat afoot

Indeed, such a style of inference looks useful in helping to establish the general physicalist claim that everything either is physical or is grounded in the physical, by helping show that the biological is grounded in the physical via the chemical. After all, if this style of inference were invalid then there would arise the worry that, even though the biological is grounded in the chemical and the chemical is grounded in the physical, the biological still might not be grounded in the physical.

The assumption of transitivity is also formally useful. Given transitivity together with the widely accepted principle of irreflexivity,[7] one gets a relation which induces a strict partial ordering over the set of entities in its range (which I am currently treating as facts). Strict partial orderings provide metaphysical structure. This structure is what allows one to speak of fundamental entities as minimal elements in the ordering, and to apply the resources of directed acyclic graphs needed for structural equation models (cf. Schaffer manuscript). For instance, the style of inference seen in 1–3 is useful in establishing a hierarchy with physics underlying chemistry, and chemistry underlying biology.

That said, the matter of formal utility needs qualification. For one can always define the transitive closure R^* of an intransitive relation R. So one could just define grounding* as the transitive closure of grounding, and then revise physicalism to require only that everything be either physical or grounded* in the physical, while retaining partial ordering structure via the grounding* relation. So the formal utility of transitivity is best understood in terms of preserving simpler and more intuitive accounts of physicalism and of structure.

---

[7] Though see Jenkins 2011 for an objection to irreflexivity. See Section 4.3.2 for a brief application of contrastivity to Jenkins's argument.

4.2   COUNTEREXAMPLES

So far I have introduced the notion of grounding and discussed how the assumption of transitivity is widespread, plausible, and useful (Section 4.1). The stage is now set for the counterexamples. I will offer three.

Of course I can only claim to make a reasonable case. With each example, the stalwart defender of transitivity can always reject one of the two linking premises, or "bite the bullet" and accept the chained conclusion. (Likewise with the counterexamples to the transitivity of causation, which I take to have roughly equal force as my counterexamples.[8]) Part of my purpose in providing three counterexamples is to exhibit their diversity, and thereby show just how stalwart a defender of transitivity must be.

4.2.1   *The dented sphere*

Imagine a slightly imperfect sphere, with a minor dent. The thing has a precise maximally determinate shape which English has no ready word for, but which I will dub "shape S." The thing also falls under a determinable shape which English also has no ready word for, but which I will dub "more-or-less spherical," understood as covering a range of maximally determinate shapes centered around the perfectly spherical but permitting some minor deviations. Now consider the following grounding claim:

> 4. The fact that the thing has a dent grounds the fact that the thing has shape S

Claim 4 is plausible since the presence of the dent helps make it the case that the thing has maximally determinate shape S. Were it not for the dent the thing's shape would have been different. If one wonders why the thing has shape S, the fact that it has a dent is part of the reason.

Now consider:

> 5. The fact that the thing has shape S grounds the fact that it is more-or-less spherical

Claim 5 is an instance of the generally plausible claim that something's having a determinate property grounds its having the relevant

---

[8] For discussions of the various counterexamples to the transitivity of causation, see for instance McDermott 1995, Hall 2000, Paul 2000, Hitchcock 2001, Sartorio 2006, and Hall and Paul forthcoming, §5. Virtually everyone in the causation literature seems now to accept at least some of these counterexamples as genuine, with the notable exception of Lewis (2000).

determinable (cf. Rosen 2010, p. 126). If one wonders why the thing is more-or-less spherical, the fact that it has precise shape S is part of (indeed perhaps the whole of) the reason.

But given 4 and 5, transitivity would force us to conclude:

6. The fact that the thing has a dent grounds the fact that it is more-or-less spherical

And 6 is implausible, since the presence of the dent makes no difference to the more-or-less sphericality of the thing. The thing would be more-or-less spherical either way. The presence of the dent in no way helps to support the more-or-less sphericality of the thing, but is if anything a *threat* to the more-or-less sphericality of the thing. The thing is more-or-less spherical *despite* the minor dent, not because of it.[9]

4.2.2 *The third member*

Let S be a set with exactly three members, a, b, and c: $S = \{a, b, c\}$. Now consider the following grounding claim:

7. The fact that c is a member of S grounds the fact that S has exactly three members

Claim 7 is plausible since c's being a member of S helps make it the case that S has exactly three members. Were c not a member of S then S would have had two members and not three. If one wonders why S has exactly three members, the fact that S has c as a member is part of the reason.

Now consider:

8. The fact that S has exactly three members grounds the fact that S has finitely many members

Claim 8 is plausible (along lines similar to claim 5) since *having finitely many members* is a determinable, of which *having three members* is a determinate. If one wonder why S has finitely many members, the fact that it has three members is part of (indeed perhaps the whole of) the reason.

---

[9] Trogdon (forthcoming, §4) worries that my example equivocates between partial and whole grounding, since 4 is only a truth of partial grounding but 5 is a truth of whole grounding. But of course any whole ground is also a partial ground, and so 5 is *both* a truth of partial grounding and a truth of whole grounding. The example thus should go through on the intended reading of "grounds" in terms of partial grounding. (Trogdon goes on to offer an "easy fix" to the worry, which is to replace the fact that the thing is more-or-less spherical with the disjunctive fact that the thing is more-or-less spherical or snow is white, in both 5 and 6. This works too.)

But given 7 and 8, transitivity would yield:

9. The fact that c is a member of S grounds the fact that S has finitely many members

And 9 is implausible, since c's being a member of S in no way helps contribute to the fact that S is finite. S would be finite either way, with or without c as a member. If anything, S remains finite not because of but *despite* taking on c as an additional member.

4.2.3   The cat's meow

Imagine that Cadmus the cat is meowing. The fact that Cadmus is meowing is partly grounded in the various facts that make this cat *Cadmus*. Perhaps – given the essentiality of origins (Kripke 1980) – these include origin facts such as the fact that this creature was produced from the meeting of this sperm and that ovum; or perhaps – given the essentiality of species membership – these include wider historical facts that key this creature into the species *felis catus*. So consider:

10. The fact that the creature was produced from the meeting of this sperm and that ovum grounds the fact that Cadmus is meowing

Claim 10 is plausible (given origin essentialism), since being produced from the meeting of this sperm and that ovum helps make the creature Cadmus as opposed to some other cat. If one wonders why *Cadmus* is meowing, the facts that make the meowing creature Cadmus are part of the reason.

The fact that Cadmus is meowing in turn grounds various "higher level" facts that are independent of the "Cadmus aspect" but rather stem from "the meowing aspect," such as:

11. The fact that Cadmus is meowing grounds the fact that something is meowing

Claim 11 is plausible since the fact that Cadmus is meowing provides a factual witness for the existential generalization that something is meowing, and factual witnesses ground existential generalizations (Fine 2010b, p. 101; Rosen 2010, p. 117). If one wonders why it is the case that something is meowing, then the fact that Cadmus is meowing provides sufficient reason.

But given 10 and 11, transitivity entails:

12. The fact that the creature was produced from the meeting of this sperm and that ovum grounds the fact that something is meowing

And 12 is implausible, since the present extrinsic and historical fact that the creature was produced from the meeting of this sperm and that ovum (as opposed to some other sperm-and-ovum duo) makes no difference to the creature's present intrinsic physical state, which is what is crucial to its ability to witness the existence generalization that something is meowing.[10] Whether the creature counts as Cadmus or some other cat, it is meowing all the same. The fact that the creature was produced from the meeting of this sperm and that ovum helps make it be *Cadmus* meowing, but doesn't help make it be Cadmus *meowing*.

I thus conclude that there are plausible counterexamples to the transitivity of grounding. Such a conclusion befits the idea that grounding is akin to metaphysical causation, since there are known to be plausible counterexamples to the transitivity of causation.

4.3 CONTRASTIVITY

I have offered counterexamples to the transitivity of grounding (Section 4.2). But it would be unsatisfying to leave the matter at that. For given that transitivity is itself a natural, plausible, and useful assumption (Section 4.2), one wants a *replacement* which not only avoids the counterexamples but explains why transitivity seemed plausible, while preserving its use in generating structure.[11] Indeed, one might hope for a replacement which is *unified* in at least two respects. First, the replacement might furnish a unified diagnosis of the diverse counterexamples. Secondly, the replacement might cover not just grounding but causation as well, as an analogue notion whose transitivity is equally in doubt. I will thus

---

[10] Of course, there may well be a *causal* connection from the *past* meeting of sperm and ovum to the *present* meowing. But that must be distinguished from the question of whether there is a *grounding* connection from the *present* extrinsic and historical fact of origin to the *present* intrinsic fact of physical state.

[11] As Hall and Paul (forthcoming, Chapter 5) aptly note with regard to the counterexamples to the transitivity of causation: "What's needed is a more subtle story, according to which the inference from "*C* causes *D*" and "*D* causes *E*" to "*C* causes *E*" is safe, *provided* such-and-such conditions obtain – where these conditions can typically be assumed to obtain, except perhaps in odd cases . . . [S]pelling out the needed conditions – or providing some other explanation for why causation can often safely be assumed to be transitive – is a crucial bit of unfinished business."

conclude by sketching a replacement which is unified in both of these two respects, based on *contrastive* treatments of both causation and grounding.

I should clarify that I am only claiming to offer one such unified replacement principle. There may well be other unified replacements to consider. I am also not going to defend a contrastive treatment of causation or the application of contrastive causation to the transitivity of causation (beyond providing one illustrative example), since I have discussed this elsewhere (Schaffer 2005, especially §5). And I am not going to try to defend a full contrastive treatment of grounding. My primary purpose is rather to extend the contrastive treatment of transitivity for causation to the case of transitivity for grounding, and thus exhibit at least one respect in which a contrastive treatment of grounding holds promise.

4.3.1   Contrastive treatments

In the causal case, the contrastive treatment involves viewing causation not as a binary relation between two actual distinct events but as a quaternary relation including a non-actual causal contrast and a non-actual effectual contrast, of the form:

C rather than C^* causes E rather than E^*

Here C and E are required to be actual distinct events, but C^* is required to be a non-actual alternative to C, and E^* is required to be a non-actual alternative to E. In the grounding case (continuing to restrict the relata to facts), the contrastive treatment involves viewing grounding as having the form:

The fact that φ rather than φ^* grounds the fact that ψ rather than ψ^*

The fact that φ and fact that ψ are required to be obtaining facts, but the fact that φ^* is required to be a non-obtaining alternative to the fact that φ, and the fact that ψ^* is required to be a non-obtaining alternative to the fact that ψ.[12]

Contrastive treatments might at first seem implausibly radical, but in fact they are now quite orthodox for causation.[13] Indeed, the leading treatments of causation work within *structural equation models* (cf. Pearl 2000), with events represented via variables each of which is allotted

---

[12] In both the causal and grounding cases the contrast slots can be expanded to allow for sets of contrasts, but for simplicity I will stick with the case of the single contrast in the main text.
[13] Contrastive treatments of causation are defended in Hitchcock 1996, Woodward 2003, Maslen 2004, Schaffer 2005, 2010c, and forthcoming, Craver 2007, Menzies 2007 and 2009, and Northcott 2008, inter alia.

a range of permitted values. The range of permitted values constitutes a *contrast space*.[14] What range of values is permitted affects causal outcomes (Schaffer 2010b, §1.3). And so structural equation models are inherently contrastive. Given that grounding is akin to causation, this provides one initial motivation for extending a contrastive treatment to grounding.

A further motivation for a contrastive treatment of both grounding and causation is the idea that both back forms of explanation.[15] Now explanation is widely thought to be contrastive (cf. van Fraassen 1980, Garfinkel 1981). Thus explaining why *Adam* ate the apple is a different matter from explaining why Adam *ate* the apple, or why Adam ate *the apple*. To explain why *Adam* ate the apple one needs information that distinguishes Adam from other possible apple eaters such as Eve, whereas to explain why Adam *ate* the apple one needs information that distinguishes the actual eating from other possible actions Adam might have engaged in with the apple such as ignoring it, and to explain why Adam ate *the apple* one needs information that distinguishes the apple from other possible things Adam might have eaten such as the nearby pear. Contrastive treatments of both causation and grounding cast both causation and grounding in an apt form to back explanation.

Some confirmation of the applicability of a contrastive treatment is that focal differences can make for truth-conditional differences. In the case of causation, Achinstein (1975) notes that it may be true to say that Socrates' *drinking hemlock* at dusk caused his death, yet false to say that Socrates' drinking hemlock *at dusk* caused his death. One wants to say: what he drank matters, when he drank it did not. The contrastivist can put this as follows: Socrates' drinking hemlock at dusk rather than wine caused his dying rather than surviving, but Socrates' drinking hemlock at dusk rather than dawn did not cause his dying rather than surviving (Schaffer 2005, p. 308).[16] An analogous point holds with grounding. The grounds for Socrates' *drinking hemlock* at dusk should involve the relevant features of the physical system that make the liquid be

---

[14] More formally, a causal model may be formalized as a pair $<S, F>$ where S (the *signature*) is a triple $<U, V, R>$ with U being a set of exogenous variables, V being a set of endogenous variables, and R being a function associating each variable $X \in U \cup V$ with a range of at least two allotted values. R is what encodes the contrasts for a given event $X=x$. (The other element of the model, F, then associates each endogenous variable $X \in V$ with a function f_X mapping values of X's parent variables to values of X.) See Halpern 2000 for further formal treatment.

[15] Or perhaps better: there is a general notion of explanation which can be backed by causation or by grounding (inter alia), or in some cases by a mixture of the two. After all, to explain a macro-effect from a micro-cause, one needs a "diagonal" explanation that crosses both times and levels.

[16] As Menzies (2009, p. 361) notes, discussing this very example in connection with structural equation models: "The point of the contrastive focus in the event nominals is to indicate the range of values of the relevant variables."

hemlock rather than, say, wine. While the grounds for Socrates' drinking hemlock *at dusk* should involve the relevant features of the physical system that situate it at dusk rather than, say, dawn.

That said, the prospects for contrastive treatments depend on a detailed assessment of fully developed frameworks. In my view the best framework for treating causation is that of structural equation models which incorporate contrastive information. I think that structural equation models can be extended to provide fruitful treatments of grounding relations, but such a claim requires its own full-length discussion (Schaffer manuscript).

4.3.2   *Differential structure*

Grounding – when conceived of as a binary relation – is widely thought to be irreflexive, asymmetric, and transitive. Indeed, such principles impose partial ordering structure (Section 4.2). What happens to all these principles in a contrastive framework?

The simplest and most natural extension of all of these principles into a contrastive framework is to think of them all as holding, not between individual facts, but between *differences*. Continuing to work with a fact-restricted singular–singular relational schema for grounding (Section 4.1.1), think of "The fact that φ rather than φ^*" as one such difference, grounding the difference "the fact that ψ rather than ψ^*." Irreflexivity, asymmetry, and transitivity can then be understood as holding between these differences, as per the following schemata:

> *Differential Irreflexivity:* It is not the case that the fact that φ rather than φ^* grounds the fact that φ rather than φ^*

> *Differential Asymmetry:* If the fact that φ rather than φ^* grounds the fact that ψ rather than ψ^*, then it is not the case that the fact that ψ rather than ψ^* grounds the fact that φ rather than φ^*

> *Differential Transitivity:* If the fact that φ rather than φ^* grounds the fact that ψ rather than ψ^*, and the fact that ψ rather than ψ^* grounds the fact that ρ rather than ρ^*, then the fact that φ rather than φ^* grounds the fact that ρ rather than ρ^*

Thus one retains partial ordering structure, albeit not over individual facts but over differences.[17]

---

[17] As mentioned in Section 4.1.2, Jenkins (2011) objects to irreflexivity since she thinks that one could coherently hold both that (a) the fact that neural state *n* exists grounds the fact that mental state *m*

One thus recovers the idea of a *fundamental difference* as a minimal element in the ordering over differences:

> *Differential Fundamentality:* The fact that φ rather than φ* is fundamental $=_{df}$ there is no difference ψ rather than ψ* that grounds the fact that φ rather than φ*

One can moreover speak of a fundamental fact *simpliciter*, as a fact occupying the first slot ("φ") of a fundamental difference:

> *Absolute Fundamentality:* The fact that φ is absolutely fundamental $=_{df}$ there is a possible fact φ* such that the fact that φ rather than φ* is fundamental

The fundamental facts are the obtaining portions of fundamental differences. One can likewise speak of a fundamental entity *simpliciter* as an entity that a fundamental fact concerns. One can thus retain the plausibility of grounding-based formulations of physicalism: all differences are physical differences or grounded in physical differences. Or: all absolutely fundamental facts are physical facts.

One can then consider various structural restrictions on the difference ordering. By way of illustration, one might or might not require differential well-foundedness, now understood as the idea that every difference which is not fundamental is grounded in a difference which is fundamental:

> *Differential Well-foundedness:* If the fact that φ rather than φ* is not fundamental, then there is a difference ψ rather than ψ* which is fundamental and which grounds the fact that φ rather than φ*

In short, a contrastive treatment of grounding augmented with *Differential Transitivity* preserves much of what was promising about transitivity. If transitivity is intuitive, *Differential Transitivity* represents its intuitive extension. If transitivity is plausible in application to physicalist

---

exists, and that (b) the fact that neural state *n* exists is identical to the fact that mental state *m* exists. In response she considers the option of treating grounding as a four-place relation between <fact, aspect> pairs, so as to be able to say that <the fact that the state in question exists, neural aspect> grounds <the fact that the state in question exists, mental aspect>. A contrastive approach outfitted with *Differential Irreflexivity* can equally resolve her objection (while enjoying the motivations of a contrastive treatment: Section 4.3.1, and naturally extending the structural principles used in binary approaches: Section 4.3.2). The contrastive treatment has it that the fact that the state in question exists rather than a state with this other neural feature grounds the fact that the state in question exists rather than a state with that other mental feature.

inferences, and useful (with irreflexivity) in yielding metaphysical structure, *Differential Transitivity* (with *Differential Irreflexivity*) can claim comparable virtues.[18]

4.3.3   Counterexamples resolved

A contrastive treatment of grounding augmented with *Differential Transitivity* can resolve the counterexamples to transitivity presented in Section 4.2, just as a contrastive treatment of causation can resolve the counterexamples to the transitivity of causation via the analogous principle:

> *Differential Transitivity of Causation:* If C rather than C^* causes D rather than D^*, and D rather than D^* causes E rather than E^*, then C rather than C^* causes E rather than E^*

With causation the key idea is to show that all the counterexamples to transitivity require illicit shifts in the middle contrast, only fitting the schema: C rather than C^* causes D rather than D^*, and D rather than D^{**} causes E rather than E^* (where $D^* \neq D^{**}$). Cases that only fit such a schema are no counterexamples to *Differential Transitivity of Causation*.[19]

I will not discuss the contrastive treatment of the transitivity of causation save to provide an illustrative example (*nudgings*, from Schaffer 2005, pp. 309–10). Thus imagine that when Suzy throws a rock through a window, her rock is ever so slightly deflected in midair (from trajectory1 to nearby trajectory2) by a mote of dust. Then it might seem as if the following holds:

13. The dust mote's nudging the rock causes the rock to reach the midpoint of trajectory2

---

[18] To the extent that contrastive structure is understood as a concomitant of using structural equation models (where variables are contrast spaces), the structural principles need to force the structure *over the variables* into the structure of a directed acyclic graph (Schaffer manuscript). In the case of binary variables the principles in the main text suffice. But for variables allotted more than two values, the principles need to be extended to take on sets of contrasts. In any case, what bears emphasis is that the relevant structure in structural equation models is not a structure over outcomes (actual values of variables) but a structure over contrast spaces (variables themselves, each with a range of allotted values). Thus from a structural equation modeling perspective the partial ordering needed is not of the form that transitivity might provide but rather of the form that *Differential Transitivity* provides.

[19] If one thinks of the contrasts as supplied by the context when left implicit, this is to say that all the counterexamples to transitivity require illicit *context shifts*. Any statement of the transitivity schema (for either causation or grounding) will be valid *in any fixed context*, given that a fixed context supplies a fixed stock of implicit contrasts.

14. The rock's reaching the midpoint of trajectory2 causes the window to shatter

Indeed 13 and 14 each seem validated by the simple *counterfactual dependence* test for causation, which is at least an excellent test. But given 13 and 14, the transitivity of causation would entail:

15. The dust mote's nudging the rock causes the window to shatter

But clearly the dust mote's nudging the rock does not cause the window to shatter. At most it makes the tiniest difference in how the window shatters, but the window will shatter either way.

It should be evident how the contrastive treatment holds promise for 13–15. The difference that the dust mote's nudging the rock rather than missing the rock makes is:

13*. The dust mote's nudging the rock rather than missing the rock causes the rock to reach the midpoint of trajectory2 rather than the midpoint of trajectory1

But the rock's reaching the midpoint of trajectory2 rather than the midpoint of trajectory1 does not cause the window to shatter rather than remain intact. The window will shatter either way:

14*. The rock's reaching the midpoint of trajectory2 rather than the midpoint of trajectory1 does NOT cause the window to shatter rather than remain intact

What does cause the window to shatter rather than remain intact are differences such as the rock's reaching the midpoint of trajectory2 *rather than dropping directly to the ground*:

14**. The rock's reaching the midpoint of trajectory2 rather than dropping directly to the ground does cause the window to shatter rather than remain intact

But of course the dust mote's nudging the rock does not make the difference as to whether the rock reaches the midpoint of trajectory2 rather than dropping directly to the ground. There is no differential chain running from the dust mote's nudging the rock to the window's shattering.

Returning to grounding, the key idea is thus to show that the counterexample to transitivity require shifts in the value of the middle contrast, only fitting the following schema (where $\psi^* \neq \psi^{**}$):

The fact that φ rather than φ* grounds the fact that ψ rather than ψ*

The fact that ψ rather than ψ** grounds the fact that ρ rather than ρ*

X Thus: the fact that φ rather than φ* grounds the fact that ρ rather than ρ*

Cases that only fit such a schema are of course no counterexamples to *Differential Transitivity*.

With this idea in mind, return to the case of the dented sphere (Section 4.2.1). Consider the fact that the thing has a dent, as compared to the natural alternative of it being undented. What difference does the presence of the dent make? It makes the difference between the thing having its precise shape S, and its having a slightly different (and more perfectly spherical) shape S*:

4*. The fact that the thing has a dent rather than having no dent grounds the fact that the thing has shape S rather than S*

But the fact that the thing has shape S rather than S* makes *no difference* to whether the thing is more-or-less spherical. The thing will be more-or-less-spherical either way:

5*. The fact that the thing has shape S rather than S* does NOT ground the fact that the thing is more-or-less spherical rather than not

What does make a difference as to whether the thing is more-or-less spherical are differences such as between the thing's having its precise shape S and its having a completely different flat-as-a-pancake shape S**:

5**. The fact that the thing has shape S rather than S** grounds the fact that the thing is more-or-less spherical rather than not

But of course the presence of the dent does not make the difference between the thing's having S or S**. There is no differential chain running from the presence/absence of the dent to the thing's being more-or-less spherical or not.[20]

One can of course find features of the thing that do make the difference between its having its precise shape S and the flat-as-a-pancake shape S**. But these features *do* make the difference between the thing's being more-or-less spherical rather than not. In general, consider any features of the thing that

---

[20] Indeed it may be natural to think of the case of the dented sphere as the grounding-theoretic analogue to the example of nudgings. One might think of the dent as nudging the location of the sphere in the determination space for shape.

make a difference to its shape. Either these features make a difference to whether the thing is more-or-less spherical, or not. If not then the analogue of 5 will fail (as was seen with 5*). But if so then the analogue of 6 should hold (as was seen with 5**). Either way, *Differential Transitivity* stands.

Similar comments apply to the case of the third member (Section 4.2.2). What difference does having *c* as a member make to *S*?

7*. The fact that *c* is a member of *S* rather than not a member of *S* grounds the fact that *S* has exactly three members rather than exactly two members

But whether or not *S* has exactly three members or exactly two members, *S* will remain finite:

8*. The fact that *S* has exactly three members rather than exactly two members does NOT ground the fact that *S* is finite rather than infinite

What does make the difference as to whether *S* is finite are differences such as between *S*'s having exactly three members and its having as many members as there are natural numbers:

8**. The fact that *S* has exactly three members rather than as many members as there are natural numbers grounds the fact that *S* is finite rather than infinite

But of course the fact that *c* is a member of *S* does not make the difference between *S*'s having exactly three members rather than as many members as there are natural numbers. There is no differential chain running from *c*'s membership-or-not in *S* to *S*'s being finite-or-not.

In general, consider any alternative supposition to *S*'s having *c* as a member. That alternative will either preserve *S*'s finitude or not. If so then the relevant analogue of 8 will fail, and if not then the relevant analogue of 9 will hold. *Differential Transitivity* stands either way.

Similar comments apply equally to the case of the cat's meow (Section 4.2.3). Being produced from the meeting of this sperm and that ovum rather than a different sperm and ovum makes the difference between it being Cadmus who is meowing and it being some other cat (say, Cilix) who is meowing:

10*. The fact that the creature was produced from the meeting of this sperm and that ovum rather than a different sperm and ovum grounds the fact that Cadmus is meowing rather than Cilix meowing

But whether it is Cadmus or Cilix who is meowing, there will still be something meowing:

11*. The fact that Cadmus is meowing rather than Cilix meowing does NOT ground the fact that something is meowing rather than nothing meowing

What does make the difference as to whether something is meowing rather than nothing meowing are differences such as between the creature's intrinsic physical state being this way rather than that:

11**. The fact that the creature is in this intrinsic physical state rather than that intrinsic physical state grounds the fact that something is meowing rather than nothing meowing

But of course the present historical fact that the creature was produced from the past meeting of this sperm and that ovum does not now help ground the difference between the creature being in this intrinsic physical state rather than that intrinsic physical state. (The meeting of this sperm and that ovum may have had various causal repercussions across time, but at the present moment it makes no difference to the intrinsic physical state of the system.) There is no differential grounding chain running from the present historical fact of production from this sperm and that ovum, to the present fact of being in this intrinsic physical state rather than that.

In general, consider any alternative supposition to the creature's having been produced from the meeting of this sperm and that ovum. The alternative will either preserve the fact that something is meowing or not. If so then the analogue of 11 will fail; if not then the analogue of 12 will hold; either way *Differential Transitivity* stands.

Putting all this together, I have argued that a contrastive treatment of grounding not only comes with strong initial motivations (Section 4.3.1), but also provides a natural unified replacement principle of *Differential Transitivity* which can help generate metaphysical structure (Section 4.3.2), while resolving the plausible counterexamples to transitivity (Section 4.3.3). For these reasons I think that a contrastive treatment of grounding holds promise. But whatever one may think of contrastivity as a corrective, I would contend that the assumption of transitivity was a mistake.[21]

[21] Thanks to Karen Bennett, Fabrice Correia, Laurie Paul, Raúl Saucedo, Alex Skiles, Joshua Spencer, Kelly Trogdon, and audiences at the Geneva-Barcelona Workshop, the Australian National University, and the Australian Metaphysics Conference.

CHAPTER 5

Violations of the Principle of Sufficient Reason (in Leibniz and Spinoza)

Michael Della Rocca

You may ask: is this chapter an endeavor in the study of the history of philosophy or is it an endeavor in contemporary philosophy? And I may answer: it's both. Instead of wondering about how this chapter fits with prior notions of what is good or bad work in either of these domains, just sit back and enjoy the ride.

My central concern here – violations of the Principle of Sufficient Reason (hereafter: 'PSR') – does indeed stem from my engagement with two figures from the history of philosophy: Leibniz and Spinoza. Both of these philosophers are big fans of the Principle of Sufficient Reason, the principle according to which each thing that exists has an explanation.[1] Indeed, a strong case can be made that each of these thinkers structures his entire system around the PSR more or less successfully.[2] However, despite these similarities, the character of each philosopher's commitment to the PSR differs, and the differences have illuminating implications for our understanding of the power of these

---

[1] Spinoza: see *Ethics* 1p11d2. Leibniz: see *Monadology* §32. I use the standard system for referring to passages from the *Ethics*. Thus, e.g., 1p11d2 = *Ethics* Part 1, Proposition 11, second demonstration. Unless otherwise noted all references to Spinoza are to the *Ethics*.

I use the following abbreviations:

(i) Editions of Spinoza's works: *Spinoza Opera*, Gebhardt 1925: Geb.
(ii) Editions of Leibniz's works: *Sämtliche Schriften und Briefe*, Berlin Academy: A
Opuscules, Couturat 1903: C
Die Philosophischen Schriften, Gerhardt 1875–1890: Ger
Leibniz: Philosophical Essays, Ariew & Garber: AG
Philosophical Papers and Letters, Loemker 1969: L
De Summa Rerum, Parkinson 1992: DSR
New Essays on Human Understanding, Remnant and Bennett: NE
Fragmente zur Logik, Schmidt 1960: S

[2] Spinoza more, Leibniz less!

rationalist systems and for the metaphysical issues these philosophers take up that concern us today. One way to distill these differences is by exploring the perhaps surprising ways violations of the PSR arise for Leibniz and Spinoza. It will turn out that Leibniz is, or would be, unable to handle such violations, while Spinoza can handle them more or less in stride in his more resilient and, in some ways, more exotic, rationalist system.

To elicit these violations of the PSR, I would like to highlight an important strand in Leibniz's wonderfully rich thinking about relations. I don't pretend to capture all that Leibniz says about relations throughout his career. But I aim to articulate at least some of his commitments on this topic. As is well known, Leibniz thinks that relations are (somehow) not in, not states of, the things (apparently) related and that they are (somehow) ideal. I will return to the ideality of relations briefly later, but mostly I want to focus on one of Leibniz's reasons for thinking that relations are not states of the things (apparently) related. I think that this line of thought is rather good and that it is of a piece with Leibniz's best uses of the PSR. After drawing out this good strategy in Leibniz, I will extend this rationalist line of thought perhaps further than Leibniz himself does in order to reveal the violations of the PSR in Leibniz. This revelation – unwelcome from Leibniz's point of view – will set the stage for a comparative evaluation of the resources that Leibniz and Spinoza may have for handling such violations.

So one of my goals is to play Leibniz and Spinoza off each other. Because these figures are two of the greats and because their systems are still not well understood, I think we should care about this investigation. But I believe we should care also because of the philosophical issues at stake: the arguments that Leibniz and Spinoza develop have – as I will stress – considerable power. In particular, in the course of elucidating Leibniz's and Spinoza's commitments to the PSR, I will present an argument for – and at least tentatively endorse – Leibniz's view that the states of a thing are due only to the nature of the thing itself, a view that can be seen as a version of Leibniz's famous predicate in subject principle (hereafter: PISP). On the basis of this argument, I will also present an argument for – and at least tentatively endorse – an extreme form of the theory that the world itself is the only thing that exists. That is, I will tentatively argue for a monism of the kind to be found in Spinoza.

5.1   GROUNDING RELATIONS

Leibniz advances the following controversial principle:

If x is F, then the state of being F must be due to, explained by, x's nature exclusively.[3]

In other words, anything true of x is, for Leibniz, due to x's nature alone. The explanatory basis for states of an object is simply the object's nature. Leibniz sometimes puts the point in terms of the idea or notion of an object. We find evidence – from various stages in Leibniz's career – for this reading. Thus we find Leibniz saying in 1686 in the *Discourse on Metaphysics*:

all true predication has some *basis* [*quelque fondement*] in the nature of things. (*Discourse on Metaphysics* §8, Ger IV, p. 433; my emphasis)

See also *Discourse on Metaphysics* §14:

what happens to each [substance] is a *consequence* of its complete idea or notion alone (*ce qui arrive à chacune n'est qu'une suite de son idée ou notion complete toute seule*). (My emphasis; translation altered, Ger IV, p. 440)

See also "Primary Truths" (*c.* 1686):

the predicate or consequent is always in the subject or antecedent, and the nature of truth in general or the connection between the terms of a statement, consists in this very thing . . . The connection and inclusion of the predicate in the subject is explicit in identities, but in all other propositions it is implicit and must be shown through the analysis of notions. (C, p. 518; AG, p. 31)

See also *New Essays* (*c.* 1703):

Whenever we find some quality in a subject, we ought to believe that if we understand the nature of both the subject and the quality we would conceive how the quality could arise [*résulter*] from it. (p. 66)

See also the following passage from around 1695 in Leibniz's logic notes:

If there is somebody who is Strong, Brash, Learned, a King, General of an army, Victor in the battle of Arbela, and the other things of this kind that are ascribed to Alexander the Great, God, intuiting the individual essence of Alexander the

---

[3] Leibniz does use the term "state" as well as "accident," "property," and others. (For Leibniz's uses of "state" see "De Affectibus" in Grua 1948, II, pp. 512–13. For other related terms, see Clatterbaugh 1973, p. 2.) There are important distinctions here, not all of which are clear in Leibniz, but I won't dwell on them, for in each case in which a thing has a property or accident or is in a certain state, there must be something in virtue of which this is the case.

Great, will see a complete concept ... from which those things all follow [*consequuntur*]. (S, pp. 475–6, quoted in Mates 1986, p. 85, n5)

In general for Leibniz, as I mentioned,

> If x is F, then the state of being F must be due to, explained by, x's nature exclusively.

Notice that in the passages just quoted, Leibniz sees the nature of a thing as the basis for its properties and as being that of which certain changes are consequences. This terminology suggests that the nature of a thing serves as the explanatory ground of its states. This claim is, in effect, a version of Leibniz's PISP.

But *why* does Leibniz hold this claim? He sees the principle as importantly connected to the PSR ("Primary Truths," C, p. 519; AG, p. 31; see also *Discourse on Metaphysics* §13), and indeed, he proclaims that if this principle is not true, then "I don't know what truth is" (G II, p. 56; L, p. 337). Unfortunately, many of Leibniz's readers have been tempted to call his bluff here. We are inclined to say that although Leibniz is right, e.g., that my being wise has something to do with my nature, we are also inclined to say that it may also be due in part to other factors such as the wisdom pills I take every morning with my breakfast. My being wise seems not to be due to my nature alone. Why then does Leibniz hold that the properties of a thing are due to its nature alone?

To begin to articulate some of Leibniz's reasons for the PISP, it will help to see that this claim is a specific and implausible version of a general and much more plausible claim. The general claim is this:

> (**1) If an object x is in a certain state (or has a certain property or whatever), then there must be some thing or things in which this state is grounded, some thing or things in virtue of which the thing is in that state.

Unlike the PISP, (**1) allows that my being wise may be due in part to things other than my nature. (**1) requires only that there be some thing in virtue of which I am in that state. Although this claim is not itself a commitment to the full-blown PSR, it is a rationalist claim in that it issues a demand for an explanation, a demand that there be an explanation for certain states. Because this claim is rather plausible, I have placed asterisks before it. (Throughout this section, I will use the asterisks to mark what I see as plausible claims in a rationalist spirit.)

I want to show how one can get from the plausible (**1) to Leibniz's implausible PISP. To begin the process, I want to consider a specific kind of state that *x* may be in – what might be called a relational state. Since *x* is in the state of being related in some way to *y*, it follows from (**1) that there is some thing or things in virtue of which *x* is related to *y*. In the spirit of (**1), it seems right to say that this state depends on, at least, *x*.

If the relational state *x* is in of being related to *y* is grounded in (at least) *x*, what is the relation between *x* and *y* dependent on? Just as it seems natural to demand that there be a ground for states, so too it seems natural to demand that there be some ground for relations. Just as states are not free-floating but are, instead, states of, and grounded in, something, so too relations are relations *between* or *among* things and so they seem to be grounded in those things. The general demand here is that relations, like states, must be grounded.

So here is another plausible principle:

(**2) If objects *x* and *y* stand in a relation, then there must be some thing or things in which that relation is grounded.

I believe Leibniz accepts this demand. This is clear when he says to Des Bosses that a power of determining oneself without any cause implies a contradiction for it implies a relation without a foundation.[4] Here Leibniz explicitly affirms that relations must be grounded. This is evident also from the passages quoted below in which Leibniz seeks the ground of relations. One can see (**2) as following more or less directly from the PSR which demands an explanation for each thing. But one can also see this as simply a plausible demand for grounding along the lines of (**1). By seeing how Leibniz tries to meet this plausible demand for explanation, we will have a way of seeing how he would motivate the PISP. Thus my goal in this section is to place asterisks before the PISP.

Let's focus for now on relations between substances. Take a case in which a substance *x* stands (or apparently stands) in a relation to another substance *y*. According to (**2), this relation must be grounded in some thing or things. We can see that Leibniz – in order to reveal the nature of this ground – carries out a three-step argument. I will be focusing primarily on the first two steps.

Leibniz's first step is to say that the relation between *x* and *y* cannot be a state of *x* in particular as opposed to *y*, because there is no reason to locate the relation in *x* exclusively, to see the relation as grounded in *x* exclusively,

---

[4] Leibniz to Des Bosses, 8 Feb. 1711, Ger II, p. 420.

given that there is equally good reason to see the relation as grounded in y instead. Similarly, the relation cannot be a state of y exclusively because if it were, then there would be no good reason that the relation is not grounded in x instead. In general, because grounding the relation in one of x or y exclusively would be arbitrary, the relation cannot be grounded in x or y exclusively. This first step in Leibniz's argument relies on something like the PSR.

At this point, a natural thing to say is, of course, that while the relation cannot be grounded in one of x or y but not the other, it is grounded in x and y together, i.e. the relation depends on x and also depends on y, and is thus grounded in both together. In other words, the relation is partially grounded in x and partially grounded in y. Although this is more plausible than seeing the ground of the relation in only one of x or y, Leibniz rejects this view too: for Leibniz, a relation cannot be a state of, or grounded in, the two apparently related substances in this joint manner. Leibniz denies, as he puts it to Des Bosses in 1716,

the existence of an accident that can, at the same time, be in two subjects and has one foot in one, so to speak, and one foot in the other. (29 May 1716, Ger II, p. 517; AG, p. 203)[5]

Leibniz denies that relations between substances can be, as it were, pants that pairs of substances wear. This rejection of pants, this denial that a relation is a state of the related substances together is the second key step in Leibniz's investigation of the explanatory basis of relations.

But now we must ask: how then is the relation grounded if not in x or y individually or together? Leibniz will not, of course, have recourse to the claim that the relation is not grounded – that would be to go against the plausible (**2), not to mention that it would be to go against the PSR. Instead, Leibniz claims that the relation is grounded in a mind that compares x and y. Leibniz makes clear that ultimately the relevant mind is God's mind. So the relation between x and y consists, for Leibniz, simply in the fact that God has ideas of x and y and that these ideas are linked in God's intellect, that God somehow compares x and y. Thus Leibniz says:

[5] Leibniz also says to Des Bosses "I do not believe that you will admit an accident that is in two subjects at the same time" (21 April 1714, G II, p. 486; L, p. 609), and to Clarke, "an accident in two subjects, with one leg in one and one in the other" is "contrary to the notion of accidents" (Ger VII, p. 401; L p. 704; AG, p. 339). Cf. Avicenna: "Therefore in no way may you think that one accident is in two subjects" (Henninger 1989, p. 5).

It appears that relations are not other than truths. In themselves, relations are not things which can be created: they are born by virtue of the divine intellect alone. ("Notes on Aloys Temmnik's *Philosophia Vera Theologicae et Medicinae Ministra*" (1715 or 1716), quoted in Mugnai 1992, p. 21)

Relations and orderings are to some extent "being of reason," although they have their foundations in things; for one can say that their reality, like that of eternal truths and of possibilities, comes from the Supreme Reason. (NE, p. 227)

The reality of relations is dependent on mind, as is that of truths; but they do not depend on the human mind, as there is a supreme intelligence which determines all of them from all time. (NE, p. 265)

God not only observes each single monad and all its modifications, but also the relations between them. The reality of relations and truths consists in this. (Notes for Des Bosses, 5 February 1712, Ger II, p. 438; AG p. 199)

And so, by making this final, idealist move, Leibniz believes he is able to make the existence of relations compatible with the demand that relations be grounded.

We can see all three steps at work – in compressed form – in the following important passage from Leibniz's correspondence with Des Bosses:

orders, or relations which join two monads, are not in one monad or the other, but equally well in both at the same time, that is, really in neither, but in the mind alone. (*Ordines . . . , seu relationes, quae duas monades jungunt, non sunt in alterutra monade, sed in utraque aeque simul, id est, revera in neutra, sed in sola mente.*) (29 May 1716, Ger II, p. 517; AG, p. 203)

Here Leibniz makes the first move out of what seems to be a concern to avoid arbitrariness. Relations "are not in one monad or the other, but equally well in both at the same time." At the same time, he makes the second move: relations are "equally well in both at the same time, that is, really in neither." Finally, he makes the idealist move: relations are "in the mind alone." And, again, this train of thought seems to depend on the plausible grounding claim (**2).

Before evaluating this three-step argument for the ideality of relations, I want to examine a popular line of interpretation that might be thought to limit the anti-relational import of this argument. On some interpretations, although Leibniz rejects the reality of relations for something like the reasons I have just outlined, he nonetheless accepts the reality of relational states or relational accidents of individual substances. If this interpretation is correct, then Leibniz is friendly to the reality of relationality of some kind, even if not to the reality of relations themselves. Proponents of this reading often appeal to passages such as the following.

First, Leibniz says in the fifth letter to Clarke in a passage part of which was already quoted:

The ratio or proportion between two lines L and M may be conceived three ways: as a ratio of the greater L to the lesser M, as a ratio of the lesser M to the greater L, and lastly, as something abstracted from both, that is, the ratio between L and M without considering which is the antecedent or which the consequent, which the subject and which the object ... In the first way of considering them, L the greater, in the second, M the lesser, is the subject of that accident which philosophers call "relation". But which of them will be the subject in the third way of considering them? It cannot be said that both of them, L and M together, are the subject of such an accident; for, if so, we should have an accident in two subjects which is contrary to the notion of accidents. Therefore, we must say that this relation, in this third way of considering it, is indeed out of the subjects; but being neither a substance nor an accident, it must be a mere ideal thing. (G VII, p. 401; L, p. 704; AG, p. 339)

Similarly, Leibniz writes to Des Bosses:

My judgment about relations is that paternity in David is one thing, sonship in Solomon another, but that the relation common to both is a merely mental thing whose basis is the modifications of the individuals. (21 April 1714, G II, p. 486; L, p. 609)

In these passages, Leibniz might seem to regard relational states, such as paternity in David, states which are located non-arbitrarily in one particular substance, as real (and not ideal). At the same time, he seems to regard more abstract relations (as opposed to relational states), such as the relation between a father and son or the similarity between similar substances, as things that can only be arbitrarily located in one particular substance and thus as things that are not real (and are ideal).[6]

Without being able to do full justice to this subtle reading, I will make two observations which, jointly, cast doubt on seeing Leibniz as endorsing the reality of relational states but not the reality of relations.

(1) Even if substances have relational states or accidents, for Leibniz, he may nonetheless regard these accidents as not fundamental, but rather as grounded in non-relational accidents. Nothing in the passages just quoted indicates that the relational accidents are fundamental. They may be grounded in intrinsic, non-relational, perhaps perceptual, accidents.[7] It is significant that, even in the letter to Clarke just cited, it is not clear that Leibniz accepts the reality of relational accidents. In that passage,

---

[6] See Kulstad 1980, McCullough 1996, pp. 172–5, and Clatterbaugh 1973, pp. 61–73.
[7] This line of interpretation is developed by Cover and O'Leary-Hawthorne 1999.

Leibniz merely invokes an accident that, he says, "philosophers call 'relation'." It is clear from this that, for Leibniz, when, e.g., *a* is lesser than *b*, *a* is the subject of an accident. But it is not clear that, for Leibniz, the accident of which *a* is the subject is genuinely relational. Leibniz simply says that philosophers call this accident a relation; he himself does not call it a relation or even a relational accident. A similar point may apply to the David–Solomon example in the letter to Des Bosses. There is a real accident in David and this accident leads philosophers to say that David stands in a certain relation to Solomon. But, for all Leibniz says here, it may be that the genuine accident of which David is the subject is not a relation or even a relational accident.

(2) The hybrid position articulated in the alternative reading – i.e. no real relations, but real relational accidents – may not be philosophically coherent. One way to raise this worry is as follows. On most interpretations of Leibniz, although two substances are real and not dependent on being perceived by a mind, relations between the two substances are ideal in that they require that a mind (God's mind) compare the two substances. If this is the case, then it seems natural to say – in contrast to the hybrid reading – something similar about so-called relational accidents: these items are ideal in that they require that a mind compare the relevant substances. Thus just as the relations do not appear or show up without a mind getting in the act, so too so-called relational accidents – unlike intrinsic accidents – do not appear or show up without a mind getting in the act. For Leibniz to deny the reality of relations while affirming the reality of relational accidents would thus be, it seems, for him to draw an invidious distinction. The burden is thus on the proponents of the hybrid position to explain away the apparent tension between the two views such proponents attribute to Leibniz.

Thus, I believe there is good reason to see Leibniz as rejecting the reality not only of relations, but also of relational accidents. Further, I think that if Leibniz's three-step argument against the reality of relations succeeds, then he also has good reason to reject the reality of relationality in general – to reject the reality of relations and of relational states.[8]

So let's return to that three-step argument against the reality of relations in order to see if it is successful. And to do this, I will work backwards through the three steps and test for plausibility. The idealist move seems the least plausible of the three. Normally, we would say that when a mind compares two things, the mind picks up on relations that are already out

---

[8] For a fuller treatment of problems with the hybrid interpretation, see Mugnai forthcoming.

there, independently of the mental comparing. But, on the Leibnizian view, the relations are, in effect, constituted by a mind. This seems to get things backwards. But given that Leibniz has already, in the previous two steps, denied that the relations are grounded in x or y themselves and given that – because of a plausible application of the PSR – he holds that this relation must be grounded, what choice does he have other than to ground the relation in a mind? I believe that there is an alternative, one that Spinoza adopts, as I will argue later. Fortunately, in the justification I offer below for Leibniz's PISP, I will not have to rely on the idealist step in Leibniz's argument concerning relations.

Let's turn to Leibniz's second step in his account of the grounding of relations. Why does Leibniz reject the view that the relation between x and y is grounded jointly in the nature of x and in the nature of y? That is, why does Leibniz deny that x and y can have pants?

When Leibniz rejects pants in the correspondence with Clarke, he does not seem to offer a justification. However, I think we can see Leibniz's reasons here as turning on the plausible grounding principle about relations, (**2). If the relation between x and y were a state of x and y jointly, then this relation would be determined by, explained by, grounded in, x and y together. The "jointly" and "together" here are crucial, for these terms indicate that the relation is grounded at least in part in the fact that x and y are together, the fact that they *coexist* with certain natures, i.e. the fact that they are related somehow. So the relation between x and y is grounded in their standing in a certain relation. But this is hardly an illuminating explanatory ground: at best it merely passes the buck to another relation that needs to be explained (and thus threatens to lead to an infinite regress of relations), at worst it is an out-and-out circular explanation. It's not an option for Leibniz (or for a proponent of the PSR) to say that the relation is ungrounded or is grounded in other relations which are grounded in other relations and so on ad infinitum. To adopt such a view would be to say that ultimately there is no *thing* or things in virtue of which x and y stand in this relation. This result would violate the plausible grounding principle (**2) (and also the PSR). So if we appeal to pants to explain the relation, the relation remains unexplained.

One might object that the line of thought sketched in the previous paragraph mischaracterizes what it is for a and b together to ground a relation. It might be argued: For a and b together to ground a relation, R, is just for a to be a partial ground of R and for b to be a partial ground of R. a can stand in a partial grounding relation to R and so can b without it being the case that R is grounded in relations in a circular fashion or in a way that ineliminably appeals to relations. *a* partially grounds R and *b* partially grounds R, and because *a*'s partial grounding of R is not dependent on *b* (*a* acts on its own, as it were), it is not the case that R itself is dependent on *a* and *b* *as well as* some relation between *a* and *b*. Rather, R depends simply on *a* and *b* or, as one might put it in order to make clear the absence of a relation as among the grounds of R: R is grounded simply in *a, b*. By means of this counterargument, one might think that pants are, after all, legitimate.

However, this strategy won't avoid the result that the relation cannot legitimately be grounded in *a* and *b* together. Consider the claim – implicit in this objection – that in order for R (a relation between *a* and *b*) to hold, *a* must partially ground R. This claim is simply a more specific version of (**2). (**2) says, in effect, that in order for a relation to hold it must be grounded in things. The claim I have just invoked makes the more specific point that in order for a relation between *a* and *b* to hold, the relation must be partially grounded in *a* (and also partially grounded in *b*). Call this relation of partial grounding (between *a* and R) R'. So R holds in part because R' holds. Why does R', the relation of partial grounding between *a* and R, hold? There's a relation, R', of partial grounding between *a* and R only because *a* coexists with *b*. Call the relation of coexistence R". Were it not for R", the coexistence of *a* and *b*, *a* wouldn't be able to partially ground R and thus, were it not for R", R' – the relation of partial grounding between a and R – wouldn't hold at all. So R exists in part because of R' which exists in part because of R". Now in virtue of what do *a* and *b* coexist, i.e. in virtue of what does the relation, R", of coexistence hold? Just as R' obtains in part because *a* and *b* coexist, so too R" obtains because *a* and *b* coexist. This is because R" obtains in part because *a* partially grounds R". But, *a* partially grounds R" in virtue of *a*'s coexistence with *b* – it's in part because *a* coexists with *b* that *a* is able to partially ground R". Without the coexistence of *a* and *b*, *a* couldn't partially ground R". Thus, R" obtains in part because *a* partially grounds R" and *a* partially grounds R" in part because *a* and *b* coexist. But the coexistence of *a* and *b* just is R". So R" holds in part because R" holds. That is, *a* and *b* coexist in part because *a* and *b* coexist. More fully: the coexistence of *a* and *b* depends on the partial grounding of this coexistence by *a*, and the partial grounding depends on the coexistence of *a* and *b*. And so the coexistence depends on the coexistence. And here we reach a circular explanation of a relation. This circular explanation of R" undermines the explanation of our original relation R itself. R obtains in part because of R' which obtains in part because of R" (the relation of coexistence), and R" obtains in part because of R″ itself. Since R″ is not properly explained, neither is R which is explained in part in terms of R″. But if R is not properly explained, then it seems that R is not properly grounded in objects and so (**2) would be violated.

Thus we can see again that if we allow pants, if we allow R to be partially grounded in *a* and partially grounded in *b*, then R must be ultimately ungrounded. This result violates (**2), and thus we can see why Leibniz might reject pants and – precisely because (**2) is plausible – not only Leibniz but also we have reason to reject pants. Thus:

(**3) The relation between *x* and *y* cannot be a state of *x* and *y* together.

There are strong indications that Leibniz relies on this kind of argument for rejecting pants when he voices concern about an infinite regress of relations. First, consider an unpublished passage quoted by Mugnai in which Leibniz says that if relations were real, they would be simultaneously in two subjects and they – the relations – "would go into infinity."[9] Leibniz seems to be worried, as Mugnai puts it, that "if we admit that relations are real entities, we have to admit that so also are relations of relations, and so on, accepting an unjustifiable proliferation of entities which are all equally real" (p. 18). The concern here is about precisely the kind of infinite regress that I have said relations as pants would lead to.

Here is another such passage:

It is not surprising that the number of all numbers, all possibilities, all relations or reflections are not distinctly understood; for they are imaginary and have nothing that corresponds to them in reality. For example, suppose that there is a relation between *a* and *b*, and that that relation is called *c*; and let a new relation be considered between *a* and *c*, and let that relation be called *d*, and so on to infinity. It does not seem that any one may say that all those relations are true and real ideas. Perhaps only those things are purely intelligible which can be produced; that is, which have been or will be produced. ("Notes on Metaphysics," December 1676, A VI 3, pp. 399–400; DSR, p. 115)[10]

Again, in rejecting the reality of relations Leibniz seems to be worried about an infinite regress of relations.

---

[9] "*Si relationes essent entia in rebus ipsis realia aliter quam per conceptionem, forent accidentia simul in duobus subiectis, nam relatio pari iure in utroque est; relationes praeterea irent in infinitum.*" Cited in Mugnai 1992, p. 18, n9.

[10] I am indebted to Tom Feeney here. This passage is also cited in this connection in Mugnai forthcoming.

Thus the reason I gave earlier for denying pants, a reason based on Leibniz's own view that relations must be grounded, would certainly appeal to Leibniz. It is worth noting that the above argument for the denial of pants is in the spirit of F. H. Bradley's famous regress argument concerning relations (*Appearance and Reality*, Book 1, Chapters 2 and 3). Bradley, like Leibniz (and Spinoza), is a fan of the plausible grounding principle (**2) and, indeed, of the PSR.[11] However, as we'll see, this reason for denying pants leads to a kind of monism that Bradley embraces (and Spinoza too), and that Leibniz for much of his life struggled against.

Finally, let's turn to Leibniz's first step, i.e. his claim that

(**4) The relation between x and y cannot be a state of x in particular (as opposed to y) or a state of y in particular (as opposed to x).

As we saw, this claim seems to be at work in the compact passage from the correspondence with Des Bosses.[12] And, as you can already see by my having just slapped asterisks on this claim, I regard this claim as plausible and, indeed, as a plausible application of the PSR. The relation between x and y is beholden to x and to y, dependent on x and on y. And so it would seem arbitrary, inexplicable, and indeed just plain unfair for x to get to be the subject of the relation between x and y, while y just sits around (and similarly if we located this relation in y exclusively).

Here's another way to make this point: if the relation depends on both x and y, but is a state of only one, there must be something to statehood over and above dependence. But what would that something be? There seems to be no way to articulate the difference other than to say unilluminatingly: statehood is the special kind of dependence that is statehood. There would, then, be two kinds of dependence, but no illuminating way to explain the difference between them. This difference would thus be a brute fact. It would also then be a brute fact that there's any state at all in this case over and above mere dependence, and so, a fortiori, it would be a brute fact that there is a certain state located here and not there.[13]

---

[11] This argument is also in the spirit of certain medieval arguments against the reality of relations, arguments to be found in Henry of Harclay and in William of Ockham. See Henninger 1989, pp. 110–12, 121–2. For more on the connection between Bradley and Leibniz, see Mugnai manuscript. For the PSR as the driving force behind Bradley's regress, see van Inwagen 2008, p. 45, and Russell 1910, p. 374.

[12] It's also at work in Leibniz's claim that "a relation is with equal right in both [subjects]." This passage is quoted in Mugnai 1992, p. 18, n9, and is, indeed, the clause immediately before Leibniz's complaint, mentioned earlier, that real relations would go into infinity.

[13] The reasoning here is closely related to what can be seen as one of the greatest hits of rationalism: Leibniz's argument against the absoluteness of space (especially in the correspondence with Clarke).

Recall where we left things. Leibniz holds the PISP, i.e. the view that each state of a thing is a consequence of the nature of that thing alone, but it is not at all clear how Leibniz would motivate that view. I will now argue that Leibniz's first two steps in his argument concerning the reality of relations go a long way toward justifying the PISP.

For the purposes of a reductio, let's say that the PISP is false and, in particular, that x has a feature F or that x is in a state of being F and that this state is due in part to something other than x (and its nature), say y. In this case, there is a relation of dependence between x and y. In order for this case to be a counterexample to the PISP, this relation of dependence must be real: the PISP is compatible with there being merely ideal relations of dependence between substances, but not with real relations of dependence. Since the relation is to be real, what is it in? Applying the reasoning in the discussion of relations in general, we can see that the relation between x and y cannot be a state of one of these substances to the exclusion of the other. (This is Leibniz's first move.) Nor can the relation be a state of both of the substances together. (This is the second move, the denial of pants.) Thus the relation of dependence between x and y – if real – has no legitimate ground.

Because the purported counterexample to the PISP – i.e. a case in which x's state of being F is due to a distinct substance y – entails that there is an ungrounded relation between x and y, and because Leibniz's rationalism dictates that there are no ungrounded relations, it follows that the purported counterexample to the PISP is illegitimate. In other words, there is no case in which x has a feature that is due to some other substance. Thus all of x's features must be due to x alone, and this result is basically the PISP.

In brief, the argument is that features of a substance that are due to some other substance presuppose unintelligible relations of dependence, and so there cannot be features of a substance that are due to other substances. To reach this radical conclusion, all Leibniz needs are his first two rationalist moves concerning relations which can be seen as stemming, in part, from the general claim, (**2), that relations must be grounded. If you want to reject Leibniz's PISP (and not many people don't), then you must find a way to reject one or both of Leibniz's first two moves both of which are, as I have argued, plausible, and which

Just as God cannot arbitrarily locate an extended object in one location rather than another in absolute space, so too a relation cannot be arbitrarily grounded or "located" in one relatum rather than another.

reflect the plausible general claim, (**2), concerning the grounding of relations. In light of this defense of the PISP, I am prepared to place – somewhat tentatively – asterisks on the PISP:

> ** If x is F, then its being F must be due to, explained by, x's nature alone.

This way of defending the PISP helps us to see that Leibniz is committed to a general assimilation of dependence and statehood and that Leibniz has good grounds for being so committed; in other words, there are good reasons to hold that a state depends on a substance, x, if and only if that state is a state of x. That is, a certain state of being F depends on a substance if and only if that state is a state of that substance and that substance is therefore F. (See especially *Discourse on Metaphysics* §14, quoted earlier.) Let's look at both halves of this biconditional. Obviously, if something, S, is a state of x, then S depends on x. As we have just seen, the converse also seems to be true: if a state S depends on a substance x, then S is a state of x. I will refer to this coextensiveness simply as the assimilation of statehood and dependence.

One of the breathtaking things about Leibniz's PISP is that with it he gives us a well-motivated account of statehood: statehood is nothing more than dependence. Or, at least this is what Leibniz and the rest of us are committed to by (**2) and by Leibniz's plausible first two moves regarding relations. In Leibniz's case, this commitment stems from his commitment to the PSR which undergirds this line of thought. But we will see that he quickly violates his own commitment here.

5.2 REAL RELATIONS AND A RATIONALIST DILEMMA

To begin to see such violations, let's turn to a kind of relation that Leibniz labels as not real – i.e. causal relations. Leibniz denies that there are any real causal relations between distinct substances – or at least between distinct finite substances. As we will see soon, the infinite substance generates important and problematic exceptions. If substance x causally interacts with substance y, then we may ask: what grounds this causal relation? The relation cannot be a state of x exclusively or of y exclusively (this is the first Leibnizian move) nor can it be a state of the two substances together (this is the second Leibnizian move). Leibniz concludes that causal relations between distinct (finite) substances are not real. The non-reality of causal relations between finite substances is, of course, at the heart of Leibniz's pre-established harmony (*Monadology* §78; NE, p. 440).

One relation in this area will be particularly important for my argument, i.e. the relation of being passive. If y causes a change in x, then x stands in the relation of being passive, being acted on. But, for Leibniz, this passivity proves to be elusive: it cannot legitimately be a state of any substance. Notice that although x seems to be acted on, the passivity cannot simply be a state of x. This is because the passivity of x, i.e. x's being acted on, is due also to y. Given Leibniz's assimilation of statehood and dependence (i.e. given the PISP), it follows that this state is also a state of y. But the passivity can in no way be a state of y because, as we've stipulated, y is active here and not passive. We can see then that, for Leibniz, nothing can legitimately ground the state of being passive in this case. x cannot serve as the complete ground of the passivity because the passivity is not due to x alone. And y cannot, in this case, be passive at all because y is the cause and not the effect.

So the passivity in a case of an alleged causal relation between x and y can, at best, be partially grounded (in x itself) and thus would be a brute fact. One finite substance cannot genuinely be passive in relation to another in Leibniz's system, and Leibniz can be seen as rejecting real intersubstantial finite causation for this reason. Indeed, as we will now see, Leibniz also seems committed to the view that nothing can be genuinely passive in relation to any other thing. And this is where Leibniz's problems begin.

This problem arises most explicitly in the case of the causal relation that is creation. God creates finite substances that are in some way distinct from himself (see, e.g., *Theodicy* §395, *Monadology* §55, "On the Ultimate Origination of Things" in Ger VII, pp. 302–8; AG, pp. 149–55; L, pp. 486–91). This causal relation is real and not merely ideal. If there were no genuine causal relations between God and finite substances, then what can account for the existence of finite substances? Surely, Leibniz would stress, finite substances cannot account for their own existence. So the existence of the finite substances would be a brute fact if God does not really do the work of causing them to exist. And, of course, Leibniz rejects brute facts.

But by allowing these real causal relations, Leibniz still gets stuck with brute facts, as we can see by applying the Leibnizian reasoning we have outlined concerning relations in general to the specific case of creation. Let's ask what are by now our usual litany of questions: what substance is the ground of the real causal relation between God and, say, substance x? The relation is, at best, partially grounded in x, but it cannot be fully grounded in x because this relation is due to God as well. Nor can the relation be fully grounded in God's nature for the relation is in part a function of the nature of *x*. As in the other cases, it would seem unfair, arbitrary and a brute fact to locate the relation in one only of the two substances. This is the first Leibnizian move. Further, the relation cannot be a state of both God and *x* together. To say that it is would be to regard two substances as having pants and, as we have seen, Leibniz's plausible, second move in the argument regarding the reality of relations is to reject pants.

So where can the causal relation – the causal relation of creation – between God and *x* be grounded if not in God or *x* separately or together? As we have seen, this relation cannot be grounded in a mind instead of being a real relation between the substances. And so there seems to be nowhere for Leibniz to turn in order to find the ground for the reality of the relation of creation. This real causal relation thus seems to be – on Leibniz's own terms – a not-fully grounded, partially free-floating, brute fact, a violation of the plausible grounding principle (**2) and, indeed, of the PSR.

I will not, however, stress this problem concerning creation because the notion of creation is often thought to be fraught for Leibniz (and for anyone else). I want to turn instead to a much more insidious problem in this vein. This problem arises when we turn from relations between one substance and another and look instead within each substance. Here we find another relation that Leibniz regards as real, i.e. the relation between a single substance and its states. For Leibniz each substance, finite or not, causes its own states. These states are not caused by any other (finite) substances, and this causal relation is not ideal. Indeed, the reality of this kind of intrasubstantial causal relation is what grounds the merely apparent causal relations between one finite substance and another. To begin to see what the problem is with this (intrasubstantial) causal relation, just ask: what is this causal relation grounded in? In this case, it would, as before, seem arbitrary for the causal relation to be grounded in either the substance or its state to the exclusion of the other. Further it would seem problematic for the relation to be grounded in both the substance and its state together: pants internal to a substance would be as objectionable as (and just as prone to infinite regresses or circles as) pants that straddle two substances. Thus while we can go some distance toward grounding the relation by pointing to either the substance or its state, we cannot fully ground it in either, nor can we ground it in the two together. The intrasubstantial relation of dependence thus seems to be at best only partially and not fully intelligible.

We can see this problem perhaps even more clearly when we turn to the passivity a state exhibits in relation to the substance of which it is a state.

The state, call it S, is passive in relation to the substance – after all, the substance causes it. S itself thus has a state, the state of being passive, and so the passivity is grounded in state S, but is only partially grounded in S. The passivity of the state also depends, of course, on the substance itself: the state is passive because it is a state of that substance. Given the assimilation of statehood and dependence, the passivity in this case must itself be a state of the substance. That is, the substance itself is passive in this matter. But how can this be? In this matter, the substance is active and the state is passive. And so we cannot say that here the substance is – as the assimilation of statehood and dependence would lead us to say – in some way passive. Thus although we can go some distance toward grounding the reality of the state of passivity in S itself (and perhaps in other passive states), we cannot fully ground the passivity in S or in other states or in the substance itself. Thus passivity is not fully intelligible. Once again, we find that passivity cannot find a proper home. This is the elusiveness of passivity *within* each substance and not, as before, between God and finite substances.

Thus Leibniz seems to be committed to a real relation of passivity within finite substances, a relation that is not grounded properly and is thus a brute fact. Indeed, most, if not all, features of states of substances would be similarly unintelligible at least to some extent. Thus take the following feature of a state of a substance: its being a state. What would the state's state of being a state be a state of? The state's state of being a state cannot be fully intelligible in terms of the state of which it is a state. This is because the state's state of being a state is dependent on something else, i.e. on the substance in question. But the state of being a state cannot be a state of the substance because then the substance itself would be a state and that would be contradictory. Thus being a state is not fully intelligible as a state of the state nor can it be a state of the substance. Nothing, then, truly has the state of being a state. This is the elusiveness of statehood, and it shows that the state of being a state is ultimately unintelligible and not properly grounded, for Leibniz. Thus once again, there seems to be a pervasive brute fact in Leibniz that arises from Leibniz's own strategy – dictated by the plausible (**2) and ultimately by the PSR – of denying the reality of relations.

Leibniz thus faces a dilemma. (**2) leads to the conclusion that real relations between distinct things and, indeed, real relations between a thing and its states are ruled out. On this view, there can be no genuine multiplicity of objects that stand in relations of dependence and no genuine states of objects that depend on those objects. Such multiplicity and such states are precluded by our assiduous application of (**2). Thus if Leibniz is committed to the real existence of a multiplicity of objects and to the existence of states of objects (and he certainly seems to be by his talk of creation and intrasubstantial causation), then he must give up the plausible claim that relations must be grounded in a thing or things. So Leibniz's dilemma is this: EITHER give up the claim that there is a multiplicity of objects and that there are states of objects OR give up the claim that relations are grounded.

Indeed, it is not just Leibniz who faces this dilemma, but any of us who is committed to the existence of a multiplicity of objects and to the existence of states of objects and also committed to the principle that relations must be grounded. The dilemma is particularly acute for Leibniz because to take the second horn of the dilemma – to deny that relations must be grounded – would be to deny the PSR. This is because the principle calling for the grounding of relations is an implication of the PSR. Thus at stake in this dilemma, for Leibniz, is the fate of the PSR itself, the cornerstone of his system. For Leibniz, the dilemma boils down to this: either deny multiplicity or deny the PSR. Since Leibniz is not willing to deny either of these things, the dilemma seems intractable for him.

But even for those of us not explicitly committed to the PSR, the dilemma is troubling, and that is because it seems so plausible to think both that there is a multiplicity of objects (etc.) and that relations must be grounded in something. So for those not explicitly committed to the PSR, the dilemma boils down to this: either deny multiplicity or deny that relations are grounded. Is there any way for Leibniz or us to get out of this dilemma? For guidance in this troubled time, let us turn to Spinoza, who faces this dilemma too.

5.3   DEGREES OF EXISTENCE AND A WAY OUT OF THE DILEMMA

Spinoza does not develop a theory of relations with as much sophistication and care as does Leibniz. But Spinoza would surely – guided as he is by the PSR – accept the grounding of relations (and states generally). Even more importantly, Spinoza is perhaps more explicit than is Leibniz on the assimilation of statehood and dependence. Spinoza's treatment of the relation of being in something (i.e. inhering in something), the relation of being conceived through something and the relation of being caused by something as coextensive suggests strongly that Spinoza endorses the assimilation of statehood and dependence.[14]

Because of these shared rationalist commitments, Spinoza – like Leibniz – faces the problem of the intelligibility of certain intrasubstantial relations. The problem, for Spinoza, would be couched not in terms of states of substances, but rather in terms of states of modes of substance. Modes are literally in the substance, i.e. they are states of substance, i.e they are ways in which substance exists. Modes as states are dependent on substance, they are passive in relation to substance. How can this passivity of modes be understood? Just as we saw in the case of states of substances, the passivity of a mode cannot be understood as a state of the substance which the modes are in, for that substance, i.e. God, is in no way passive. The passivity of a mode also cannot be fully grounded only in the mode itself, for this feature of the mode is dependent not only on the mode, but also on something other than the mode itself, i.e. on the substance. Thus the passivity of the mode seems not to be adequately grounded, seems not to be fully unintelligible, seems to be a brute fact, just as passivity does in Leibniz's system. Similarly, given Spinoza's commitment to the PSR, he would find problematic the relations that come with any multiplicity of objects. Thus both Spinoza and Leibniz face the same dilemma: either reject a multiplicity of objects and states or reject the PSR. And, as before, the dilemma need not be put in terms of the PSR, but can be articulated in terms of the more plausible claim that relations must have some ground in the world. Thus, for Spinoza as for Leibniz as for us, the dilemma is this: either reject a multiplicity of objects and states or reject the claim that relations are grounded.

When faced with this dilemma which is in part a threat to the PSR itself, what does Spinoza, a good rationalist, do? We can see his response in two ways. One way of putting the Spinozistic response is this: "if you can't beat 'em, join 'em." If you can't avoid the brute facts, then embrace them. The response (seen in this way) is to take the second horn of the dilemma: either reject multiplicity or reject the PSR. Alternatively, the Spinozistic response may also be portrayed this way: there is no multiplicity of objects and states. The response (seen in this way) is to embrace the first horn of the very same dilemma. Thus, Spinoza takes both horns of the very same dilemma. Like the great philosopher and baseball player, Yogi Berra, who said, "When you come to a fork in the

---

[14] See Della Rocca 2008a.

road, take it," when Spinoza comes to a fork in the road, he takes it. How is this possible? Allow me to demonstrate.

Let's say that Spinoza holds that existence is not an either–or matter, rather existence comes in degrees. Let's say also that Spinoza holds that intelligibility and unintelligibility also come in degrees. (We saw degrees of intelligibility in the case of intrasubstantial relations: the relation between a substance and its state is partially intelligible in terms of the substance and in terms of the state, but not fully intelligible in terms of either or both together.) Finally, let's say that Spinoza holds that things that exist to a lesser degree do so precisely to the extent that they are unintelligible. Thus, on this view, existence is coextensive with intelligibility. (In fact, on this view, existence would, I believe, be identical with intelligibility, but the claim of coextensiveness is all we need for our purposes.) Existence and intelligibility rise and fall together, and because intelligibility comes in degrees, so too does existence. On this view, then, to be is coextensive with being intelligible, and to be intelligible to some degree goes hand in hand with existing to some degree.

If we (or Spinoza) allow for degrees of existence in this way, then it seems natural to offer the following corollary of the PSR. As initially stated, the PSR is the principle that whatever exists has an explanation. But if things can exist only to some degree, and if existence goes along with intelligibility, then we would expect that those things would be unintelligible, inexplicable, to some degree as well. In this light, a proponent of the PSR who sees existence as equivalent to intelligibility should be willing to grant this corollary:

Things exist to the extent that those things are intelligible.

This principle allows that there may be, somehow, things that are unintelligible to some degree, but requires that these things do not fully exist. The principle would rule out not unintelligible things per se, but rather unintelligible things that exist to exactly the degree that fully intelligible things do. There would be a correspondingly modified version of (**2), the plausible claim that relations must be grounded. This corollary would be:

Relations exist to the extent that they are grounded.

The notion of degrees of existence – and thus the formulation of the corollary of the PSR and the corollary of (**2) – is unusual, at least from the point of view of contemporary philosophy, and it might be thought to be incoherent. I don't believe it is incoherent, though I do not have the space here to address the puzzles that the notion of degrees of existence might be thought to raise.[15] Here I merely want to point out that, if Spinoza accepts the notion of degrees of existence and the corollary of the PSR, he can allow unintelligible things within his system, as long as those things do not fully exist. In this way, Spinoza could allow that passive things – to the extent that they are passive – are not intelligible and involve brute facts and do not exist. Spinoza can also allow relations between substance and modes as long as he also specifies that these unintelligible things, these passive things, do not fully exist. Similarly, Spinoza can allow that there is somehow a multiplicity of objects as long as he specifies that this multiplicity qua multiplicity is not fully intelligible and thus does not fully exist. This move would enable Spinoza to avoid the dilemma that Leibniz and the rest of us face. Yes, the PSR and the claim that relations are grounded lead to the view that passivity and multiplicity and relations as such are unintelligible, but the PSR with its corollary, also lets us incorporate unintelligibility within our philosophical system as long as passivity and multiplicity and relations are given the lesser ontological status they so richly deserve, i.e. the lesser status of existing only to some degree. So, in a way, Spinoza takes the second horn of the dilemma: he denies the PSR by allowing for violations of it. But these violations do not fully exist and so they are not in conflict with the modified PSR which allows for degrees of intelligibility and degrees of existence. At the same time, Spinoza takes the first horn of the dilemma: he denies that there is a multiplicity of states and relations. But this denial is qualified: while there is no multiplicity, no states, and no relations that fully exist, there can be such things as long as they exist to a lesser degree. It is by accepting the notion of degrees of existence and thus by accepting the modified PSR (and the modified grounding principle concerning relations) that Spinoza is able, as Yogi Berra recommends, to take the fork in the road. Spinoza can thus avoid the unpleasant choice between denying multiplicity and denying the PSR (or denying the grounding principle concerning relations). Or, to put the point another way: without accepting the notion of degrees of existence, Spinoza would be faced with a very unpleasant choice indeed, a choice between rejecting multiplicity and rejecting the PSR (and the plausible grounding principle). And if we too accept multiplicity and accept (at least) the plausible grounding principle concerning relations – and most of us do – then we too are required to accept the notion of degrees of existence.

---

[15] I take up one such puzzle – raised by David Lewis – in Della Rocca 2008b, p. 269.

Does Spinoza hold this view of existence? He certainly seems to. The heart of this view is the equivalence of existence and intelligibility: it is this equivalence that makes it natural, as I argued, to embrace the corollary of the PSR. And we do find that Spinoza embraces the equivalence of existence and intelligibility and does so because of the PSR itself. Spinoza explicitly identifies God's essence and God's existence in 1p20. As I have argued elsewhere, since God's essence is just God's being conceived through itself (1def3, 1def6), God's existence for Spinoza is just God's conceivability, i.e. God's being intelligible through itself. Further, Spinoza's naturalism and the PSR dictate that just as God's existence is God's conceivability, so too the existence of things in general is just their conceivability or intelligibility: to think otherwise would be to see God and other things as playing by different rules.[16]

Given the equivalence of existence and intelligibility, and given also Spinoza's commitment to the view – stemming from the Leibnizian reflections concerning the reality of relations – that passivity and multiplicity and relations are not fully intelligible, Spinoza is committed to the view that passivity and multiplicity and relations do not fully exist.

Thus Spinoza's acceptance of the coextensiveness of existence and intelligibility and his corresponding commitment to degrees of existence is at least part of what enables Spinoza to avoid the Leibnizian dilemma that we all face. And, as I've suggested, if we know what's good for us, we too will accept the notion of degrees of existence and thus avoid the dilemma. It might seem as though Leibniz can make a similar move. After all, Leibniz does seem to accept that passive things have a lesser ontological status than active things (see, e.g., *Monadology* §41), and perhaps this would lead him to allow that there may be some unintelligible things (that exist only to some degree). Finally, perhaps this would lead him to accept the corollary of the PSR. In this way, Leibniz could escape the Leibnizian dilemma.

5.4 MOSES AND MONISM

But matters are not so simple. There is more – and necessarily there is more – to the Spinozistic strategy than the acceptance of degrees of existence. For Spinoza, although unintelligible things do exist to some degree, the perspective on the world according to which there are (to some degree) brute facts is not the best or most accurate one. If the PSR is true,

---

[16] See Della Rocca 2008a, p. 36, and Della Rocca 2003, pp. 82–8.

then the world is fully intelligible and there must be a perspective on the world from which there are no brute facts. Further, if the PSR is true, this perspective must be fully accurate. But if brute facts exist even to some degree, then it seems that the PSR is just false. There would be no true view of the world according to which there are no brute facts. To avoid this worry, there must be a way to "cash in" the brute facts that exist only to some degree and redeem them so that they find their place in a fully intelligible reality.

How is this possible?

Notice first that there will be brute facts as long as there is passivity or multiplicity or relations, as long as there are individual finite things that limit one another. So in this light consider two ways to view the world. First, we can see the world as full of more or less separate things which have the relations of activity and passivity that finite things enter into. Because these things are passive, they don't exist, at least insofar as they are passive, and this passivity is a brute fact, one that doesn't fully exist.

Now consider the world as consisting of only one thing. On this view, we quantify over only one thing (one substance, if you will). On this view, there are no individual finite things, rather there is only the active world, the active substance. Finally and importantly, on this view, there is no passivity and no distinct things to be related, and so there is none of the unintelligibility, none of the brute facts that passivity and relations inevitably bring. There is only the active substance.

Next compare these two ways of viewing the world. Given the PSR, the second way must be more accurate, more true, because only it is a view according to which the world is fully intelligible, does not contain brute facts, and does not contain passivity. The first point of view is not completely illusory, it captures reality to some degree and the objects recognized on this view exist to some degree. But whatever reality is captured by this first point of view is also captured by the second point of view which recognizes only one object. The finite, passive individuals drop out as we shift perspectives in this way, but all that is really lost in the transition is the passivity, the unintelligibility, the brute facts. And, in light of the PSR, to lose such things is to lose nothing at all. The passive, finite individuals, insofar as they are passive, are nothing, no thing.

Thus the PSR may dictate a view of relations according to which certain things exist only to some degree and are intelligible only to some degree. But, if one simply remains with these somewhat unintelligible things, one will be unable to do justice to the PSR which requires that the most accurate perspective on the world is one on which there are no brute facts at all. It is for that reason that a proponent of the PSR who wants to avoid the Leibnizian dilemma must advance the view that there are ultimately no finite, determinate, passive things, rather what there really is is only one thing. Thus, if one accepts the PSR, then, to avoid the dilemma, the unintelligibility that comes with finite individuality must be cashed in for the full intelligibility and reality of the one active substance.

This is, I believe, the route Spinoza takes. First, note that he endorses the view that individuals, insofar as they are passive, are nothing. We can see Spinoza as getting at this point in his famous dictum "determination is negation" (*determinatio negatio est*, Letter 50). And we can see him discussing the shift in perspective in his letter on the infinite (Letter 12). Finite individuals are seen as real from a limited, less accurate perspective and drop out when the shift is made to a more accurate, monistic perspective:

> if we attend to quantity as it is in the imagination, which is what we do most often and most easily, we find it to be divisible, finite, composed of parts, and one of many. But if we attend to it as it is in the intellect, and perceive the thing as it is in itself, which is very difficult, then we find it to be infinite, indivisible and unique. (Geb IV, p. 56)

I think we can see Spinoza's views on privation in a similar light. From the perspective according to which the world consists of more or less separate, unintelligible things, privations seem real (just as passivity does). But from the absolute, monistic perspective, the privations drop out (just as passivity does). As Spinoza puts the point, a certain "privation can be said only in relation to our intellect, not in relation to God's" (Letter 19, Geb IV, p. 92).

For Spinoza, finite things qua finite do not exist, but what is real about finite objects is captured more perfectly from the divine perspective, according to which only the active God exists. Thus we can see that the corollary of the PSR that Spinoza may be willing to endorse is acceptable only if he also holds that, instead of fully existent finite things, there is only one substance. On this view there can fully exist no relations between distinct things, on this view there can fully exist no creation by God of things distinct from God, and on this view monism is true.

So although Spinoza does not directly take on the dilemma that emerges from Leibniz's rationalist account of relations, I think Spinoza does see clearly that for the PSR to be true, one must quantify over only the one substance, reject the notion of creation, and view finite and passive things as, to some extent, unreal.

And here we can see more clearly why Leibniz cannot adopt Spinoza's way out of the dilemma, for Leibniz is, of course, unlike Spinoza, wedded to creation and to the denial of monism. Spinoza is thus better able than Leibniz to deal with the dilemma and the brute facts that relations bring with them. And the tragic irony is that despite all his wonderful work in delivering us from confusion about relations and getting us to appreciate the rationalist underpinnings of the theory of relations, Leibniz is unable to resolve the dilemma he so insightfully helps us to see. Like Moses, Leibniz can lead his followers to the promised land – in this case, the rationalist promised land – but he cannot himself enter it.

But can we enter the promised land and should we? Certainly if we – like Spinoza – accept the PSR, then, given the Leibnizian arguments concerning relations, we should enter the promised land of monism. But can we get to the promised land without invoking something as strong as the PSR? Yes, I believe that all we need to invoke is the plausible claim that relations must be grounded. Given this relatively uncontroversial claim, it follows – as we have seen – that relations are not fully real and that the only thing that fully exists is the one world. Of course, this relatively uncontroversial claim and the PSR itself are in need of further scrutiny before we can confidently accept the results advanced in this chapter.[17] But, in the meantime, we emerge from this historical/non-historical investigation of relations and violations of the PSR not only with a better understanding of Leibniz's and Spinoza's rationalist systems but also with at least the outlines of a strong case for monism. And just as this argument for monism seeks to elide the apparent differences among objects, so too the example of this chapter seeks to elide the apparent differences between historical and non-historical approaches to philosophy.[18]

---

[17] In Della Rocca forthcoming, I explore in a rationalist spirit some problems for the rationalist position developed here.

[18] Versions of this chapter were presented at a faculty discussion at Yale, at the Society for Early Modern Philosophy at Yale (SEMPY), at the Leibniz/Spinoza conference at Princeton in September 2007, at colloquia of the philosophy departments at Michigan State University (the McCracken Lecture), Bloomsburg University, the University of South Carolina, and Northern Illinois University, at an early modern workshop at Harvard, a conference at the University of Washington, and at the Second International Conference of the European Society for Early Modern Philosophy in Berlin in February 2010. I would like to thank the many people at these events for their warm reactions and helpful comments. I am especially grateful for helpful discussions and correspondence with Gaurav Vazirani, Leslie Wolf, Sung-il Han, Omri Boehm, Julia von Bodelschwingh, John Grey, Tomis Kapitan, Tom Feeney, Kelley Schiffman, Pedro Stoichita, Anja Jauernig, Ken Winkler, Sukjae Lee, Stephan Schmid, Massimo Mugnai, Mark Kulstad, Dan Garber, Dennis Deschene, Selim Berker, and Brian Schnieder.

CHAPTER 6

Requirements on reality

J. Robert G. Williams

There are advantages to thrift over honest toil. If we can make do without numbers we avoid challenging questions over the metaphysics and episte-mology of such entities. Authors such as Field (1980) have developed a detailed, integrated, and attractive metaphysics free of numbers, sets and other abstracta. I'll assume that radically minimal metaphysics such as this is *internally* coherent. My focus in this chapter is how *revisionary* we need to be about wider theory, in order to incorporate the minimal metaphysics. In Section 6.1 I outline a 'Moorean' epistemological challenge: that overly revisionary or error-theoretical theories of the world will *not be reasonable to believe* for those that start off with a fair share of common sense and a healthy respect for the testimony of best science. I outline two strategies for responding to this challenge by reconciling educated common sense and minimal metaphysics – 'structured metaphysics', in the mode of Fine and Schaffer, and the linguistic strategies favoured by Quine and contemporary fictionalists. Section 6.2 focuses on some familiar 'representational' strat-egies; and Section 6.3 develops my own favoured version of this strategy.

6.1 THE MOOREAN CHALLENGE

Field (1980) and Yablo (2001) say that there aren't really any numbers. When speaking literally, they deny that the number of moons of Mars is two – while agreeing that Phobos and Deimos are distinct moons of Mars, and the only such. Van Inwagen (1990), Dorr (2002), and Merricks (2001) say that really, there are no tables; though there are subatomic particles arranged in table-like fashion.

Such philosophical theories conflict with the opinions of 'the many and the wise' – with common sense and with science-as-it-is-currently-practiced. If we accept Field's theory, we should stop believing seeming platitudes about the number of things in front of us, and distrust the best confirmed results published in the science journals. It's not surprising that people have felt that this is *too radical* a shift for philosophical argumentation to accomplish.

6.1.1   An initial Moorean challenge

Jonathan Schaffer argues recently that Field's position is *obviously* incorrect:

contemporary existence debates are trivial, in that the entities in question obviously do exist ... Start with the debate over numbers. Here, without further ado, is a proof of the existence of numbers:

1. There are prime numbers.
2. Therefore there are numbers.

> 1 is a mathematical truism. It commands Moorean certainty, as being more credible than any philosophers argument to the contrary. Any metaphysician who would deny it has ipso facto produced a reductio for her premises. And 2 follows immediately, by a standard adjective-drop inference. Thus numbers exist. End of story. (Perhaps there are no completely knock-down arguments in metaphysics, but this one seems to me to be as forceful as they come ...) (Schaffer 2009b)

One thing that we should concede to Schaffer is that his 'proof' of the existence of numbers is valid. And most of us believe the premise. But then, most of us don't start off as mathematical nominalists (it's supposed to be a radical position, after all). Nominalists like Field should be non-plussed by this argument as stated. For he has urged that we *should* reject both premise and conclusion – and he takes himself to provide forceful arguments for this change in view.

The interesting part of Schaffer's discussion isn't so much the highlighted argument itself, but his commentary on the premise – that it commands 'Moorean certainty' and 'is more credible than any philosopher's argument to the contrary'. Here is a classic expression of the same sentiment from David Lewis:

I'm moved to laughter at the thought of how *presumptuous* it would be to reject mathematics for philosophical reasons. How would you like the job of telling the mathematicians that they must change their ways, and abjure countless errors, now that philosophy has discovered that there are no classes? (Lewis 1991, p. 59)

So what is the argument expressed in the commentary? One idea is that it claims we are *better justified* in our educated common-sense beliefs (e.g. 'I have hands', 'the number of my hands is two', 'there are prime numbers') than we could be in any philosophical premises incompatible with them. If so, then we always turn arguments against the existence of hands around, and treat them as a 'reductio' of the premises, as Schaffer suggests.

But this threatens to be a game of bait-and-switch. The premise about numbers in the simple inference seems obvious to most of us. But the epistemic claims about justification required in the commentary are *highly* non-trivial. And they're also ones that nominalists discuss at length: one of the central arguments for nominalism is an argument that we exactly *lack* good justification for mathematical claims such as there being prime numbers. So appealing to relative justification just takes us back into the original first-order dispute in the philosophy of mathematics.

6.1.2   A better Moorean argument

The most impressive Moorean considerations focus, not on the relative *justification* for one's beliefs, but on conditions under which it is *rational to change one's beliefs*.

I presently have a vast array of beliefs that, according to Field, are simply false – beliefs about the number of fingers on my hand, on the approximate length of my table, various beliefs about the size of the national debt and the function that describes the trajectory of objects in gravitational fields. Set aside the issue of whether these beliefs are all-things-considered justified. Something that all sides can agree on is that the belief state I would have to be in to consistently *accept* Field's view is very different from the one I accept now.

The epistemological concern to press is: *under what circumstances is it rational for me to change my beliefs to this drastic extent?* The suggestion is not that it's impossible for anyone to rationally come to believe that there are no numbers. It's simply that *given my starting point* it's irrational for *me* to come believe there are no numbers – at least without much more impressive evidence than philosophy has so far provided.

Here is one picture of belief change that dramatizes the concern. In order to assess an empirical theory, we need to measure it against relevant phenomena to establish theory's predictive and explanatory power – how *good* a theory it is. But these phenomena include platitudinous statements about the positions of pointers on readers, statements about how experiments were conducted, and whatever is described by records of careful observation. Field's account entails the falsity of numerical records of experimental data. So – for one starting from a common-sensical, science-respecting starting point – the natural conclusion is that his nominalism fails to fit with the data.

(This case only goes through if something that was conceded earlier is in fact correct – that we *do currently* believe in abstracta, in macroscopic things, and the like. One way of resisting the Moorean charge is to resist this description of ourselves, arguing that *we never believed mathematical (or mathematicized physical) claims in the first place.* The idea might be that we only *pretend* or *act under the supposition* that numbers exist. The *hermeneutic* figuralism of Steve Yablo defends exactly this position.)

This is an interesting Moorean challenge – and one that captures the sentiment that trying to *persuade* people of an error theory opens the philosopher to mockery. It relies, of course, on substantive positions in first-order epistemology. But while claims about the relative justification of mathematical vs. philosophical claims took us back in a tight loop to the question of whether mathematical claims are justifiable in the first place, this time we make progress since we have connected the debate to general issues about observation and rational belief-change – for example, of the theory-ladenness of observation.

Interestingly, Field (1989) preempts some of this discussion. He points to cases he thinks analogous, where *scientific evidence* has forced a radical change in view. He argues that when a serious alternative to our existing system of beliefs (and rules for belief-formation) is suggested to us, it is rational to (a) bracket relevant existing beliefs and (b) consider the two rival theories on their individual merits, adopting whichever one regards as the *better* theory. The revolutionary theory is *not* necessarily measured against our best *current take* on what the data is, but against what the *revolutionary theory says* the data is. For example, in the grip of a geocentric model of the universe, we should treat 'the sun moves in absolute upward motion in the morning' as an observational datum. However, says Field, even for those within the grip of that model, when the heliocentric model is proposed, it is rational for them to measure its success against the *heliocentric description* of the content of our observations (which does not describe sunrises in terms of absolute upward motion). Notice that on this model, there's effectively no 'conservative influence' constraining revolutionary belief-change – since when evaluating new theories, one's prior opinions on relevant matters are *bracketed.* Field can agree that the case for nominalism is disanalogous to the case for heliocentrism in terms of the *weight of evidence* supporting revolution. But this is irrelevant: what is important is that the model of belief-change has no inherent conservative bias, and so the Moorean attack fails.

The Moorean-friendly description of rational belief change has considerable appeal. If we are to trust a theory's own take on its fit with data and other virtues, can we rule out 'self-aggrandizing' theories that say of themselves that they possess theoretical virtues, or who say silly things about what the data is? It's especially hard to accept that this could be a sensible policy when we are fully aware that the theories are making crazy claims about what the data is – it seems positively irresponsible to bracket this knowledge. But even if we can *sometimes* end up doing this, it beggars belief that we do this *whenever* a prima facie coherent revolutionary alternative to extant best theory arises. A moderate form of the Fieldian proposal would require there to be extant reasons for dissatisfaction with current theory (a 'crisis in normal science') in order to justify radical reappraisal. The Moorean can then question whether the distinctively *philosophical* worries of the nominalists may count as creating crisis conditions in the relevant sense.[1]

This Moorean case against error-theoretic nominalism – which can with equal justice be pressed against error-theoretic mereological nihilism – worries me deeply. Can we have the best of both worlds? Can we have a Fieldian metaphysics, while avoiding the error-theory that it seemingly brings with it?

6.1.3 Two reconciliation strategies

How should the radically minimal metaphysician respond to the Moorean challenge? The strategy I will be interested in here is one of breaking the supposed connection between radically minimal metaphysics and revisionism/error-theory. On a traditional conception, metaphysics is concerned with *how things fundamentally are*. If the idea of 'fundamental reality' makes sense, then it seems we should be able to distinguish two claims: the claim that *in fundamental reality there are no abstracta* (which on this conception articulates the key nominalist claim) vs. the claim *that there are no abstracta* (commitment to which leads to the revisionary rejection of abstracta-strewn scientific and folk theory). The radically

---

[1] There's a second line of response to the Moorean objection we can take from Field. Field compares success in philosophical theorizing to *placing the right bet*. If we compare philosophical theories (of roughly comparable detail), then the analogy is that we need only make the case that the favoured theory is more likely to be true than its competitors. This is quite compatible with it being unreasonable to *believe* the theory. However, unless philosophical theories must meet some reasonable threshold of credibility, I think this simply isn't a good representation of the aim of presenting a philosophical theory. And for any reasonably high threshold (say, over 0.4) I think an analogue of the Moorean case can be pressed.

minimal metaphysician I have in mind endorses the former, but not the latter. Thus Jonathan Bennett:

> The work of any interesting metaphysician involves two or more levels. I do not mean levels of reality: the metaphysicians I am talking about do not describe reality as stratified; rather, they stratify their accounts of it. At the basic level of speech, thought and conceptualization, they express truths that directly reflect the metaphysical situation; at the less basic level, they say things that are still true, but, as stated, are bad pointers to the metaphysical situation, and one needs an account of what their truth amounts to, comes down to, arises from, in terms of facts expressed at the basic level. The non-basic level gets a hearing only because it involves ordinary, familiar ways of saying things.
>
> . . .
>
> Anyone who thinks he has metaphysical news about the world will distinguish levels of speech about it. (Bennett 2001, pp. 147–8)

Interesting metaphysicians may balk at Bennett's characterization in a couple of ways. Perhaps raising the banner of Quine, they insist that Bennett's talk of 'direct reflection' and the like are weasel words. What one needs for metaphysics is the existential quantifier and a serious tone of voice – one should be willing to affirm the 'ontological implications' of everything one affirms, in van Inwagen's phrase. This view has the attraction that we're able to endorse metaphysical views without bringing in special-purpose vocabulary ('substance', 'fundamental', 'basic') against which critics of metaphysics have traditionally cavilled. For these con-servatives, the error-theory is the *honest* consequence of a minimal metaphysics.

The opposite reaction to Bennett's characterization is that it does not go far enough. A leading theme of contemporary metaphysics is a picture of the world 'structured' into the derivative and the fundamental (or, in some versions, into the grounded and the things that do the grounding) – the stratification within reality that Bennett distances himself from. The view works itself out in various ways in the recent literature, in particular in the work of Fine (2001) and Schaffer (2009b). Schaffer, for example, argues for a metaphysics structured by the *grounding* relation. Fundamental entities are those that are not grounded in anything, but themselves ground other things. Schaffer can accept the nominalist claim that there are no abstracta in *fundamental reality* – but since there are 'emergent' abstracta he faces no problem reconciling this with common sense.

Schaffer's contention is that – appropriately understood – a stratified metaphysics can give respect to the insight of the nominalists, while avoiding conflict with 'obvious' truths. We endorse the Moorean truth that there are numbers by finding a place in our metaphysics for abstracta (as derivative existents). But we can engage with 'nominalist-like' projects by a (redescription) of them as positing 'dependency relations' between numbers and nominalist-friendly relations of congruence and betweenness instantiated by space-time points. Fundamental reality may be nominalistic, even if there are, derivatively, numbers.

I am a fan of the Bennettian picture. Mind-independent reality is thus-and-so (perhaps an ontology of concreta spread through space-time, characterized by the instantiation of various natural properties). The relation between this reality and *representations of it* – including the sentences of natural language and the language of thought – is complex and demands analysis. When the dust settles, some of these representations will turn out to be *true*. But – for example – all that may be required of reality for the representation 'there are tables' to be true, is that certain simple particles stand in certain arrangements.

But it's one thing to open up the possibility of an 'indirect representation' account reconciling minimal metaphysics with common sense. It's another to pin down what story about representation achieves this. The next section outlines some familiar representational strategies, and some natural misgivings about them. The final section explores what the best version of deflationism about the derivative might look like. I think that this will leave us *talking* somewhat like Schaffer and Fine – but with a very different conception of what we're up to.

6.2 RECONCILIATION THROUGH THE PHILOSOPHY OF LANGUAGE

In this section, I will discuss two extant proposals for reconciling minimal metaphysics and common sense: Quinean paraphrase, and revisionary syntax.

6.2.1 Translate-and-deflate

Quine was sensitive to the need to reconcile 'desert landscape' ontology with (certain savable portions of) common sense. His favoured method of reconciliation was paraphrase. We are a given body of common-sensical claims – perhaps involving apparent quantification over glints, quirks, and other unQuinean beasts. Quine offers a choice: reject portions of common sense, or *provide a translation* into kosher vocabulary.

Quine certainly makes room for error-theory (the parts of common sense that are rejected, not paraphrased). But what *is* the status of the paraphrase relationship? How does it interact with the kind of bridge principles described above?

Quine's views on the philosophy of language kick in at this point.[2] His favoured take on 'truth', 'reference', and so on is *disquotational.* Schemas such as: 'The beetle is black' is true iff the beetle is black; give what looks like an extensionally adequate definition of truth as applied to (at least a fragment) of one's own language. But if we want to call sentences in other languages true or false, we need something extra (you can't disquote *French* sentences into English). Thus the role for translation/paraphrase. If we use 'dtruth' for the disquotationally defined notion, we can say:

S is true iff *S* is translated to a dtruth

Thus, 'la neige est blanche' is true, because it translates as 'snow is white', which is dtrue because snow is white.

Given this translation-augmented disquotationalism (I'll call it the 'translate-and-deflate' account of language), we can see that *for Quine*, giving paraphrases is a way of *avoiding* error theory. Suppose that part of a paraphrase involves mapping 'Harry kept quiet for Larry's sake' to 'Harry kept quiet out of concern for Larry'. Even if, in reality, there are no sakes, the first sentence can be true, since it translates to a sentence that is dtrue.[3]

---

[2] I here follow Field's presentation of Quine's views in Field 1994. Though Field famously rejected the Quinean approach in his early writings (roughly, the 1970s and 1980s), he has since come to advocate it. However, (especially in the light of criticisms due to Stewart Shapiro) he has come to doubt whether paraphrase is the best device in extending dtruth to truth proper. See the paper cited before, and especially the addenda included in the collected version.

[3] Of course, much more needs to be said about the methodology when we're applying it in the *intralinguistic* case. For suppose we think that, in reality, there are no sakes, and hence a fortiori, Harry did not keep quiet for Larry's sake. Then our original sentence is dfalse. If the trivial paraphrase (every sentence maps to itself) is plugged into the above scheme, we then read off that it is false. Yet with the paraphrase given above, we get that it is true! Likewise, if paraphrase is symmetrical, then 'Harry kept quiet for Larry's sake' will count as true (since paraphrased to a dtruth) but 'Harry kept quite out of concern for Larry' will count as false (since paraphrased to something dfalse). My own view is that this is best developed by understanding paraphrases (and translations) as non-symmetric mappings from a set of sentences Γ into a set of sentences Δ; and treating the above biconditional as invoking a *specific* paraphrase relation. The biconditional invoking the trivial paraphrase will be a *rival* account of truth to one invoking the paraphrase that maps sake-involving sentences to paraphrases in terms of concern. Of course, this raises the question of *which* such paraphrase to use – is one singled out? We're here in the territory of Quine's discussion of the inscrutability of reference and ontological relativity, and I won't examine such issues further here.

The Quinean view on philosophy of language has the resources to *deny* the bridge principles that take us from radical minimal metaphysics to error theory. Consider the Field position on the constituents of reality. If we found an acceptable *paraphrase* from mathematics, or mathematized physics, into nominalistically acceptable (and dtrue) talk, then for the Quinean there would be no error theory. In reality, there would be no numbers. But compatibly with that, 'there are numbers' would be true.

Of course, it is by no means obvious that such an acceptable paraphrase exists. What I want to emphasize, however, is that the idea that paraphrase is relevant to ontological commitment prima facie requires the distinctively Quinean translate-and-deflate philosophy of language. Suppose one rejects such a view for a more robust account of semantic properties such as truth (see, for example, Field (1972)). There's simply no obvious role for any appeal to 'paraphrase' within such an account of the conditions for a sentence to be true – and so it's utterly unobvious what one would be up to in constructing such 'paraphrases' from apparently committal talk into a nominalistically respectable theory.[4]

Often, it's not very clear to what end metaphysicians offer paraphrases. Van Inwagen (1990), for example, offers a paraphrase from ordinary macro-talk into plural talk of microscopic things arranged this way or that. What is the status of this paraphrase? Is it intended as part of a Quinean account saving the truth of common sense? Or does it rather point to an alternative way of speaking, that would *give up* common sense claims? I don't think it's clear from the text *what* we're supposed to do with it.

The idea that providing appropriate paraphrases shows that the paraphrased theory is not 'ontologically committed' to problematic entities makes perfect sense within a certain highly contentious philosophy of language. When advocated by those who do not endorse that particular position, absent further explanation it is baffling.

---

[4] Interestingly, there might be something we could do. In Montague's suggested treatment of semantics for natural language, we have an initial paraphrase from natural language into a certain rich intensional language; and then semantic theorizing is done via the latter rather than the former. This is interestingly close to Quine's translate-and-deflate idea, except rather than deflating, one gives a substantive characterization of truth-conditions. But in the same fashion, one could say that *S* has semantic property *P* iff it translates to *S'* which has property *P'*. Whether there's any need for this sort of paraphrase step is however controversial. And even in Montague's hands, the idea is not to treat the 'paraphrase' as liberally as Quine would have.

6.2.2   Syntactic or semantic rescue

Very different from the Quine translate-and-deflate view is a proposal that Field (1989) suggests (but does not endorse). Rather than regarding 'there are infinitely many primes' as false, he canvasses the view that this should be read as something like: *necessarily, if Ω, then there are infinitely many primes* – where Ω is an axiomatization of arithmetic. Now, it's easy to see what the *paraphrase* that's being suggested is here. But we ask the question: what's the significance of this paraphrase? Field's view at the time was that is was a proposal concerning the *syntactic structure* of mathematical utterances (or their language-of-thought analogue).

On this view, paraphrase isn't an autonomous part of the analysis of truth, as it was for Quine; but rather codes for certain underlying facts about a more familiar conception of the properties of language – syntactical, in this case – appreciation of which would remove apparent tension between the view of reality advocated, and the common-sense claim at issue.

In the literature on fictionalism various proposals of this kind have been floated. Most endorse interesting and unexpected claims about some aspect of our ordinary language use in the disputed area. As well as the syntactic revisionism of Field (1989) and Rosen (1990), it's been suggested that the *existential quantifier* as it features in discourse about abstracta has a distinctive semantic interpretation – perhaps 'there exists' in English has exactly the syntax it appears to, but picks out the same function from properties to truth-values as the complex phrase 'if there were mathematical objects, there would exist . . .'. This would be semantic rescue from error-theory, parallel to the syntactic ones just mentioned. Of course, if you want to make such claims, you better be prepared to defend them to people with an expertise in the relevant areas (philosophers of language and mind, linguists, psychologists). You can't make a sentence of natural language or the language of thought have a underlying conditional syntax or semantics just by wishing it were so. Field agreed – though he canvasses the possibilities hereabouts, he prefers to stick with error-theory.

The positions just described illustrate that there are perfectly *familiar* ways of reconciling minimal metaphysics with what the many and the wise say. But I don't find either of these particular proposals appealing. I don't like the *global* view of the nature of representation required for the first; and I don't believe the *local* claims about syntax and semantics required for the second. The jury on the Bennettian framework is still out.

6.3   REALITY-REQUIREMENTS AS MEDIATOR

We can distinguish between the *apparent* ontological commitments of mathematics (or macro-talk, or whatever), and its real commitments – what is required to exist in reality in order for the relevant claims to be true. Each of the theories above have ways of cashing out claims like: 'All that is required of reality, in order that "there are numbers" be true, is that Peano Arithmetic be conservative over nominalized science'; or 'All that is required of reality, in order that "Billy is sitting" be true, is that the things that are arranged Billy-wise are also arranged sitting-wise.' For the Quinean, we might talk of suitable paraphrases relating one claim to the other. For syntactic or semantic revisionists, we might talk about the underlying as opposed to superficial syntactic form or semantic interpretation. Even the Yablo-style figuralist has a notion of the 'real content' of an assertion made in the scope of a certain pretence – the way that reality must be in order that, within the pretence, certain pretended-assertions are licensed. The notion of a (potentially non-disquotational) requirement on reality is what groups these approaches together.

We have a general notion of what is required of reality for a claim to be true – with *ontological* commitments being the special case where the requirement is *existential*.[5] This raises the following thought. Each of the accounts above took a common notion of reality-requirements, and proposed a particular reduction to something more familiar: to syntax, semantics, or translation.

But why go so quickly to questions about what constitutes these properties of language? We should start by getting clear what the properties are, by formulating a theory of reality-requirements directly – if it turns out to be reducible to some other features, so much the better. What we want to defend is the view that what is required for 'Billy is sitting' to be true, is that, in reality, the things arranged Billy-wise be arranged sitting-wise. If accepted, this would seem to effect the kind of reconciliation between common sense and minimal metaphysics we were looking for. My proposal is that if this is what we believe, we should come straight out and say so, without tying this in the first instance to contentious claims about translation, syntax, and the like.

---

[5] We should say that S is ontologically committed to Fs if *that Fs exist* is part of the reality-requirement of some *consequence* of S – but the detailed formulation of a criterion of ontological commitment is rather delicate, and in any case I take reality-requirements to be the more primitive notion.

The remainder of this section is an investigation of the prospects for and constraints on such a theory. In the first subsection I propose some constraints and explanatory obligations on an autonomous theory of reality-requirements. In the second subsection I sketch a view on which truth-conditions and reality-requirements, though different, are jointly determined by metasemantics. And in the final subsection, I compare the emerging position to that of the advocate of a stratified reality.

6.3.1   Formulating requirements on reality

I noted earlier that once the Quinean translate-and-deflate account of truth is given up, it's no longer clear what is being done when one 'gives a paraphrase'. Once we separate off *giving a theory of meaning* (or truth) from *saying what's required of reality for a sentence to be true*, we have a new role for paraphrase. For we can let semantic theory take care of itself (assigning to words functions from macroscopic possibilia to truth-values, or whatever), and offer the paraphrase as an autonomous story about 'what truth requires of reality'.

The very name 'paraphrase' may be misleading, since it brings with it overtones of synonymy, translation, and other semantic notions that we can now disavow. What's really going on is a certain function f from sentences of English to sentences of some metaphysically revealing language ('Ontologese', if you like) is being described. And our account then takes the form: for all S, what it required of reality for S to be true, is for $f(S)$ to hold.[6]

Thus, suppose van Inwagen's paraphrase of macro-talk succeeded in pairing intuitively true natural language claims with true statements of 'Ontologese'. On the current picture, semantics itself, formulated in English, need not change. But when we ask, not about what words refer to or what proposition is assigned to which sentence, but rather about *what is required of reality for 'Billy is sitting' to be true*, we'd look to the paraphrase relation to give our answer. Likewise, on a Fieldian position, we might give a completely orthodox semantics and syntax for mathematical discourse, and pair that with a paraphrase construed

---

[6] I'm going to use 'holds' as a placeholder for a disquotational truth-predicate. This aids formulation. We could instead try to replace sentence-to-sentence paraphrase with the definition of a certain *paraphrasing operator* – but I think this would leave the discussion largely unchanged.

as articulating reality-requirements, that maps a set-theoretical claim p to the true modalized claim $\Box(\Omega \rightarrow p)$.[7]

Not any old mapping from sentences to sentences is plausible as a 'possible first-order theory of reality-requirements'. Some will be wildly false – saying that 'Billy sits' requires of reality that dragons stalk the Earth. But there are interesting questions about whether we should impose any formal constraints on acceptable paraphrase – systematicity, finitude, in principle surveyability, etc.

In a related context, Melia (2005) and Cameron (2008a) explicitly reject the need to give a *systematic* story about how arbitrary sentences are made-true by the world (they may indeed adopt something more radical, saying – in my terminology – that even in an individual case there may be no finitary paraphrase stating the reality-requirements of a single sentence). This is perfectly coherent territory to explore. However, a theory of reality-requirements that people like us can *actually articulate* in a finitary way is desirable – even if there's no transcendental proof that it's necessary. I take it that there's no transcendental proof that physical theories are finitely graspable. But surely the best confirmed ones will be, simply due to the fact that they're the ones we're in a position to actually weigh up! One shouldn't forget the pessimistic possibility that the true theory of some area is beyond our ken – but I don't see there's any more reason to believe that reality-requirements are ineffable than that any other particular theory would be.

If we do need to actually lay out a theory of reality-requirements, the natural way to do that is by some kind of systematic recursion. After all, there are infinitely many sentences to assign reality-requirements! Similarly, surely there will be recurring patterns between the requirements of complex sentences and the requirements of their simpler parts. And we should prefer a theory that predicts such patterns to one that takes them as brute. So while I am sympathetic to much that Melia and Cameron say in principle, I think they underplay what would be needed to build up a believable account of the reality-requirements of our discourse.

There's one area in particular that I think we face explanatory obligations, and that concerns the question: What makes it the case a given theory T of

---

[7] There are others who might use this framework to articulate relations between language and what really exists that are *more* demanding than a disquotational reading might suggest. Thus, one form of truth-maker theory might insist that *all* requirements must end up as requirements that such-and-such exists. If so, the appropriate paraphrase should be from 'Sparky is charged' to something existential, for example *the trope of Sparky's charge exists*. See Cameron 2008b, Cameron 2008a for one take on the truth-maker project, and its use in augmenting or minimizing ontological commitments.

reality-requirements is the right one? Reality-requirements are after all *contingent* features of sentences. 'Snow is white' might have meant something completely different, and if so, surely its reality-requirements would vary. Just as we face the metasemantic challenge to ground the truth-conditions of sentences in more primitive features of the world, we need to similarly ground whatever reality-requirements they carry. Furthermore, reality-requirements aren't *unrelated* to meaning-facts; they stand in all sorts of interesting counterfactual dependencies to them. If 'Billy sits' had meant what 'Sally runs' in fact means and vice versa, then presumably their reality-requirements would also have been switched. Our answer to the question of what grounds reality-requirements should offer an explanation of these connections.

(We might attempt to finesse these points. Suppose our semantics took the form of associating to each sentence a structured proposition. Then perhaps the structured proposition has both its truth-conditions and its reality-requirements, essentially. But this just shifts the bump in the carpet. Either there are (different) structured propositions with the same truth-conditions but different reality-requirements, or there are not. If there are, then we face the question of why our sentences pick out the structured propositions with *those* particular reality-requirements, rather than the alternatives. If there are not, we face the question of why only our favoured structured propositions exist, and the others do not.)

The reductive treatment of reality-requirements in the syntactical rescue and translate-and-deflate traditions are excellently placed to answer such questions. No mystery in the counterfactual correlations, since reality-requirements reduce to aspects of meaning. And given the reduction, whatever we say to ground the meanings of language in general will *en passant* ground reality-requirements. But if we think of reality-requirements as autonomous, then we can't avail ourselves of these features. So as well as the challenge to articulate a definite theory of reality-requirements for a whole language, we need to make a case that by positing this new layer of properties of language, we're not generating metaphysical mysteries.

6.3.2 *Reality-requirements, semantics, and metasemantics*

There are two main aspects to the theory I favour. One is the detailed view on what the reality-requirements of (say) number talk in a nominalist world turn out to be. The other is the development of a broad framework for specifying these requirements, that is capable of addressing the concerns just raised. I'll sketch my favoured view of each in turn (I develop the view fully elsewhere (Williams 2010), so I will concentrate here on the key themes, rather than the nitty gritty details. My views on these matters are heavily influenced by the work of Rayo (2008)).

On the question of the reality-requirements for number talk, I favour a kind of fictionalism – but the sense in which it is 'fictionalist' needs to be handled very carefully. The kind of fictionalism in question is not committed to the psychological claim that we only make-believe that there are numbers (as Yablo may be); nor is it committed to a fictive syntax (the view Field considers) or non-standard semantic values for existential quantifiers, or any other of the familiar slate of options. Instead, the key strategy is to piggyback on what one might initally think of as the reality-requirements for a sentence – that 'there are numbers' requires that *there be numbers*. Let's call this putative committal reality-requirement R. Then the view is that the actual reality-requirement is that the world be such that, *according to the fiction that there are numbers*, R holds. Notice that it is not *required of reality* that it contains fictions, or that fictions have things true according to them. Rather, we *use* fictionality to *characterize* what's required. (This strategy has strong similarities to Yablo's notion of the 'real content' of a fictive utterance – though I emphasize again that my use of the notion in no way presupposes the kind of pschological/semantic deployment of the notion that Yablo favours.) If this specification of reality-requirements works, then the reality-requirements of 'there are prime numbers' will be met, even if reality is as Field describes it.

But having committed myself to this position, I face the more metaphysical questions outlined in the previous sections. Why should we think that this is the right account to give of reality-requirements? And how can we explain the correlation of reality-requirements and truth-conditions (e.g. that the roles for the symbols for 2 and 1 were reversed, then '$1 + 1 = 4$' would have the truth-conditions, and the reality-requirements, that '$2 + 2 = 4$' actually does)? I favour tackling these questions simultaneously. Reality-requirements are specified, not by providing a paraphrase independently of semantic theory, but by specifying reality-requirements in a compositional way *in the course of giving a semantic theory.*

Just to illustrate how this might come about, we can envisage the following kind of semantic axioms being provided:

'Larry' refers to x iff x's simple parts are the yy, and in reality, the yy are arranged Larry-wise.

x satisfies 'sings' iff x's simple parts are the yy, and in reality, the yy are arranged singing-wise.

With the usual compositional clause, the canonical theorems provable in such a theory would include that 'Larry sings' is true iff there's some x with simple parts yy, such that (i) in reality, the yy are arranged Larry-wise, and (ii) in reality, the yy are arranged singing-wise. We earlier canvassed reading off reality-requirements from paraphrases, by saying that what's required of reality for 'S' to be true is that S^*, where 'S^*' is the paraphrase of S. We now propose reading off reality-requirements from canonical theorems of the form just sketched, by saying that what's required of reality for S to be true is that the conditions on reality spelled out on the right-hand side of its canonical theorem, be true. In the case above, what we ask of *reality* is that it contain some simples, arranged in various ways (we also talk of parthood and macroscopic objects, but we don't explicitly say anything about whether they exist *in reality*).[8]

(I said earlier that I wanted a theory of reality-requirements that is autonomous – I didn't want to start telling natural language semanticists that they weren't sufficiently mindful of the metaphysical issues. But that the above is a correct specification of the semantic values of sentences is perfectly compatible with the correctness of specifications of semantic clauses that don't use these special operators. If 'Larry' refers to Larry because Larry is the things whose simple parts are, in reality, arranged Larry-wise, then it's also true that 'Larry' refers to x iff x is Larry. So there's no inconsistency between saying that a certain style of semantic theory is of particular interest to the metaphysician (and perhaps only to them) – and that certain less 'loaded' descriptions of the semantic properties of language are entirely appropriate for the purposes of semanticists and philosophers of language.)

There are immediate advantages from moving from a paraphrase to a compositional specification of reality-requirements of the sort just mentioned. A paraphrase must assign to whole sentences a claim about fundamental reality that is purified of any unwholesome elements. And as Melia (1995, 2000) emphasizes, demanding that such purification be achievable in a finitary way can seem an unreasonable constraint. But from our current perspective, only what occurs within the scope of the

---

[8] Compare Azzouni 2004. As he notes, if our view is that a minimal metaphysical base (say, atoms arranged this way and that) is sufficient to allow talk of macroscopic things to be true, then we should be able to happily use such talk within a range of theoretical projects. Why shouldn't that include giving a semantic theory? Or indeed, in the present case, in saying what reality has to contain in order for the sentences to be true? Just because one's view is that, in reality, there are no sets, numbers, or macroscopic things, one needn't forgo appeal to such things in articulating what you *do* think reality contains.

'in reality' operator in the canonical theorems need meet this condition on the view just sketched – which increases considerably the expressive power we can achieve (and allows, I think, a more minimal metaphysics to be defended).

Equally vital is the connection forged between reality-requirements and semantic values. A theory such as the above both specifies semantic values of terms, and specifies the reality-requirements of sentences. But if we can give a theory of *what makes a theory of this particular form correct for a given natural language*, we will thereby be able to explain both what makes reality-requirements what they are (directly from that theory), and why this will be correlated with truth-conditions (since the story about how they get fixed will be one and the same). The earlier theory explained counterfactual dependencies between meaning and reality-requirements by reducing one to the other. I propose to explain them by pointing to a common cause – a simultaneous reduction of both to the underlying meaning-making facts about usage and the wider world.

My favoured metasemantic account is in the broadly 'radical interpretation' camp – particularly as developed by David Lewis (1984, 1975).[9] As I read him, Lewis's idea is that the correct meaning-fixing theory is that one which is (a) simplest; and (b) fits with a certain set of privileged 'correlations' between sentences and propositions.[10] Condition (a) imposes a bias towards *simpler* specifications of semantic theory – but only when doing so wouldn't give a gross mismatch between the assigned truth-conditions of S and the conventions of usage.

Applying this to a theory of requirements, the trade-off of these two factors gives an explanation of how non-obvious specifications, with weakened reality-requirements, arise. In a Fieldian nominalistic world, or a mereologically nihilistic world, the most natural, simple specification of semantic values would say, for example, that an object x is in the extension of 'sings' iff in reality, it sings. This is less complex than the sort of clauses mentioned above – and to that extent, a semantic theory for English that embeds this clause is pro tanto better. However, in a nihilistic world, such specifications lead to error theory. On grounds of charity,

---

[9] I discuss it as applied to meaning in Williams 2005, 2007, and 2008. In Williams 2007, I raise *objections* to Lewis's version of this theory – but I've always been sympathetic to the general approach, and I think a principled modification of Lewis's position is available.

[10] In my view, (a) is what underlies Lewis's famous appeal to 'eligibility' and 'reference magnets' – see Williams 2007 for discussion of the relation. On (b), Lewis appeals to his theory of conventions to explain these correlations – they are certain kinds of entrenched regularities of uttering S only when one believes that p.

then, the rival specification is pro tanto better, as it *weakens* the reality-requirements so they are satisfiable even in a nihilistic world. All things considered, the small sacrifice in simplicity of the slightly twisted assignment of reality-requirements is worth it, for the massive gains in charity (fit with conventions of usage) that it stands to gain.[11]

The full theory has of course not been set out here. But even at this stage, we've seen that there's no *principled* obstacle to giving an autonomous account of reality-requirements that doesn't make the reality-requirements possessed by a given natural language simply brute – and which also articulates expected connections between reality-requirements and truth-conditions. And if this can be done, the sort of quasi-fictionalist story about the reality-requirements for statements talking about numbers or macroscopic objects becomes available, without having to adopt a revisionary position on syntax, semantics, or buy into the radical translate-and-deflate position of Quine himself.

6.3.3   Comparison with structured metaphysics

There's a way of reporting the views that I've just been advocating that makes it sound close to the views of Schaffer, Fine, and other friends of stratified metaphysics. For on this view, a certain image of *what there is* is projected from total theory. 'There are numbers', 'there are macroscopic objects', and the like will be *true* according to view developed. To put it less coyly and without qualification: numbers and macroscopic objects exist. What could be more natural than to call the totality of what exists our 'ontology'? Within the ontology, there are some entities that not only exist, but are such that they form the 'requirement-base' for the rest – that is, such that what is 'required' of reality, in order that the truths be true, never invokes anything outside of this base. We could call this 'fundamental ontology', and call any part of ontology that isn't part of fundamental ontology 'merely derivative'.

---

[11] Just to be clear: the basic commitment here is that the radical interpretation story be run to pick a theory of requirements that specifies semantic values. That already gives us a story about what the semantic properties of natural language expressions are. It's then an open question about whether we defend the 'unloaded' textbook versions of the semantic clauses by running radical interpretation a *second* time, on the revised understanding of the metalinguistic modals, or just see it as a true and far more convenient way of communicating information about what the semantic values and truth-conditions of sentences are. I'm presently agnostic about how this is to be best thought of – it probably depends very much on one's conception of what the explanatory ambition of textbook semantic theory is to be.

While I earlier suggested that the existential component of reality-requirements be called 'ontological commitments'; why not call it instead 'fundamental ontological commitments', and allow a standard understanding of 'ontological commitments' *simpliciter*, in terms of what must feature as the values of our variables for a sentence or theory to be true? Insofar as the existence of *a* is part of what's required for '*b* exists' to be true, we might choose to say that *b* is *grounded in a*. And so forth.

In this way, a simulacra of the sort of talk that the friends of stratified metaphysics engage in might be built up. But before we hastily conclude that the view I've been outlining is stratified metaphysics in disguise, it's worth noting that the more traditional representational approaches can give similar speeches. A fan of Quinean paraphrase may say that 'there are numbers' is true – because it is paraphrased to some dtruth (involving fictional operators and the like). Quine identifies 'ontological commitments' with the values of variables of total theory once it is properly paraphrased. But why not let the ontological commitments be the values of the variables of total true theory? Even if one demands nominalistic paraphrases before conceding that mathematical talk is true, the Quinean may admit that numbers are ontological commitments *in the sense just defined*. We'd then need some alternative terminology for the traditional focus of Quinean metaphysics – so to coin a phrase we call the values of the variables of the properly paraphrased version of the theory, 'fundamental ontological commitments'.

In describing the Quinean view, a terminological stipulation tying 'ontological commitment' closely to the true existential sentences would be highly misleading. And I'm inclined to say the same about the analogous stipulation in the context of the theory I favour. Ultimately, however, the terminology isn't important – what is significant is the theoretical setting in which the terminology is explained. Schaffer includes a primitive relation of grounding, and explains other distinctions in terms of it. However, my working primitive is broadly linguistic – the reality-requirements of a sentence – and I think that we can and should explain what in non-linguistic reality makes it the case that sentences have the reality-requirements that they do. I say this not to claim any superiority over Schaffer's proposals, but just to emphasize that they are different enterprises. I'm happy to allow that in Schaffer's theoretical setting, a tie between 'ontological commitments' and true existentials is natural; I don't think to insist on such a tie in the setting I favour would be to obscure the differing conceptions we have about the relationship between words and the world. (In any case, whatever verbal agreement we might achieve will I think quickly dissolve when we get down to details – I doubt that I can have a sense of 'grounding' that doesn't relate entities immediately down to the fundamental, for example, whereas theorists like Schaffer and Fine can posit whole chains of grounding. I suspect in many respects, my views will end up more like those of a fictionalist, rather than someone in the Fine/Schaffer camp – and my disagreements with extant fictionalists will be fought over the correct way to theorize about language, rather than over metaphysics.)[12]

6.4 CONCLUSION

We started by supposing we had some 'first-order' reasons to favour a radically minimal metaphysics – and a candidate description of reality that we supposed to be at least internally coherent (Field's nominalistic metaphysics can be taken as representative here). It is natural to think that this sort of metaphysics is going to lead to revisionism – to a mathematical error theory. That's only bad if the error theory itself is a bad thing – and I sketched one 'Moorean' way of running interference on this front. Of course, *any* way of reconciling the tension between radical metaphysics and common sense/science is likely to involve taking a stand on some contentious issues. But we have a choice about where to take that stand. One option (that Field himself advocates) is to engage with the epistemology of theory change that lay behind the Moorean objection I outlined. A philosophy of language of the Quinean translate-and-deflate kind might do the job. But I favour addressing the issue in the most direct way – giving a theory of 'reality-requirements' directly. I hope in this way to minimize the hostages to fortune given to best theory in epistemology or semantics.

But we cannot avoid issues of theoretical integration altogether. My own view is that such theories owe a two-fold explanatory debt. If they're at all interesting (i.e. if they're not merely disquotational) then it'll be unattractive to treat the theories as *brutely true* – we'll need to say something about what *makes them correct*. And we also need to make intelligible the relation between requirements on reality and meaning.

The best way I know to achieve these desiderata is to build requirements directly into the specification of semantic theory. We can do this in a way

---

[12] Just as a matter of autobiography – my thinking on these matters was initially prompted as a possible interpretation of Fine (2001) and his advocacy of the use of a distinction between what is true 'in reality' and what is merely true. I've since come to think that Fine should be read in a more inflationary way.

that does not affect what semantic values are assigned to expressions; nor does it cast doubt on the cogency of the more standard ways of specifying the semantic values that we find in philosophy of language and linguistics. So the proposal is semantically and syntactically non-revisionary. A meta-semantic theory I find independently attractive – radical interpretation – then completes the package by grounding the *choice* of the reality-requirement-specifying semantic theory.

CHAPTER 7

Varieties of ontological dependence

Kathrin Koslicki

7.1

A significant reorientation is currently under way in analytic metaphysics. Following W. V. O. Quine's seminal article, "On What There Is" (Quine 1948), metaphysics and its central component, ontology (the study of being), insofar as they were thought of as meaningful enterprises at all, were for most of the second half of the twentieth century construed as concerned primarily with questions of existence, i.e., questions of the form, "What is there?" More recently, though, a number of writers (e.g., Kit Fine, Gideon Rosen, and Jonathan Schaffer) have urged that many of the most central questions in metaphysics and perhaps philosophy in general are more profitably understood not as asking about the existence of certain apparently problematic sorts of entities (e.g., abstract objects), but rather as asking whether one type of phenomenon (e.g., a smile) is in some important sense dependent on another type of phenomenon (e.g., the mouth that is smiling). Existential questions, it seems, can often be answered trivially ("Yes, of course, there are numbers; after all, $2 + 2 = 4$"); but even after these questions have been answered, the status of the entities in question still remains to be clarified, e.g., whether they are derivative of another class of phenomena (e.g., concrete spatiotemporal particulars). The reorientation that is currently underway within contemporary metaphysics really constitutes a return to older traditions, such as those of Aristotle and Husserl, who recognized and emphasized the importance of questions of dependence in metaphysics and philosophy in general.

In order for this approach to metaphysics to stand on firm ground, a good grasp of the notion of dependence is obviously needed. For several decades, it was widely believed that dependence, at least as it concerns systematic connections between entire realms of phenomena (e.g., the mental and the physical or the evaluative and the non-evaluative) could be analyzed by means of the notion of supervenience, i.e., the idea that any difference with respect to one type of phenomenon (e.g., the mental) entails a difference with respect to another (e.g., the physical). However, after a period of lively interest in supervenience, even its most committed champions were forced to conclude that this notion is not strong enough and lacks the right formal profile to yield a relation of genuine and asymmetric dependence (cf. Kim 1993). For one thing, supervenience is not in and of itself an asymmetric relation. Secondly, supervenience serves to mark merely a relation of necessary covariance between its relata. But, following considerations raised in Fine 1994, we now have reason to believe that no relation that is defined in purely modal terms could yield a genuine relation of dependence. For example, while the singleton set containing Socrates arguably depends on Socrates, the reverse intuitively does not hold; however, since necessarily each exists just in case the other does, necessity coupled with existence alone cannot capture the asymmetric dependence at issue.

Surprisingly, despite the central role dependence has played in philosophy since its very inception, this relation has only recently begun to receive the kind of attention it deserves from contemporary metaphysicians.[1] In this chapter, I would like to contribute to the recent surge of interest in this subject by helping to develop a better grasp of the notion of ontological dependence. In doing so, I am not interested primarily in defending particular positions in first-order metaphysics, e.g., trope theory or Aristotelianism about universals. Rather, the focus of this current project is to become clearer about the kinds of dependence relations to which philosophers who assert or deny these positions in first-order metaphysics appeal. I take this project to be a crucial component of defending a realist position in metaphysics, according to which substantive disagreements in ontology are possible.

Due to space limitations, I presuppose for the purposes of this chapter that construals of ontological dependence in terms of existence and modality do not capture all that is encompassed by this notion.[2] Instead, I focus on the more tempting account of ontological dependence in terms

---

[1] See for example Correia 2005; Fine 1991, 1995a, 1995b, 2001, this volume, manuscript; Lowe 1994, 1998, 2005b, 2006a; Mulligan, Simons, and Smith 1984; Rosen 2010; Schaffer 2009b, 2010a; Schnieder 2006a, 2011; Sider 2011; Simons 1982, 1987; Smith and Mulligan 1982.

[2] Aristotle's dependence claim in the *Categories*, according to which all the other entities are in some way dependent on the primary substances, is often read in a primarily modal/existential way: if the primary substances did not *exist*, then it would be *impossible* for anything else to *exist*. For a defense of a non-existential reading of Aristotle's dependence claim, see Corkum 2008 and Peramatzis 2008. See also Lowe 1994 for convincing counterexamples to a straightforwardly modal/existential construal of ontological dependence, according to which an entity, Φ, modally/existentially depends on an entity, Ψ, iff necessarily if Φ exists, then Ψ exists. A more interesting non-modal existential construal of ontological dependence is offered in Correia 2005 and Schnieder 2006a; I must leave a detailed discussion of their proposal for another occasion.

of a non-modal and sufficiently constrained conception of essence developed in Fine 1995a. I argue below that even this essentialist account is, as it stands, not fine-grained enough to recognize different varieties of dependence which ought to be distinguished even within the realm of ontology.

7.2

The kind of dependence relation on which I want to focus in this chapter concerns not so much systematic connections between two entire realms of phenomena (e.g., the mental and the physical), but rather relations among entities, their characteristics, the activities they are involved in, their constituents, and so on. For example, smiles depend in some fashion on mouths; but mouths do not in turn appear to depend on the smiles they are manifesting. (As Alice notes, in Lewis Carroll's *Alice's Adventures in Wonderland*, it is not unusual to see a cat without a grin; but to see a grin without a cat is the most curious thing she has ever seen.) I consider the relationship between a mouth and its smile to be a good illustration of what I will call "ontological dependence." (In what follows, whenever I speak of dependence simpliciter, I can be assumed to have in mind ontological dependence, unless otherwise indicated.) Notice that ontological dependence can be, and often is, asymmetric: thus, the dependence smiles exhibit with respect to mouths is plausibly taken to be one-directional and not reciprocated by mouths which may or may not exhibit smiles.

There surely are different varieties of dependence relations and many of them are not relevant to the sorts of cases I have in mind here. For example, one such dependence relation is causal dependence (according to a Humean notion of causation), e.g., the way in which Caesar's death depends on Brutus' stabbing. A second is logical dependence, e.g., the way in which the truth of the conclusion of a valid argument for example depends on the truth of the premises. A third is probabilistic dependence, e.g., the way in which the decay of a particle depends on its half life or the way in which my recovery from strep throat depends on my having taken penicillin. None of these varieties of dependence are instances of what I would categorize as ontological dependence.

Quite possibly, the following examples are cases in which entities stand in an ontological dependence relation of some kind: (i) smiles and mouths; (ii) sets and their members; (iii) events or states of affairs (e.g., lightning or heat) and their participants (e.g., electrons or molecules); (iv) chemical substances (e.g., water) and their molecular/atomic constituents (e.g., H_2O-molecules);[3] (v) tropes (e.g., the redness of a particular tomato) and their "bearers" (e.g., the tomato);[4] (vi) Aristotelian universals (e.g., redness) and their "bearers" (e.g., objects that are red); (vii) holes (e.g., the holes in a piece of Emmentaler cheese) and their "hosts" (e.g., the piece of Emmentaler cheese); (viii) boundaries (e.g., the boundary around a football field) and their "hosts" (e.g., the football field).[5] In all of these cases, the dependence relation in question is plausibly taken to be asymmetric.

The examples just cited are perhaps plausible candidates for cases which exhibit an ontological dependence relation of some sort. But until we have had a chance to sort out the details more carefully, we should not presuppose that there is just a single relation which deserves to be called by the name, "ontological dependence." In fact, I will be proposing below that the cases considered so far really present us with more than one

---

[3] In what follows, I will on most occasions (unless I am paraphrasing the views of other philosophers) use the more general terms "constituent" and "complex entity," in place of "part" and "whole." I intend these terms, "constituent" and "complex entity," to be understood in a broad and neutral way which allows for different specific construals of constituency and complexity that is appropriate to different cases. One kind of case in which an object is a constituent of a complex entity is when the former is related to the latter in the straightforward mereological way in which a proper part is related to a whole (e.g., the sense in which an arm for example is a proper part of a body). But we might also count an object as a constituent of the singleton set of which it is the sole member, even though constituency here cannot be understood in a straightforwardly mereological way. Moreover, according to certain approaches to the metaphysics of properties, the redness of a tomato for example might count as a constituent of the tomato whose redness it is. This constituency-based conception of the relation between objects and their characteristics for example might be congenial to trope-theorists or to those who embrace an Aristotelian conception of universals, according to which universals are in some sense "present in" the particulars to which they can be truly attributed.

[4] Not every trope-theorist would endorse this dependence-claim. For example, those who take a reductive approach to particular objects might in fact think the dependence relation in question points in the opposite direction: for example, if particular objects are viewed as bundles of tropes, then it might seem more plausible to take a bundle of tropes to be dependent on the tropes that are being bundled, rather than the other way around. I do not intend to put this example forward as a claim that would be endorsed by all trope-theorists.

[5] I might also have included on the list that follows items that exhibit the relation Husserl, in the *Logical Investigations*, calls "foundation," i.e., the relation that holds between moments and their fundaments. To illustrate, Husserl regards the relation between color and extension as paradigmatic of a dependence relation he calls "foundation"; both of the relata in this case are moments. A color-moment, in Husserl's view, requires supplementation by an extension-moment; and he considers both to be proper parts of a more inclusive whole of which they are moments. Thus, every whole which has a color-moment as a part also must have an extension-moment as a part. Moreover, the relation of foundation here is reciprocal, in Husserl's view: color-moments and extension-moments are mutually founded, in the sense that every color-moment requires an extension-moment that is part of the same more inclusive whole of which the color-moment is part in order for the color-moment to exist, and vice versa. However, the relation between color-moments and extension-moments, on the one hand, and the more inclusive whole of which they are proper parts, on the other hand, is not reciprocal, but asymmetric. I will in what follows assume that the case of Husserlian moments can be assimilated to that of tropes.

underlying relation which merits this title. Thus, if my suggestions in what follows are correct, we should adopt a sufficiently fine-grained approach to ontological dependence that allows us to recognize several species of dependence even within the domain of ontology.

7.3

How, then, do smiles depend on mouths? An attractive idea proposed in Fine 1995a is that smiles are ontologically dependent on mouths roughly in that mouths are constituents in the essences of smiles. The asymmetry in the relationship between mouths and smiles, on his account, is captured by the fact that while mouths are constituents in the essences of smiles, the reverse is not the case; smiles are not also constituents in the essences of mouths. In Fine's view, the being, nature, or essence of an object, x, is the collection of propositions that are true in virtue of x's identity, where "it is true in virtue of the identity of x that . . .," for Fine, denotes an unanalyzed relation between an object and a proposition. The collection of propos-itions which are true in virtue of x's identity can also be considered a real definition of x. (Real definitions contrast with nominal definitions and concern objects themselves, rather than the linguistic expressions we use to refer to objects or the concepts we use to conceive of them.) Thus, an entity, Φ, is ontologically dependent on an entity, Ψ, on Fine's conception, just in case Ψ is a constituent of a proposition that is true in virtue of Φ's identity; in cases where this holds, Ψ is a constituent of an essential property of Φ:[6]

> (ODE) *Ontological Dependence – Essentialist Account* (Fine):
> An entity, Φ, ontologically depends on an entity (or entities), Ψ, just in case Ψ is a constituent (or are constituents) in Φ's essence.

Essence, on this account, cannot be understood in the traditional modal way, for reasons laid out in Fine 1994. Such a construal of essence would not capture the asymmetric manner in which for example singleton sets ontologically depend on their sole members, while their sole members do not in turn ontologically depend on the singleton sets of which they are the sole members.

Fine's approach to ontological dependence crucially relies on a distinc-tion between essence, narrowly constructed ("constitutive essence"), and essence, more widely constructed ("consequential essence"). Unless some

---

[6] Fine's account assumes that we may think of objects as constituents of properties and propositions.

such "narrow/wide" distinction for essences can be drawn, Fine's account of ontological dependence threatens to become vacuous, since everything will turn out to depend ontologically on everything else. This result follows because, in whatever way exactly we draw the constitutive/consequential distinction, the consequential essence of any entity, on Fine's conception, will be closed under logical consequence and all the logical truths will therefore end up in the consequential essence of everything whatsoever. Since for example the proposition that the number 2 is self-identical is a logical truth, the number 2 will turn up as a constituent in the consequential essence of every object whatsoever. And because the number 2 here was picked arbitrarily and every object is self-identical, every object will by the same reasoning turn up as a constituent in the consequential essence of every other object. Thus, if an entity were to count as being ontologically dependent on all those objects which figure as constituents in propositions that belong to its consequential essence, then the notion of ontological dependence would have been trivialized and every object would turn out to be ontologically dependent on every other object. It is thus important, at least for the purposes of providing an informative account of ontological dependence in terms of essence, that the approach in question can avail itself of some more restrictive conception of essence than what is given by the notion of consequential essence.

To this end, Fine considers two distinct methods by which to draw the constitutive/consequential distinction for essences.[7] The first proposal for how the constitutive/consequential distinction might be drawn is outlined in the following passage:

A property belongs to the *constitutive* essence of an object if it is not had in virtue of being a logical consequence of some more basic essential properties; and a property might be said to belong to the *consequential* essence of an object if it is a logical consequence of properties belonging to the constitutive essence (a similar account could be given for the case in which the essence is conceived in terms of propositions rather than properties). (Fine 1995a, p. 276; his emphasis)

Since the "more basic essential properties" in question presumably just are the ones that figure in the constitutive essence of an object, the method outlined here amounts to taking as basic the notion of constitutive essence and defining that of consequential essence in terms of it by way of logical closure. A proposition then belongs to the consequential essence of an

---

[7] I am here relying primarily on Fine 1995a, pp. 276–80; but similar thoughts (though presented in a more condensed fashion) are also found in Fine 1995b, Sections 3–4.

object, according to this first approach, if it is a logical consequence of a proposition that belongs to the object's constitutive essence (which of course is not itself to be taken as closed under logical consequence). For example, if the proposition that Socrates' singleton set contains Socrates as its sole member belongs to the constitutive essence of Socrates' singleton set, then the proposition that Socrates' singleton set contains some member or other is admitted into the consequential essence of Socrates' singleton set by logical closure. Since the logical truths are logically entailed by any proposition whatsoever, these propositions will end up in the consequential essence of any object whatsoever by this procedure.

In case the idea of taking the notion of constitutive essence as basic is found to be objectionable in a context in which our aim is to give an account of ontological dependence, Fine also considers a second approach to the constitutive/consequential distinction:

It is therefore preferable, in the interest of conceptual economy, to see if the notion of dependence can be explained in consequential terms, without appeal to an underlying constitutive conception. To this end, we need an independent way of distinguishing between those objects that enter into the consequential essence as a result of the logical closure and those that enter in "their own right", i.e., by way of the constitutive essence. But this is readily done. For when an object enters through logical closure, it can be "generalized away". (Fine 1995a, p. 277)

According to Fine's second proposed method of drawing the constitutive/consequential distinction, we are to take as basic the notion of consequential essence and define that of constitutive essence in terms of it. The central idea underlying this second procedure is this: if an object enters as a constituent into a proposition belonging to the consequential essence of another object only through logical closure, then such an object can be "generalized away." For example, the proposition that the number 2 is self-identical belongs to the consequential essence of Socrates' singleton set; but so does, for every object whatsoever, the proposition that that object is self-identical. In this way, the number 2 can be "generalized out" of the proposition that the number 2 is self-identical, which belongs to the consequential essence of Socrates' singleton set. Following this second method of drawing the constitutive/consequential distinction, then, only those objects which function as constituents of propositions belonging to the consequential essence of a given entity and which cannot be "generalized out" of these propositions make it into the constitutive essence of the entity in question as constituents of propositions belonging to its constitutive essence. In this way, it seems that Fine can avoid the result that Socrates' singleton set ontologically depends on the number 2 (and, more generally, on any object whatsoever).[8]

The trouble is that Fine's second method of drawing the constitutive/consequential distinction for essences (i.e., taking for granted consequential essence and defining constitutive essence in terms of it), as it stands, cannot be assumed to take us all the way to an object's constitutive essence. The second proposed method of drawing the constitutive/consequential distinction is based on the idea that those constituents that are intuitively irrelevant to the essential nature of the entity under consideration can be "generalized out" of propositions belonging to an object's consequential essence. But Fine's "generalizing out" procedure is really effective only in removing the logical truths from the consequential essence of an object, since this procedure takes advantage of a special feature of logical truths, i.e., that they remain true under all re-interpretations of the non-logical vocabulary. The "generalizing out" procedure thereby leaves us with a *restricted* conception of consequential essence, i.e., the collection of propositions consisting of an object's unrestricted consequential essence minus the logical truths. But this restricted notion of consequential essence cannot in general be expected to deliver the suitably narrow conception of essence that is needed for an account of ontological dependence along the lines of (ODE). For, unless the narrow notion of constitutive essence is already implicitly presupposed (as is done by the first method of drawing the constitutive/consequential contrast), the entities on which an object depends ontologically need not match exactly those which figure as constituents in propositions that belong to an object's restricted consequential essence.

---

[8] The following is a more precise characterization of the notion of "generalizing out" (cf. Fine 1995a, pp. 277–8). Consider a proposition P(y), which has an object, y, as a constituent. For example, P(y) might be the proposition that Socrates is identical to Socrates for y=Socrates. Fine's first step is to define the notion of a "generalization" for propositions, rather than objects (i.e., constituents of propositions): the generalization of a proposition, P(y), is the proposition that P(v) holds for all objects, v. Thus, the generalization of the proposition that Socrates is identical to Socrates is the proposition for all objects, v, that v is identical to v. (To obtain the generalization, P(v), of a proposition, P(y), all occurrences of the constituent, y, must be replaced by occurrences of v.) Given the notion of a generalization, defined for propositions, we can now make sense of the idea that an *object* can be "generalized out" of a collection, C, of propositions in the following way: an object, y, can be generalized out of a collection, C, of propositions if C contains the generalization of a proposition P(y), whenever it contains the proposition P(y) itself. Finally, these defined notions are now applied to the analysis of ontological dependence in the following way: an object, x, depends ontologically on an object, y, according to this method of drawing the constitutive/consequential distinction, just in case y cannot be generalized out of the consequential essence of x, i.e., just in case some proposition P(y) belongs to the consequential essence of x without it being the case that the generalization of P(y) also belongs to the consequential essence of x.

Consider for example the proposition that the number 2 is not a member of Socrates' singleton set. If this proposition belongs to the unrestricted consequential essence of Socrates' singleton set, then, in accordance with the second method of drawing the constitutive/consequential distinction just considered, the "generalizing out" procedure will pass it on into the constitutive essence of Socrates' singleton set as well. Since this proposition is not a logically necessary truth, it does not remain true under all re-interpretations of the non-logical vocabulary. For it is not true in general for every object, v, that v is not a member of Socrates' singleton set, since Socrates, after all, is a member of Socrates' singleton set. The number 2 therefore will not "generalize out" of the proposition that 2 is not a member of Socrates' singleton set and it seems the proposition in question, by the second method of drawing the constitutive/consequential distinction, will therefore wrongly end up in the constitutive essence of Socrates' singleton set with the result that Socrates' singleton set will again turn out to depend ontologically on the number 2 (and, by the same reasoning, on any object other than itself whatsoever), on the assumption that an entity ontologically depends on just those objects that appear as constituents in propositions belonging to its constitutive essence.

Suppose, on the other hand, that the proposition that the number 2 is not a member of Socrates' singleton set is excluded from the unrestricted consequential essence of Socrates' singleton set. Now, it seems, the second method of drawing the constitutive/consequential distinction has really collapsed into the first. For it is difficult to see on what grounds the proposition that the number 2 is not a member of Socrates' singleton set could be excluded from the unrestricted consequential essence of Socrates' singleton set, unless it is excluded on the grounds that this proposition pertains to the essential nature of Socrates' single-ton set neither directly nor indirectly, by being logically entailed solely by those propositions that directly pertain to the essential nature of Socrates' singleton set. But if these are in fact at least implicitly the grounds on the basis of which the proposition in question is to be excluded from the unrestricted consequential essence of Socrates' singleton set, then the procedure for determining whether a proposition belongs in an object's unrestricted consequential essence is tacitly defined by reference to an object's constitutive essence. And this is of course just the way in which the first method of drawing the constitutive/consequential distinction proceeds, i.e., by taking as basic constitutive essence and defining unrestricted consequential essence in terms of it by way of logical closure.

In light of these considerations, it thus seems that there is really only one method by which to approach the constitutive/consequential distinction, namely the first one: to take as basic constitutive essence and define consequential essence in terms of it by means of logical closure (restrictedly or unrestrictedly). And while there is nothing in principle wrong with taking as basic constitutive essence, we should note that, in the context of giving an account of ontological dependence in terms of constitutive essence, Fine's first proposed procedure for drawing the constitutive/consequential contrast does not really give us an independent handle on the notion of ontological dependence. Fine himself is well aware of this feature of his account:

It is, of course, no surprise that dependence can be defined in terms of the objectually constrained form of essential truth; for the notion of dependence is already built into the constraints by which the relevant notion of essential truth is understood. But even without the constraints, a definition could still be given. For we may say that x depends upon y just in case, for some property φ not involving y, it is true in virtue of the nature of x that y φ's and yet not true in virtue of the nature of x that every object φ's; the dependees are the objects which cannot be "generalized out". Thus we do not have, in the notion of dependence, an idea that is genuinely new. (Fine 1995c, p. 243)

Thus, although nothing prevents us from defining a notion of ontological dependence in terms of constitutive essence as proposed above, we should be conscious of the fact that we have not thereby accomplished more than to state what is at bottom a single ontological relationship in two different, but interdefinable, ways, i.e., either by means of a suitably restricted notion of essential truth or by means of a suitably restricted notion of ontological dependence. To illustrate, it helps to return once more to the proposed asymmetry in the relation between Socrates and Socrates' singleton set. Thus, to say that it is a properly constitutive essential truth about Socrates' singleton set that it has Socrates as its sole member (while it is not also a properly constitutive essential truth about Socrates to be the sole member of Socrates' singleton set) is really just another way of saying that Socrates' singleton set ontologically depends on Socrates (while Socrates does not also ontologically depend on Socrates' singleton set); and vice versa. As Fine puts it in the passage just cited: "the notion of dependence is already built into the constraints by which the relevant notion of essential truth is understood"; and, given (ODE), a suitably narrow conception of essence is also already built into the constraints by which the relevant notion of ontological dependence is understood.[9]

---

[9] Like Fine, Aristotle also recognizes a distinction between what belongs to the essence proper of an object and what merely follows from its essence proper, i.e., the so-called "propria" or "necessary

7.4

According to Fine's essentialist account of ontological dependence, as discussed in the previous sections, an entity, Φ, is ontologically dependent on an entity or entities, Ψ, just in case Ψ is a constituent in Φ's essence, where "essence" here must be understood in some appropriately narrow sense. Fine assumes that, for the purposes at hand, essences can be identified with collections of propositions that are true in virtue of the identity of a particular object or objects. Fine also simultaneously thinks of such collections of propositions that are true in virtue of the identity of an object or objects as real definitions for the object or objects in question. There is not, then, on this approach, much of a distinction between essences and real definitions.

But we may wish to proceed somewhat differently and leave room for a less propositional conception of essences, such as that endorsed by Aristotle for example. For Aristotle, the essence of a kind of thing includes at least its form. (Whether the essence of a kind of thing also includes additional components besides the form, e.g., the matter, is a controversial question which I will not try to address here.) For example, the essence of a living being, in Aristotle's view, encompasses at least its soul, i.e., the form of the living being. But, given Aristotle's association of the soul with certain kinds of powers or capacities [*dynameis*], e.g., the

accidents." But Aristotle's "narrow/wide" distinction for essences does not exactly line up with Fine's. For example, for Aristotle, it is part of the essence of planets that they are heavenly bodies that are near; but it is merely a necessary (but non-essential) feature of planets that they do not twinkle. The latter proposition, in Aristotle's view, states a feature which merely follows from, but is not itself included in, the essence of planets. But the relevant notion of "following from" that is operative in this context, for Aristotle, cannot simply be that of logical consequence. The (explanatorily less basic) proposition that planets are heavenly bodies which do not twinkle is logically entailed by the (explanatorily more basic) proposition that planets are heavenly bodies that are near together with auxiliary premises (e.g., the proposition that heavenly bodies that are near do not twinkle). But the same holds also in the opposite direction: the (explanatorily more basic) proposition that planets are heavenly bodies that are near is also logically entailed by the (explanatorily less basic) proposition that planets are heavenly bodies that do not twinkle together with auxiliary premises (e.g., the proposition that heavenly bodies that do not twinkle are near). Thus, the relation of logical entailment alone (as is brought out in a more contemporary context by Sylvain Bromberger's "flagpole" objection against Hempel's deductive-nomological model of scientific explanation) is not sufficient to capture the asymmetry of scientific explanation. In Aristotle's system, the relevant notion of asymmetric consequence that is operative in his model of scientific explanation is that of *demonstration*, as developed theoretically in his *Posterior Analytics* and (according to my reading of Aristotle) applied practically for example in his biological treatises. A scientific explanation is asymmetric, for Aristotle, because (if accurate) it is the theoretical and/or linguistic reflection of an asymmetric real-world relation of *causal* priority, where causation here of course must be construed along Aristotelian (and not Humean) lines. These issues are explored further in Koslicki 2012.

capacity for growth and nourishment, locomotion, perception and thought, it would be strange to think of the soul of a living being as a collection of propositions. It is perhaps more natural to take real definitions, which Aristotle regards as linguistic entities [*logoi*] of some sort, i.e., formulas or statements of the essence, as collections of propositions or perhaps as only a single proposition, if there is only a single canonical way of stating the essence of a kind of thing.[10]

The basic idea underlying Fine's essentialist approach to ontological dependence can be reformulated in terms of real definitions as follows:

(ODD) *Ontological Dependence – Real Definition:*
An entity, Φ, ontologically depends on an entity (or entities), Ψ, just in case Ψ is a constituent (or are constituents) in a real definition of Φ.[11]

In what follows, I will use the phrase, "*essential dependence*," to stand for the dependence relation defined in (ODD).

A real definition, I will assume for present purposes, has at least the following features. It is expressed by a statement containing a noun-phrase standing for Φ, the entity to be defined (i.e., the *definiendum*), together with a noun phrase standing for Ψ, the entity or entities in terms of which Φ is to be defined (i.e., the *definiens*). Moreover, these two expressions are connected by a relational term of some kind which stands for the definitional relation holding between the definiendum and the definiens in a real definition. A common way of formulating a real definition in English is by way of the "To be Φ is to be Ψ" or the "For something to be Φ is for it to be Ψ" construction. To illustrate, the Aristotelian real definition for human beings can be stated as follows: "To be a human being is to be a rational animal" or "For something to be a human being is for it to be a rational animal." Here, the phrase "a human being," which is embedded in the "To be . . ." construction occurring on the left-hand side of the

---

[10] In fact, it would be wise, I think, for a proponent of a non-modal conception of essences, such as Fine's, to draw a firm distinction between essence (non-propositionally construed) and real definition (propositionally construed). For it is difficult to see how essences could really do the requisite work of *grounding* the derivative necessary (but non-essential) features of objects in any interesting sense if they are conceived of along quasi-linguistic lines. I will not attempt to defend this claim here, since such a project would exceed the confines of the present context; but see Koslicki forthcoming for further exploration of these issues.

[11] The formulation of (ODD) in the text contains "*a* real definition," rather than "*the* real definition," since I want to leave it open for the time being whether an entity can have more than one real definition. This possibility would obtain if two different propositions (or collections of propositions) could be equally explanatory of the essential nature of the entity in question.

definitional relation stands for the entity, Φ, to be defined, i.e., the species, human being. The phrase, "a rational animal," which is embedded in the "to be ___" construction occurring on the right-hand side of the definitional relation stands for the entities, Ψ, which are doing the defining, i.e., the genus, animal, and the differentiating feature, rationality, which distinguishes the particular species in question from all other species that fall under the same genus.

A real definition, if successful, must at least entail an identity: that is, the two noun phrases flanking the relational expression in a statement expressing a real definition must be at least extensionally equivalent. Assuming that identity-statements, if true, are necessarily true, the two noun phrases flanking the relational expression are not only contingently, but necessarily, extensionally equivalent. And yet a statement expressing a real definition must also accomplish more than simply to offer two different ways of singling out the same entity or entities, since the definiens must also be explanatory of the essential nature of the definiendum. Thus, I take it, a pure identity-statement, such as "Hesperus is Phosphorus," could not be transformed into a good candidate ("To be Hesperus is to be Phosphorus") for a statement expressing a real definition of the planet, Venus, since we do not learn anything about what it is to be this particular planet, Venus, by learning that the two names, "Hesperus" and "Phosphorus," are used to pick out the single object in question. Nor is the fact that Venus appears at a certain position in the evening sky and at a certain position in the morning sky explanatory of the essential nature of Venus.

The approach to definition at work here is perhaps somewhat unfamiliar to those who have been reared on the conception of definition to which Quine famously objects in his critique of the analytic/synthetic distinction (see, e.g., Quine 1948, 1951a). First, as noted above, in contrast to the notion operative in Quine's critique, we are currently assuming a real, as opposed to a nominal, conception of definition: in a real definition, the definiendum as well as the definiens are entities, while in a nominal definition they are expressions belonging to a particular language or concepts belonging to a particular conceptual system. Thus, I assume for example that Aristotle's attempt in the *Posterior Analytics* at defining thunder as a kind of noise in the clouds caused by the extinction of fire is directed at arriving at a scientific understanding of the natural phenomenon, thunder, itself, rather than at the elucidation of the meaning of a word of the Greek (or any other) language or a concept belonging to a particular conceptual system.

Secondly, and relatedly, the present approach does not presuppose that real definitions are in general based on a priori connections between concepts or the meanings of words. For example, we might consider "To be water is to be a chemical substance composed (predominantly) of H_2O-molecules" to be a perfectly good example of a statement expressing a real definition of the chemical substance in question, but the connections between the substance, water, and its molecular and atomic constituents are presumably a posteriori, at least assuming that a Kripke/Putnam-style approach to natural kinds and the semantics of natural kind terms is in its basic outline correct.

Thirdly, according to the approach taken here, one does not automatically succeed in giving a real definition for a certain entity by stating necessary and sufficient conditions which single out the entity or entities in question and distinguish them from all other relevant entities in the vicinity. An example may help to illustrate this point: the conditions, being the successor of the successor of the number 0 and being the predecessor of the number 3, both do the job we expect necessary and sufficient conditions to do, i.e., they single out the number 2 and differentiate it from a certain contrast-class (i.e., the rest of the natural numbers). However, one might reasonably adopt the attitude that the first condition (being the successor of the successor of the number 0) is more explanatory of the essential nature of the number 2 than the second condition (being the predecessor of the number 3), since the first mirrors more closely than the second does the method by which the number 2 is constructed from a basic entity, the number 0, together with a relation that is taken as primitive, i.e., the successor relation.[12]

Similarly, the case involving Socrates and Socrates' singleton set also illustrates the point that real definitions, on the current conception, must accomplish more than to specify necessary and sufficient conditions that single out and delineate the entity to be defined from the rest. For if it is part of the essence of Socrates' singleton set that it has Socrates as its sole member, but not part of the essence of Socrates that he is the sole member of Socrates' singleton set, then we would expect a real definition of Socrates' singleton set to include in its statement of what it is to be the set in question that it has Socrates as its sole member, whereas a real definition of Socrates should not include in its statement of what it is to be Socrates that he is the sole member of Socrates' singleton set. However, if all we require from real definitions is that they provide necessary and sufficient conditions that single out and delineate the entity in question

---

[12] Thanks to Graeme Forbes for helpful discussion of this point (as well as many others relevant to this project).

from some relevant contrast class, then both of the conditions just cited (i.e., being the set that has Socrates as its sole member and being the entity that is the sole member of Socrates' singleton set) would do equally well in accomplishing their intended task in providing real definitions, respectively, for the entities in question, i.e., Socrates' singleton set and Socrates.[13]

A statement that purports to express a real definition thus is successful, according to the current approach, if it not only uniquely identifies and delineates the entity to be defined, but also states what it is to be the entity in question, i.e., if it is explanatory of the essential nature of the definiendum. In a statement of the form, "To be Φ is to be Ψ," which purports to express a real definition, the same thing is being referred to on either side of the definitional relation, by the phrases "to be Φ" and "to be Ψ," i.e., the essence of the entity to be defined. But in order for a real definition to accomplish its intended job of being explanatory of the essential nature of the entity to be defined, the phrase, "to be Ψ," occurring on the right-hand side of the definitional relation must present a distinct way of referring to the essence of the entity to be defined, Φ; otherwise, no illumination would have been achieved by the alleged real definition in question. Thus, in the statement, "To be a human being is to be a human being," the essence of the entity to be defined (i.e., the species, human being) is being referred to on both sides of the definitional relation; but we have not thereby accomplished a real definition of the

---

[13] Relatedly, a conception of real definition according to which such propositions or collections of propositions must do more than simply provide necessary and sufficient conditions that single out and differentiate the entity to be defined from some intended contrast class also pits us against a venerable tradition within contemporary metaphysics which has enjoyed popularity among those who take a modal approach to essence (see for example Plantinga 1974, p. 60; Forbes 1985, pp. 146–8; Mackie 2006, p. 19; et al.). According to the approach in question, the primary job of essences is to *individuate* the entities whose essences they are across worlds and times at which these entities exist. Such a primarily individuative conception of essence also seems to be at work in E. J. Lowe's approach to ontological dependence (cf., Lowe 1994, 1998, 2005b, 2006a). But, as is already brought out by the cases discussed above (i.e., the relation between the number 0 and the rest of the natural numbers as well as the relation between Socrates and Socrates' singleton set), such a modally inspired and primarily individuative conception of essence and real definition, not surprisingly, will turn out to be not sufficiently fine-grained for our present purposes: for there are many ways in which an entity can be located in every world and at every time at which it exists which cannot plausibly be taken to be explanatory of what it is to be the entity in question. The phrase, "the instance of redness of shade S_n I am actually currently thinking about," for example, arguably uniquely picks out a particular redness trope at every time and in every world in which it exists; but the condition in question should not strike us as being explanatory of the essential nature of the redness trope in question. (This example is a modified version of one which is discussed in Wedgwood 2007, pp. 139ff, with a similar aim.) Thus, essences, on the current picture, must do more than individuate the entities whose essences they are; and real definitions must do more than state conditions which uniquely identify and delineate the entities under consideration at every time and in every world in which they exist.

entity to be defined, since the statement in question does not succeed in stating a condition that is explanatory of the essential nature of, or what it is to be, a human being. In order for a statement that purports to express a real definition to do so, the phrase, "to be Ψ," occurring on the right-hand side of the definitional relation, must reveal the essence of the entity, Φ, in a way in which the phrase, "to be Φ," occurring on the left-hand side of the definitional relation, does not. We will investigate the question of how such a feat might be accomplished in more detail in the next section.

7.5

In light of these observations concerning the notion of real definition, we can now return to our initial list of examples in (i)–(viii) and evaluate these putative cases of ontological dependence in accordance with the schema given in (ODD). When approached through the lense of (ODD), these cases are analyzed as follows:

(i′)   Smiles ontologically depend on mouths: mouths are constituents in real definitions of smiles.

(ii′)   Sets ontologically depend on their members: the members of sets are constituents in real definitions of sets.

(iii′)   Events/states of affairs ontologically depend on their participants: the participants in events/states of affairs are constituents in real definitions of events/states of affairs.

(iv′)   Chemical substances ontologically depend on their molecular/atomic constituents: the molecular/atomic constituents of chemical substances are constituents in real definitions of chemical substances.

(v′)   Tropes ontologically depend on their "bearers": the "bearers" of tropes are constituents in real definitions of tropes.

(vi′)   Aristotelian universals ontologically depend on their "bearers": the "bearers" of Aristotelian universals are constituents in real definitions of Aristotelian universals.

(vii′)   Holes ontologically depend on their "hosts": the "hosts" of holes are constituents in real definitions of holes.

(viii′)   Boundaries ontologically depend on their "hosts": the "hosts" of boundaries are constituents in real definitions of boundaries.

There are of course no uncontroversial examples of real definitions in philosophy; but, for the sake of concreteness, it helps to have before us some potential candidates in order to illustrate how one might approach the account given in (i′)–(viii′) of the putative dependence relations in question. My concern at present is not so much with the substantive content of these candidate real definitions, but with certain general questions concerning the relation between ontological dependence and real definition which need to be sorted out. Among other things, (i′)–(viii′) in their present formulations, using plural rather than singular expressions, leave open the question of whether real definitions are best construed as applying to entities at the level of kinds or to entities at the level of individuals. (In what follows, I use the terms, "individual" and "particular" interchangeably.) Understood in the former way, as applying to entities at the level of kinds (indicated below by the subscript "$_K$"), rather than to entities at the level of individuals, we can use the following as potential candidates for statements expressing real definitions of the entities at hand:

(SMILE$_K$) To be a smile is to be a state resulting from an activity of smiling engaged in by a mouth.

(SET$_K$) To be a set is to be a collection of members that satisfies the axioms of set theory.[14]

(LIGHTNING$_K$) To be an occurrence of lightning is to be an event in which energy is discharged by electrons (in a certain way).

(WATER$_K$) To be a quantity of water is to be a quantity of a chemical substance composed (predominantly) of H_2O-molecules.[15]

(TROPE$_K$) To be a trope is to be a property instance had by some object.

[14] Here, the phrase "that satisfies the axioms of set theory" is meant to be an abbreviation of the actual content of the axioms in question which spell out in detail what kind of collection a set-theoretic collection is.

[15] (LIGHTNING$_K$) and (WATER$_K$) contain occurrences of nouns that are standardly used as mass terms, i.e., "lightning" and "water." I have added the phrases, "occurrence of" and "quantity of," simply to allow me to use singular count noun phrases (i.e., "an occurrence of lightning" and "a quantity of water") or plural count noun phrases (i.e., "occurrences of lightning" or "quantities of water"), so that these cases may be treated in a manner analogous to the remaining cases in (i)–(viii). Just as in these other cases, the statements in question are to be understood as concerning the kind of entity, lightning or water, in question, rather than as statements concerning particular instances of the kind in question.

(UNIVERSAL$_K$)   To be an Aristotelian universal is to be a property present in all objects that are alike in a certain respect.

(HOLE$_K$)   To be a hole is to be an opening present in an object.

(BOUNDARY$_K$)   To be a boundary is to be a demarcation of the interior of an object from its exterior.

The statements in (SMILE$_K$)–(BOUNDARY$_K$) all purport to state what it is to be a certain kind of entity (i.e., a smile, a set, an occurrence of lightning, etc.) in general.[16] But even if we are sympathetic to the idea that (ODD) yields a serviceable general schema by which to approach these putative cases of ontological dependence, it is still possible to dig deeper in our diagnosis of *why* the entities whose real definitions are purportedly stated above are ontologically dependent on the entities which allegedly feature in these real definitions. In what follows, I will suggest that our present range of data as presented by (i)–(viii) calls for the recognition of at least two more fine-grained species of essential dependence, which I will refer to below as "constituent dependence" and "feature dependence."

The first variety of ontological dependence, constituent dependence, has some prima facie plausibility with respect to (SET$_K$), (LIGHTNING$_K$), and (WATER$_K$). In these cases, it is natural to think that the entities that are being defined (i.e., sets, quantities of water, and occurrences of lightning) are complex, in the sense that they have a certain constituent structure, and that the entities in terms of which they are being defined (i.e., members of sets, H_2O-molecules, and electrons) figure as constituents in these complex entities themselves, according to some notion of constituency, and not merely in their real definitions. To characterize cases in which the constituent structure of the real definition in this way mirrors the constituent structure of the complex entity that is being defined, I will employ the term, "*essential constituent*," defined as follows:

(EC) *Essential Constituency:*
   An entity, Ψ, is an *essential constituent* of an entity, Φ, just in case (i) Ψ is a constituent in a real definition of Φ; and (ii) Ψ is also a constituent of Φ itself.

---

[16] It is a difficult and interesting question whether real definitions can be given for individuals as well, what form such real definitions for individuals take, and how they are related to the kind-level statements just listed. Since these issues are well worth exploring in detail, I will reserve discussion of them for a different occasion and confine my attention in what follows to real definitions as applying to entities at the level of kinds.

We can now apply (EC) to the first group of cases in the following way:

(SET$_C$) A set is a complex entity of a certain sort (i.e., a certain kind of collection) which contains its members as essential constituents.

(LIGHTNING$_C$) An occurrence of lightning is a complex entity of a certain sort (i.e., a certain kind of physical event) which contains electrons as essential constituents.

(WATER$_C$) A quantity of water is a complex entity of a certain sort (i.e., a quantity of a certain kind of chemical substance) which contains H_2O-molecules as essential constituents.

When interpreting (SET$_C$)–(WATER$_C$), we should bear in mind the following three caveats. First, different notions of constituency will be appropriate in different cases: thus, the sense in which an entity is a constituent of a proposition, operative in (ODD), is presumably quite different from the sense in which for example a set has its members as constituents or the sense in which quantities of water contain H_2O-molecules as constituents.[17] Secondly, we are currently only dealing with real definitions as applying to entities at the level of kinds; thus, I am in the present context leaving open for example the question of whether a particular occurrence of lightning is essentially tied to the *very* electrons which are in fact involved in this event, or whether a particular quantity of water is essentially tied to the *very* H_2O-molecules or the *very* hydrogen and oxygen atoms of which it is in fact composed. Only the respective kind-level claims are directly relevant for our present purposes, i.e., that it is essential to occurrences of lightning in general that electrons figure in them as constituents (according to some notion of constituency) and that it is essential to quantities of water in general that they contain H_2O-molecules as constituents (according to some notion of constituency).[18]

[17] Though tempting, "constituency" cannot be construed along mereological lines across the board. For example, in the case of sets, although the subset relation is formally analogous to the parthood relation of classical mereology, it is not plausible to think of the members of a set as parts of the set. Among other things, parthood is generally taken to be a transitive relation; but set-membership is not a transitive relation, since a member of a member of a set, S, need not itself be a member of S.

[18] The analogous claims for sets is much less controversial. For not only is it a commonly accepted fact about (non-empty) sets in general that they are certain kinds of collections (i.e., set-theoretic collections) of their members; it is also a commonly accepted fact about particular sets that they are essentially tied to the *very* members of which they are in fact composed. But this easy transition

Thirdly, (SET$_C$), (LIGHTNING$_C$), and (WATER$_C$) are not to be read as attempting to capture the full content of (SET$_K$), (LIGHT-NING$_K$), and (WATER$_K$). In the case of sets, in order to indicate what it is for a collection to be a set, it must also be said what sort of collection a set-theoretic collection is, i.e., that it is one which has the characteristics detailed by a particular axiom system for set theory. For the very same objects that are members of a given set might also function as essential constituents of other non-set-theoretic collections, e.g., committees or mereological sums, which do not behave in accordance with the axioms of set theory. In the case of lightning, in order to indicate what it is for an event to be an occurrence of lightning, it is not enough to state that certain sorts of objects (i.e., electrons) are essential constituents of such an event; it must also be said (depending on the particular conception of events under consideration) for example what sorts of changes these essential constituents must undergo in order for a physical event to count as an occurrence of lightning, i.e., that energy must be discharged by the electrons that are essential constituents of such events in the particular way that is characteristic of occurrences of lightning. In the case of water, to say what it is for a chemical substance to be water, it is also important for example to indicate that its atomic constituents (hydrogen and oxygen atoms) must be arranged in the form of H_2O-molecules. The molecular arrangement of these atomic constituents itself plays a crucial role in an account of the chemical properties and behavior that are characteristic of water, as contrasted with other chemical substances.

We can now formulate a more fine-grained variety of essential dependence which seems to work well for this first group of cases as follows:

(CD) *Constituent Dependence:*
　　An entity, Φ, is constituent dependent on an entity (or entities), Ψ, just in case Ψ is an essential constituent (or are essential constituents) of Φ.

(CD) is to be read as a species of ontological dependence, as stated in (ODD): in order for an entity, Φ, to be constituent dependent on an entity (or entities), Ψ, it must be the case not only that Ψ is a constituent (or are constituents) in a real definition of Φ, as required by (ODD), but

from claims about the essences of sets in general to claims about the essences of particular sets is peculiar to sets and should not be taken as representative for the whole group of cases exhibiting constituent dependence.

also that Φ itself is a complex entity which includes Ψ among its constituents, according to some notion of constituency.

We may think of cases exhibiting the variety of essential dependence described in (CD), in more vivid terms, as involving entities that have the character of *collections* or *constructions*, i.e., entities that are in some way built up from the constituents on which they are ontologically dependent. Sets for example are collections of a specific sort that are constructed from their members by means of the operation of set-formation. Similarly, quantities of water may be thought of as constructed from their atomic and molecular constituents by means of some building operation (e.g., mereological composition). Finally, those who take events or states of affairs to be ontologically dependent on their participants presumably view these entities as well as resulting from an application of an item-generating operation of some sort which takes these participants as building blocks and yields an event or state of affairs as output. (CD) thus provides one parameter in accordance with which entities that have the character of collections or constructions may be categorized as ontologically dependent and hence perhaps as deserving an ontologically derivative status with respect to such notions as substancehood, fundamentality, basicness, priority, and the like.[19]

It is not obvious, however, that the constituency-driven model of real definition just outlined applies equally well to all of the cases considered above; for it is not always natural to think that constituency in a real definition and constituency in the entity being defined itself go hand in hand in the way suggested by (CD). Plenty of philosophers who subscribe to particular conceptions of tropes, Aristotelian universals, holes, or boundaries view these entities as ontologically dependent on their "bearers" or "hosts" in some way, but not in the way described in (CD), i.e., not as being built up or constructed from their "bearers" or "hosts" as constituents, analogously to the way in which a set is built up or constructed from its members. Such philosophers, I take it, would not find the analogues of (SET_C)–$(WATER_C)$ for tropes, Aristotelian universals, holes, or boundaries congenial to their first-order commitments; rather, if anything, they might in fact favor the negations of these statements, as stated in $(TROPE_{not-C})$–$(BOUNDARY_{not-C})$, over their positive counterparts:

[19] Cases of this first kind, in which the defined entity is complex and the real definition reveals its constituent structure, are also dealt with in Johnston 2006. If my observations in this section of the chapter are correct, however, then we ought to allow that not all real definitions fall into the same mold, i.e., of revealing the constituent structure of a complex entity. The role of operations of construction in ontology is also investigated for example in Fine 1991 and Bennett 2011.

(TROPE$_{not-C}$)   A trope is **not** a complex entity which contains the object in which it is present as an essential constituent.

(UNIVERSAL$_{not-C}$)   An Aristotelian universal is **not** a complex entity which contains the objects in which it is present as essential constituents.

(HOLE$_{not-C}$)   A hole is **not** a complex entity which contains the object in which it is present as essential constituent.

(BOUNDARY$_{not-C}$)   A boundary is **not** a complex entity which contains the object in which it is present as an essential constituent.[20]

To illustrate, according to (TROPE$_{not-C}$)–(BOUNDARY$_{not-C}$), we ought not to think of a piece of Emmentaler cheese for example as *being* a constituent of the holes it contains or to think of a football field as *being* a constituent of the boundary which demarcates its interior from its exterior. We may point out in favor of these observations that a piece of Emmentaler cheese after all is *bigger* than, and hence occupies regions of space time not occupied by, the holes it contains; similarly, a football field is *bigger* than, and hence occupies regions of space time not occupied by, its boundary, if boundaries are even spatially extended at all.

Trope-theorists, if anything, tend to think that the constituency relation between a trope and its "bearer," if it is applicable to this case at all,

---

[20] This is not to say that *all* philosophers who subscribe to particular first-order conceptions of the entities under discussion would prefer (TROPE$_{not-C}$)–(BOUNDARY$_{not-C}$) over their positive counterparts. One might hold for example that tropes and events belong to a single ontological category (see for example Bennett 1988). But this thesis could be interpreted in one of two ways. First, the identification of events with tropes (or tropes with events) could lead one to believe that tropes therefore should be taken to be complex entities that have constituents, if one is also of the opinion that events are complex entities that have constituents. Alternatively, one could also take the attitude that events therefore *lack* a constituent structure, because tropes do and events are to be identified with tropes. A philosopher who adopts the second type of view would not take issue with (TROPE$_{not-C}$), but instead would object to (LIGHTNING$_C$). (For illustrations of the second type of view, see for example Campbell 1990 and Lowe 2006a.) What matters for present purposes is only that either thesis concerning the nature of tropes (and events) commits one to an interesting and controversial position within first-order metaphysics with which other reasonable philosophers may very well disagree. In order to represent a disagreement of this sort as the substantive dispute that it appears to be, however, we must be able to have recourse to an alternative conception of ontological dependence which does not subsume every case of ontological dependence under the same rubric as the relation that holds between a collection or constructed entity and the constituents from which it is constructed.

points in the opposite direction, i.e., that the tomato *has* its redness trope as a constituent, not that the tomato *is* a constituent of its redness trope. Similarly, in the case of Aristotelian universals: perhaps the most significant difference between those who are Aristotelians about universals and those who are Platonists about universals is that Aristotelians seem to want to say that universals are, in some sense, constituents of the particular objects they characterize, while Platonists place universals in a realm separate from that inhabited by the particulars they characterize. According to such a view, then, if the constituency relation is applicable to the case of Aristotelian universals at all, it would again point in the opposite direction compared to what we observe in the case of (SET$_C$)–(WATER$_C$): according to the Aristotelian, it is not the particular red objects, say, that *are* constituents of the universal, redness; rather, the particular red objects, if anything, *have* the universal, redness, as a constituent.

In the case of holes or boundaries, to speak of constituency at all seems a bit of a stretch.[21] For to think of a hole, which after all marks the *absence* of cheese in a piece of Emmentaler cheese, as being a constituent of a piece of cheese would require quite an unusual notion of constituency, to say the least. Similarly, in the case of boundaries: the boundary around a football field indicates where the football field ends and where the surroundings of the football field begin. But that demarcation, which itself may not be spatially extended at all, presumably should not be thought of as still included in the football field; otherwise, the boundary marking the end of the football field would be pushed out a little further beyond what we initially thought of as its boundary.

Since it is controversial to what extent (if at all) the notion of constituency applies to the cases currently under consideration, it is advisable to look for a different, and more neutral, notion in terms of which to formulate our second more fine-grained variety of essential dependence. To this end, I avail myself of the distinction between an object and its *features*:

(TROPE$_F$)   A trope corresponds to a certain feature had by an object.

(UNIVERSAL$_F$) An Aristotelian universal corresponds to a certain feature shared by some objects.

(HOLE$_F$)   A hole corresponds to a certain feature had by an object (i.e., an opening).

---

[21] Though for the case of boundaries see for example Chisholm 1994, p. 505, who offers an account (inspired by Brentano) of boundaries, points, lines, surfaces, and the like according to which these entities do count as constituents of the objects they delineate.

(BOUNDARY$_F$)   A boundary corresponds to a certain feature had by an object (i.e., a demarcation of its interior from its exterior).

I use the intentionally vague expression, "corresponds to," in such a way as to leave room for different positions concerning the question of how exactly we should approach the relation between the entities to be defined (tropes, Aristotelian universals, holes, and boundaries) and the features had by an object when one of these entities is present in it. For example, one might take the relationship indicated by "corresponds to" in these statements to be simply that of identity: a trope for example, on this conception, simply *is* (numerically identical to) a certain feature had by a particular object; and so on. But one might also take the position that the entities to be defined (tropes, Aristotelian universals, holes, and boundaries) are distinct from, though no doubt tightly linked to, the presence of certain features in the objects in which they reside. For example, whenever a hole is present in an object, the object in question has certain spatial features (i.e., is perforated in a certain way); but, according to this second approach, we are nevertheless to distinguish the spatial features had by the objects in question from the holes that are present in them, perhaps because an attempt at an outright identification of holes with certain spatial features of objects faces difficulties. (For discussion, see for example Lewis and Lewis 1970.)[22]

I will state this new species of ontological dependence, which I call "feature dependence," as follows, where the phrase "corresponds to" is to be construed as leaving room for the sorts of possibilities indicated above:

(FD) *Feature Dependence:*
    An entity, Φ, is *feature dependent* on an entity (or entities), Ψ, just in case (i) Ψ is a constituent (are constituents) in a real definition of Φ; (ii) and Φ corresponds to a feature of Ψ.[23]

---

[22] A further issue on which we may currently remain neutral is whether the presence of tropes, Aristotelian universals, holes, or boundaries in an object is *explanatorily prior to* the presence of the corresponding features in the object in question; or whether instead the reverse is the case and the corresponding features that are present in these objects are in fact explanatorily prior to the presence of tropes, Aristotelian universals, holes, or boundaries in them. I will only note here that, if the latter were the case, I wonder what purpose is served by being committed to tropes, Aristotelian universals, holes, or boundaries in the first place, if they cannot be appealed to in order to explain the presence of the corresponding features in these objects in which they are present.

[23] The notion of inherence is often used to describe the variety of ontological dependence I am calling "feature dependence," at least in cases in which the features in question are accidental to their "bearers." In his classic paper, "Inherence," G. E. L. Owen uses the term "inherence" as a technical term to apply to cases which, in the view of Aristotle's *Categories*, exhibit the relation, being in a subject, as when we accidentally predicate of a tomato for example that it is red. If features may also be essential to their

We may think of cases exhibiting this variety of essential dependence, in more vivid terms, by availing ourselves of the notion of *abstraction*, without supposing that this notion must be given an explicitly epistemic construal. Thus, a tomato's redness trope for example might be thought of as the result of an application of a process of abstraction of some sort which takes the tomato as its starting point and arrives at its redness trope by in some way blocking out all the other features present in the tomato that are not relevant to its color. And while it is of course possible to stake out a position within first-order metaphysics according to which entities which appear to be abstractions of some sort (e.g., tropes, Aristotelian universals, holes, or boundaries) are in fact best understood as constructions of some sort, such a thesis should be regarded as a highly ambitious, controversial, and substantive commitment, and not as one that is either trivially true (perhaps because it straightforwardly follows from a definition) or trivially false (perhaps because its contradiction straightforwardly follows from a definition).[24]

The one remaining case which has yet to be considered is that of smiles. Smiles are tricky entities and, depending on how one conceives of them, they could in principle be assimilated to either of the two paradigms of ontological dependence I have just distinguished, constituent dependence or feature dependence. One way of thinking of smiles would be to regard them as amenable to the constituency-driven model of ontological dependence, perhaps because they are viewed as instances of the category of events or states of affairs, e.g., as comparable to lightning or heat. According to this conception, smiles turn out to be complex entities that are in some way constructed from mouths as their constituents. Alternatively, smiles might also be regarded as amenable to the feature-driven conception of real definition and ontological dependence, perhaps because they are viewed as instances of the category of tropes or Aristotelian universals. On this view, smiles are taken to correspond to features (and perhaps constituents) of the objects in which they are present. According to both models, smiles may be thought of as essentially dependent on mouths, in the sense that mouths figure as constituents in real

"bearers," then Aristotle's notion of being said of a subject (i.e., essentially predicating of something, e.g., Socrates, that it belongs to a certain taxonomic category, e.g., the species, human being, or the genus, animal) may also be subsumed under my notion of "feature dependence."

[24] Similar remarks apply to the reverse position, according to which all entities which appear to be constructions of some sort are in fact best understood as abstractions of some sort. Such a position should also be understood as involving a substantive commitment over which reasonable philosophers may very well meaningfully disagree.

definitions of smiles. But the first conception of smiles has the consequence that smiles are to be viewed as constructed entities of some sort that *have* mouths as constituents, while the second conception might lead one to think that smiles are abstracted entities which, if anything, *are* constituents of mouths. My aim, for present purposes, is not to adjudicate between these two alternative ways of thinking of the relation between smiles and mouths, the constituency-driven model or the feature-driven model, but only to indicate how the two varieties of ontological dependence just distinguished would lead to quite different ways of conceiving of the relationship between smiles and mouths.[25]

7.6

In conclusion, I began by noting that a certain kind of asymmetric dependence holds between smiles and mouths and other candidate pairs of entities; I called this relation "ontological dependence." A plausible account of ontological dependence is proposed in Fine 1995a, according to which this notion is to be understood in terms of a non-modal and properly constrained notion of essence. According to Fine, an entity, Φ, ontologically depends on an entity (or entities), Ψ, just in case Ψ is a constituent (or are constituents) of the essence, narrowly construed, of Φ. I commented above on the possibility of defining the narrower notion of essence ("constitutive essence") that is needed for this account in terms of a wider one ("consequential essence") and concluded that there is no way around taking either a properly constrained conception of essence or a

---

[25] I do not intend to imply that the two varieties of ontological dependence I distinguish here necessarily exhaust the whole spectrum of relations in the vicinity of ontological dependence that need to be recognized. For one thing, it might turn out to be necessary to recognize further species of ontological dependence, in addition to the ones discussed here. Moreover, it is quite plausible to think that additional relations that are interestingly different from, but also related to, ontological dependence will be needed to give a full account of such notions as substancehood, fundamentality, priority, basicness, non-derivativeness, and the like. For example, several writers (e.g., Correia 2005; Fine 2001, this volume, manuscript; Rosen 2010; Schnieder 2011) have recently focused on a relation they call "grounding" which differs from the relations of ontological dependence I have considered, among other things, in that the relata of the grounding relation are typically taken to be facts or propositions, while the relata of ontological dependence, as I have been construing it, are objects and their characteristics, activities, constituents, and so on. As noted earlier, an Aristotelian non-modal approach to essence also appeals to a grounding relation of some sort in order to explain how the necessary (but non-essential) features of objects are related to basic facts about essences. My only claim for the time being is that, even when we confine ourselves to cases involving relations between objects, their characteristics, activities, constituents, and so on, a distinction between at least two types of ontological dependence is needed; this is of course compatible with there being further relations in the vicinity of what I have been calling ontological dependence which also deserve to be recognized.

properly constrained conception of ontological dependence as basic in an attempt to define the other notion. To make room for a less propositional conception of essence than that assumed by Fine, I urged that we distinguish more firmly between essences, on the one hand, and real definitions, on the other, which state these essences in the form of propositions or collections of propositions.

Even if we are sympathetic to the idea that this approach gives us a serviceable general characterization of ontological dependence along essentialist lines, I have argued above that we nevertheless ought to try to go deeper in our diagnosis of *why*, in a given case, an entity is essentially ontologically dependent on another. In cases of what I have called "constituent dependence" (e.g., the relation between a set and its members), the dependent entity, Φ, is complex and has a certain constituent-structure; and the dependee entity or entities, Ψ, figure not only as constituents in Φ's real definition, but also as constituents in the defined entity, Φ, itself, according to some notion of constituency. We may think of the ontologically dependent entity here as resulting from an application of an operation of *collection* or *construction* of some sort, which takes the constituent entities as building-blocks and constructs the resulting entity from them by means of an item-generation operation of some sort. But this constituency-driven model is not obviously applicable to all cases in which we want to classify an entity as ontologically dependent on another. For, in some cases (e.g., a tomato's redness trope), it may be more natural to think of an entity as essentially dependent on another in the sense of what I have called "feature dependence," according to which the dependent entity corresponds to a feature that is present in a "bearer" or "host." In a case of feature dependence, the ontologically dependent entity may be thought of as the result of an application of a process of *abstraction* of some sort which takes the "bearer" or "host" as its starting point and arrives at the abstracted entity by in some way blocking out all the other features present in this object that are irrelevant to the case at hand. It is useful not to collapse these two varieties of essential dependence into one another, since they yield two potentially very different measures of ontological fundamentality (or substancehood, basicness, primacy, non-derivativeness, priority, and the like). Moreover, reasonably minded philosophers may certainly engage in what appear to be substantive disagreements over which (if either) notion of ontological dependence is appropriate in a given case.

As a number of writers have noted, it is plausible to think that dependence and explanation are related in something like the following way: an explanation, when successful, captures or represents (e.g., by means of an argument or an answer to a "why"-question) an underlying real-world relation of dependence of some sort which obtains among the phenomena cited in the explanation in question. Thus, a successful causal explanation for example gives expression to (linguistically or otherwise) an underlying real-world relation of causal dependence which obtains between events or whatever the preferred relata of the causal relation are.[26] If this connection between explanation and dependence generalizes, then we would expect relations of ontological dependence to give rise to explanations within the realm of ontology, in the sense that a successful ontological explanation captures or gives expression to an underlying real-world relation of ontological dependence of some sort. If my remarks in this chapter are on the right track, then at least some characteristically ontological explanations take the form of real definitions, i.e., propositions that are explanatory of the essential nature of, or what it is to be, a certain kind of entity. Our grasp of such characteristically ontological explanations is thus advanced by developing a deeper and more fine-grained understanding of what may be accomplished by a real definition.[27]

---

[26] For remarks along these lines, see for example Audi forthcoming, manuscript c; Correia 2005; Fine 1995a, 2001, this volume, manuscript; Kim 1994; Lowe 1994, 2005b, 2006a; Rosen 2010; Ruben 1990; Schnieder 2006a, 2011; Strevens 2008.

[27] The connection between ontological dependence and explanation is certainly very suggestive and deserves to be worked out in much more detail. If at the end of the day we want to be left with a substantive notion of ontological dependence (as well as related concepts, such as those of priority, primacy, basicness, non-derivativeness, fundamentality, substancehood, and the like), the type of explanation at work here cannot be viewed as one that is to be understood in primarily subjective, pragmatic, or epistemic terms. Although it is very common these days to think of explanation in this way, other approaches to explanation, which are more conducive to a realist understanding of this notion, are available. For example, one might hold that any explanatory connection between a phenomenon, Ψ, and a phenomenon, Φ, can be traced back to there being a *law* connecting Ψ and Φ. And at least some philosophers who have a relatively easy time hearing the explanatory "because" as a highly pragmatic, subjective, epistemic, and/or context-sensitive connective may perhaps find it more difficult to swallow that what counts as a law should similarly be tailored to interests or other occasion-dependent features. Aristotle's famous doctrine of the four causes or explanatory factors also allows for a realist approach to explanation: matter (material cause), form (formal cause), telos (final cause), and source of change (efficient cause), in Aristotle's view, are real and privileged constituents of the world, even though which of these aspects is of particular importance to us, when we ask a specific "why"-question, may of course vary from occasion to occasion.

CHAPTER 8

Asymmetrical dependence in individuation

E. J. Lowe

Very often, it seems, entities of a certain kind have their identities 'fixed' by *other* entities of different kinds. For example, *events* plausibly have their identities fixed at least partly by their *subjects*. Thus, *which* death a certain death is, is plausibly determined, at least partly, by *whose* death it is: for instance, the identity of Caesar's death is at least partly determined by its being *Caesar's*, as opposed to that of any other living being. I say 'at least partly' because it may well be contended that the *time* of an event is another determinant of its identity. (It might be supposed that, on the assumption that a living being can die only once, the time of Caesar's death is irrelevant to its identity. However, it would be controversial to assume that Caesar could not have died a different death from the death that he actually died, if he could have died at a different time and indeed in a different manner.) Now, of course, it is also plausibly true that Caesar's death couldn't have been the event that it is without its being a *death*: that event is surely no less essentially a *death* than it is essentially *Caesar's*. However, its being a death doesn't help to determine *which* particular event it is, only what *kind* of event it is, whereas its being Caesar's helps to determine *which event of that kind* it is: in other words, it is part of its *individual* essence that it is Caesar's death, but only part of its *general* essence that it is a death. But the case of events is not the simplest that we have to hand, to illustrate the general point that I am trying to make. Similarly, and less controversially, *which* set a certain set is, is clearly determined by – and indeed *solely* by – its *members*. For instance, the set of the intrajovian planets has its identity fixed by the planets Mercury, Venus, Earth, and Mars, which are its sole members. It is they, and they alone, that determine *which* set this particular set is.

Now for some technical terminology which will prove useful later: the entities that fix the identity of a given entity, *x*, may be called the *individuators* of *x*. Individuation – in the metaphysical, as opposed to the cognitive, sense of the term – is, then, a metaphysical determination relation between entities: it is the relation of *identity-dependence*.[1] A principle of individuation for entities of a certain kind K specifies what the individuators of Ks are. Such a principle provides a so-called *trans* world criterion of identity for Ks, not merely an *intra*world criterion – a point that we shall explore in more detail later.

Identity-dependence would appear to be an asymmetrical, or at least an *anti*symmetrical relation, with the implication that no two distinct entities can be *each other's* individuators – even if we can allow, as I believe we should, that some entities are *self*-individuating. This point is related to the fact that circular explanations are inadmissible. For identity-dependence is clearly a species of explanatory relation, in the metaphysical – rather than the merely epistemic – sense of 'explanation'. The identity of a death is *explained*, at least partly, by the identity of its subject. As it may otherwise be put, a death has its identity at least partly 'in virtue of' the identity of its subject – and not the other way around.

However, some so-called 'structuralist' ontologies seem to threaten the contention that two or more entities of a certain kind cannot all fix each other's identities. For instance, it is sometimes suggested that the identities of events can be fixed by *other events* in a causal structure to which they all belong, provided that this structure is suitably asymmetric in form. Similar claims are sometimes made about the identities of *powers*, or more generally about the identities of *properties*. If these suggestions are correct, then it would seem that, in principle, all facts about the identities of entities of any kind may 'supervene' upon relational facts about certain structures to which those entities belong. Hence, no identity fact would be metaphysically basic or foundational. In the present chapter, this line of thought will be challenged and thereby a case be made out for the claim that some entities in any coherent system of ontology must be self-individuating, with these entities ultimately explaining the identities of all other entities in the system.

8.1 CRITERIA OF IDENTITY AND PRINCIPLES OF INDIVIDUATION

Let 'K' denote a putative kind of entities. Suppose, furthermore, that we believe that Ks *exist*, perhaps because we espouse Quine's criterion of ontological commitment – 'To be is to be the value of a bound variable' – and are

---

[1] For more on the distinction between individuation in the metaphysical sense and individuation in the cognitive sense, see Lowe 2003. For more on the notion of identity-dependence, see Lowe 1998, pp. 147–51.

convinced that scientific theories that we believe to be true *quantify over Ks*.[2] Perhaps we shall then also want to espouse Quine's other famous dictum – 'No entity without identity' – and thus accept that we are obliged to offer a *criterion of identity* for *Ks*, on the grounds that no clear sense can be made of certain entities being possible values of our variables of quantification if no principled account can be offered of the identity and distinctness conditions of such entities.[3] A criterion of identity for entities of a kind *K* is supposed to be a principle which specifies the identity (and thereby also the distinctness) conditions of *Ks* in an *informative or non-trivial* way – a principle that can be stated in the following form:

(CI)   If *x* and *y* are entities of kind *K*, then $x = y$ iff *x* and *y* stand to one another in the relation R_K,

where 'R_K' denotes some equivalence relation (other than identity itself) on entities of kind K.[4] It is often assumed that one condition on the adequacy of a criterion of identity is that such a principle should be *non-circular* – not just in the obvious way which is excluded by not allowing R_K to be the relation of *identity*, but also in any more roundabout way. However, this last assumption has been questioned in some quarters: and this is an issue to which I shall return later. It also appears to be assumed by some philosophers that talk about identity criteria is straightforwardly interchangeable with talk about *principles of individuation* – that an 'identity criterion' for *Ks just is*, in other words, a 'principle of individuation' for *Ks*. But, whether or not this charge can be made to stick and doesn't rest merely on differences in terminology, the assumption in question is one that I certainly want to challenge.

Here is how I would distinguish between the two kinds of principle. Criteria of identity concern 'identity' conceived as a *relation* – the relation that logicians standardly represent by means of the *equality sign*, '='. Hence, it is such criteria that are required in order to put on a firm footing statements of *number* concerning entities of any kind. On the other hand, principles of individuation concern 'identity' understood in

---

[2] See Quine 1969b. I do not mean to imply that I am convinced by this criterion myself.
[3] See Quine 1969c. I say 'perhaps' because, as I have emphasized elsewhere, we should not lightly assume that there can be determinate facts about identity and distinctness only in the case of entities for which an informative criterion of identity can in principle be supplied: see Lowe 2009, p. 23. However, this is a complication that I shall set aside for present purposes as it plausibly has no bearing on the cases that I shall be discussing.
[4] See Lowe 1989a.

the sense of *individual essence*: what John Locke famously called 'the very being of any thing, whereby it is, what it is'.[5] As I remarked earlier, individuation in the metaphysical (as opposed to the cognitive or epistemic) sense, is a *determination relation between entities*: the relation that obtains between entities x and y when x determines or 'fixes' (or at least *helps* to determine or 'fix') *which* entity of its kind y is.[6] When x stands in such a relation to y, x is the (or at least an) *individuator* of y. Entities that *have* individuators obviously warrant being called 'individuals'. We shouldn't automatically assume that *all* entities are individuals in this sense, however. Nor should we automatically assume that *only individuals* can be provided with criteria of identity. For instance, it is debatable whether sub-atomic particles – such as electrons – are individuals in our sense, even if they can be supplied with a satisfactory criterion of identity. For it seems that there may be circumstances in which it is a determinate fact that we have *two distinct electrons* – orbiting, say, a helium nucleus – and yet there is no determinate fact of the matter as to *which* electron each of these two electrons is.[7] That the electrons are *not identical* is guaranteed by the fact that they differ in their direction of spin, this being required by the Pauli Exclusion Principle. However, it appears that there is no determinate fact of the matter as to *which* of the electrons is spin-up and *which* is spin-down.

8.2 IMPREDICATIVE IDENTITY CRITERIA AND THE CIRCULARITY PROBLEM

Although I said a moment ago that we should not *confuse* identity criteria with principles of individuation, it is also clear that a principle of individuation for *K*s can provide us with a criterion of identity for *K*s, but not necessarily vice versa. Thus, suppose it were correct to hold, as some philosophers do, that token *powers* (or dispositions) are individuated by their *manifestation-types, possessors*, and *times of possession*.[8] For instance, it might be maintained that a particular glass vase's token power of *fragility* is individuated by its manifestation-type, which is *shattering* (or, perhaps,

---

[5] Locke 1975: III, III, 15.

[6] See again Lowe 2003. I say more about individuation in this sense as well as in the *cognitive* sense – the sense in which individuation is the singling out of an entity in thought – in Lowe 2007.

[7] See Lowe 1998, pp. 62–3, and Lowe 2005a. See also French and Krause 2006.

[8] This is George Molnar's view in Molnar 2003, where he says that 'each power gets its identity from its manifestation ... [and] each power has one manifestation' (p. 195). He is, clearly, talking here about power-*types* rather than *token* powers. For the view that a single power-type may have many different manifestation-types, see Heil 2003, p. 83.

shattering under light impact), its possessor, which is *the vase*, and its time of possession, which might well be *the whole lifetime of the vase*, unless the glass is of a kind that could be treated so as to render it non-fragile. (Other token powers, clearly, can be much shorter-lived than this.) Some philosophers, it is true, would want to specify a token power's *stimulation*-type as an additional individuating factor, with *light impact* being the relevant stimulation-type in the case of fragility. But, as implied above, one might instead be able to build this factor into the power's manifestation-type, if need be. In any case, it makes no significant difference to the issues to be discussed below whether or not we regard token powers as being individuated by their stimulation-types *as well as* their manifestation-types, so that to make matters simpler we may assume for present purposes that they are not. It is important, incidentally, that we take *token* powers to be partly individuated by their manifestation-*types*, rather than by their manifestation-*tokens*, because a token power may happen *never* to be actually manifested, as in the case of a fragile glass vase which is never shattered – and in such a case the token power has *no* manifestation-tokens and hence none that could help to individuate it. Moreover, in the case of a token power which can be manifested more than once, such as the elasticity of a piece of rubber, it is an entirely contingent matter *which* and *how many* token manifestations the power displays during the course of its existence. All of this being accepted, we may state the following as a plausible criterion of identity for token powers:[9]

(CIP)   If p and q are token powers, then $p = q$ iff p and q have the same manifestation-type, possessor, and time of possession.

Now, (CIP) *seems* to meet all of the desiderata for an adequate criterion of identity. First, it is *non-trivial*. An important point in this connection is that a power is never identical with its own manifestation-type. This is obviously true of *token* powers, since types cannot be identical with tokens. But it is also true of power-*types*. Clearly, even though a power can be a power to acquire *another power*, a power cannot be a power to acquire *itself*: it cannot *be* its own manifestation-type. Secondly, (CIP) is *formally correct* inasmuch as it specifies the identity conditions of token powers in terms of *an equivalence relation* (distinct from identity itself) on token

---

[9] Evidently, the corresponding criterion of identity for power-*types* would simply be this: if P and Q are power-types, then $P = Q$ iff P and Q have the same manifestation-type. I concentrate for present purposes on *token* powers only because all of the other criteria of identity with which I want to compare (CIP) also concern tokens rather than types, or particulars rather than universals.

powers, namely, the relation of having the same manifestation-type, possessor, and time of possession. However, there is a further issue that needs to be considered here and that is whether (CIP) involves any kind of *circularity* that would serve to vitiate it as a criterion of identity. This turns on the question of whether, as some philosophers believe, *the manifestation-types of all powers are or involve the acquisition of other powers*. For if they do, one may worry that (CIP) is implicitly circular in a vicious way.

An obvious analogy is with the well-known criterion of identity for token *events* once proposed (and later retracted) by Donald Davidson:[10]

(CIE)   If *e* and *f* are token events, then *e* = *f* iff *e* and *f* have the same causes and effects.

The first thing to observe about (CIE) is that it illustrates our earlier point that criteria of identity are not just the same as principles of individuation. It is not plausible to maintain that an event's causes and effects are *essential* features of it and thus qualify as its *individuators*, because it is very plausible to suppose that the same event *could have had* different causes and effects from those that it actually has. Another illustration of this point is provided by the 'Lockean' criterion of identity for *material objects* – 'Lockean' because Locke maintained that no two material objects of the same sort (for example, two *cats* or two *tables*) could exist in the same place at the same time:[11]

(CIM)   If *x* and *y* are material objects, then *x* = *y* iff *x* and *y* are objects of the same sort and have the same spacetime trajectory.

For, once again, it is not plausible to maintain that a material object's spacetime trajectory is an *essential* feature of it: any cat or table, for instance, surely *could have occupied* different spacetime locations from those that it actually occupies. More immediately important for present purposes, however, is the fact that (CIE) appears to be *viciously circular*, at least if one supposes that all causation is *event* causation, for this implies that all of an event's causes and effects are *themselves events* and so subject to (CIE). In short, (CIE) is an *impredicative* identity criterion, because the equivalence relation on events to which it appeals in order to specify the identity conditions of events itself involves *identity relations between events*.

---

[10] See Davidson 1980. He retracts it in his reply to Quine in Lepore and McLaughlin (eds.) 1985. Note that Davidson himself does not explicitly distinguish, as I think we should, between criteria of identity and principles of individuation.

[11] See Locke 1975: II, XXVII, 1.

(Clearly, if all causation is event causation, then to say that events e and f have *the same causes and effects* is just to say that *the same events* are causes of both e and f and that *the same events* are effects of both e and f.)

Now, a number of philosophers, myself included, have observed that impredicativity *as such* need not be fatal in a criterion of identity.[12] Consider, for instance, the *Axiom of Extensionality* of set theory, conceived as providing a criterion of identity for sets. So conceived, it may be formulated thus:

(CIS)   If x and y are sets, then $x = y$ iff x and y have the same members.

But it is not a fatal objection to the status of (CIS) as a perfectly adequate criterion of identity for sets that *sets themselves* may be members of sets, with the implication that – at least in some cases – sets x and y are identical purely in virtue of the fact that *the same sets* are members of both x and y. For, at least in standard set theory, every set has in its transitive closure either certain *non*-sets or at least the (unique) empty set, with the consequence that, by repeated applications of (CIS), we can be guaranteed that this criterion will serve to identify or distinguish *any* two sets x and y, even if they contain other sets in their transitive closure. (CIS) itself, of course, establishes the uniqueness of the empty set, because sets with *no* members trivially have *the same* members. And it might be thought that similar considerations can save (CIE) from vicious circularity. Thus, it may be pointed out that the causal structure of events in a given world could be such that, *as a matter of fact*, each event's place in that structure is uniquely specifiable in causal terms, in a way that makes (CIE) satisfied by those events.[13] In a very simple case, for example, such a structure might contain just three events, e, f, and g, such that e has no causes and has f as its only immediate effect, while g has only f as its immediate cause and has no effects. See Figure 8.1.

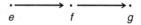

$$e \qquad\qquad f \qquad\qquad g$$

Figure 8.1 A causal structure in which (CIE) is satisfied.

In this structure, there is *just one* event with no causes and exactly two effects (event e), *just one* event with exactly one cause and exactly one effect (event f), and *just one* event with exactly two causes and no effects

[12] See Lowe 1989b.
[13] I discuss this point in Lowe 2002, pp. 226–8. See also Horsten 2010 and Ladyman 2007.

(event *g*). (Here we are assuming, of course, that causation is transitive, but it would make no material difference for present purposes if it were not.) Thus, each event is uniquely specified by its place in the causal structure, in a way that makes (CIE) satisfied by those events: for, given the above causal facts about the structure, it follows that each member of the pairs {*e*, *f*}, {*f*, *g*}, and {*e*, *g*} differs from the other member in respect of at least some of its causes or effects. And who is to say that the *actual* world is not a world whose causal structure similarly provides a unique specification for every event in it, in a way that makes (CIE) satisfied? In which case, would not (CIE) be vindicated?

My answer to this question is that *it would not.* One thing that philosophers who take this line of thought may forget is that a criterion of identity for entities of a kind *K* is supposed to be a *metaphysical* principle, telling us what the identity and distinctness of *Ks consists in*, to use Locke's well-known phrase.[14] As such, it is a principle that should hold for *Ks* in *any* possible world in which *Ks* exist. (CIE) does not meet this requirement, because there are surely worlds in which there are events but in which, owing to a *symmetry* in the causal structure of the world in question, (CIE) *fails to determine*, with respect to every pair of events in that world, whether or not they are identical. See, for example, Figure 8.2, in which events *g* and *h* are distinct but (CIE) is incapable of distinguishing them, because they both have the same causes (*e* and *f*) and effects (none).

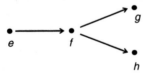

Figure 8.2 A causal structure in which (CIE) is not satisfied.

Other examples are easy to construct. Perhaps there are possible worlds in which some events are *causally isolated* from one another. If there are such worlds, as seems perfectly conceivable, then (CIE) clearly fails in, for instance, a world in which there are just *six* events, each belonging to just one of two three-event structures of the form depicted in Figure 8.1. See Figure 8.3. Such a world is symmetrical in the relevant sense, even though each of these three-event structures is asymmetrical. In such a world, (CIE) fails to determine to *which* of the two exactly similar

---

[14] Locke 1975: II, XXVII, 9.

asymmetrical event-structures a given event belongs. For example, it fails to distinguish between *g* and *j* in Figure 8.3.[15]

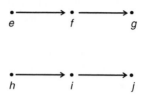

Figure 8.3 Another causal structure in which (CIE) is not satisfied.

It may well be the case that, in a certain world – perhaps even the actual world – a certain proposition of the *form* (CI) happens to be made true by the fact that a unique place within a certain structure is occupied by *every entity* of a certain kind *K* in that world: but we cannot conclude simply from this that the proposition in question qualifies as a bone fide *criterion of identity* for *K*s in that world. We should not be misled in this matter by the set-theoretical example discussed earlier: for, of course, given the correctness of standard set theory, (CIS) serves to determine, with respect to every pair of sets *in any world whatever*, whether or not they are identical. (CIE), by contrast, only does the same for events in *some* worlds – and that is not good enough for it to qualify as a genuine criterion of identity for events. For it doesn't serve to tell us what the identity and distinctness of events, considered purely as such, *consists in.* This cannot be supposed to depend on contingent features of just some worlds in which events exist, since it is a fact about the very nature of events.

It will be seen, now, to what conclusion we are driven with regard to the question of the identity and individuation of token *powers*. Suppose it is maintained, as mentioned earlier, that the manifestation-types of all powers *either are or involve the acquisition of other powers*: this is what the doctrine that all properties are 'pure' powers contends, because on this view there are no *non*-power properties (no purely 'categorical' or purely 'qualitative' properties) for the manifestation-types of some powers to be. It might still be thought that this fact would not necessarily vitiate a criterion of identity for powers framed in terms of their manifestation-types, such as (CIP) above. For it might be supposed, analogously with the case of (CIE), that the *power-structure* of a world could be such that every power in it occupies a unique structural position with respect to all

[15] I am indebted to Kit Fine for suggesting this example in discussion.

other powers in that world.[16] There might be a kind of circularity involved, in that the identity or distinctness of every pair of powers in that world turns on the identity or distinctness of *other* pairs of powers in that world – but not, it may be urged, a *vicious* one. (Note that it is not crucial here whether we are right to assume that a single power has only *one* manifestation-type, since the same issues arise on the assumption that it can have more than one.) So, the thought might be that, whatever may be the case in *some* possible worlds, at least in the *actual* world (CIP) might turn out to be an adequate criterion of identity for powers, even though the equivalence relation on powers to which (CIP) appeals itself involves *identity relations between powers*, rendering (CIP) *impredicative* like (CIS) and (CIE). Of course, my objection to this suggestion is, as with the case of (CIE), that an adequate criterion of identity for entities of any kind *K* must be satisfied by *K*s in *any* world in which *K*s exist. And while (CIS) passes this test, (CIP) does not, if the supposition now at issue is correct, any more than (CIE) does – this supposition being, recall, that the manifestation-types of all powers either are or involve the acquisition of other powers. For, surely, we cannot just rule out a priori the existence of possible worlds with *symmetrical* power-structures.

8.3 TRANSWORLD VERSUS INTRAWORLD CRITERIA OF IDENTITY

At this point, it is worth returning to another important matter discussed earlier: the difference between *criteria of identity* and *principles of individuation*. I remarked that a criterion of identity may be derived from a principle of individuation, but not necessarily vice versa. A significant difference between (CIP) and (CIS), on the one hand, and (CIE) on the other is that the former derive from principles of individuation but the latter does not. One way to think of this difference is as follows: (CIP) and (CIS) both have the status of putative *transworld* identity criteria, but (CIE) has only the status of a putative *intraworld* identity criterion. In advancing (CIE), Davidson had no intention of implying that every event must have the same causes and effects *in every possible world in which it exists* – just that any 'two' events existing in a certain possible world which have the same causes and effects *in that world* are, in virtue of that fact, *identical* events, that is, that no two

---

[16] See Bird 2007a.

distinct events can be such that there is *some* possible world in which they have the same causes and effects.[17] By contrast, because (CIS) derives from the principle of individuation of sets – which is that they are individuated by *their members* – it *does* serve as a transworld identity criterion for sets: any set must indeed have the same members in every possible world in which it exists, for *which* set it is, is entirely determined by *which* things are its members. Likewise, then, because (CIP) derives from the putative principle of individuation of powers, it should serve as a putative transworld criterion of identity for powers: if (CIP) is correct, any token power must have the same manifestation-type, possessor, and time of possession *in every possible world in which it exists.* In this connection, it is important not to confuse the point that some criteria of identity, such as (CIS), are *transworld* criteria of identity with the point that any adequate criterion of identity for Ks must be *satisfied in every possible world in which Ks exist.* The latter point applies equally both to criteria like (CIS), which are transworld criteria, and to criteria like (CIE), which purports only to be an intraworld criterion. The mere fact that (CIE) purports only to be an intraworld criterion does not exempt it from the requirement of being satisfied in every possible world in which events exist – a requirement which, as we have seen, it fails to meet.

Now, if a criterion of identity qualifies as a transworld criterion, because it derives from a principle of individuation, then we know that it must be satisfied in *every* possible world if it is satisfied in *any*. A criterion of identity, *C*, cannot be satisfied *across* certain possible worlds unless it is also satisfied *within* all of those worlds. To deny this commits one to the absurdity of having to allow that there might be 'two' entities, *x* and *y*, both of which exist in each of two worlds, *w* and *v*, such that, according to *C*, *x* in *w* is identical with *y* in *v* and yet *C does not determine* whether or not *x* in *v* is identical with *y* in *v*. If *C* determines that *x* in *w* is identical with *y* in *v*, then a fortiori it determines that *x* in *v* is identical with *y* in *v*. For, if *C* is satisfied *across w* and *v*, then it must, obviously, determine that *x* in *v* is identical with *x* in *w* – whence, by the transitivity of identity, it

---

[17] Some philosophers do, of course, appear to believe that every event has all of its causes and effects essentially, because they hold that causal necessity is nothing other than metaphysical necessity: see, for example, Shoemaker 1998. But it is evident that this view is not compatible with an endorsement of (CIE), given the metaphysical possibility of causal structures such as that depicted in Figure 8.2. For, given the latter possibility, (CIE) delivers the false verdict that *distinct* events, such as *g* and *h* in Figure 8.2, are *identical*, in virtue of having the same causes and effects in the world there depicted (and thus, indeed, in *every* world, according to this view).

determines that x in v is identical with y in v. See Figure 8.4, where an arrow from one term to another signifies that the designation of the first term is identical with the designation of the second term.

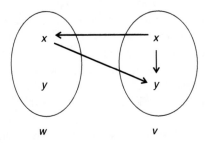

Figure 8.4 Transworld satisfaction entails intraworld satisfaction.

Thus, for example, it was possible for Davidson's putative criterion of identity for events, (CIE), to turn out to be satisfied in *some* possible worlds but *not* in others: but this was because it was only supposed to qualify as an *intra*world criterion.

The foregoing fact gives us an additional reason for contending that (CIP) is inadequate as a criterion of identity for token powers if it fails to be satisfied even in just *one* possible world, whether or not that world is the actual world. For (CIP), like (CIS), is derived from a principle of individuation and so should be satisfied in *every* possible world in which powers exist, if it is satisfied in *any*. Adherents of (CIP) cannot therefore allow there to be *any* possible world in which it is not satisfied – even setting aside my own earlier contention that all adequate criteria of identity, including merely *intra*world criteria, ought, in any case, to be satisfied in every possible world in which entities of the kinds that they concern exist. But it appears that this is what they *must* allow, if they think that the manifestation-types of powers always are or involve the acquisition of *other powers*. For then it seems that they must allow that there are worlds containing powers in which the power-structure is such that (CIP) does *not* serve to identify a unique position in that structure for every power, on account of some kind of symmetry in the structure. If powers really are *individuals*, then there cannot be *any* world in which there are *unindividuated* powers. But if powers are always individuated at least in part by *other powers*, then there can be no guarantee that all of the powers in a possible world are fully individuated, because 'two' powers may stand in the same power-structure relations to all 'other' powers, such that nothing in that structure determines *which* power either of these powers is. Once again, it surely will not do to proclaim as an a priori truth that the power-structure of any possible world *must* exhibit asymmetries which permit the assignment of each power in that world to a unique position in the structure. (Essentially the same objection may be raised against any philosopher who – unlike Davidson himself – maintains that (CIE) qualifies as a *trans*world criterion of identity. It simply isn't credible to suppose that causal structures like that of Figure 8.2 are *metaphysically impossible* – and yet this is what must be maintained by any philosopher who holds that (CIE) derives from the *principle of individuation* of events.)

I conclude that those philosophers who think that only a benign circularity need be involved in the claim that all powers are at least in part individuated *by other powers* are deceiving themselves. First, they are failing to distinguish properly between criteria of identity and principles of individuation. Second, they are failing to recognize that even those criteria of identity, such as (CIE) and (CIM), which purport only to function as *intraworld* criteria, still need to be *satisfied* in every possible world in which entities of the kinds that they concern exist – which is why (CIE) itself turns out to be inadequate.

8.4 THE DOCTRINE OF 'PURE' POWERS

Of course, I haven't so far discussed *why it is* that certain philosophers are tempted to suppose that the manifestation-type of any power always is or involves the acquisition of other powers, beyond saying that this is an implication of the doctrine that all properties are 'pure' powers. But, clearly, it is only this supposition that has raised a dispute about the adequacy of (CIP), or something very close to it, as a criterion of identity for token powers. (It might be contended, as remarked above, that at least some token powers may have *more than one* manifestation-type, contrary to what (CIP) implies: but that would not materially affect the current dispute.) Suppose, however, that it were to turn out that power-types and their manifestation-types are always organized into well-founded *hierarchies* of descending orders, such that each power-type of order n is the first of a sequence of power-types of successively lower orders, with each power-type in the sequence apart from the last having as its manifestation-type a power-type in the sequence of the *next* lower order, terminating in a *first*-order power-type whose manifestation-type is a *non*-power property. Then, in that case, (CIP) would be guaranteed to be free of vicious circularity, for the same sort of reason that (CIS) is according to standard set theory, where the Axiom of Foundation provides the corresponding guarantee. But why should any philosopher doubt that precisely this *can* and indeed *must* be the case?

Some do, it seems, because they think that the very notion of a '*non-power* property' of a concrete object makes no sense because – they suppose – such a property would have to be causally *perfectly inert*. For this sort of reason, some philosophers contend that there are really no purely 'categorical' or 'qualitative' properties – *only* power properties, even if some of them may also be in some way 'qualitative' or have a 'qualitative aspect'.[18] For instance, they urge that even a *shape* property, such as sphericity, cannot be coherently thought of as being a pure non-power property, because that, they think, would imply that sphericity made no difference whatever to a spherical object's causal behaviour – in which case we couldn't even *tell* whether or not an object was spherical, because perception of an object's properties requires some sort of causal interaction between the perceiver and the object. Such philosophers typically urge that part of what it is *to be* a spherical object – part of the *essence* of sphericity – consists in the powers that an object has in virtue of its sphericity, such as the power to roll down an inclined plane or to cast a circular shadow when it is illuminated from a suitable angle or, indeed, to *look* spherical to a normally sighted person. For my own part, I am by no means convinced by such reasoning, but since I have expressed my dissatisfaction with it in some detail elsewhere, I shall not say much more about it here.[19] I shall simply voice my considered opinion that a geometrical property such as sphericity is not *itself* a kind of power, even if, in virtue of possessing it along with certain other appropriate properties, an object can possess a certain power, such as the power to roll down an inclined plane, by observing the manifestation of which we can acquire evidence of the object's sphericity. The manifestation of a power to roll is *rolling* and by *observing* an object to roll we can acquire evidence about its *shape*. Rolling, however, is not *itself* a power, in any sense that I can understand, for I cannot understand what its 'manifestation' would be. It is just a kind of *activity*. So, amongst *non*-power properties, I would include *geometrical properties* such as

---

[18] Compare Heil 2003, pp. 76–8 and 111–13, although he emphatically eschews all talk of 'aspects' in this connection. Molnar, on the other hand, does countenance the existence of some non-power properties – but very few, and he doesn't include properties of shape: see Molnar 2003, p. 160. For further discussion of Molnar's theory, see Lowe 2006a, pp. 136–40. For further discussion of Heil's theory, see Lowe 2006b.

[19] See again Lowe 2006b. See also Lowe 2010, in which the nature of powers is discussed in far more detail than it is here.

sphericity and *activities*, such as rolling. And there may well be other types of non-power properties in addition to these.

My conclusion thus far, then, is that (CIP) *can* in principle function as a perfectly adequate criterion of identity for powers, and is *not* threatened by vicious circularity, precisely and only because *not* all powers have as their manifestation-types other powers. In order for (CIP) to be adequate, there are *and must be* first-order powers whose manifestation-types are *non*-power properties (such as *rolling*). Were this not so, then (CIP) would indeed be inadequate because viciously circular. And this is why no adherent of the doctrine of 'pure' powers can afford to endorse (CIP). On the other hand, it seems that adherents of this doctrine have *no option* other than to adopt (CIP), or something very close to it which is subject to the same difficulty. So the implication of all this is that the doctrine of 'pure' powers is simply untenable. Adherents of the doctrine should think again about their arguments against the existence of non-power properties, for it is these arguments that have placed them in the predicament that I have just described. One need not compromise one's belief in the reality and importance of powers by acknowledging that *not all* properties are powers. Indeed, if my foregoing arguments are correct, one can rationally believe in the reality of powers *only if* one is prepared to acknowledge that there are also non-power properties, for without these powers must lack an adequate principle of individuation.

8.5 AGAINST 'STRUCTURALIST' ONTOLOGIES

The criticisms that I have just raised against the doctrine of 'pure' powers are ones which, *mutatis mutandis*, can be raised against any type of 'structuralist' ontology which maintains that *all* of the entities of a certain kind are *mutually individuating*. The basic problem is that it just doesn't seem intelligible to suppose that different entities of the same kind can be *each other's sole individuators*. Imagine, for instance, that someone were to try to counter my earlier suggestion that the two electrons orbiting a helium nucleus are not 'individuals' (in my sense) by contending that *each* of them is in fact *the other's* individuator. The obvious and, in my view, correct reply would be that this suggestion is futile, because viciously circular. Two different entities of the same kind cannot both individuate *each other*. Nor indeed, more generally, can *any* plurality of entities of the same kind all be individuated solely by other members of the same plurality. Consider first the two-entity case. Two distinct *K*s cannot *each* determine *which K* the other one is, because unless it is *already* determined which *K* one of them is, this *K* cannot fix the identity of the other. And the two-entity case surely generalizes.

Note that the point at issue here exclusively concerns *principles of individuation* as such, not *criteria of identity*. (CIP), for instance, conceived *merely* as a criterion of identity, can certainly be satisfied in every possible world containing powers – even if all powers have other powers as their manifestation-types – *provided* that every such world has a suitably asymmetric power-structure. But this doesn't entail that in *any* such world all, or indeed any, of the powers will be properly *individuated* – only that, for every pair of powers in such a world, (CIP) will determine *whether or not the members of that pair are identical.* This is not at all the same as saying that the *identity* of every power in such a world will be fixed. Once again, we always must distinguish clearly between 'identity' understood as a *relation* and 'identity' in the sense of *individual essence* – and it is the latter notion that is now in play.

Here it is helpful to consider the case of the *natural numbers.* It seems entirely reasonable to say that each number *except the first* in the series of natural numbers is individuated *by its predecessor* and hence solely by *another number in the series.* The first number, 0, is not individuated in this way, however. In fact, 0 seems to be *self*-individuating, in virtue of its being *part of its essence* that it is the sole natural number with *no* predecessor. Something exactly similar may be said of the empty set: it too is self-individuating, in virtue of its being *part of its essence* that it is the sole set with no members. But it is only *because* there is one number in the natural number series that is *not* individuated solely by other numbers in the series that *other* numbers in the series can be individuated by their predecessors and thus solely by other numbers in the series. So, even if there are no relevant symmetries in the power-structure of a world, I still contend that it cannot be the case that every power in that world is individuated *solely by other powers in that world.* Either some power would have to be somehow self-individuating, by analogy with 0 or the empty set, or else some powers would have to be individuated by *non*-powers. However, a moment's reflection reveals that no power *could* be self-individuating, given that all powers must have manifestation-types and that every power is individuated by its manifestation-type. For, as was pointed out earlier, no power can be *its own* manifestation-type and hence every power's individuator must be an entity that is distinct from itself. The conclusion must therefore be that some powers must have *non*-powers as their manifestation-types. The only other possibility is that it is part of the essence of some power that it has *no* manifestation-type, rather as it is part of the essence of o that it has no predecessor. If there were necessarily only *one* such power, it could be the manifestation-type of *another* power, thereby individuating that other power, thus beginning a sequence of individuation which could ultimately incorporate all other powers. However, it really makes no sense to suppose that there could be a *power* which had no manifestation-type, because it is part of the essence of any power that it is a power *to* φ, for some manifestation-type φ. A 'power' that was not a power *to do* or *to be* anything would not really be any kind of power at all. If it were anything at all, it would have to be some kind of *non*-power property – in which case we are back to the conclusion that some powers must have *non*-powers as their manifest-ation-types. This isn't to deny that there might perhaps be some powers which are *unmanifestable*, that is, which are such that it is impossible for their manifestation-types to be instantiated. For these powers, strange though they might be, would still *have* manifestation-types, just no *tokens* of those types.

What is common to all 'structuralist' ontologies is the idea that *all* of the entities of a certain kind K occupy unique positions within a certain asymmetrical *relational structure*. In the case of 'pure' power structuralism, of the sort that we have been examining, the relation in question is the *power–manifestation relation*: the relation that a power has to the property that is its manifestation-type, where this property is taken to be *another* power. In a structuralist ontology of *events*, the relation in question might be taken to be the relation of *direct causation*: the relation that an event has to any other event of which it is a direct cause. All such structures, both symmetrical and asymmetrical, can be represented by *directed graphs* (or *digraphs*) consisting of *nodes* (or *vertices*) connected to one another by *arrows* (standardly called *arcs*), as depicted in Figures 8.1 and 8.2 above.[20] Now, clearly, we have to distinguish carefully between a graph *diagram*, such as those displayed in Figures 8.1 and 8.2, a *graph* conceived as an abstract mathematical structure *depicted* by such a diagram, and a *concrete structure of entities and relations* which is *representable* by such a mathemat-ical structure. For instance, a set of *events* standing in *causal* relations to one another is not itself an abstract mathematical structure, because the entities and relations in question – *events* and *causal* relations – are concrete in character.[21] However, their structure may be *represented* by

---

[20] For more on graph theory and its ontological applications, see Dipert 1997 and Bird 2007b, pp. 139–46.

[21] For more on the concrete/abstract distinction, see Lowe 1995, pp. 509–24.

an abstract mathematical structure, such as a directed graph, and the latter may be *depicted* by a graph diagram, of the sort displayed in Figures 8.1 and 8.2. Now, in the case of *graphs themselves*, conceived as abstract mathematical structures, the question arises as to how their *nodes* or *vertices* are individuated. And it *may* be perfectly proper to say that they are individuated by their 'positions' in the graph, if this is suitably asymmetrical. (If the graph is *not* suitably asymmetrical, it may be proper to say instead that at least some of the nodes are *not* in fact individuated, and so do not qualify as 'individuals' at all – something which may not matter for some *mathematical* purposes, any more than the non-individuality of electrons matters for some quantum-mechanical purposes.) After all, it is plausible to contend that there can be nothing more to the *essence* of a node than its position in the graph, relative to the positions of all other nodes of the graph. For instance, in the graph depicted in Figure 8.1 above, the node labelled '*e*' occupies a position which is unique in the graph, being connected by an arrow to another node, labelled '*f*', which is in turn connected by an arrow to a third node, labelled '*g*'. No other node in the graph is so characterized in terms of its relations to other nodes. If, for example, we switched the labels '*e*' and '*f*', the nodes that they would then designate would have *different* graph-theoretic properties from those possessed by the nodes that are *actually* designated by those labels. But although the *labels* can be switched in this manner, it surely makes no sense to suppose that *the nodes that they designate* could be so switched. And this is because it is surely *part of the essence* of any node that it possesses the graph-theoretic properties that it does – indeed, those properties very plausibly *exhaust* its essence.

However, a vital point to keep in mind now is that a *concrete* structure which may be *represented* by a graph – which may in turn be *depicted* by a graph diagram – cannot coherently be *identified* with such a graph, the latter being a purely *abstract* structure. Moreover, of course, *different* concrete structures may well be representable by the *same* graph. For instance, the graph depicted in Figure 8.1 may represent a possible concrete structure of *events*, but it could equally represent a possible concrete structure of *powers*, or indeed of any other set of suitably interrelated concrete entities. For these very reasons, however, what applies to the *nodes* of the graph cannot automatically be taken to apply, *mutatis mutandis*, to the concrete entities *representable* by those nodes, namely, that they are individuated by their 'positions' in the concrete structures to which they belong. For the latter to be the case, it would have to make no more sense to say, for example, that a given event could have occupied a different position in the same or another *event-structure* than it does to say that a given node could have occupied a different position in the same or another *graph*. Moreover, we should not lose sight of the fact that concrete structures contain *relations* as well as the entities that are the relata of those relations, just as directed graphs contain *arrows* (or *arcs*) as well as nodes. As far as *graphs* are concerned, this seems to present no problem of intelligibility. But where, say, an event-structure is concerned, which contains *causal* relations as well as events, we need to be able to say how *they* are individuated, not merely how the *events* are. After all, as I remarked a moment ago, it seems perfectly possible that an *event*-structure and a *power*-structure could both be represented by the *same* directed graph, such as that depicted in Figure 8.1. But if it were now to be alleged that the events and the powers are individuated by their 'positions' in their respective concrete structures, then, since these structures are *ex hypothesi* isomorphic, the only way to prevent the absurd conclusion that the events are *identical* with the powers is to provide some account of what distinguishes the *causal* relations between the events from the *power–manifestation* relations between the powers. However, the obvious and I think proper thing to say is that we need to explain the distinction between causal relations and power–manifestation relations in terms of the difference between events and powers, not vice versa. Indeed, where *token* causal and power–manifestation relations are concerned, it seems proper to say that they are individuated at least partly *by their relata*, the individual events and powers that they relate.

The upshot of all this is that, while a 'structuralist' ontology may well be apposite in the case of certain abstract mathematical structures such as graphs, there is no good reason at all to suppose that the same can be said with regard to *concrete* entities of any kind, such as events, powers, and material objects. Some kinds of concrete entities do plausibly have *relational essences*, in that it is part of the essence of an entity of one of these kinds that it stands in a certain relation to one or more entities of the same or another kind. For example, as I noted at the outset, it is plausible to say that it is part of the essence of a certain event not merely that it is a *death*, but that it is the death *of a particular person*, say of *Caesar*. Caesar, then, is something that helps to individuate this event, perhaps along with its time of occurrence. But I think we have seen enough now to conclude that it is simply impossible for *all* of the entities in a given system of ontology to be individuated entirely by *other* entities in that system, in the manner that the 'structuralist' ontologist aspires to. *Some* entities in any coherent system of ontology, I conclude, must simply be *self*-individuating, if any other entities in that system are to be properly individuated at all.

We should not, I think, regard the notion of *self*-individuation as mysterious or repugnant to reason. Individuation in the metaphysical sense is, recall, the relationship between entities *x* and *y* which obtains just in case *which* entity *y* is, is (at least partly) determined by *which* entity *x* is – the relation of *identity-dependence*, as I call it. But I see no reason to deny that it is possible, at least in the case of some kinds of entity, that an entity *x* of that kind *itself* determines which entity of that kind it is. Indeed, we saw plausible examples of precisely this earlier in the cases of the number 0 and the empty set. These are entities which plausibly do *not* have relational essences. And I see no reason to deny that the same may be true of at least some *concrete* entities.[22]

---

[22] I am grateful for comments received when previous papers on some of the topics of this chapter were presented to audiences at the Universities of Durham and Oxford, and when an earlier version of the present chapter was delivered at the 'Because' Conference at the University of Geneva in February 2008.

CHAPTER 9

Simple metaphysics and "ontological dependence"

Jody Azzouni

9.1 BACKGROUND AND STAGE-SETTING FOR SIMPLE METAPHYSICS (I): FOUR PRINCIPLES

I've claimed in earlier work (Azzouni 2004) that a de facto community criterion for what exists is independence from our (from any, actually) linguistic and psychological processes. Call this *the independence criterion*. By describing the independence criterion as *de facto*, I mean that no analysis of the concept of "existence," or of "reality," or of "being," or of any other purportedly related term, can yield it (or any criterion, for that matter) as a result. Any such analysis, relying as it must on perceived "meanings," offers only indeterminate fruit. By describing the independence criterion as a *community* criterion, I allow for exceptions – "deviants" (to use Quine's language[1]) – and in this particular case many such deviants (unsurprisingly) are found among philosophers. "Deviance," so understood, isn't the deviant's varying on the perceived meanings of such words: the deviant philosophers I'm speaking of continue to use these words in accord with their perceived meanings. Rather, they deviate from the ordinary person's views about when such words can be used truly. Ordinary people take (for example) Santa Claus, Mickey Mouse, Zeus, holes, and similar items, *not* to exist.

Meinongians should be included among the deviants so described, despite their agreement with the letter of the last statement. A "Meinongian position" is any from a family of positions that take non-existent beings, despite their non-existence, to have substantial ontological and/or semantic roles. Contemporary Meinongians, for example, think that non-existent objects have properties. They also think that how non-existent objects are (what properties they have) are the truth-makers for sentences about those objects.

[1] Quine 1969a, p. 88, footnote 7.

I diagnose the thought that truths must be due to what there is – specifically, that what a statement is *about* determines the truth-value of that statement – as the source of Meinongianism. Even truths about Mickey Mouse (one thinks when in this mood) must be due to the properties that *Mickey Mouse* has. And indeed, the statements of ordinary people about non-existent objects seem to attribute properties to those objects. No metaphysical result directly follows from this fact about the statements of ordinary people, however. This can be seen by means of a distinction between *object-based property attributions* and *truth-based property attributions*. Object-based property attributions are ones based on properties that objects have. We can correctly attribute the property of being gray to the table because the table *is* gray. By contrast (given a nominalist view of numbers), the property attribution, "2 has the property of being an even prime," is true not because there is an object that has such a property but only because "2 is an even prime" is true. Ordinary usage, therefore, doesn't invite Meinongian doctrines, let alone provide evidence for them – not all by itself, anyway.

I've argued in other work (Azzouni 2010a, 2010b) that ordinary usage admits only two ontological statuses: existence and non-existence. Further, only things that exist have properties. Truths about those things, therefore, correspondingly correctly describe those properties, and attribute those properties to those things. Anything that doesn't exist has no properties, for anything that doesn't exist isn't in any way at all. Therefore: no thing that doesn't exist can be talked about (because there is nothing *to* talk about). That these sound like evident truisms, and indeed, that they sounded like evident truisms to Plato and Parmenides, isn't an indication that these are constraints on the *meaning* of words like "exist" and "nothing," or phrases like "there is," and "no thing." Nothing that strong follows. It *is* an indication, however, of an aspect of our *ordinary* understanding of metaphysics, of our ordinary and fundamental understanding of what there is and what there isn't.

Four of the five principles of *Simple Metaphysics* have emerged. There is, first, the assumption of only two ontological statuses, existence and non-existence (*the dichotomy assumption*); there is, second, the claim that metaphysically speaking, everything has the status of existence (nothing lacks the status of existence), and that only things that exist have properties (*the monopoly assumption*); there is, third, *the univocality assumption*: ordinary usage treats "exist," "real," "being," etc., when utilized in an ontologically relevant manner, as cognates. And lastly, there is the earlier mentioned *independence criterion*. A *simple metaphysician* (a proponent of Simple Metaphysics) accepts all of these principles.

Notice that these principles of Simple Metaphysics are – at first glance – ones about specific ordinary usages of words such as "there is," "exist," and so on. But they are simultaneously metaphysical principles: they describe how we take the world to sort out with respect to certain ontological concepts – when these words are used to express those concepts. According to the dichotomy and the univocality principle, objects either exist or they don't. They're either real or they're not. Furthermore, objects exist if and only if they're real.

Ordinary usage may seem to violate these assumptions of Simple Metaphysics. Consider the sentence:

(1) Some of the characters in William Gaddis's *The Recognitions* exist, and some don't.

This statement with its apparent quantification over characters described as having and lacking the property of existence invites an easy refutation of Simple Metaphysics. This sentence quantifies over characters, and attributes existence to some of them while apparently denying that property to other ones. To quantify over something (one might think) is to attribute a kind of "being" to it. One can say, somewhat archly, "There be characters in William Gaddis's *The Recognitions* that exist and there be characters in William Gaddis's *The Recognitions* that don't exist." One or another flavor of Meinongianism seems to follow.

Such a Meinongian lesson being drawn from ordinary usage – I protest – requires the antecedent assumption that ordinary language quantifiers bestow on what they're "about" some ontological status or other (e.g., "being"); no such assumption is supported by either the (ordinary language) semantics of such quantifiers or by their use. Indeed, one or another version of this assumption commonly arises (on the part of that philosopher imputing some sort of ontological claim as implicitly involved in ordinary usage): that whenever "exist," "real," "to be," etc., are used, they invariably involve the attribution of "being" of some sort. On the contrary. These are neutral idioms: they're sometimes used in an ontologically committing manner and they're sometimes used in an ontologically irrelevant manner.[2]

---

[2] See Azzouni 2007, 2010a for the ordinary-language data that support this claim. In anticipation of the discussion at the beginning of Section 9.5, I should note that perceptual idioms such as "see" and

9.2 BACKGROUND AND STAGE-SETTING FOR SIMPLE METAPHYSICS (II): THE SEPARATION THESIS FOR ONTOLOGY AND TRUTH

Consider statements like:

(2) Every object I've ever hallucinated has been purple.
(3) Some orcs are depicted in the Lord of the Rings as rather evil.

The claim that such statements are *true* may seem to pose a problem for simple metaphysicians: What factors – after all – can possibly be operative in making such statements true when those statements contain terms that refer to (or quantify over) nothing at all? Indeed, if (i) we reject the idea that fictional and hallucinated objects actually exist, (ii) we accept that positive statements about fictional and/or hallucinated objects are true, and (iii) we accept that the various paraphrase or replacement strategies fail, it may seem that only the Meinongian strategy is left standing.

This isn't so, say I, because sentences with non-referring noun phrases can nevertheless be true. An immediate objection to what I say is that the resulting attribution of truth-values looks unconstrained. After all, the other options acknowledge truth-makers: on those views, a statement is true *because of* the properties of the objects that statement is about. Without such truth-makers, what's left to constrain truth and falsity?

A broader model of what it is that forces truth-values on statements supplements correspondence factors with *indispensability considerations*. If attributing truth to a class of statements is indispensable (to us) because of the deductive and evidential roles that they play in ordinary life and in the sciences, then we *must* take those sentences to be true.[3] The

---

"observe" are also ontologically neutral idioms. (Indeed, I hypothesize that all the idioms of natural languages are ontologically neutral.) "I'm hallucinating again. I can tell because I can see that elf that I always see whenever I begin to hallucinate." These are ontologically non-committing uses of "see." Similarly: "I'm hallucinating again. I can tell because there's that elf I always see whenever I begin to hallucinate." Here there's a non-ontologically committing use of "there's that," in addition to a non-ontologically committing use of "see." In this way, the ordinary language "see" is similar to the ordinary language "there is" and even the ordinary language "exist": such words are ontologically neutral because there are both ontologically committing and ontologically non-committing usages of such.

[3] There are evident analogies between so-called "coherence" views of truth, and the indispensability considerations I'm now invoking. Both approaches accept that at least some truths don't require "correspondence"; some truths don't require their truth to depend on how it is with the referents of the noun phrases in those truths or to how it is with the objects that fall within the range of their

indispensability of such truths is what prevents assignments of truth values to them being unconstrained. Consider the sentence:

Sherlock Holmes is depicted in the Conan Doyle stories as living in London.

The failure of the paraphrase option, coupled with this sentence's evidential and deductive role, makes it indispensably true. However, it isn't true *because* there is an object (Sherlock Holmes) that those stories depict as living in London. Rather, the sentence is true because its truth correlates to the pretend-acts of fictionalizing that occur in the Conan Doyle stories. But how is such a correlation between what such a statement says, and pretend-acts of fictionalizing achieved without reference providing the connections between the terms *in* that sentence and things with properties?

Consider this analogy. Goya has a nightmare about an evil (living) gargoyle. He then draws that nightmare accurately. In doing so, it's not that he interacts with *the gargoyle*, for there is no gargoyle for him to interact *with*. Rather, he captures the *nightmare* accurately, and in doing so, his drawing can be derivatively described as "capturing the gargoyle accurately" because (and only because) it captures (certain aspects of) the visual contours of his *nightmare*.[4]

The indispensability model of truth treats it as a mistake to regard the truth-aptness of sentences as necessarily determined by the objects the noun phrases in such sentences refer to: sometimes there are no such objects. Instead, we should accept the separation thesis with respect to truth and reference: Truth-aptness doesn't *require* objects. "Mickey Mouse was invented by Walt Disney" is true even though there is no Mickey Mouse. What makes this sentence true is a state of affairs with respect to Walt Disney and certain drawings that he created. But for a state of affairs to be why a sentence is true doesn't require that the state

---

quantifiers. Traditional coherence views – however – tend to be global and exclusionary: all truths require coherence (with, say, other background truths); none involve correspondence. That's not what's on offer here with respect to indispensability considerations. There can be truths – just as the correspondence theorist demands – that truly describe the states of affairs regarding what their noun phrases refer to and what their quantifiers range over. This isn't the case, however, with *all* truths. Another important difference is of stress: traditional coherence views focus on truths fitting in – according to one or another requirement – with other truths. Indispensability considerations focus instead on such truths being *required* by the areas of application of those truths: our current evidential and deductive needs in the sciences, for example.

4 For the purposes of this analogy I'm treating nightmares – psychological events – as things that exist. That events exist (as opposed to the entities that participate in events) is something the simple metaphysician might challenge. See Section 9.5.

of affairs contain objects that are the relata of noun phrases that occur in the sentence. Sometimes this happens: "Mickey Mouse was invented by Walt Disney," is made true by a state of affairs that involves an actual object Walt Disney that's referred to by "Walt Disney." But it doesn't correspondingly also involve another object (Meinongian or otherwise): Mickey Mouse.

Supplementing correspondence factors with indispensability considerations for how truth-values are forced on statements allows recognition of the fact that there are many ways that the truth of classes of sentences can become indispensable to our evidential and deductive practices in a subject area. One way has been illustrated by our indispensable talk of fictions. In this case, there is a pretence-practice of talking about characters and objects. Descriptions that correlate to this practice can be evidence for, or premises in deductions to, other statements that don't correlate to such pretence-practices. These indispensable descriptions that correlate to our pretence practices can't be given without "quantifying over non-existent objects" – without using non-referring noun phrases, and so this is one way that the truth of a class of statements becomes indispensable to our evidential and deductive practices.

There are other ways. Suppose that in fact it's true that the noun phrases in mathematical truths – "1," "function," "Hilbert space," and so on – refer to nothing at all. The indispensability of these referentially empty truths arises not because they correlate to some pretence-practice but because scientific practice quite directly requires the deductive (and evidential) use of such truths. This, if right, is a different way in which a class of statements can be indispensably true.

Valuable at this juncture is a distinction between *truth-makers* and *truth-value inducers*. Both sets of items are "how it is"s (to coin a particularly ugly locution) with things that exist. When a statement has noun phrases all of which relate to things in the world, to which that statement attributes properties and relations, I'll describe how those relata are as the *truth-maker* of that statement. That Socrates is wise is how Socrates is, and that's the truth-maker of "Socrates is wise." This characterization of "truth-maker" is *similar to* that of some theorists who describe the truth-maker of "Socrates is wise" as Socrates' wisdom or the fact that Socrates is wise. There are important differences, however. First, those theorists often take Socrates' wisdom or facts to exist. I don't. (See the rest of this chapter.) This is why I prefer the locution "how Socrates is" as a characterization of the truth-maker of "Socrates is wise."[5] Another difference is that I require the truth-makers to be how it is with the existing items that are referred to by noun phrases in the statements the truth-makers are of.

It follows immediately that many statements either have no truth-makers at all, or have truth-makers that only go part of the way towards explaining the truth-values (true or false) of the statements they are the truth-makers of. In particular, when a statement has noun phrases that don't relate to things in the world, then what also contributes to the truth value of that statement are *truth-value inducers*: how it is with items that *aren't* referred to by the noun phrases of the statement. For example, consider how it is with the items that determine mathematical practice in various ways, the forms that mathematical languages can take, the role of mathematics in science, and so on. All this (vaguely described, admittedly) are the truth-value inducers of "2 is a prime number."[6]

The foregoing is an argument that Simple Metaphysics should include the separation thesis with respect to ontology and truth, that the truth of statements doesn't have to depend on how it is with the objects those statements are about.[7] Hereon, Simple Metaphysics is so understood.

---

[5] Some theorists understand a truth-maker of a statement to be something whose existence *entails* the truth of that statement. I don't. I instead characterize the statement as describing how it is with what it refers to. If, indeed, that *is* how it is with the referents of the noun phrases in the statement, then the statement is true by virtue of that (otherwise it's false by virtue of the truth-maker). I should add this: How it is with something isn't something that *entails* anything, on my view. It's something that can be *described*, however, correctly or incorrectly. And, as I'll indicate later in this chapter, truth-makers on my view, explain the truth (or falsity) of the statements they are the truth-makers for. So there is an explanatory role for truth-makers, as I understand them. I should stress, as will become clear later in the chapter, that although how it is with some collection of objects is objective, it isn't an existent. Only the objects exist, not how they are. *Mea culpa*: I've sometimes spoken in earlier work in ways that make it sound like truth-makers and truth-value inducers are the existing objects that are themselves this way or that way. That use of "truth-maker," however natural, deviates far too much from how the rest of the philosophical profession currently uses "truth-maker."

[6] Traditional truth-maker views, depending on how they specify their truth-makers, often face problems with complex statements: conjunctions and negations, for example. This in turn motivates some of those theorists to treat truth-makers as items that *entail* statements. A view that helps itself both to truth-makers (narrowly construed) and truth-value inducers has more resources. For example, "There are no flying horses," has no truth-makers, on my view. It does have truth-value inducers, however: How it is with everything are the truth-value inducers of that statement.

[7] There is a lot to say about how the separation thesis bears on semantics – specifically on truth-conditional semantics. See Azzouni 2010b for this.

9.3 FORMAL MODES OF SPEAKING AND MATERIAL MODES OF SPEAKING

The remainder of this chapter will focus on the independence criterion. I'll start by raising an apparent problem for the simple metaphysician who is committed to it. An easy way to set up the problem is to temporarily adopt a paradigmatic Meinongian perspective. Imagine that you are faced with two objects, and that you want to ascertain their ontological statuses. Suppose further that one of the objects is Mickey Mouse and that the other is Barack Obama. Sense can be made of "applications" of the independence criterion in such a context. You examine (as it were) each object to determine whether it is, indeed, independent of anyone's psychological and linguistic processes; and how the result of this examination should go is also clear: there is no Mickey Mouse apart from all the Mickey-Mouse-talk and Mickey-Mouse-thought that's due (originally) to Walt Disney. Barack Obama, by contrast, is something apart from (and in addition to) all the Barack-Obama-talk and Barack-Obama-thought that *he's* (largely) the source of.[8]

There is a sense, however, in which – although the Meinongian can take the above exercise as a literal one (in both cases some object or other is directly studied in order to recognize whether a certain property holds of it or not) – a simple metaphysician can only understand the exercise, when it comes to Mickey Mouse, as sheer metaphor. If no object is Mickey Mouse, then one can't examine *Mickey Mouse* to determine what properties *it* has. There is no relatum of "Mickey Mouse" that *has* properties.

There is, one might think, a curious asymmetry between ontological independence and its negation, ontological dependence. Ontological independence may be taken to describe a property that everything has. Ontological dependence on the other hand is empty. The result is a lack of contrast that apparently prevents the purported criterion from being an ontological *test*. How, then, are we supposed to apply it – even in principle? If ontological independence applies to everything, there won't be anything left for ontological dependence to apply to.

---

[8] Compare Russell 1919, p. 170: "If no one thought about Hamlet, there would be nothing left of him; if no one had thought about Napoleon, he would have soon seen to it that some one did." I'm leaving aside, of course, the possibility of various skeptical scenarios (e.g., everyone around you is a hallucination induced by one or another species of demon: everyone around you is ontologically dependent on the demon).

Couching this concern metaphysically, in terms of the extensions of predicates and their negations, misdirects it. The concern shouldn't be that a particular property is to apply to everything and that its negation is to apply to nothing. There's nothing particularly wrong with pairs of properties like that. The point is this: Although it's reasonable to describe any property of everything as a "criterion for what exists," it's hard to see the relevance of the complement of such a property to the non-existence of Mickey Mouse or to that of orcs. After all, it surely isn't because these "items" are lacking this particular property that they don't exist: to speak this way is to desert Simple Metaphysics for the speech patterns of Meinongians.

It's important to keep clear what the attribution of properties to non-existent objects means. Certain truths hold; but there are no objects those truths are (really) about. So to think that there is an object Mickey Mouse that's really "dependent on" our psychological and/or linguistic processes is confused. *It* isn't dependent on our psychological and/or linguistic processes because it *isn't* at all.

I should dwell on the indispensability of "the material mode of speech," an indispensability that's operative regardless of the onto-logical status of what's spoken of. Such a mode of speech is intrinsic-ally misleading (at least to a certain kind of philosopher). When we can, therefore, we should recast what's going on in the "formal mode of speech," or at least we should try to locate our philosophical vantage point at the level of words rather than things. In particular, the simple metaphysician's "criterion for what exists" isn't a metaphysical property (or set of properties) that's to be applied to each thing in order to distinguish it from nothing. Instead what's on offer is a tool to be applied to noun phrases, quantifiers, and, ultimately, to the sentences containing such. Relatedly, what's on offer is a tool to be used to evaluate *thoughts*, to determine when reference-apt parts of those thoughts actually refer and when they don't.

The beginning of the last paragraph was written *in* the material mode of speech because I was there writing of items and their ontological statuses. Putting the point "formally" instead yields: "I should dwell on the indispensability of 'the material mode of speech,' an indispensability that's operative regardless of the ontological-imputing status of the uses of one's words." I repeat that I'm definitely *not* claiming that it's possible or even desirable to everywhere replace or try to replace the material mode of speech with the formal mode. I take the lesson of indispensability arguments (e.g., the Quine–Putnam indispensability argument) to be that we can't – ultimately – escape the material mode of speech with respect to non-existent entities.[9] That is to say, we *can't* systematically restrict our quantifiers and names *only* to what exists. But if we are to truly evaluate how we are to understand criteria for what exists (formally: But if we are to truly evaluate how we are to understand criteria for sorting the ontological-imputing status of the uses of one's words), we must endeavor to avoid the confusions the material mode of speech engenders. Much of the difficulty in this area of metaphysics arises directly from philosophical misinterpretations of the (indispensable) material mode of speech. Because of their training, philosophers automatically read ontological commitments into the material mode of speech. Doing so prevents their seeing a real option in logical space, that any such a mode of speech has an ordinary usage that's ontologically irrelevant.

9.4 PROPERTIES, RELATIONS, AND TROPES, AND WHY THEY DON'T EXIST

One always observes an object *being in a certain way*, as *having certain properties* (and not others) as *participating in a state of affairs*, and so on.[10] I'm going to treat all these ways of speaking – including there being "facts" or "facts of the matter" about such objects – as interchangeable language.

We can ask the following question. In observing objects being certain ways, do we therefore observe two kinds of *things* interacting, objects *and* the properties those objects manifest? We do not. That an object *has* such and such properties is something we see; that an object *is* a certain way and not another way is something we see. But *ways that objects are* are not additional objects that we see alongside the objects that manifest those ways.[11]

Precisely here the independence criterion of the simple metaphysician and various language-based approaches to ontology definitively part ways. For some philosophers, that the various *ways* that objects are (the various

---

[9] This sentence itself is in the material mode. Formally (instead): "I take the lesson of indispensability arguments (e.g., the Quine–Putnam indispensability argument) to be that we can't – ultimately – escape the material mode of speech with respect to noun phrases that don't refer." Arguments for the claim can be found in Azzouni 2004, 2009.

[10] There is the genuine worry that one may, instead of observing a property of the object, be instead engaged relationally to the object in a way that doesn't yield an observation of a property of *it*. Seeing the colors of objects is a notorious case, one where the status of colors as properties of the objects seen has been long debated. I'm leaving this issue aside.

[11] Notice that in *this* context, uses of "see" and "observe" and so on, are ontologically weighted.

properties that objects have) admits of *nominalization* – labeling by noun phrases and quantification into the places of those noun phrases – is a prima facie indication that such ways are themselves suitable ontological commitments. This is not so for the simple metaphysician. The simple metaphysician recognizes that nominalization is a (mere) tool of language that facilitates the exposure of logical tissue: it enables inferences to become visible.[12] Indeed, the facilitation of inference is why nominalization and quantification are so ubiquitous to how we (indispensably) describe the world. But contrary to the dictates of Quine's criterion for what a discourse is committed to, serious ontologizing shouldn't take its orders from the (indispensable) use of nominalization (and concomitant quantification).

The upshot is this: the simple metaphysician rejects ontological commitments to properties, to relations, and to tropes despite the fact that many of these are named by noun phrases, and despite the fact that in many contexts quantifications over such occur, and may even be indispensable. For properties, relations, and tropes are all of these no more than *ways* that objects can be. The simple metaphysician concedes that it's an objective matter how things are. That doesn't, however, require that the ways things are – properties, relations, or tropes – be *objects.* And the independence criterion provides the simple metaphysician with his motivation for not taking on any additional ontological commitments to properties, relations, and so on, in contrast to language-based ontology proponents.

Let's pursue this issue a little further. The simple metaphysician is committed to the independence criterion. Furthermore, the simple metaphysician admits that the only empirically known way to establish the existence and properties of objects is to observe those objects (or, more generally, to instrumentally engage with them). That is, just as whether an object exists or not is an objective matter only to be discovered empirically, so too what *properties* that object has is an objective matter as well. So why, an opponent can ask, doesn't the simple metaphysician's independence criterion establish the existence of properties exactly as it establishes the existence of objects?

---

[12] This point, to my knowledge, is first made forcefully by Davidson 1967, 1977. He additionally urges an ontological commitment to events as a result of the needed quantification over such. Rejecting Quine's criterion for what a discourse is committed to – as the simple metaphysician urges – enables resistance to Davidson's ontological pleas on behalf of events, at least on *those* grounds. I discuss events further in Section 9.5.

It's true that the simple metaphysician grants that it's an objective fact that objects have certain properties and not others. Indeed, the distinction – in Section 9.1 – between object-based property attributions and truth-based property attributions has its source in the idea that object-based attributions are true because of the objective fact of the *objects* in question being a certain way (and not another way). But there is a lot of distance between the objectivity of the way that an object is, and that way *itself* (therefore) being an object. And there is nothing in what we observe of objects (or in how we instrumentally interact with objects that are out of the range of our senses) that can be used to establish the claim that the *ways* (that objects are) are *themselves* objects.

Someone might urge that I've misdescribed how we actually interact with objects. Such an opponent might say: The only way to interact with a material object is by interacting with its features: we stand in direct causal relations to the features (tropes), and the material object itself is only causally efficient through those features. When it comes to contact or access, the features of an object come first, and the material object comes second. In this way someone might try to establish the existence of tropes.[13]

The previous paragraph doesn't establish the existence of tropes; it presupposes them. Consider a massive magnetic object *o*. And suppose I interact with it magnetically. That's one kind of causal interaction with *o*. If I instead interact with *o* via its mass (gravitationally), that's a different kind of causal interaction with *o*. These are two different ways to relate to *o* (resulting in two different "how it is"s between me and *o*). In interacting with *o* in these two different ways, it can't be said that I'm actually interacting with two distinct *features* of *o* (and mean these features to exist) unless it's already been established that there are such features for me to so interact with. Furthermore, what are actually different kinds of causal interactions (with an object), and ordinarily recognized as such, are instead treated by an opponent who presupposes features as the same "causal interaction," but now with one feature and then with another.[14]

---

[13] My thanks to Benjamin Schnieder for this characterization of a traditional motive for trope theory.
[14] Consider the electromagnetic field generated by an electron. That such a field is *itself* something we should be ontologically committed to isn't to be trivially established by the sorts of considerations raised by trope theorists. Additional considerations – about how such fields are themselves interacted with – must be brought into play.

Notice: I'm *not* claiming that a trope theorist can't recharacterize our interactions with objects in a way compatible with an antecedent commitment to tropes or features. I'm pointing out that our ordinary interaction with objects of course takes such an interaction to occur *via* one way or another: how it is with us and how we interact with the object can be one way or another. But there is nothing in our ordinary interactions with objects that obviously presupposes a *veil of features*: that instead of interacting with the *object* in different ways, we are instead interacting with its different features.[15]

Some philosophers try a different maneuver: they try to root an argument for an ontological commitment to properties, relations, or tropes in the requirement that truths of various sorts must be *explained* by how the world is. That is, not only is it that truths are to be about things in the world, it's also that the fact that certain statements are true (and others are not) is itself to be explained by the machinations of objects *and* properties, where properties are themselves a kind of object. Notice, in any case, that it's intuitively natural to ask why a (particular) statement is true: in asking this, one is asking for an explanation for why the statement is true. And the explanation sought isn't a causal one: one doesn't expect to be told what *caused* the statement to be true.

This second maneuver doesn't work either. "That table is gray" is true, presumably, *because of* the way that table is; the explanation for the truth of "That table is gray" is given by the way the table is. This requires *that table* to be a certain way; it doesn't require that *that way* be itself an additional piece of furniture in our ontology. Furthermore (and crucially), the demand that *every* truth is to be explained by the machinations of objects that are the relata of the quantifiers and grammatically referring expressions of that truth is, anyway, rejected by the simple metaphysician. I'll dwell on this important point again.

The simple metaphysician accepts that a non-causal explanatory relation exists between truths on the one hand, and the world on the other. What isn't accepted by the simple metaphysician is that this explanatory relationship always has to take the form of a relationship between the truth and the ways that the *truth-makers* of that statement are. This is the case only if all the noun phrases of that

---

[15] It's surprising, upon analysis, how close this argumentative motivation for tropes is to the traditional argument from hallucination.

truth (and what it quantifies over) exist. Consider the true sentence: "That table is that particular shade of gray."[16] As noted, this sentence is true because of the table and because the table is indeed that particular shade of gray. So the truth of this sentence is *explained* by the table being a certain way (by its being a particular shade of gray and no other). It's explained by the table being in one and not in a different state of affairs, where "state of affairs," "ways that things are," and so on, are all noun phrases that the simple metaphysician no more takes to refer to objects than he takes "property" or "trope" to so refer.

But given the simple metaphysician's rejection of an ontological commitment to numbers, the truth of "2 is a prime number" is *not* to be explained by the number 2 being a certain way. There is no number 2, and so that this statement is true must be explained in some other way entirely. It must be explained at least in part by the indispensability of the truth of the statement to science and to our daily lives; correspondingly, the attribution of primeness to 2 is a truth-based property attribution in contrast to the attribution of that particular color to the table which instead is an object-based property attribution.

One may demur.[17] After all, that "'2 is prime' is true because 2 is prime" seems to be one example of a very intuitively sounding schema: If "*S*" is true, then "*S*" is true because *S* (where "*S*" is a schematic letter replaceable by sentences). Why, therefore, reject this as an explanation? The reason to reject it is because we *also* have the intuition that successful explanations can't be trivial or circular. If I explain that the reason why 4 isn't prime is that 4 isn't prime, the rejection of my explanation isn't that what I've said isn't true, it's that I've just repeated what it is that's to be explained. A circular explanation does the same thing, although not so obviously: eventually, what's been explained presupposes what's to be explained.

Now consider "'2 is prime' is true because 2 is prime." According to the simple metaphysician, there are no prime numbers. Furthermore, that 2 is prime is itself a *truth-based* property attribution. But if this is right then that "2 is prime" is true is being ultimately explained in terms of the statement itself being true. And that *is* circular – which makes it unacceptable as an explanation.

---

[16] "That particular shade of gray," when used as a noun phrase, picks out (let's say) a purported trope borne by the table.

[17] Benjamin Schnieder so demurred. The objection that follows is his.

I qualified the nature of the explanation of the truth of "$2 + 2 = 4$" as being *in part* due to indispensability considerations. In point of fact, I think in the case of "$2 + 2 = 4$" the explanation is entirely in terms of indispensability considerations. Or perhaps, because of the ubiquitousness of the application of the truth "$2 + 2 = 4$" to *many* domains of discourse, we can say that the explanation for its truth turns both on how the world is (in *general*) and the form that our language must take.[18] But the most interesting sorts of truths are ones where the explanations we can give for their truth turns in part on indispensability considerations and in part on the ways that certain *specific* objects are in the world. I turn to examples of these now.

9.5 TRUTHS ABOUT HOLES, BOUNDARIES, AND EVENTS

Let's return to holes. We apparently *see* holes in Swiss cheese, but we see them in many other places as well. Not only can we apparently see holes, but if holes move about (in a certain kind of gel, say) then we can apparently track the locations of those holes over time. It's only with a little care that we recognize that in fact the *objects* involved here aren't the holes but instead the things the holes are in. We speak of seeing a hole, but that use of "see" isn't ontologically committing: as we ordinarily use "see," we can see things that aren't there. And if something isn't there, then there isn't anything we're *actually* observing because there is no such object. Instead, our perceptual experience of it is based on our sensory interaction with something else and it's only the something else that exists.

Paraphrasing our language appropriately, so that sentences in which the non-referring noun phrase "hole" occurs are replaced with other sentences in which no such noun phrase appears, isn't an option.[19] Instead, we can recognize that statements about holes are yet another example of indispensable statements with non-referring terms. We can continue to speak of seeing holes, digging holes, etc., provided we recognize these statements to be true for reasons other than how the holes they refer to are.

Consider the statement:

(4) That piece of Swiss cheese is full of holes.

---

[18] The truth of indispensable statements of broad applicability – such as those of mathematics – are hard to provide explanations for, at least if those explanations are to be couched in terms of *specific* aspects of the world.

[19] See Lewis and Lewis 1986 for an illustration of the difficulties of paraphrase in the case of holes.

(4) has one truth-maker, namely the piece of Swiss cheese itself. What makes (4) true is a way that piece of Swiss cheese is, in particular, the way it's *perforated*.[20] The *explanation* for the truth of (4) turns on *more* than the way this truth-maker is, however. It also turns on indispensability facts about the resistance faced by attempts to recraft (4) into a statement that can play the same role (4) does but which refers to – or quantifies over – only the piece of Swiss cheese and not over its holes.

To recognize the role that indispensability considerations play in the explanation of any truth is to recognize a schematic framework for where to look for explanations for why certain statements are true. Such explanations don't take the same form in every case. With specific statements about specific holes, one must focus not only on the fact that talk of "holes" is indispensable language, but on the particular objects that the holes are the perforations in. More accurately, one must focus on the particular object (that the hole is in) and the ways that object is. For it is the ways that object is (the ways that object is perforated) that provide the factual basis for the particular claims about the hole that's in it. The object and how it's perforated provides part of the explanation for why a particular statement about a hole in that object is true. More precisely, the object – and how it's perforated – are the truth-value inducers of the statement in question: they are part of the explanation of the truth of the statement.[21] But the holed object (and how it is) is only *part* of the explanation because the indispensability of the use of the idiom "hole" to represent particular truths about that object and how it's perforated is part of the explanation for the truth of those truths (instead of there being other truths that don't refer to or quantify over holes).

Consider, for example, a particular holed object *o*. And consider the predicate R which holds of an object if and only if it is holed in precisely the way that *o* is holed. R*o*, therefore, is true, and it's true precisely because of its truth-maker, how *o* is (*o* is R). However, R*o* is relatively useless to us as a descriptive truth. Consider this different

---

[20] Or indented: perforations – strictly speaking – are punctures. But we also use "hole" to describe indents in something if they are appropriately shaped (e.g., not too shallow). Hereafter, I'll use "perforated" to include appropriately shaped indents.

[21] In some cases, the object the hole is in is referred to by a term in a sentence, as in: The hole in that donut is too large. But not always: That hole is larger than it looks. In the first case, *how the object the hole is in* is a truth-maker of the sentence in question; in the second case it's only a truth-value inducer for the sentence in question.

(and far more valuable) statement: "There are seventeen holes in *o* which are perfectly spherical and which can be linearly ordered according to the strictly increasing lengths of their diameters." This statement indispensably quantifies over the holes in *o*. The explanation for its truth, therefore, turns both on the fact that *o* is R and on the fact that we can't represent aspects of how *o* is R without quantifying over holes, as our more valuable statement does.[22]

Statements referring to (or quantifying over) boundaries of objects are understood similarly. For how an object is contoured is just as much a way that that object is as how it's perforated.[23]

I turn now to smiles. Smiles evidently raise new considerations beyond those previously discussed, even though smiles are only particularly appealing contours that faces – more specifically mouths – can take. The essential point is that smiles (sadly) are fleeting: they are ways that faces are only for short times. Smiles, that is, are *events* that mouths undergo.[24] Events, in turn, are ways that objects behave (or have) *over time*. Unlike "smiles" (apparently), many events are often, but not invariably, labeled by noun phrases that cover the doings of a *number* of objects over a period of time, for example, a war, a competitive race, an explosion.

Consider:

(5) The explosion was dangerous.

(5) has no truth-makers. It has, however, a complicated set of truth-value inducers. The explosive event referred to in (5) involves (let's say) an indeterminate number of actual objects that individually participate in various individual events of their own – specifically, they each experience their own individual trajectories. Let's simplify the particular explosion described in (5) by treating it as a large number of specific objects that traject in a number of different ways over a specified time. The indispensability of (5) can be measured (in a sense) by realizing that to eliminate the non-referring noun phrase "explosion," (5) would have to be replaced by numerous individual statements, each describing the

---

[22] The indispensability point becomes even clearer if we replace R with a giant set of predicates each of which describes certain aspects of the way that *o* is.

[23] It's interesting how intuitions come apart here. Although it's very natural to think of holes in an object as things that don't exist, it's much less natural to think of the boundaries to an object as similarly non-existent. Nevertheless, just as we don't *actually* observe holes but only the objects with holes (or, at least, the material around a hole) so too we don't *actually* observe boundaries but only the objects that have those boundaries.

[24] Mouths are parts of faces. Whether that means that mouths exist isn't an issue I'm going to pursue in this chapter.

trajectories of different objects. And, somehow, a condition on the individual trajectories of these objects would have to enable a characterization of why (collectively) they are dangerous. Furthermore, characterizations of these trajectories – even relative to other objects – require quantifications over space and time.

Nevertheless, the foregoing is at least a qualitative picture of the explanation of the truth of (5), one that turns both on the actual ways that a certain set of existing objects are (a collection of truth-value inducers), and particular details of the indispensability of stating the content of (5) in terms of the non-referring term "explosion."[25]

9.6   ONTOLOGICAL DEPENDENCE FOR EXISTENTS

Explanations (based on explanatory relations) must be explanations of *something*. On behalf of the simple metaphysician, I've accepted the demand that truths one and all demand explanations: one is obliged to explain why truths are true. The *correspondence realist* handles the explanation of the truth of any statement in terms of objects, and how they are (truth-makers): that the statement correctly corresponds to those truth-makers. But given the broad range of indispensable truths that there are, this approach requires all manner of objects: numbers, fictional entities, hallucinated entities, holes, boundaries, properties, and so on. If no explanation of why any statement is true were possible except one in terms of truth-makers (in terms of how the relata of a sentence are), the simple metaphysician would be at a disadvantage because that metaphysician would be forced to claim that some statements are true for no reason at all – the truth of some statements is without an explanation. I've endeavored in the foregoing to blunt that sort of attack on the simple metaphysician.

Let's turn to issues of nomenclature, in particular to my use of "ontological dependence." Nomenclature is treacherous in a field where it's so easy to misunderstand complexities that (often) turn on "single-hair" distinctions. No wonder that even the most emotionally austere of philosophers can get so upset over bungled terminology as to let loose an obscenity or two (although only in private, of course).

---

[25] I've not, however, established that "explosions" don't exist – at least I haven't done so in terms of the criterion of ontological independence that's fundamental to the creed of the simple metaphysician. (I think there are subtleties and complications in this case that I can't get into now.) So this should be viewed as only an illustration, one based on the presumption that explosions don't exist.

"Ontological independence" and "ontological dependence" are such terms. I've used them for over a decade as shorthand notation for what I've urged is a criterion for what we take to exist. "Ontological independence," "ontological dependence," and other quite similar terms are used, however, by other philosophers to describe the relationship that some items – such as, say, smiles, events, states of affairs, tropes, Aristotelian universals, holes, boundaries, etc.,[26] items that *they* take to genuinely exist – bear to other items that also exist. Consequently, such philosophers treat the "ontological dependence" relation as a substantial relation between kinds of objects that's to be studied in metaphysics.

The simple metaphysician disagrees. The ontological dependence relation that such philosophers presume to detect as holding between a collection of objects and the state of affairs they are in, or tropes and the objects that bear them, holes and the objects they are in, and so on, are (on the view of the simple metaphysician) only the recognition that a set of truths (that quantify over, or refer to, what doesn't exist – e.g., states of affairs, tropes, holes, ...) has as part of their explanatory basis certain actual objects the ways of which are the truth-inducers of these truths.

Indeed, the various intuitions that certain "entities" are ontologically dependent on other things, holes and boundaries on what they are the holes and boundaries of, tropes and Aristotelian properties on the entities that manifest them, events and states on the objects participating in those events and that are in those states, are for the simple metaphysician only evidence of the subliminal recognition that there actually are no such things as holes, properties, events, and so on. To repeat: ontological dependence comes to nothing more than that the truth of certain statements with certain nominalizations and quantifications (to the non-existent) are to be explained by the ways that certain other objects are plus the indispensability of those nominalizations and quantifications.

It should be clear, therefore, why I've labeled the position I've urged in this chapter *simple* metaphysics. Because if it's right, there aren't a lot of metaphysical entities *left* to study in metaphysics: there are no properties, no tropes, no facts of the matter, no states of affairs, no abstracta, no fictional entities, no Meinongian objects, no etc. Correspondingly, however, explanations for why certain statements are true become more complicated because the easy reach to an explanation in terms of a correspondence to entities (and how they are) is gone.

----

[26] I draw this list, with some omissions, from Koslicki this volume.

No doubt it's a motivation for some philosophers to keep the explanations simple for why true statements are true: just use correspondence, and just coin new entities into existence whenever the entities already around aren't enough to provide the needed correspondences. I think on the contrary that such a methodological approach to ontology is a bad one. It should be recognized, instead, that explanations are often hard to find, and that they should never be trivialized by wanton entity-positing. Indeed, entity-positing as it occurs in the sciences issues clear guidelines about this. Posit entities if needed; but then attempt appropriate epistemic access to them in order to verify that there are such.

Why does wanton entity-manufacturing trivialize explanations? In a word because when doing so we are making up the explanation along with the entities (that we're making up) instead of trying to determine what's really behind what it is we're trying to provide an explanation for. This is a point that's relevant not just to explanations of truths, but one that's relevant to explanations in general.

I should add this final remark: one good reason for my continuing to use "ontological dependence" the way I have is precisely because the items that many metaphysicians treat as ontologically dependent are the ones I deny existence to altogether. On the view of the simple metaphysician, therefore, ontological dependence, if it's mistakenly treated as a relation between things that exist, is only a symptom of an already bloated ontology.[27]

[27] My thanks to Benjamin Schnieder for valuable comments on the penultimate version of this chapter. My gratitude to the participants at 2009 Colorado conference on dependence where I presented a much earlier version of this chapter.

CHAPTER 10

Truth-makers and dependence

David Liggins

This chapter discusses the significance of non-causal dependence for truth-maker theory. After introducing truth-maker theory (Section 10.1), I discuss a challenge to it levelled by Benjamin Schnieder. I argue that Schnieder's challenge can be met once we acknowledge the existence of non-causal dependence and of explanations which rely on it (Sections 10.2 to 10.5). I then mount my own argument against truth-maker theory, based on the notion of non-causal dependence (Sections 10.6 and 10.7).

10.1 SOME TRUTH-MAKER THEORY

It's true that Mulligan exists; that is, <Mulligan exists> (the proposition *Mulligan exists*) is true. Is there anything in virtue of which it is true? It is very natural to think that the proposition is true in virtue of Mulligan. Let us define the term *truth-maker* as follows: *o* is a *truth-maker* for *P* just in case *P* is true in virtue of *o*. Then Mulligan is a truth-maker for <Mulligan exists>; the proposition is *made true* by Mulligan. 'In virtue of' is an explanatory locution: we can explain why the proposition is true by pointing to the existence of Mulligan. Indeed, quite generally, if *o* is a *truth-maker* for *P* then *P* is true because *o* exists (Horwich 2006; MacBride 2005, p. 133).

Many philosophers will agree that true existential propositions, such as this one, have a truth-maker. But truth-maker theorists go further. Some of them (e.g. Armstrong 2004, p. 5) claim that every true proposition has a truth-maker;[1] more cautious truth-maker theorists specify a class of true

---

[1] Or, more strictly, is made true by some things collectively. For instance, Restall 1996, p. 332, suggests that three performances collectively make <Pärt's *Magnificat* has had three performances> true, though none of the performances is a truth-maker for the proposition. In common with most writers on truth-maker theory, I will ignore this complication.

propositions, going beyond the existential truths, and claim that each of these truths has a truth-maker. For instance, Rodríguez-Pereyra maintains that each synthetic truth has a truth-maker: for each synthetic truth, there is some entity in virtue of which it is true (Rodríguez-Pereyra 2006b, p. 979).

What entity could serve as truth-maker for <The wall is turquoise>? Perhaps it is plausible to think that this proposition is made true by the wall. However, truth-maker theorists generally accept the following claim (see, e.g., Armstrong 1997, pp. 115–16):

Necessitarianism: If *o* a truth-maker for a truth *P*, then the proposition that *o* exists entails that *P* is true.

And it follows from this that the wall does not make <The wall is turquoise> true; since the wall would have failed to be turquoise if it had been painted a different colour, <The wall exists> does not entail that <The wall is turquoise> is true. If this proposition has a truth-maker, as many truth-maker theorists will claim, then it must be something whose existence entails that the proposition is true. And the same goes for other inessential predications. Different truth-maker theorists offer different candidates to play the role of truth-maker for such truths: competitors include tropes (Mulligan, Simons, and Smith 1984) and facts (or 'states of affairs') (Armstrong 1997).

As is well known, Necessitarianism cannot be extended to the biconditional:

o is a truth-maker for a truth *P* *if and only if* the proposition that *o* exists entails that *P* is true.

Let me give two reasons why. First of all, this principle implies that every entity is a truth-maker for every necessary truth: thus Restall's refrigerator makes the Goldbach conjecture (or its negation) true (Restall 1996, p. 334). But it is obvious that if the conjecture is true, it is not true in virtue of any consumer durable. The second reason is similar. Consider again the true proposition <The wall is turquoise>. The existence of any of the following entities will entail that the proposition is true: the event of my discovering that the wall is turquoise, the singleton of this event, my knowing that the wall is turquoise, the singleton of this process … and so on. The principle under discussion therefore implies that each of these is a truth-maker for the proposition; but it is clear that it is not true in virtue of any of these entities (Smith 1999, Section 5).

Not every theory which has been called a truth-maker theory accepts all the above doctrines. For instance, the version of truth-maker theory defended in Rodríguez-Pereyra 2002 does not incorporate Necessitarianism (see Rodríguez-Pereyra 2003). In this chapter, I'll consider theories which claim that some non-existential truths have truth-makers and accept Necessitarianism. It is these theories which Schnieder sets out to challenge (Schnieder 2006c, pp. 21–2).[2]

IO.2   SCHNIEDER ON EXPLANATION

Schnieder's challenge to truth-maker theory is based on some doctrines concerning explanation. According to Schnieder, there are two basic types of explanation: *causal* and *conceptual*. The term 'causal explanation' is a familiar one, and it applies to explanations such as:

(1) The tree fell because de Selby hit it with an axe.

Conceptual explanations include:

(2) Thorsten is Benjamin's brother-in-law, because he is married to Benjamin's sister

and

(3) Xanthippe became a widow, because Socrates died.

(All the examples in this section are from Schnieder 2006c – though, to avoid imposture, I have changed 'my' to 'Benjamin's'. I retain Schnieder's numbering.) Schnieder (Schnieder 2006c, p. 32) says that conceptual explanations 'are based on certain conceptual relations'. For instance, the concept *brother-in-law* can be analysed as follows: x is y's brother-in-law iff x is a man who is married to a sibling of y or a brother of y's spouse: (2) trades on this analysis. Similarly, (3) trades on the obvious analysis of *widow* as *woman whose husband has died*. But not all conceptual explanations are quite like this, Schnieder (Schnieder 2006c, p. 33) tells us:

(4) This vase is coloured because it is red

is a conceptual explanation, but the concept *being coloured* cannot be analysed in terms of individual colours. Nevertheless, (4) trades on a conceptual connection: that everything red is coloured.

---

[2] Rodríguez-Pereyra 2006a provides a more detailed overview of truth-maker theory.

In (2), (3), and (4), the concepts invoked in the explanandum are more complex than those invoked in the explanans. Schnieder holds that this is generally the case with conceptual explanations:

The direction of conceptual explanations seems to be owed to factors of conceptual complexity and primitiveness; in general, statements involving complex or elaborated concepts are explained in recourse to more primitive concepts (which may or may not enter into an analysis of the complex concepts). (Schnieder 2006c, p. 33)

According to Schnieder, some explanations combine conceptual and causal elements. For instance,

(6) Xanthippe became a widow, because Socrates drank the cup of hemlock

factors into a conceptual explanation:

Xanthippe became a widow, because Socrates died

and a causal one:

Socrates died because Socrates drank the cup of hemlock.

Call such explanations *hybrid*. Although he never makes the claim explicitly, Schnieder's discussion presupposes that every explanation which is neither causal nor conceptual is hybrid.

It seems that we can explain why some propositions are true: for instance

(9) It is true that Thorsten is Benjamin's brother-in-law because he is Benjamin's brother-in-law

(10) It is true that Thorsten is Benjamin's brother-in-law because he is married to Benjamin's sister.

According to Schnieder (Schnieder 2006c, p. 35), these are conceptual explanations.[3]

Schnieder introduces the notion of *the most direct explanation* of a phenomenon: $<p>$ is the most direct explanation of why r iff there is no proposition $<q>$ such that both (i) r because q and (ii) q because p. Informally, 'r because p' is the most direct explanation of why r iff it is not a telescoped version of some longer chain of explanations, such as 'r because q; q because p', or 'r because q; q because t; t because p'.

---

[3] See Künne 2003, pp. 154–5, and Dodd 2007, pp. 399–400, for similar claims.

For instance, (6) does not give the most direct explanation of why Xanthippe became a widow, since it can be expanded into the chain of explanations 'Xanthippe became a widow, because Socrates died; Socrates died because Socrates drank the cup of hemlock.' It is plausible that the most direct explanation of why Xanthippe became a widow is that Socrates died, since it is hard to think of a sentence which could fill both blanks in the following to yield a pair of correct explanations:

Xanthippe became a widow because _____; _____ because Socrates died.[4]

Schnieder (Schnieder 2006c, p. 38) argues that (9) gives the most direct explanation of why it is true that Thorsten is his brother-in-law:

Statement (9) hooks on the operator which governs the whole statement – the sentential operator 'it is true that'. Any other explanation with this *explanandum* will relate to something *inside* the scope of this operator; this will make such an explanation less direct than (9) (this is equally true for causal explanations as for conceptual ones).

Similarly, he argues that any instance of

(T) It is true that p because p

gives the most direct explanation of its explanandum.

10.3   SCHNIEDER'S CHALLENGE TO TRUTH-MAKER THEORY

Schnieder offers the following argument. Consider first truth-maker theorists who claim that tropes make true inessential predications true. These philosophers claim (for instance) that the trope *Socrates' paleness* is a truth-maker for <Socrates is pale>. On such views:

(?S) It is true that Socrates is pale because Socrates' paleness exists.

Now consider the claim:

(S-T) It is true that Socrates is pale because Socrates is pale.

This is an instance of (T). Schnieder has already argued that each instance of (T) gives the most direct explanation of its explanandum: if that is right, then (S-T) gives the most direct explanation of why it is

---

[4] 'Xanthippe's husband died' is perhaps a suitable substitution (see Ruben 1990, pp. 218–20, on 'identity explanations'). If so, then 'Xanthippe's husband died' will be the most direct explanation of why Xanthippe became a widow.

true that Socrates is pale. It follows that (?S) does *not* give the most direct explanation, and so the explanans in (?S) should also explain (S-T)'s explanans – that is:

(S-1) Socrates is pale because Socrates' paleness exists.

Schnieder argues that (S-1) is false: rather,

(S-2) Socrates' paleness exists because Socrates is pale.

To establish (S-2) and argue against (S-1), Schnieder (Schnieder 2006c, p. 41) notes that '[I]t is part of our understanding of "Socrates' paleness" that it denotes an entity that exists if *Socrates is pale*.' There is a conceptual connection between the concept of the trope *Socrates' paleness* and other concepts such as *Socrates* and *paleness*. Whichever of (S-1) and (S-2) is correct will trade on this connection. But which of them *is* correct? Schnieder argues that we can settle this question by considering relative conceptual complexity: the concept of the trope *Socrates' paleness* is more complex than *Socrates*, *paleness*, and whatever further concepts are required to understand the sentence 'Socrates is pale'. In conceptual explanations, the explanadum employs more complex concepts than the explanans. Hence, Schnieder claims, we should reject (S-1) and accept (S-2).

Nothing hangs on the particular choice of example here: we may go through the same argument whenever a trope is claimed to be the truth-maker of the proposition expressed by a true subject-predicate sentence. Moreover, we can also apply a parallel argument to theories which posit facts, rather than tropes, as truth-makers. If the fact that Socrates is pale makes <Socrates is pale> true, then that proposition is true because the fact exists. But that cannot be the most direct explanation of why the proposition is true, since (S-T) is the most direct explanation. The question then arises: is Socrates pale because the fact exists – or does the fact exist because Socrates is pale? The concept of the fact that Socrates is pale seems to be more complex than the concepts required to understand 'Socrates is pale', so (Schnieder argues) it is the second of these explanations that is correct. That is bad news for theorists of facts-as-truth-makers, since their theory implies the correctness of the first, and presumably they can't both be correct.

In short: expressions picking out tropes and facts

are understood on the basis of our understanding the components of the atomic statements. But because of that, they cannot be invoked for a conceptual explanation which would have to hold for them to be truth-makers. (Schnieder 2006c, p. 41)

At one point, Schnieder (Schnieder 2006c, p. 39) claims to have established that truth-maker theories stem from a 'capital philosophical mistake'. But right at the end of his article, he concedes that his argument can be seen as a twofold challenge to truth-maker theory:

> Given that my analysis of truth-making is correct, [truth-maker] theorists can be required to tell us *firstly* what explanatory relation could justify the truth of the explanations they need for their theory to work, explanations such as (S-1). And *secondly* they should either undermine the conceptual explanation I tried to establish with respect to (S-2), or explain how it can be that in this special case, we have an explanation running in both directions. (Schnieder 2006c, p. 42)

One way to respond to these challenges would be to dispute their legitimacy. For instance, one might argue that the first challenge is illegitimate on the ground that one can be confident that something is an explanation without being able to classify it. (One can recognize a tree without being able to tell what sort of tree it is.) But I take it such a response would be unsatisfying.

Another style of response would be to dispute the reasoning which leads up to the challenges. For instance, one might choose to attack Schnieder's claim that understanding 'Socrates' paleness exists' involves more complex concepts than understanding 'Socrates is pale.' But issues of analysis are delicate ones; I am not sure how to go about settling them. So I will grant Schnieder all his claims about relative conceptual complexity. Another option would be to argue that Schnieder's term 'the most direct explanation' is not well-defined: perhaps we can have 'p because q' and 'p because r' where neither of these explanations is a telescoped version of a longer chain. I will not attempt to establish that here. A further possibility would be to attack the claim that instances of 'It is true that p iff p' are conceptual truths, on the grounds that they are not conservative over logic.[5] In Sections 10.4 and 10.5, I offer truth-maker theorists a way to meet Schnieder's challenges head on.

10.4 HOW TRUTH-MAKER THEORISTS CAN REPLY
TO THE FIRST CHALLENGE

For definiteness, let's build conceptual priority into the notion of a conceptual explanation: in order for an explanation to count as conceptual,

---

[5] 'Either p or not p. If p, then $<p>$ is true. If not p, then $<$not $p>$ is true. Either way, something is true. Thus something exists.' Philosophers suspicious of a conceptual proof that something exists will think that the more likely candidates for conceptual truth are the conditionals 'If $<p>$ exists, then: $<p>$ is true iff p.' Compare Field 1984.

an explanation must employ less complex concepts in the explanans than in the explanandum. This is purely a matter of notation; it would be possible to say everything I am going to say while using the expression 'conceptual explanation' in a wider sense, but it would take longer.

With that stipulation made, it is plausible that there are correct explanations that are neither causal nor conceptual nor hybrid. Here are some examples.

(a) This act is morally wrong because it produces pain just for fun.
(b) These things constitute a table because they are arranged table-wise (in the sense of van Inwagen 1990, p. 109).
(c) The tea is poisonous because it contains arsenic.

These are clearly non-causal. Neither are they conceptual (*pace* Thomasson 2006): for instance, it is not analytic that if there are things arranged tablewise, they constitute a table (see Sider 2009, Section 4). And it is hard to see them as hybrid: what could the intermediate explanations be? Thus there seem to be at least three explanations which escape Schnieder's taxonomy.

It should come as no surprise that there are such explanations: their existence is implied by some plausible theses which I will now set out.

Kim (1994, p. 68) put forward the idea that explanations often track instances of dependence (see also Ruben 1990, Chapter VII). For instance, when a causal explanation of the form 'E occurred because F occurred' is correct, that is because F stands in the causal relation to E. The causal explanation is underpinned by an instance of causal dependence.

It is plausible that there is also *non-causal dependence*. For instance, it is commonly supposed that many of the properties of wholes depend on the properties of their parts, that the values of things depend on their non-evaluative features, and that the possession of higher-level properties depends on the possession of lower-level properties which realize them.

Regarding (a), Mackie (1977, p. 41) asked: '[J]ust what *in the world* is signified by this "because"?' This question led to a rich debate concerning supervenience. But Mackie's question was about dependence – which is not the same thing as supervenience. To see this, note that necessities supervene upon everything, but they do not depend on everything. The existence of Socrates supervenes on the existence of his singleton set, but does not depend on it: plausibly, the dependence runs the other way (see Fine 1995a, p. 271). Philosophers have discussed supervenience extensively in the last forty years or so, whereas non-causal forms of dependence are just beginning to receive thorough investigation.

The non-causal dependence connected with realization, constitution, and value underwrites explanations such as (a), (b), and (c). These explanations are clearly non-causal; it is no surprise that non-causal dependence does not underwrite causal explanation. But are they conceptual, in the sense of that term I introduced above? It is not plausible to think so. If these explanations were conceptual, then what depends on what would be mirrored in the complexity of the concepts we use to think about these things; sentences reporting dependent phenomena would involve more complex concepts than those reporting the things on which they depend. But there is no obvious reason to expect this. Indeed, there seem to be cases where this mirroring does not obtain: the concept *arranged tablewise* can be analysed into *table* and other concepts (see van Inwagen 1990, p. 109).

There are, therefore, explanations which are not causal, not conceptual, and not hybrid; moreover, if explanation often tracks dependence, then we have a theoretical reason to expect such explanations to exist. Let us call such explanations *determinative*. Truth-maker theorists can use this category to reply to Schnieder's challenge. They can accept that (S-1) does not fall into any of the categories which he sets out; but they can claim that there are more types of explanations than Schnieder's philosophy allows for: (S-1) is determinative. And so are the other explanations whose nature Schnieder asks the truth-maker theorist to specify.

10.5   HOW TRUTH-MAKER THEORISTS CAN REPLY
TO THE SECOND CHALLENGE

I have shown that truth-maker theorists are free to endorse (S-1), but as yet I have done nothing to counter Schnieder's argument for (S-2). I take it that the truth-maker theorist does not want to end up endorsing both (S-1) and (S-2) though, so they must explain where Schnieder's argument for (S-2) has gone wrong. In other words, they must meet the second challenge.

To do so, truth-maker theorists should first point out that, although Schnieder's (2) and (3) appear to be true, they do not feel very explanatory. When you ask why someone is a widow, it is less than satisfying to be told that her husband is dead, true though this may be. These phenomena could be explained if in (2) and (3) 'because' does not signal the presence of an explanation but has some other function. What could this function be? Well, we know that 'because' sometimes functions as an inference-marker: for instance, one might say 'Somebody has taken the diamonds, because they're not where I left them.' In these instances, 'because' works like 'therefore' or 'so'. Perhaps the same is occurring in

(2) and (3): in these sentences, 'because' could be signalling the presence of an inference rather than an explanation. For instance, we might see (2) and (3) as summaries of the following arguments respectively, or of similar arguments with extra premises:

> Thorsten is married to Benjamin's sister.
> For all x and y, if x is a man who is married to y's sister, x is y's brother-in-law.
> Therefore, Thorsten is Benjamin's brother-in-law.

> Xanthippe was married to Socrates.
> Socrates died.
> Every woman whose husband has died is a widow.
> Therefore, Xanthippe became a widow.

We can explain why one might be tempted to mis-classify (2) and (3) as explanations by acknowledging that 'because' does often signal the presence of an explanation. And we can go further. Consider the following pair of arguments:

> Thorsten is married to Benjamin's sister.
> For all x and y, if x is a man who is married to y's sister, then 'is the brother-in-law of' applies to x and y (in that order).
> Therefore, 'is the brother-in-law of' applies to Thorsten and Benjamin (in that order).

> Xanthippe was married to Socrates.
> Socrates died.
> 'Is a widow' applies to a woman just in case her husband has died.
> Therefore, 'is a widow' applies to Xanthippe.

I take it that the premises of these arguments explain their conclusions. Quite generally, we can explain why certain things satisfy a predicate by citing its application conditions; these two arguments are examples. They can be summarized as follows:

> (2′) 'Is the brother-in-law of' applies to Thorsten and Benjamin (in that order) because Thorsten is married to Benjamin's sister.
> (3′) 'Is a widow' applies to Xanthippe because Socrates died.

We can explain why one might be tempted to class (2) and (3) as explanations by mentioning the danger of confusing them with genuine explanations which are closely similar, namely (2′) and (3′).

So far in this section, I have concentrated on two of Schnieder's examples of conceptual explanations. I counsel truth-maker theorists to say corresponding things about (S-2): it seems true, but does not feel very explanatory, and that is because it is an elliptical version of the following argument:

> Socrates is pale.
> If Socrates is pale, then Socrates' paleness exists.
> Therefore, Socrates' paleness exists.

If (S-2) is really a deduction, rather than an explanation, then no explanatory circularity follows from endorsing (S-1) and (S-2) together. Moreover, there is a ready explanation of why we might feel sympathetic to the mistaken idea that (S-2) is an explanation: we confuse (S-2) with a genuine explanation to which it is intimately related, namely:

> 'Exists' applies to Socrates' paleness because Socrates is pale.

which is a compressed version of the following:

> 'Exists' applies to Socrates' paleness just in case Socrates is pale.
> Socrates is pale.
> Therefore, 'exists' applies to Socrates' paleness.

In this way, truth-maker theorists can meet Schnieder's second challenge.

10.6 A RELATED ARGUMENT AGAINST TRUTH-MAKER THEORY

We have seen that the notion of non-causal dependence enables truth-maker theorists to overcome Schnieder's challenges. In the rest of the chapter, I will show that non-causal dependence also poses a problem for truth-maker theory, by using that notion in an attack on truth-maker theory. In a nutshell, my charge is that truth-maker theory cannot be integrated into an attractive general account of non-causal dependence.

To provide a motivation for their theories, truth-maker theorists look to truth's dependence on reality. As Rodríguez-Pereyra writes:

[T]he root of the idea of truth-makers is the very plausible and compelling idea that the truth of a proposition is a function of, or is determined by, reality. ... In other words, truth is not primitive. If a certain proposition is true, then it owes its truth to something else: its truth is not a primitive, brute, ultimate fact. (Rodríguez-Pereyra 2005, p. 21)[6]

In order to capture this dependence, truth-maker theorists invoke the relation of *grounding*, a dependence relation which truth-makers bear to propositions (Armstrong 1997, pp. 128–31; Rodríguez-Pereyra 2005, pp. 26–7). This relation is non-causal (Armstrong 2004, p. 5). It is cross-categorial, in that it relates propositions to non-propositions. (It may *sometimes* relate a proposition to a proposition: for example, perhaps every proposition is a ground of <There is a proposition>.) According to Necessitarian versions of truth-maker theory, grounding is related to entailment as follows: if *o* grounds <*p*>, then <*o* exists> entails that <*p*> is true.

We saw in Section 10.1 the following principle fails:

o is a truth-maker for a truth *P* if and only if the proposition that *o* exists entails that *P* is true.

Since truth-making concerns the non-causal dependence of truth on reality, the failure of this principle should come as no surprise: it is just a special case of the thesis that non-causal dependence cannot be captured in modal terms (see Fine 1995a, pp. 270–2; Leuenberger 2008, pp. 755–8).

According to truth-maker theorists who regard tropes as truth-makers,

(?S) It is true that Socrates is pale because Socrates' paleness exists.

Corresponding to this, these truth-maker theorists claim that the trope *Socrates' paleness* grounds <Socrates is pale>. The explanation is under-pinned by this instance of non-causal dependence. Likewise, truth-maker theorists who posit facts will claim:

<Socrates is pale> is true because the fact that Socrates is pale exists.

and they will explain why they regard this explanation as correct by asserting that the fact grounds the proposition.

I am highly sympathetic to the idea that the truth-values of propositions are typically determined by extra-propositional reality. But I am not yet convinced that this dependence involves a relation which

---

[6] Horwich (2008, p. 262) suggests that truth-maker theory is not about truth: truth-maker theorists use the truth-predicate merely to articulate generalizations which are not about truth. In the light of their motivation, the suggestion is implausible.

propositions bear to other things (and sometimes to propositions). Other options deserve consideration. I will now sketch a couple of general accounts of non-causal dependence, and show how they can accommodate the dependence of truth on reality without invoking the truth-maker theorists' grounding relation.

First, consider the *fact–fact theory*. On this view, the non-causal dependence relation always relates facts to facts. This relation is invoked when we use the following locutions:

p in virtue of its being the case that *q*.
The fact that *q* makes it the case that *p*.
The fact that *p* obtains in virtue of the fact that *q*.
The fact that *p* is grounded in the fact that *q*.
The fact that *p* is constituted by the fact that *q*.

Let us write 'Nom(q)' for the nominalization of the sentence 'q': for instance, Nom(The rose is scarlet) is 'The rose's being scarlet'. The operator turns declarative sentences into noun phrases. Then further expressions can be added to the list:

p in virtue of Nom(q).
Nom(q) grounds Nom(p).

The fact–fact theory says that each of these explanations has the same underlying metaphysics: the non-causal dependence relation relates the fact that *p* to the fact that *q*.

At first sight, the theory might seem implausible, since it appears that non-facts are often involved in ontological dependence. For instance, the dependence of {Socrates} on Socrates appears to involve a set and a philosopher, neither of which is a fact. But these cases can be accommodated by the fact–fact theory, which regards them as misleadingly reported dependences between facts. According to the theory, the claim expressed by the sentence '{Socrates} depends on Socrates' is more perspicuously expressed by '{Socrates} exists in virtue of its being the case that Socrates exists' and 'The fact that Socrates exists makes it the case that {Socrates} exists.' And these sentences, the theory maintains, require only fact–fact dependence. Apparent counter examples to the theory are thus paraphrased away. The theory resembles accounts of causal dependence which claim that causal relata always belong to some particular category (such as the category *event*) and that sentences which apparently report causation of or by things outside that category are misleading and do not genuinely do so.

The fact–fact theory seems to have no problem accommodating the dependence of truth on reality. Take an instance of (*T*):

(S-T) It is true that Socrates is pale because Socrates is pale.

The fact theory accounts for the correctness of this explanation by positing two facts: the fact that <Socrates is pale> is true, and the fact that Socrates is pale. On this account, the former obtains in virtue of the latter; no dependence relation borne by a proposition is involved. Indeed, it is very natural to spell out the dependence of truth on reality by using fact-talk: see the quotation from Rodríguez-Pereyra above.

Let me bring onto the stage another general account of non-causal dependence: the *operator theory*. This account is suggested by some remarks of Kit Fine's. In his 2001, Fine generally talks of dependence as a relation between true propositions. But he suggests (p. 16) that we could use a sentential operator to express grounding claims. He claims that this 'shows that there is no need to suppose that a ground is some fact or entity in the world'. I doubt that Fine regards the availability of this way of expressing dependence claims as *establishing* that dependence is not a relation, or group of relations: rather, the point is that the assumption that dependence should be accounted for in relational terms stands in need of justification. The operator theory asserts that dependence claims should be understood as involving sentential operators, and denies that there is any relation of non-causal dependence. It thus resembles the account of conjunctive sentences which says that they can often be true even though 'and' does not pick out any relation.[7]

The operator theory seems to be able to accommodate the dependence of truth on reality. Those who endorse it need not deny (S-T); and they will challenge their opponents to show that (S-T) requires for its truth the obtaining of any non-causal dependence relation.

The fact–fact theory is elegant and economical. If causes and effects are always facts, it offers us a pleasingly unified theory of dependence. For all that, we do not yet know whether the fact–fact theory of non-causal dependence is true. More importantly for my argument, we do not yet have conclusive grounds to rule it out.[8] Since the fact–fact theory is incompatible with truth-maker theory, the onus is on truth-maker theorists to explain what

---

[7] See Melia 2005 for a related account of truth-making.

[8] Correia 2005 and Rosen 2010 explore the logic of dependence. Although Rosen adopts a fact-based approach while Correia remains metaphysically neutral, both these philosophers' logical investigations can be exploited by fact–fact and operator theorists alike.

is wrong with this account of non-causal dependence. Similar remarks apply to the operator theory: its apparent availability challenges truth-maker theorists to demonstrate that non-causal dependence is relational.

In response to this argument, truth-maker theorists might claim that truth-maker theory can be extended to form a general theory of non-causal dependence – and that this theory is just as good as the operator or the fact–fact theory. In the remainder of this section, I will bolster my argument by showing that this response is not only implausible but methodologically unsound.

First of all, we must ask what shape a theory of non-causal dependence modelled on truth-maker theory would take. The most obvious extension says that, just as there is a dependence relation (namely, grounding) which objects bear to the propositions they make true, there is another dependence relation which objects bear to the acts they make morally wrong, another dependence relation which objects bear to the things they make poisonous, and so on. Perhaps the trope *the act's producing pain just for fun* bears the relevant relation to the act and is therefore its wrongmaker. Or perhaps the tea's poisonmaker is the fact that it contains arsenic.

The dependence relations posited by this theory cannot be identical. (Identifying these relations would imply that poisonous cups of tea and morally wrong acts have truth-makers and are therefore true.) It would be more economical to see each of these dyadic relations as derived from a triadic one: instead of a dependence relation between the wrongmaker and the act, the truth-maker theorist might introduce a relation between the wrongmaker, the act, and the property of being morally wrong; and it could be the same relation which relates the poisonmaker, the cup of tea, and the property of being poisonous. Fixing the property generates the dyadic relations. The most perspicuous notation for claims of non-causal dependence would thus involve a three-place predicate such as 'x is made F by o'. On this account of dependence, making true is just a special case of making F.

The problem with this account of non-causal dependence is that there are plenty of plausible cases it cannot accommodate. Consider

{Socrates} depends on Socrates.
There is a singleton set in virtue of the existence of Socrates.
Grass is not red, in virtue of grass being green.
Every particle that is among some particles arranged tablewise is part of a table, because every group of particles arranged tablewise constitutes a table.

Necessarily, water contains hydrogen, in virtue of the essence of water.
Kasparov and Karpov cannot both win, owing to the laws of chess.
Birds are able to fly, thanks to their having wings.
If this stone were to be dropped, it would fall, owing to the direction
of the gravitational field.

It is most unlikely that all these cases can be stated using '*x* is made *F*
by *o*' – whereas the fact–fact theory and the operator theory have no
problems in accommodating them. The moral is that there is more to
non-causal dependence than *making*. Truth-maker theory is thus a poor
model for accounts of non-causal dependence.

Moreover, there is a methodological error in beginning with truth-maker
theory and then seeking to extrapolate an account of non-causal dependence
from it. As we have seen, there are lots of plausible instances of non-causal
dependence which do not involve the truth of a proposition depending on
some entity. When investigating the metaphysics of non-causal dependence,
we should bear all these phenomena in mind and hunt for an attractive
theory which does justice to as many of them as possible. This is not to say
that metaphysicians of non-causal dependence must consider *all* the putative
examples (or types of examples) of the phenomenon from the outset of their
inquiry. That approach threatens an unmanageable overload, so it may be
preferable to start off with a case study and then proceed to a general theory of
non-causal dependence. But then the case study may have to be rethought
once further data is brought into consideration. Any results based on a subset
of the available evidence must be regarded as provisional. (For a parallel,
consider a philosopher of causation who began by arguing for a metaphysics
of the causation of bodily movements and then sought to extend this account
to other cases of causation. It would be reasonable to doubt that this
procedure would lead to the best over-all metaphysics of causation.) Truth-
making is only a small province of the broader republic of non-causal
dependence – and we have no reason to think it a representative one. In
plumping for an account of the metaphysics of truth's dependence on reality
without considering other cases of non-causal dependence, truth-maker
theorists have succumbed to methodological myopia.

10.7 OBJECTIONS AND REPLIES

'Truth-maker theorists have provided successful arguments for their
theories. These arguments thereby refute the fact–fact theory and the
operator theory.'

Reply. As Dodd (2002, pp. 69–70) and Merricks (2007, p. 2) have noted, truth-maker theorists rarely offer detailed arguments for their views. When they do offer argument, truth-maker theorists appeal to truth's dependence on reality (e.g. Armstrong 2004, p. 7): but we have just seen that there is a substantial gap between that idea and the grounding claims made by truth-maker theorists.[9] Rodríguez-Pereyra 2005 offers a detailed argument for truth-maker theory on the basis of truth's dependence on reality, but this argument is, in my view, inconclusive (see Section v of my 2008). It raises the same questions concerning the ontology of non-causal dependence which I have been discussing here.

'If the fact–fact theory is true, then a grounding relation of the sort posited by truth-maker theorists can be defined. So the fact–fact theory is compatible with truth-maker theory.'

Reply. According to the fact–fact theory, non-causal dependence only ever relates facts to facts. So it entails the non-existence of the truth-maker theorist's grounding relation. It is true that the fact–fact theorist can define a *predicate* as follows:

o grounds* $<p>$ iff the fact that o exists grounds the fact that $<p>$ is true.

But this is a predicate whose satisfaction-conditions, given by the right-hand side of the biconditional, do not require the existence of a grounding relation which could have a proposition among its relata. The same goes for the operator theory: although the operator theorist can define a predicate 'grounds**' in similar fashion, their theory also entails the non-existence of the truth-maker theorist's grounding relation, and thus that this predicate will not pick out that relation.

10.8 CONCLUSION

I have argued that Schnieder's challenge to truth-maker theory can be met once we acknowledge the existence of non-causal dependence and of explanations which appeal to it. But non-causal dependence is at present only dimly understood. In particular, its metaphysics is unsettled. It remains to be seen whether truth-maker theorists' claims about grounding can be integrated into an attractive general theory of the

---

[9] Liggins 2008, Section IV, argues that it is very difficult to see how the groundedness of truth in reality supports truth-maker theory.

metaphysics of non-causal dependence. In the second half of this chapter, I have argued that the prospects for such an integration are slim. We should acknowledge truth's dependence on reality without claiming that any relation of dependence is borne to propositions.[10]

[10] For comments, discussion, and encouragement, I would like to thank Chris Daly, Ezequiel Zerbudis, Hugh Mellor, Gonzalo Rodríguez-Pereyra, Julian Dodd, Michael Clark, the editors of this volume, and an anonymous referee. Thanks also to audiences in Amsterdam, Buenos Aires, Ghent, and Geneva.

CHAPTER 11

Expressivism about making and truth-making

Stephen Barker

11.0 INTRODUCTION

The facts of truth are not primitive facts. Unless we accept the identity theory of truth – and equate truth and fact – the fact that a proposition is true must obtain in virtue of something: how things are with its subject matter.[1] We might express this thought as the idea that truth supervenes on, is asymmetrically determined by, being (see Bigelow 1988). But that would be misleading, since it suggests that truth is not part of being. The facts of truth, that certain propositions are true or false, are part of how things are, and so, are aspects of being. We should say rather that the facts of truth, the alethic facts, are made the case by non-alethic facts. (Still, as we shall see, that claim will need qualification.) Viewed in this way, the problem of truth-making reduces to the problem of *making*. What's *making*?

We are very familiar with causal making, that is, causation. It occurs through time linking events. Non-causal making is atemporal and operates through *levels of reality*. For just about any predicate *F*, we can discern *F-making*, that is, what makes something *F*. We might say that *making-the case* is the most basic kind of non-causal making – all kinds of non-causal making can be reduced to it. Fred's being unmarried and male makes it the case that he is a bachelor. Logically simpler facts frequently make various logically more complex facts the case. Certain facts make it the case that some propositions are true or false. And so on. Truth-making then reduces to non-causal making-the-case of facts by facts.

How do we understand making? (I leave out *non-causal* unless required.) My strategy is not to ask what making *is* with the hope of providing a metaphysical theory about its nature. It's rather to look to the language of *making*. The metaphor behind *making* refers to agency.

[1] Rodríguez-Pereyra 2005 presents this kind of argument for truth-making.

It would be absurd to suggest that claims about making, be they non-causal or causal, are claims about agency. It is not absurd, however, to propose that the concept of making somehow emerges from features to do with agency.[2] Agency resides in capacities to manipulate things. Agency theorists of causation invoke *causal recipes*, procedures for an agent to get what she wants by manipulating the world. In the case of non-causal making, the recipes are not procedures for manipulating things in the world. They are, rather, *analytic recipes*: capacities to manipulate concepts.

An analytic recipe finds its paradigm form in an introduction rule for a logical constant. Introduction rules are linked to *construction* in the sense that they reveal the canonical grounds for use of a logical constant. I liberalize the idea of introduction-rule to that of any inference whose premises are canonical grounds for the application of a concept, be that concept a logical constant or non-logical concept. Roughly, my proposal is that non-causal making-claims express commitments to derivations, as in *M* – here 'F' appended to sentences, *p*, *q*, etc. forms a term denoting a fact:

M: In asserting $<Fp_1, Fp_2, \ldots Fp_n$ *makes-the case* $Fq>$, U expresses a commitment to a derivation of *q* using only introduction rules employing all of $\{p_1, p_2, \ldots p_n\}$.

(*M* needs some qualification in the case of negation, as we shall see.) I am not claiming that making-claims are claims about inference, that is, kinds of metalinguistic claims. I am not offering reductive truth-conditions for making-claims in terms of inferential commitments. Instead, I am offering an explication of making-talk in terms of the activities and cognitive structures underpinning its production. The form of theoretical orientation naturally sees itself allied with *expressivism*. So, I am offering an expressivist treatment of making- and making-true-claims. None of this implies non-cognitivism about making-statements. They are, on this approach, truth-apt and about the world.[3]

II.I FRAMING TRUTH-MAKING

In what follows I assume that truth-bearers are propositions. Let '$<p>$' denote the proposition that *p*. For any true proposition $<p>$, I submit, the TM-sentences below are true, and their converses are false:

---

[2] That's the path taken by agency theorists of causation, such as Gasking 1955, von Wright 1971, Price 1992, and Woodward 2003.
[3] See Barker 2007 and 2011, for sketches of the expressivist framework I work with.

TM: *(i)* $<p>$ is true because p;
      (ii) $<p>$ is true in virtue of the fact that p;
     (iii) The fact that p makes $<p>$ true.

TM-sentences all convey the same basic fact about the dependency of a proposition's truth on how things are with its subject matter. But since truth-making is just one kind of making, they express the dependence of one kind of fact on another. If so, the facts that true TM-sentences express, facts like that below – here again 'Fp' means the fact that p, etc.,

    Fp *makes-true* $<p>$,

are reduced to facts of *making-the-case* as in:

    Fp *makes-the case* $F[<p>$ *is true*].

In what follows I use both locutions *makes-the-case,* and *makes-true,* depending on whether the reduction of *making-true* to *making-the-case* is being emphasized.

Many philosophers don't like facts. So they won't like my reduction of truth-making to fact-making. They may want truth-making without truth-makers. Such theorists might be happy with TM-sentences like TM *(i)*, which, on the surface, don't seem to refer to facts (Hornsby 2005). It strikes me the denial of facts is utterly implausible. If there are objects and properties, and objects instantiate properties, then there are facts. Even set-theoretic nominalists cannot deny that. To avoid facts one has to embrace a serious nominalism about properties, which is difficult to do.[4] I argue in §11.5 below that ontological concerns about facts are exaggerated, and we can make perfect sense of them.

Amongst philosophers who don't mind facts, there are those who don't like negative facts. Negative facts are standardly viewed as ontologically dubious entities (Molnar 2000, Simons 2005). These philosophers won't like my espousal of all true TM-statements, in particular TM-sentences like:

    $<\neg p>$ is true in virtue of the fact that $\neg p$.

Foes of negative facts, who want, as I think they should, negative truths to have truth-makers, have to provide alternative truth-makers for such

---

[4] If you're a fact-foe, you can treat this paper as an explication of sentences like TM *(i)*, interpreted as carrying no commitment to facts.

truths. Take Armstrong's approach. For him, truth-making is about a relation of necessitation between facts and propositions, as in **NEC**:

NEC: X truth-makes $<p>$ iff X exists, and X's existence necessitates $<p>$.

Armstrong's fact-ontology comprises positive atomic facts and one totality fact *TOT*. *TOT* is the fact that the atomic facts are all the atomic facts there are. For Armstrong, *TOT* makes negative propositions true: they are all made true by the same totality fact. It works this way. Given that Fp is not amongst the atomic facts, *TOT* necessitates $<\neg p>$. Thus, *TOT* is the truth-maker of $<\neg p>$.

The problem with Armstrong's proposal is that **NEC** is false. Armstrong is forgetting that alethic facts are part of being. Where $<\neg p>$ is true, then the alethic fact, that $<\neg p>$ is true, exists. The existence of this fact necessitates $<\neg p>$. So, the fact that $<\neg p>$ is true makes-true $<\neg p>$. But the fact that a proposition is true does not make that proposition true. Here's another aspect of the problem. Suppose $<$snow is white$>$ is true. It's true in virtue of snow's being white. Suppose proposition 1 says that $<$snow is white$>$ is true. Suppose proposition 2 says that 1 is true. Suppose proposition 3 says 2 is true. And so on, up to proposition N. Clearly, N is true in virtue of $<$snow is white$>$'s being true. But given the alethic fact, that N is true, necessitates $<$snow is white$>$, then by **NEC**, we can conclude that $<$snow is white$>$ is true in virtue of N's being true. But that reverses the order of dependency of alethic facts on other alethic facts. The order of making is inverted.

We cannot solve the problem by denying that alethic facts exist, since, surely, if there are propositions possessing the property of truth, and we accept the general category of fact, then we must accept alethic facts. We cannot deny that alethic facts can be truth-makers, since if alethic facts are facts, they must be truth-makers for the propositions that describe them.

You might think other kinds of modification of **NEC** will solve the problems. I don't think so.[5] Other approaches to removing negative facts are just as problematic for very much the same reason. Bringing in the world as a truth-maker of negatives (Cameron 2007) won't help, since the world must include alethic reality, and we will get the same problem we have just articulated. I suggest that invoking totality, or the world, to explain negative truth is not going to work. So, we have some reason to believe negativity is unavoidable. I don't think this is a problem in itself.

---

[5] See Barker manuscript for development of these issues.

The arguments against negative facts are overrated (Barker and Jago forthcoming). And as I suggested above, a general treatment of fact-talk awaits us in Section 11.5, which I think renders talk of fact, logically simple and complex, unproblematic.

Logical complexity

TM *(i)–(iii)* are not the only kinds of TM-sentences. There are also those that express the dependency of logically complex truths on logically simpler facts, such as:

Fp *makes-true* $<p \lor q>$.
Fp and Fq together *make-true* $<p \ \& \ q>$.

On the other hand, the logically complex does not make logically simpler truth. Witness:

CON: F($p \ \& \ q$) *makes-true* $<p>$.

It's false that $<p>$ is true in virtue of the fact that ($p \ \& \ q$) (even assuming that q). The reason **CON** isn't acceptable, I think, is that q has nothing to do with the securing of the fact that $<p>$ is true. Philosophers who think otherwise confuse necessitation with making. Making may involve necessitation, but it's not identical to it. If I ask you what makes something the case, I am asking how it came to be. The truth of $<p>$ necessitates the fact that p, the fact that p necessitates the truth of p. There's necessitation in both directions. So the question, how did $<p>$'s being true come to be? is not answered by a claim about necessitation. Those impressed by **NEC**, will naturally gravitate to **CON**, since the existence of F($p \ \& \ q$) necessitates $<p>$. But F($p \ \& \ q$) has nothing to do with how $<p>$ comes to be true, any more than that Fp comes to be through $<p>$'s being true. And as we have seen, **NEC** is false.

The issue concerning relevance is sharpened when we consider the fact that more than one fact can contribute to the making of another fact: there is collective making, just as there is collective causal making. The following are cases thereof:

(1) Fp, Fq (together) *make-the case* F[$p \ \& \ q$];
(2) Fp, Fq (together) *make-true* $<p \ \& \ q>$.

Togetherness requires explanatory relevance. All the facts entering into the making relation have to do their bit: they must contribute to the bringing about. So in the cases above, Fp and Fq make essential contributions to the making. They are essential parts of the explanation for the obtaining of the fact F[p & q] and the truth of <p & q>. Hence intuitively these statements (1) and (2) of collective making seem correct. In contrast those below look wrong:

(3) Fp, Fq, and Fr (together) *make-the case* F[p & q].
(4) Fp, Fq (together) *make-true* <p>.

In (3), Fr makes no contribution. The Fr has nothing to do with the explanation of the obtaining of F(p & q). Similarly, in (4), Fq makes no contribution to <p>'s truth. It's not part of how <p>'s truth comes about. This shows again that a necessitation approach is off the mark.

A friend of necessitation as an analysis of making might point out that a disjunctive truth, <p v q> could be made true by Fp and Fq, since both obtain, even though just one would be sufficient for the disjunctive truth. The right thing to answer here is that the making of the disjunctive truth is over determined, where both Fp and Fq obtain, both independently, and not collectively, make-true <p v q>. I see no fundamental problem with that idea.

My claim that all truths have truth-makers might be challenged by the case of logically necessary truths. The claim that necessary truths don't require truth-makers is odd. How can a class of facts about truths suddenly be primitive facts? One might object that they are true in virtue of meaning. That might apply to sentences, sentences *have* meanings, but not to propositions, they *are* meanings. If it is logically necessary that p v $\neg p$ for some p, then that's because it's logically necessary that there is some truth-maker of some contingent kind or another. The proposition <p v $\neg p$> is guaranteed to have a truth-maker no matter what. The truth-makers are either Fp or, allowing negative facts, F$\neg p$. In turn, the truth, <It's necessary that p or $\neg p$> has as its truth-maker a fact of necessity. This is a modal fact. This fact could be the fact that in every possible world, either Fp holds or F$\neg p$ holds. What provides the guarantee that one of these facts will always obtain? That is a matter about the making of facts, and not the making of truths, and does not undermine the claim that truths of logical necessity are true in virtue of fact.

I have been urging that facts make propositions true. But a challenge to that idea is that objects such as people, electrons, or numbers, can make propositions true. What makes existential propositions true, like <2 exists> if not 2? If one has the necessitation conception of truth-making distilled in **NEC**, this conclusion follows. But **NEC** is false. If we return to explanatory making, and the locutions through which it is expressed, we have to assert:

(5) <2 exists> is true in virtue of 2.

This may not make sense. Just as objects don't cause, objects don't make. Makers are conditions, states of affairs, and facts. Even necessitation-theorists tacitly accept this. It's X's existing that necessitates, not X itself.

II.2   MAKING-CLAIMS AND ANALYTIC RECIPES

We have perhaps said enough about the phenomenal features of making. The question now is how can we illuminate the *nature* of this relation? I don't think there is going to be any analysis to be had drawn from the usual bag of tools: supervenience, counterfactual dependence, necessitation. For example, one might think that an analysis of making in terms of necessitation with an added condition about logical complexity might work, such as:

(6) $Fp_1, Fp_2, \ldots Fp_n$ *makes-the case* Fq iff $(p_1, p_2, p_3, \ldots)$ necessitate q, and q is more logically complex than any of $(p_1, p_2, p_3, \ldots)$.

The problem with this proposal is that it will validate sentences like:

(7) $F\neg\neg p$ *makes-the case* $F[p \vee (\neg\neg q \& r)]$.

This is not in accord with the real explanatory dependence, which is as follows: Fp is the common maker of $F\neg\neg p$ and $F[p \vee (\neg\neg q \& r)]$. The path of making does not go through Fp to $F\neg\neg p$, then $F[p \vee (\neg\neg q \& r)]$.

Instead of seeking an analysis of making, I am going to recommend an alternative strategy, as I enounced in Section II.0. I won't look for an analysis of making, but of making-language. The strategy is to take the metaphor of *making* seriously, and see where it leads. This will come through a theory of what's expressed in making-claims. I have already put forward the basic proposal, with *M* (Section II.0). The metaphor in *making* is that of agency. In *making* we construct something. In logical proofs, introduction rules are linked to construction in the sense that they reveal the canonical grounds for use of a logical constant. So, I suggest, in a non-causal making-claim, a speaker expresses a commitment to a certain kind of proof construction. The proof is one linking propositions, which describe the making-facts, to the proposition describing the made-fact. The proof will only use introduction rules. (Though, as we shall see in Section II.4, proofs that underpin claims about the making of negative facts, and indeed, negative truths, involve a qualification. These proofs are reductio proofs, and reductio proofs require use of elimination rules, rather than introduction rules, in that part of the proof that unpacks consequences of accepting the hypothesis.) We liberalize the idea of introduction-rule to that of any inference whose premises are canonical grounds for the application of a concept, be that concept a logical constant or non-logical concept. I call these *analytic recipes*. So, non-causal making-statements express commitments to constructions using analytic recipes.

Applied to truth-making claims, the proposal comes out as:

TM: In asserting Fp_1, Fp_2, ...Fp_n *make-true* $<q>$, U expresses a commitment to a derivation of $<q>$ *is true* using only introduction rules using all of $\{p_1, p_2...p_n\}$.

In this account, we require that all the premises in the derivations are involved at some stage in the application of introduction rules.

What logic governs the derivations? Is it classical or relevant, or some other kind of logic? In fact, the analytic-recipe approach is fairly neutral on questions of the logic used. The logic is not the central constraint on making-statements, it's the restriction on introduction-rules that does the work. For simplicity, I shall assume classical logic.

The theses, **M** and **TM**, are not truth-condition accounts of making and truth-making claims. We are not offering truth-conditional analysis. On the other hand, we are not denying that making-statements have truth-conditions. They are truth-apt claims, and the T-schema applies to them. It's just that no illumination about making comes through looking at truth-conditions.

The required idea of *expressing* that I invoke in **M** and **TM** is one drawn from the literature on expressivism. I am not going to explore this here (see Barker 2007, 2011). Clearly, we need a kind of *cognitivist expressivism*, since truth-making claims are truth-apt.

There is some question about the psychological reality of the proposal. We do not require that speakers have an explicit grasp of introduction and elimination rules, or the concept thereof. It may be that the psychological reality for speakers involves cognitive representations of such rules, but possessing those states does not require being in possession of the concept of a derivation. It is rather that the speaker could, relatively easily, acquire such concepts.

Truth and introduction rules

Let's get down to the details of the account. Let us suppose, as seems right, that the elimination and introduction rules for the truth-predicate are those below:

Truth-I: $p \vdash \langle p \rangle$ is true.
Truth-E: $\langle p \rangle$ is true $\vdash p$.

In terms of **TM**, we now explain the basic asymmetry between being and truth and our assertion of TM-statements, Fp *makes-true* $\langle p \rangle$, and our rejection of anti-TM-statements, like F[$\langle p \rangle$ is true] *makes-the case* Fp.

It would be wrong to say that, on this theory, the asymmetric fixing of truth by being is *constituted* by facts about introduction-rules. Rather, it is that our assertion of this asymmetry involves our defending commitments to derivations involving introduction rules. Yet this assertion of a worldly asymmetry, has its correlate in a cognitive/logical asymmetry: that between introduction rules and elimination rules. But what is the latter distinction?

I argue that what characterizes an inference-rule as an introduction rule are certain cognitive and epistemic asymmetries that are linked to the idea of a canonical ground. Basically in an introduction rule, $A_1, A_2, \ldots A_n \vdash B$, there is a concept on the right-hand side, in B – expressed by a predicate, operator, or connective – not present in $A_1, A_2, \ldots A_n$. The right-hand concept characterizes the general form of the conclusion.[6]

Definitional dependency

The analytic recipe theory is meant to explain our assertion of making-statements like (8):

(8) F[Fred is an unmarried man] *makes-true* $\langle$Fred is a bachelor$\rangle$

The introduction rule for bachelor is the following:

Fred is an unmarried man $\vdash$ Fred is a bachelor

---

[6] One may be concerned about the introduction-rule for the predicate *fact*: $p \vdash$ *it is a fact that p*. If this is accepted as an introduction rule we should ideally be disposed to assert: *the fact that p makes-the case the fact that it is a fact that p*. But that looks perfectly acceptable. Note: we are committed to an infinite hierarchy of facts, Fp, FFp, etc. I find this no more problematic than an hierarchy of facts of truth.

We may worry that the vagaries of definition could get in the way here. Suppose your concept of *brother* is derived from *male sibling*. My concept of *sibling* is disjunctive: *either brother or sister*. In which case you will accept as an introduction rule:

Fred is a male sibling ⊢ Fred is a brother.

I will accept as an introduction rule:

Fred is a brother ⊢ Fred is a sibling.

You will accept the first truth-making claim, I will not. Who is right? The answer is that there is no objective fact about who is right. There does not have to be. Perhaps what we have there is a case of faultless disagreement about which facts ground which facts. That does not imply any relativity of fact or subjectivity (see Barker 2011).

Entailment and transitivity

The analytic-recipe theory drags truth-making away from entailment and towards causation. That means some familiar principles, beloved of certain theorists, have to go. One is the entailment principle (see Armstrong 2004):

> ***EP:*** If f *makes-true* $<p>$, $p \rightarrow q$, then f *makes-true* $<q>$.

From the point of view of the analytic-recipe view, there is no reason at all to think that making should be preserved by entailment. Only failure to clarify the real nature of the truth-making problem would. The closest we get to the entailment principle is:

> ***EP^{AR}:*** If U asserts f *makes-true* $<p>$, and accepts, $p \vdash q$ (only with introduction rules) then U ought to accept f *makes-true* $<q>$.

EP^{AR} is not particularly informative, since it is just a trivial consequence of the analytic-recipe view.

Transitivity of making is also validated in the recipe view. If there is a proof construction underpinning assertion of Fp_1, Fp_2, ... Fp_n *makes-the case Fq*. And one underpinning assertion of Fq *makes-the case Fr*. Then there will be one underpinning assertion of Fp_1, Fp_2, ... Fp_n *makes-the case Fr*.

Possible counterexamples

It might be objected that the analytic-recipe approach to truth-making cannot work generally. Armstrong 2005 takes the claim,

X's being H_2O makes it true that X is water,

to refute a reduction of truth-making to entailment. My recipe approach doesn't reduce making-true to entailment, nevertheless, you could wonder how it treats this case. The explanation is fairly straightforward. What underlies assertion of this TM-claim are the following introduction rules:

(9) X is water ⊢ <X is water> is true.

(10) X is the underlying stuff causing watery appearances. ⊢ X is water.

(11) X is H_2O. H_2O causes watery appearances. Nothing else does. ⊢ X is the underlying stuff causing watery appearances.

Let's explain these in turn. (9) is just the basic truth-introduction rule for the instance at hand. (10) corresponds to a canonical rule of introduction for the concept *water*. We can think of the concept of *water* as being captured in the phrase: *the underlying stuff that is causing watery appearances.* Finally, (11) is an instance of a canonical ground for use of a definite description. More schematically:

X is *N*. *N* is stuff that causes Y. Nothing else does. ⊢ X is the stuff that causes Y.

Since definite descriptions carry uniqueness implications, it's unsurprising that the canonical ground for use of a definite description should be information that a given object, *N*, uniquely satisfies a certain condition. Putting together (9) to (11), we can construct a proof, using only introduction rules, from the propositions,

X is H_2O. H_2O causes watery appearances. Nothing else does.
<X is water> is true.

Of course, the facts corresponding to the initial propositions, jointly make the proposition <X is water> true. But we can treat the second two facts as background conditions for the making-true of <X is water> by the fact that X is H_2O.

II.3 TRUTH-MAKING AND LOGICALLY COMPLEX TRUTHS

So much for the basics about TM-statements and their expression of proof constructions, that link making facts with facts made. We have some evidence that this theory captures the basic sense of the asymmetric determination of facts of truth by the facts pertaining to the subject matter of those truths. We now move on to a refinement of these ideas: making and truth-making for logically complex propositions and facts. First, let us consider, conjunction, disjunction, existential quantification, and universals.[7] I treat negation in Section 11.4, which, as we already noted, brings with it some refinements of the conception of derivations underpinning making-statements. Part of the goal is to explain our sense that logically complex truths and facts depend for their truth or their obtaining on logically simpler facts. Isn't the introduction rule-account a rather shallow explanation of that intuition? Maybe it is, but it isn't merely a stipulation of the condition that the logically complex depends on the logically simpler.

Conjunction

The treatment of conjunction is straightforward. Our acceptance of the introduction rule, $p, q \vdash (p \& q)$, means our acceptance of:

(12) Fp, Fq (together) *make-true* $<p \& q>$.

On the other hand, we accept the elimination rule, $(p \& q) \vdash p$, and so will find the truth-making claim (13) below as counter-intuitive as we do the corresponding making claim, $F[p \& q]$ *makes-the case* $F[p]$:

(13) $F[p \& q]$ *makes-true* $<p>$

The conjunctive thesis is argued against explicitly by Rodríguez-Pereyra 2006b, who sees truth-making as explanatory. Of course, those philosophers like Armstrong 2005 who do not see truth-making as explanatory do not necessarily deny (13). But my suggestion is that the latter have missed the point about truth-making in failing to see the explanatory connection.[8]

---

[7] I will not consider indicative conditionals here. That's because it is not clear at all that they have truth-conditions, and so that they are truth-apt.

[8] However, an issue of some subtlety arises in relation to the schema:

(*) $F[p \& p]$ *makes-true* $<p>$

It might seem that we should accept (*). Here's an argument from Jago 2009. He accepts:

M: Whatever truth-makes $<p>$ ought to truth-make $<p \& p>$, and vice versa.

If $F[p \& p]$ makes-true $<p \& p>$ it ought to truth-make $<p>$, but that means accepting (*). However, the current analytic recipe hypothesis won't allow us to accept (*). To assert (*) we need a derivation from $(p \& p)$ to p, to $<p>$ *is true*, but that means using an elimination rule. Is the recipe theory's denial of (*) objectionable? Jago's argument is open to dispute. M is a theoretical principle, without independent intuitive power. This is particularly so, since it asks us to have intuitions about weird sentences that we do not normally use. I mean here conjunctions of the form: *P and P*. In standard formal treatments, these are acceptable, but for natural language in which semantics and pragmatics interpenetrate they are not obviously acceptable. A conjunction $(p \& q)$ is only

Disjunction

In the case of disjunction we accept the introduction rule: $p \vdash p \vee q$. So we have the following intuitively correct making-statements:

(14) Fp *makes-the case* F$[p \vee q]$

(15) Fp *makes-true* $<p \vee q>$.

The interesting issue is the collective making-statement:

(16) Fp, Fq (together) *make-true* $<p \vee q>$.

According to our agency proposal, this cannot be right, it involves explanatory irrelevance. We use an introduction rule to derive $(p \vee q)$ from either the p or from q. Either way, one premise, either p or q, is left doing no work.

There is no reason to accept the validity of the disjunctive principle (see Read 2000 and Rodríguez-Pereyra 2006b):

DP: If Fr *makes-true* $<p \vee q>$, then Fr makes-true either $<p>$ or $<q>$.

This principle fails if we allow disjunctive facts. And that's what we are doing. Thus, F$[p \vee q]$ makes-true $<p \vee q>$ but does not make-true any of its disjuncts. If we confine ourselves to atomic facts, then **DP** is acceptable.

The rule of disjunctive elimination, $(p \vee q)$, $(p \rightarrow r)$, $(q \rightarrow r) \vdash r$, does not furnish us with intuitively correct making-statements:

(17) F$[p \vee q]$, F$[p \rightarrow r]$, F$[q \rightarrow r]$ (together) *make-true* $<r>$.

(17) does not seem right. It has the same kind of counter-intuitiveness as (6). It may be that our belief that r is brought about by a deduction using disjunction elimination. But that does not mean that the factual reality Fr is brought about by a disjunctive fact, along with certain facts of entailment.

Existential quantifications

The case of existential quantification is unproblematic, given the obvious introduction rule. So we accept:

(18) F$[T$ is a $G]$, F$[T$ is $H]$ (together) *make-true* $<$At least one G is $H>$.

Intuitively, these seem right if we consult our sense of explanatory order. Likewise the elimination rule does not furnish us with any intuitively correct making-statements.

---

well-formed if p and q don't contain each other informationally. This fact about the intuitive weirdness of $(p \,\&\, p)$ is enough to undermine appeals to the supposed intuitiveness of M.

Existential quantifications confront us with the potential over-determination of analytic making. There may be many things that are *G* and *H*. So there are many pairs of facts of the form F[*T is a G*], F[*T is H*] that in themselves (together) make-true <*At least one G is H*>. Again, that's ok with the recipe view.

Existential quantifications are related to another matter of interest. We are taking it that facts make propositions true. But propositions about existence are often cited as cases in which objects make propositions true. Is <At least one bird exists> made true by individual birds, Tweety, for example? I have resisted the idea that things, like material objects, make propositions true. Since we are being unconstrained about facts, there is no problem with our saying that it is facts of individual existence that make true, each independently, <At least one bird exists>.

Universals

Universal truths, it might seem, present us with a special problem. In terms of a Fitch-style natural deduction system, the introduction rule for universals is shown in Figure 11.1.

U-Intro

$G\alpha$

$H\alpha$

Every *G* is *H*

Figure 11.1

In this rule, α is an *eigen* variable or arbitrary object term. U-Intro involves a sub-proof in which we suppose that an arbitrary object α is *G* and derive a conclusion that it is *H*. How are we to understand truth-making of universals in terms of this rule? The answer is that it is not the proof that is the truth-maker. It is the premises for the proof that correspond to the truth-makers. What the speaker expresses in asserting a truth-making claim is a derivation from premises, that is, assertions, using introduction rules, to the truth of a claim. U-intro, unlike, say, disjunction introduction, does not specify premises, in the sense of propositions. It specifies a kind of proof. Obviously, what we want are the premises that could support application of the U-Intro, and not the derivation itself. The question now is what these premises are.

There are two cases that we have to consider in answering this question. There is the case of non-accidental universals, true by virtue of necessitation of some kind, and accidental generalities, true by virtue of brute facts.

Where *Every F is G* is an accidental truth. One might wonder in this case, how U-Intro will be applied? What is the minimal information about contingent facts required to apply U-Intro? We answer this by considering what premises we need in order to carry out a suppositional proof that begins with suppose *Fα* and ends with *Gα*. The supposition is that some arbitrary α has *F*. The answer is simple. The premises we require are the following:

$\{T_1, T_2, T_3 \ldots T_n\}$ are all the Gs
T_1 is *H*, T_2 is *H*, T_3 is *H*, $\ldots T_n$ is *H*.

If that is correct, then the following is our basic truth-making claim about universals:

(19) F[T_1 is *H*], F[T_1 is *H*], F[T_2 is *H*], F[T_2 is *H*], $\ldots$F[Every
G is in the class $\{T_1, T_2, T_3 \ldots T_n\}$] (together) *make-true*
<*Every G is H*>

This result entails that universals need facts of totality as part of their truth-makers, facts like F[Every *G* is in the class $\{T_1, T_2, T_3 \ldots T_n\}$]. This is more or less what Armstrong 2004 argues, and indeed, it seems intuitively correct. We have derived a conservative result in (19), but at least we get a principled reason for explaining an intuition shared by many people.

11.4   NEGATION

That's our account of the intuitions about positive making and truth-making. Now for negations. Let us begin that investigation with the introduction and elimination rules for negation. Take the standard introduction rule:

Suppose *p*... ⊥. ⊢ ¬*p*

There is a concern about this being an introduction rule given my analysis of what an introduction rule is – see Section 11.2. This was that the right-hand side of the rule contains a concept not present on the left. One might object: here we find ⊥, which, it could be claimed, presupposes negation. But I suggest that ⊥ does not itself presuppose negation. ⊥ is absurdity. One form of absurdity is explicit contradiction, which will require negation. But absurdity is not constituted by explicit contradiction.

Given acceptance of that introduction rule, we ought to assert truth-making claims like the following:

(20) F*p makes-true* $<\neg\neg p>$.

That fits in with intuition and the idea that logically complex truths depend on simpler facts.

We now address the promised modification of the basic proposal about introduction rules outlined in Section 11.2. Here is the issue. The analysis as we have developed it so far does not quite work. It generates the result that we should assert (21), below, but not (22):

(21) F$[\neg(p \lor q)]$ *makes-the case* F$\neg p$,
(22) F$\neg p$, F$\neg q$ (together) *make-the case* F$\neg(p \lor q)$.

The proof underpinning (21) is *P1* (Figure 11.2), and that underpinning (22) is *P2*. *P1* only used introduction rules, but *P2* uses elimination rules in the reductio sub-proof with $(p \lor q)$ as its premise.

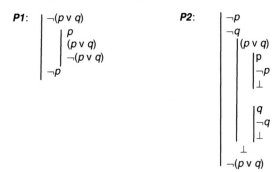

Figure 11.2

So by the lights of the hypotheses offered, (21) ought to be accepted, and (22) rejected. But surely it should be the other way around. (21) looks wrong: an atomic negative fact F$\neg p$ is not explained by the compound negative F$[\neg(p \lor q)]$. Rather, F$\neg p$ is part of the explanation of the compound fact. Accepting (21) is akin to accepting that a positive atomic fact is made the case by a conjunctive fact, which we reject. In contrast, (22) looks right. We explain why F$\neg(p \lor q)$ is the case through the negative facts corresponding to its negated disjuncts. (That's just as we explain the falsity of a disjunction by appeal to the falsity of disjuncts.)

The way out is to block proof *P1*, and allow *P2*. How can we do that given that it looks like *P1* involves only introduction rules, and *P2* has elimination rules at the second sub-proof level? The answer, which I shall justify below, is that the proofs supporting making statements can included elimination rules, under certain circumstances. Those circumstances are met in *P2*. Furthermore, elimination rules cannot be deployed under certain circumstances, and those are met in *P1*.

To motivate these ideas, we look to causation again. Consider the structure of causation of negative events or absences. (I assume these things exist.) Say that the placing of a hand in a certain position caused a shadow in the grass. The shadow is an absence, the absence of light. How is the placing of the hand able to cause the absence of light on the grass? The causing of an absence is intimately connected to the prevention of a positive event. The hand prevented light from being on the grass. How does the placing of the hand prevent the light from being on the grass? The hand excluded a condition that would have caused light on the grass. Generally speaking we can say:

> Fact/Event C causes fact $\neg E$ (C prevents E) iff C is identical to, or causes, a condition D that excludes a causally sufficient condition for E.

Exclusion here means that given the physical laws, it follows from C, and other facts, that D will not obtain.

The suggestion I want to pursue is that analytic making of negative facts works in a structurally identical way to prevention. If some facts, Fp_1, $Fp_2, \ldots Fp_n$ bring about a negative fact $F\neg q$, that is,

(23) Fp_1, $Fp_2, \ldots Fp_n$ (together) *make-the case* $F\neg q$,

then the facts Fp_1, $Fp_2, \ldots Fp_n$ do so by preventing a positive fact Fq. That means that they together exclude a condition that brings about Fq. To determine what would bring about Fq we need to apply the converse of introduction rules to q – we need to apply elimination rules to specify a condition that is explicitly incompatible with p_1, $p_2, \ldots p_n$. In other words, in the proof that supports the making judgement (23), elimination rules have to come in a specific point. That point is the following. The proof the underpins the judgement for assertion of (23) will be a reductio proof with supposition q, with premises p_1, $p_2, \ldots p_n$, with the structure in Figure 11.3 below.

In this proof, we may use introduction rules in the main line, on the premises p_1, $p_2, \ldots p_n$, but in the main line of the reductio sub-proof, beginning with hypothesis q, all the inference rules we apply to q are elimination rules.

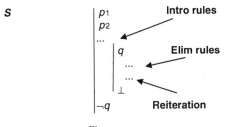

Figure 11.3

The proof structure *S* is exhibited by *P2*, but not by *P1*. In *P1* introduction rules are deployed in the reduction sub-proof, whereas they should be elimination rules for the hypothesis *p*. On the other hand, *P2* uses only elimination rules in the main line of the reduction sub-proof for hypothesis (*p* v *q*). That is the solution to our problem. We have modified the basic picture of the analytic recipe theory presented in Section 11.2, but not drastically, and in line with the intuitive idea that analytic making parallels the structure of causation. So, in sum, in making a making statement, the speaker expresses a commitment to a derivation that used introduction rules at all places, except for the rules applied to suppositions of reductio proofs.

Elimination rules of negation

We have not yet finished with analytic making and negation. We need to consider elimination rules for negation. We have assumed classical logic, and so the elimination rule is: $\neg\neg p \vdash p$. The corresponding making statement is predicted to be unintuitive:

(24) F$\neg\neg p$ *makes-true* $<p>$.

And that seems right, for already familiar reasons. The proposition $<p>$ is made true by Fp, and Fp makes-the case F$\neg\neg p$, but not vice versa.

11.5 EXPRESSIVISM, REALISM, AND METAPHYSICS

Assertions about making express commitments to derivations involving introduction rules – but with elimination rules applied in the manner specified in Section 11.4 in the case of negatives. I emphasize that it is not being proposed that statements about making are statements *about* commitments to derivations. Derivations are semantic/cognitive entities.

We are not giving the truth-conditions for statements of making. Rather we must say that statements of making are *expressions* of commitment to such derivations, where *expressing* is not a semantic relation, like representing.

Isn't the fact that we have offered an analysis of making-claims in expressivist terms an indication that there is no making after all? Compare the case of value. Expressivists propose that in asserting that *x is good*, the speaker expresses a motivational state. Values have no role in the account at all in the analysis of how value-language works. So values have been dispensed with in the explanation of our talk about value. So isn't that a good reason to conclude that values don't exist. So our talk about value needs to be understood in quasi-realist or fictionalist terms.[9] There are not values, but we talk as if there are. So, you might think the same holds for making. Making does not exist, but we talk as if it does.

Now maybe we can live with fictionalism or quasi-realism about making. But I don't think we have to accept the argument that leads to that conclusion. The argument was this: if a referent has no role in the account of talk about it, then we should conclude that the referent does not exist. But why accept this premise? Why can't we hold that value terms really do pick out values, it's just that values have no explanatory role in the account of talk about values. We are not proposing that values have no explanatory roles whatsoever. Perhaps they can have a role in explaining why people behave in certain ways. We are just denying that they have a role in the account of what goes on in the language activity of value-talk. (In the account of the causal structure of speech-acts, and the causal-account of their production.)

In taking this line, however, we really have to insist that in using value language, we are really referring to values. They are really there to be referred to. But to take this line we have to deny the following thesis, which, to some, will appear quite natural:

> **(ER) Explanatory Representationalism:** Any assignment to sentences or phrases of reference to real things *F* requires that *Fs*, or things in terms of which they can be defined, be part of the account of how the talk using those sentences and phrases function.

We must deny this thesis. So, in other words, we must be able to assert *O is referring to Fs with her terms T, but Fs have no role in the account of O's use of T.* Value-expressivism's non-representational stance to

---

[9] This seems to be the view of Blackburn 1984. It's also taken on by Kalderon 2007.

value-vocabulary cannot help but have implications for the kind of stance we take to certain other vocabularies, in particular the semantic vocabularies. So, O may say things like *The term 'goodness' is being used to refer to goodness.* If the language activity underpinning term *refers* requires an explanatory representationalist stance – explaining use of O *is referring to Fs* requires appeal to *Fs* or things in terms of which they can be defined – then that conflicts with the expressivism in relation to *goodness.* What we must do here is bite the bullet, and extend our expressivism to the semantic vocabulary. So, in explaining what goes on when a speaker U asserts O *is referring to goodness,* the referent of the term goodness cannot have an explanatory role. Generally: an expressivist about a vocabulary *D* who wants to be a realist about *D*, will have to extend their expressivism to the semantic vocabulary for talk about the semantic features of *D*.

Just what expressivism about the semantic vocabulary looks like is another matter. But let us bypass that question, which I deal with elsewhere,[10] and ask how the resulting theory will differ from straight realism. It is thought that expressivism about value is attractive because it allows us to escape questions to which a commitment to values gives rise. The feared questions are metaphysical: what are these queer beings that we call values that somehow have a compelling power on our motivational systems? I submit, however, that if our expressivism extends to the semantic vocabulary, to talk of reference and truth, then we do not have to dump realism. We can keep realism, but still escape metaphysical quandaries about value. Concerning values, we can say: values exist, but there is no theoretical requirement to give a theory of what value is. This is not to say that values are metaphysically primitives, but to say that they are without metaphysical nature. The empire of metaphysical concern cannot extend to them. In short, we have realism without an attendant obligation to uncover the metaphysical nature of things we take to exist.

If we apply this orientation to the language of making, and its subject matter, the relation of making, the result we get is this. There is making, the making that goes on when how things are with the world make propositions true, it's just that there is nothing to say about what it is. We have evacuated the question of its nature of any positive content. In other words, making is real but without any positive metaphysical nature. That conclusion seems very paradoxical. In metaphysics, we are

---

[10] See Barker 2004, 2007 for a theory about what such expressivism looks like.

very used to asking questions about the nature of *Fs* for any *F.* We always ask: *what does being F consist in?* It seems our answer in the case of values, or making, if we follow the present line, is that there is nothing these things consist in. We have realism but without any metaphysical essence to the beings concerned.

We can now turn this attitude and orientation to fact-talk itself. My strategy in relation to making-statements embraces ecumenicalism about facts. So the facts are all out there. But of course, the commitment to a plenitude of facts will offend those committed to ontological austerity problems. How can you allow all these beings? But what lies behind this fear of ontological hypertrophy about facts is an assumption that facts, if they exist, have some metaphysical nature, and the metaphysical nature of negative or universal facts will be odd indeed. So, goes the familiar line of thought, we need to deny their existence. But here's the alternative approach I want to pursue. We extend our expressivism to talk of facts, and the result will be that we can say that facts of all kinds exist, it's just that they have no inherent metaphysical nature to speak of, and so, positing them comes with no ontological cost about what they are, with the attendant fear of the supposed queerness of negative facts or universals facts. What would this expressivism about fact-talk be?

The core idea is that fact-talk involves *nominalization.* Basically, in using *the fact that p* as a referring term to refer to a fact, the speaker U asserts *p* but, through the grammatical modifier *the fact that* attached to *p*, U enables the asserted sentence to combine with a predicate to form a sentence. So in assertion of a sentence like:

F*p makes-the case* F*q*

the speaker U performs three intimately connected assertions: *(i)* U asserts that *p* and that *q*; *(ii)* U attaches 'F' to each sentence enabling the resulting expressions to combine with the predicate *make-the case*; and *(iii)* U makes an assertion with the whole sentence, which means U expresses a commitment to a proof-construction involving *p* and *q*.[11] Any assertion, of no matter what logical complexity, can be nominalized.

This analysis of fact-talk does not give facts themselves any explanatory role in the account of what goes on in the production of sentences about

---

[11] This approach needs further development to deal with embedding of fact-locutions, as in: *If Hitler had invaded England, then the fact that he invaded England would have meant all subsequent history was different.* In this case, the use of the fact locution carries no commitment to a fact.

facts. Yet, I submit, it is consistent with realism about facts. Facts exist. Of course, some people may balk at the idea that in the speech acts we perform in using *Fp* and *Fq* – nominalized assertions – we are performing referring acts. How can these terms, used in this way, really be referring terms?[12] The reason they balk at this is that they are implicitly accepting explanatory representationalism, or *ER*. *ER* implies that in order for something to be a referring term, it must be part of the explanation of what a speaker does in using the term that an object is assigned to the term. But in characterizing the function of *Fp* and *Fq*, on the nominalization model, no such function is assigned.

The expressivism we offer, however, is all for denying *ER*, and so will challenge this object. If that response works, then I think we can move towards possibly saying the following. Facts of all kinds exist, but facts as such have no metaphysical nature to speak of, and so, worries about the inherent nature of negative or even positive facts assume falsely that there is something to worry about – the metaphysical nature of facts. If this response works, then we are fully on our way to embracing a fully articulated conception of truth-making, but without the distortions that come with metaphysical austerity programs. But the way to do this is to embrace expressivism about truth-making.

---

[12] We are not saying that some asserted sentences are referring terms. It is rather that some terms of the form *that S* are derived from sentences, by addition of *that*. The resulting term has the syntax of a referring term. One might say that primary referring terms, terms that are not nominalizations, fix the syntax, which nominalizations, then borrow, enabling them to function as referring terms.

Bibliography

Achinstein, P. 1975. 'Causation, Transparency, and Emphasis', *Canadian Journal of Philosophy* 5: 1–23

Alexander, H. G. 1956. *The Leibniz-Clarke Correspondence.* Manchester University Press

Allen, R. E. 1970. *Plato's 'Euthyphro' and the Earlier Theory of Forms.* London: Routledge

Armstrong, D. M. 1997. *A World of States of Affairs.* Cambridge: Cambridge University Press

2004. *Truth and Truthmakers.* Cambridge: Cambridge University Press

Audi, P. forthcoming. 'Grounding: Toward a Theory of the In Virtue Of Relation', *Journal of Philosophy*

unpublished manuscript a. 'How Do Properties Account for Causal Powers?'

unpublished manuscript b. 'How to Rule Out Disjunctive Properties'

unpublished manuscript c. 'Non-Causal Determination'

Ayer, A. J. 1959. *Logical Positivism.* New York: The Free Press

Azzouni, J. 2004. *Deflating Existential Consequence: A Case for Nominalism.* Oxford University Press

2007. 'Ontological Commitment in the Vernacular', *Noûs* 41, 2: 204–26

2009. 'Evading Truth Commitments: The Problem Reanalyzed', *Logique & Analyse*: 139–76

2010a. 'Ontology and the Word "Exist": Uneasy Relations', *Philosophia Mathematica* 18, 1: 74–101

2010b. *Talking About Nothing: Numbers, Hallucinations and Fictions.* Oxford University Press

Barker, S. J. 2007. *Global Expressivism.* University of Nottingham ePrints manuscript. 'Alethic Reality and Truth-Making'

2011. 'Faultless Disagreement, Cognitive Expressivism, and Absolute, but Non-Objective Truth', *Proceedings of the Aristotelian Society* 110: 183–99

Barker, S. J. and Jago, M. forthcoming. 'Being Positive About Negative Facts', *Philosophy and Phenomenological Research*

Batchelor, R. 2010. 'Grounds and Consequences', *Grazer Philosophische Studien* 80: 65–77

Baumgarten, A. G. 1757. *Metaphysica.* 4th edn. Magdeburg: Hemmerde

Beebee, H. and Dodd, J. (eds.) 2005. *Truthmakers: The Contemporary Debate.* Oxford: Clarendon Press

Beebee, H., Hitchcock, C., and Menzies, P. (eds.) 2009. *The Oxford Handbook of Causation.* Oxford University Press

Bennett, J. 1988. *Events and Their Names.* Indianapolis: Hackett

2001. *Learning from Six Philosophers.* Oxford University Press

Bennett, K. 2011. 'Construction Area (No Hard Hat Required)', *Philosophical Studies* 154, 1: 79–104

forthcoming. 'By Our Bootstraps', *Philosophical Perspectives*

Bermúdez, J. L. (ed.) 2005. *Thought, Reference, and Experience: Themes from the Philosophy of Gareth Evans.* Oxford: Clarendon Press

Bigelow, J. 1988. *The Reality of Numbers.* Oxford University Press

Bird, A. 2007a. 'The Regress of Pure Powers?', *Philosophical Quarterly* 57: 513–34

2007b. *Nature's Metaphysics: Laws and Properties.* Oxford: Clarendon Press

Blackburn, S. 1987. 'Morals and Modals', in MacDonald and Wright 1986

1993. *Essays in Quasi-Realism.* New York: Oxford University Press

Bolzano, B. 1810. *Beyträge zu einer begründeteren Darstellung der Mathematik.* Prag: Caspar Widtmann

1810–12. 'Aetiologie' (manuscript, posthumously published), in *Bernard Bolzano Gesamtausgabe, Stuttgart:* 1969ff. Volume II A 5, 75–112

1837. *Wissenschaftslehre* (4 vols.). Sulzbach: Seidel

1838. 'Was ist Philosophie?', in *Bernard Bolzano Gesamtausgabe, Stuttgart:* 1969ff. Volume II A 12/3, 13–33.

Bottani, A. and Davies, R. (eds.) 2006. *Modes of Existence.* Frankfurt a. M.: Ontos

Bottani, A., Carrara, M., and Giaretta, P. (eds.) 2002. *Individuals, Essence and Identity: Themes of Analytic Philosophy.* Dordrecht: Kluwer

Bradley, F. H. 1969. *Appearance and Reality: A Metaphysical Essay.* 2nd edn. Oxford University Press

Cameron, R. 2007. 'How to Be a Truthmaker Maximalist', *Noûs* 42, 3: 410–21

2008a. 'Truthmakers and Ontological Commitment: Or, How to Deal with Complex Objects and Mathematical Ontology without Getting into Trouble', *Philosophical Studies* 140, 1: 1–18

2008b. 'Truthmakers, Realism and Ontology', in Le Poidevin 2008, 107–208

forthcoming. 'Truth-Makers', in Glanzberg, M. *Oxford Handbook of Truth.* Oxford University Press

Campbell, K. 1990. *Abstract Particulars.* Oxford: Basil Blackwell

Caputo, S. 2007. 'Truth-making: What it is not and What it Could be', in Monnoyer 2007, 275–311

Carnap, R. 1931. 'Überwindung der Metaphysik durch logische Analyse der Sprache', *Erkenntnis* 2: 219–41

1932. 'The Elimination of Metaphysics through Logical Analysis of Language', in Ayer 1959, 60–81

Chalmers, D., Manley, D., and Wasserman, R. (eds.) 2009. *Metametaphysics: New Essays on the Foundations of Ontology.* Oxford University Press

Chisholm, R. 1994. 'Ontologically Dependent Entities', *Philosophy and Phenomenological Research* 54, 3: 499–507

Clatterbaugh, K. C. 1973. *Leibniz's Doctrine of Individual Accidents.* Wiesbaden: Franz Steiner Verlag

Cohen, R., Hooker, C., Michalos, A., and van Evra, J. (eds.) 1974. *Proceedings of the 1974 Biennial Meeting, Philosophy of Science Association.* Dordrecht: Reidel Publishing

Collins, J., Hall, N., and Paul, L. A. (eds.) 2004. *Causation and Counterfactuals.* Cambridge: MIT Press

Corkum, P. 2008. 'Aristotle on Ontological Dependence', *Phronesis* 53: 65–92
forthcoming. 'Substance and Independence in Aristotle', in Hoeltje, Schnieder, and Steinberg forthcoming

Correia, F. 2004. 'Husserl on Foundation', *Dialectica* 58, 3: 349–67
2005. *Existential Dependence and Cognate Notions.* Munich: Philosophia Verlag
2008. 'Ontological Dependence', *Philosophy Compass* 3: 1013–32
2010. 'Grounding and Truth-Functions', *Logique et Analyse* 53: 251–79
2011. 'From Grounding to Truth-Making: Some Thoughts', in A. Reboul, *Philosophical papers dedicated to Kevin Mulligan* (online)
forthcoming a. 'On the Reduction of Necessity to Essence', *Philosophy and Phenomenological Research*
forthcoming b. 'Metaphysical Grounds and Essence', in Hoeltje, Schnieder, and Steinberg forthcoming

Cover, J. and O'Leary-Hawthorne, J. 1999. *Substance and Individuation in Leibniz.* Cambridge University Press

Craver, C. 2007. *Explaining the Brain.* Oxford University Press

Creath, R. 1990. *Dear Carnap, Dear Van: The Quine-Carnap Correspondence and Related Work.* Berkeley: University of California Press

Crusius, C. 1743. *De usu et limitibus principii rationis determinantis vulgo sufficientis.* Leipzig

Dancy, J. 1993. *Moral Reasons.* Oxford: Blackwell

Dasgupta, S. manuscript. 'On the Plurality of Grounds'

Davidson, D. 1967. 'Causal Relations', in Davidson 1986, 149–62
1977. 'The Method of Truth in Metaphysics', in Davidson 1986, 199–214
1980. 'The Individuation of Events', in Davidson 1986
1984. *Inquiries into Truth and Interpretation.* New York: Oxford University Press
1986. *Essays on Actions and Events.* Oxford University Press

Della Rocca, M. 2003. 'A Rationalist Manifesto: Spinoza and the Principle of Sufficient Reason', *Philosophical Topics* 31: 75–93
2008a. 'Rationalism Run Amok: Representation and the Reality of Affects in Spinoza', in Huenemann 2008, 26–52
2008b. *Spinoza.* New York: Routledge
2010. 'PSR', *Philosophers' Imprint* 10, 1–13
forthcoming. 'Rationalism, Idealism, Monism, and Beyond', in Förster and Melamed forthcoming

deRosset, L. 2010. 'Getting Priority Straight', *Philosophical Studies* 149: 73–97

Dipert, R. R. 1997. 'The Mathematical Structure of the World: The World as Graph', *Journal of Philosophy* 94: 329–58

Divers, J. 2002. *Possible Worlds*. London: Routledge

Dodd, J. 2007. 'Negative Truths and Truthmaker Principles', *Synthese* 156: 383–401

Dorr, C. 2002. The Simplicity of Everything. Ph.D. Dissertation, Princeton University. Online available at http://users.ox.ac.uk/~sfop0257/papers/SimplicityOfEverything.pdf

Field, H. 1972. 'Tarski's Theory of Truth', *Journal of Philosophy* 69, 347–75

1980. *Science Without Numbers: A Defence of Nominalism*. Library of Philosophy and Logic. Oxford: Blackwell

1984. 'Critical Notice of Crispin Wright: Frege's Conception of Numbers as Objects', *Canadian Journal of Philosophy* 14: 637–62. Reprinted in Field 1989, 147–70

1989. *Realism, Mathematics and Modality*. Oxford: Blackwell.

1994. 'Deflationist Views of Meaning and Content', *Mind* 103: 249–85. Reprinted in Field 2001, 332–60

2001. *Truth and the Absence of Fact*. New York: Oxford University Press

Fine, K. 1975. 'Review of *Counterfactuals* by David Lewis', *Mind* 84: 451–8. Reprinted in Fine 2005a

1991. 'The Study of Ontology', *Noûs* 25: 263–94

1994. 'Essence and Modality', *Philosophical Perspectives* 8: 1–16

1995a. 'Ontological Dependence', *Proceedings of the Aristotelian Society* 95: 269–90

1995b. 'Senses of Essence', in Sinnott-Armstrong, Raffman, and Asher 1995, 53–73

1995c. 'The Logic of Essence', *Journal of Philosophical Logic* 24: 241–73

2001 'The Question of Realism', *Philosopher's Imprint* 1, 1: 1–30. Reprinted in Bottani, Carrara, and Giaretta 2002, 3–41

2005a. *Modality and Tense: Philosophical Papers*. Oxford: Clarendon Press

2005b. 'The Varieties of Necessity', in Fine 2005a

2010a. 'Towards a Theory of Part', *Journal of Philosophy* 107, 11, 559–89

2010b. 'Some Puzzles of Ground', *Notre Dame Journal of Formal Logic* 51, 1: 97–118

2012a. 'The Pure Logic of Ground', *Review of Symbolic Logic* 5, 1: 1–25

2012b. 'Counterfactuals without Possible Worlds', to appear in *Journal of Philosophy*

manuscript. 'Factualist Semantics'

Forbes, G. 1985. *The Metaphysics of Modality*, Clarendon Library of Logic and Philosophy. Oxford University Press

Förster, E. and Melamed, Y. (eds.) forthcoming. *Spinoza and German Idealism*. Cambridge University Press

Fox, J. F. 1987. 'Truthmaker', *Australasian Journal of Philosophy* 65: 188–207

Bibliography

French, S. and Krause, D. 2006. *Identity in Physics: A Historical, Philosophical, and Formal Analysis.* Oxford: Clarendon Press

Garfinkel, A. 1981. *Forms of Explanation: Rethinking the Questions in Social Theory.* New Haven: Yale University Press

Gasking, D. 1955. 'Causation and Recipes', *Mind* 54: 479–87

Gillet, C. and Loewer, B. (eds.) 2001. *Physicalism and its Discontents.* Cambridge: Cambridge University Press.

Goodman, N. 1951. *The Structure of Appearance.* Indianpolis: Bobbs-Merrill Publishing Company

1954. *Fact, Fiction and Forecast.* Cambridge: Harvard University Press

Hale, R. and Hoffman, A. (eds.) 2010. *Modality: Metaphysics, Logic, and Epistemology.* New York: Oxford University Press

Hall, N. 2000. 'Causation and the Price of Transitivity', *Journal of Philosophy* 97: 198–222

Hall, N. and Paul, L. A. forthcoming. *Causation: A User's Guide.* Oxford University Press

Halpern, J. 2000. 'Axiomatizing Causal Reasoning', *Journal of Artifical Intelligence Research* 12: 317–37

Hawthorne J. 2006. *Metaphysical Essays.* Oxford University Press

Heil, J. 2003. *From a Logical Point of View.* Oxford: Clarendon Press

2004. 'Properties and Powers', *Oxford Studies in Metaphysics* 1: 223–54

Hempel, C. G. 1965. *Aspects of Scientific Explanation.* New York: The Free Press

Henninger, M. G. 1989. *Relations: Medieval Theories 1250–1325.* Oxford: Clarendon Press

Hitchcock, C. R. 1996. 'The Role of Contrast in Causal and Explanatory Claims', *Synthese* 107: 395–419

2001. 'The Intransitivity of Causation Revealed in Equations and Graphs', *Journal of Philosophy* 98: 273–99

Hocutt, M. 1974. 'Aristotle's Four Becauses', *Philosophy* 49, 385–99

Hoeltje, M., Schnieder, B., and Steinberg A. (eds.) forthcoming. *Dependence.* Munich: Philosophia Verlag

Hofweber, T. 2009. 'Ambitious, Yet Modest, Metaphysics', in Chalmers, Manley, and Wasserman 2009, 260–89

Horgan, T. and Potrč, M. 2008. *Austere Realism: Contextual Semantics Meets Minimal Ontology.* Cambridge: MIT Press

Hornsby, J. 2005. 'Truth without Truth-Making Entities', in Beebee and Dodd 2005, 33–47

Horsten, L. 2010. 'Impredicative Identity Criteria', *Philosophy and Phenomenological Research* 80: 411–39

Horwich, P. 2006. 'Red in Truth and Core', *Times Literary Supplement,* 6 January: 26

2008. 'Being and Truth', *Midwest Studies in Philosophy* 32: 258–73

Huenemann, C. (ed.) 2008. *Interpreting Spinoza.* Cambridge University Press

Husserl, E. 1900–1901. *Logische Untersuchungen.* Halle: M. Niemeyer

Jackson, F. 1998. *From Metaphysics to Ethics: A Defence of Conceptual Analysis.* Oxford: Clarendon Press

manuscript. 'Some Reflections on Representationalism'

Jackson, F. and Priest, G. (eds.) 2004. *Lewisian Themes: The Philosophy of David K. Lewis.* Oxford University Press.

Jago, M. 2009. 'The Conjunction and Disjunction Theses', *Mind* 118: 411–15

Jenkins, C. 2011. 'Is Metaphysical Dependence Irreflexive?', *The Monist* 94: 267–76

Johnston, M. 1997. 'Manifest Kinds', *The Journal of Philosophy* 94, 11: 564–83

2006. 'Hylomorphism', *The Journal of Philosophy* 103, 12: 652–98

Kalderon, M. 2007. *Moral Fictionalism.* Oxford University Press

Kant, I. 1755. *Principiorum primorum cognitionis metaphysicae nova dilucidatio.* Translation in Kant, *Theoretical Philosophy 1755–1770.* Ed. and trans. David Walford and Ralf Meerbote. Cambridge University Press, 1992, 1–45

Kim, J. 1974. 'Noncausal Connections', *Noûs* 8: 41–52

1983. 'Supervenience and Supervenient Causation', *Southern Journal of Philosophy* 22: 45–56

1984. 'Concepts of Supervenience', *Philosophy and Phenomenological Research* 45: 153–76

1993. *Supervenience and the Mind: Selected Philosophical Essays.* Cambridge University Press

1994. 'Explanatory Knowledge and Metaphysical Dependence', *Philosophical Issues Vol. 5: Truth and Rationality*, 51–69

Koslicki, K. 2008. *The Structure of Objects.* Oxford University Press

2012. 'Essence, Necessity and Explanation', in Tahko 2012, 187–206

forthcoming. 'Ontological Dependence: An Opinionated Survey', in Hoeltje, Schnieder, and Steinberg forthcoming

Kripke, S. 1980. *Naming and Necessity.* Cambridge: Harvard University Press

Kulstad, M. 1980. 'A Closer Look at Leibniz's Alleged Reduction of Relations', *Southern Journal of Philosophy* 18: 417–32

Künne, W. 2003. *Conceptions of Truth.* Oxford: Clarendon Press

Ladyman, J. 2007. 'On the Identity and Diversity of Objects in a Structure', *Proceedings of the Aristotelian Society* 81: 23–43

Le Poidevin, R. (ed.) 2008. *Being: Contemporary Developments in Metaphysics. Royal Institute of Philosophy Supplement*, vol. 83. Cambridge University Press

Leibniz, G. W. *Leibniz: Philosophical Essays.* Trans. by R. Ariew and D. Garber. Indianapolis: Hackett, 1989

New Essays on Human Understanding. Ed. and trans. P. Remnant and J. Bennett. Cambridge University Press, 1981

De Summa Rerum: Metaphysical Papers, 1675–1676. Ed. and trans. G. H. R. Parkinson. New Haven: Yale University Press, 1992

Die Philosophischen Schriften von Gottfried Wilhelm Leibniz. 7 vols. Ed. C. Berlin: Weidmann, Gerhardt 1875–1890

Gottfried Wilhelm Leibniz: Fragmente zur Logik. Ed. F. Schmidt. Berlin: Akademie Verlag, 1960

Opuscules et Fragments Inédits de Leibniz: Extraits des Manuscrits de la Bibliothèque Royale de Hanovre. Ed. L. Couturat. Reprinted Hildesheim: Olms Verlag, 1903

Philosophical Papers and Letters. Ed. and trans. L. Loemker. Dordrecht: Reidel, 1969

Sämtliche Schriften und Briefe. Darmstadt and Berlin: Berlin Academy, 1923–present

Textes inédits d'après les manuscrits de la Bibliothèque provinciale de Hanovre, vol. II. G. Grua. Paris: Presses Universitaires de France, 1948

Theodicy. Trans. by E. M. Huggard. LaSalle, Illinois: Open Court, 1985

Lepore, E. 1995. 'Quine, Analyticity and Transcendence', *Noûs* 29: 468–80

Lepore, E. and McLaughlin, B. (eds.) 1985. *Actions and Events: Perspectives on the Philosophy of Donald Davidson.* Oxford: Blackwell

Leuenberger, S. 2008. 'Supervenience in Metaphysics', *Philosophy Compass* 3: 749–62

Lewis, D. 1975. 'Language and languages', in *Minnesota Studies in the Philosophy of Science,* vol. VII. Minneapolis: University of Minnesota Press, 3–35

1984. 'Putnam's Paradox', *Australasian Journal of Philosophy* 62, 3: 221–36

1986. *On The Plurality of Worlds.* Oxford: Basil Blackwell

1991. *Parts of Classes.* Oxford: Basil Blackwell

1999a. *Papers on Metaphysics and Epistemology.* Cambridge University Press

1999b. 'New Work for a Theory of Universals', in Lewis 1999a, 8–55

1999c. 'Reduction of Mind', in Lewis 1999a, 291–324

2000. 'Causation as Influence', *Journal of Philosophy* 97: 182–97

2003. 'Things qua Truthmakers' and postscript, in Rodríguez-Pereyra 2003, 25–42

Lewis, D. and Lewis, S. 1970. 'Holes', *Australasian Journal of Philosophy* 48, 2: 206–12

1986. 'Holes', *Philosophical Papers,* vol. I. Oxford University Press, 3–9

Liggins, D. 2008. 'Truthmakers and the Groundedness of Truth', *Proceedings of the Aristotelian Society* 108: 177–96

Locke, J. 1975. *An Essay Concerning Human Understanding.* Oxford: Clarendon Press

Loewer, B. 2001. 'From Physics to Physicalism', in Gillet and Loewer, 37–56

Loux, M. J. and Zimmerman, D. W. (eds.) 2005. *The Oxford Handbook of Metaphysics.* Oxford University Press

Lowe, E. J. 1989a. 'What is a Criterion of Identity?', *Philosophical Quarterly* 39: 1–21

1989b. 'Impredicative Identity Criteria and Davidson's Criterion of Event Identity', *Analysis:* 178–81

1994. 'Ontological Dependency', *Philosophical Papers* 23, 1: 31–48

1995. 'The Metaphysics of Abstract Objects', *Journal of Philosophy* 92: 509–24

1998. *The Possibility of Metaphysics: Substance, Identity, and Time.* Oxford University Press

2002. *A Survey of Metaphysics.* Oxford University Press

2003. 'Individuation', in Loux and Zimmerman 2005.

2005a. 'Identity, Vagueness, and Modality', in Bermúdez 2005

2005b. 'Ontological Dependence', *Stanford Encyclopedia of Philosophy*. Online available at http://plato.stanford.edu/entries/dependence-ontological/ (last revised in 2009)

2006a. *The Four-Category Ontology: A Metaphysical Foundation for Natural Science*. Oxford: Clarendon Press

2006b. 'Powerful Particulars: Review Essay on John Heil's *From an Ontological Point of View*', *Philosophy and Phenomenological Research* 72: 466–79

2007. 'Sortals and the Individuation of Objects', *Mind and Language* 22: 514–33

2009. 'An Essentialist Approach to Truth-Making', in Lowe and Rami 2008, 201–16

2010. 'On the Individuation of Powers', in Marmodoro 2010

Lowe, E. J. and Rami, A. (eds.) 2008. *Truth and Truth-Making*. Durham: Acumen Publishing

MacBride, F. 2005. 'Lewis's Animadversions on the Truthmaker Principle', in Beebee and Dodd 2005, 117–40

MacDonald, G. and Wright, C. (eds.) 1986. *Fact, Science and Value: Essays in Honor of A. J. Ayer's 'Language, Truth and Logic'*. Oxford: Blackwell

Mackie, J. L. 1977. *Ethics: Inventing Right and Wrong*. Harmondsworth: Penguin

Mackie, P. 2006. *How Things Might Have Been: Individuals, Kinds, and Essential Properties*. Oxford: Clarendon Press

Mancosu, P. 1999. 'Bolzano and Cournot on Mathematical Explanation', *Revue d'histoire des sciences* 52, 429–56

Marmodoro, A. (ed.) 2010. *The Metaphysics of Powers: Their Grounding and Their Manifestations*. London and New York: Routledge

Maslen, C. 2004. 'Causes, Contrasts, and the Nontransitivity of Causation', in Collins, Hall, and Paul 2004, 341–57

Mates, B. 1986. *The Philosophy of Leibniz: Metaphysics and Language*. Oxford University Press

McCullough, L. B. 1996. *Leibniz on Individuals and Individuation: The Persistence of Premodern Ideas in Modern Philosophy*. Dordrecht: Kluwer

McDermott, M. 1995. 'Redundant Causation', *British Journal for the Philosophy of Science* 46: 523–44

Melia, J. 1995. 'On What There's Not', *Analysis* 55: 223–9

2000. 'Weaseling Away the Indispensibility Argument', *Mind* 109: 455–80

2003. *Modality*. Chesham: Acumen Press

2005. 'Truth without Truthmakers', in Beebee and Dodd 2005, 67–84

Menzies, P. 2007. 'Causation in Context', in Price and Corry 2007, 191–223

2009. 'Platitudes and Counterexamples', in Beebee, Hitchcock, and Menzies 2009, 341–67

Merricks, T. 2001. *Objects and Persons*. Oxford: Clarendon Press

2007. *Truth and Ontology*. Oxford: Clarendon Press

Molnar, G. 2000. 'Truthmakers and Negative Truths', *Australian Journal of Philosophy* 78: 72–86

2003. *Powers: A Study in Metaphysics*. Oxford University Press

Monnoyer, J.-M. (ed.) 2007. *Metaphysics and Truthmakers*. Frankfurt a. M.: Ontos

Morganti, M. 2009. 'Ontological Priority, Fundamentality and Monism', *Dialectica* 63: 271–88

Mugnai, M. 1992. *Leibniz' Theory of Relations*. Stuttgart: Franz Steiner Verlag

forthcoming. 'Leibniz's Ontology of Relations: A Last Word?', Oxford Studies in Early Modern Philosophy

manuscript. 'Leibniz-Bradley'

Mulligan, K. 2006. 'Facts, Formal Objects and Ontology', in Bottani and Davies 2006, 31–46

Mulligan, K., Simons, P., and Smith, B. 1984. 'Truth-Makers', *Philosophy and Phenomenological Research* 44: 287–321

Mumford, S. (ed.) 2003. *Russell on Metaphysics*. London: Routledge

Nolan, D. P. 2002. *Topics in the Philosophy of Possible Worlds*. London: Routledge

Northcott, R. 2008. 'Causation and Contrast Classes', *Philosophical Studies* 139: 111–23

Oliver, A. 1996. 'The Metaphysics of Properties', *Mind* 105: 1–80

Orilia, F. 2009. 'Bradley's Regress and Ungrounded Dependence Chains', *Dialectica* 63: 333–41

Owen, G. E. L. 1965. 'Inherence', *Phronesis* 10: 97–105

Paul, L. A. 2000. 'Aspect Causation', *Journal of Philosophy* 97: 235–56

Pearl, J. 2000. *Causality: Models, Reasoning and Inference*. Cambridge University Press

Peramatzis, M. 2008. 'Aristotle's Notion of Priority in Nature and Substance', *Oxford Studies in Ancient Philosophy* 35: 187–247

Plantinga, A. 1974. *The Nature of Necessity*. Oxford: Clarendon Press

Plato. 2004. *Laches*. Whitefish: Kessinger Publishing

Price, H. 1992. 'Agency and Causal Symmetry', *Mind* 101: 501–20

Price, H. and Corry, R. (eds.) 2007. *Causation, Physics and the Constitution of Reality: Russell's Republic Revisited*. Oxford University Press

Prior, A. 1971. *Objects of Thought*. Oxford University Press

Putnam, H. 1971. *Philosophy of Logic*. London: George Allen and Unwin

Quine, W. V. O. 1948. 'On What There Is', *Review of Metaphysics* 5: 21–38

1951a. 'Two Dogmas of Empiricism', *Philosophical Review* 60: 20–43

1951b. 'Ontology and Ideology', *Philosophical Studies* 2: 11–15

1960. *Word and Object*. Cambridge: MIT Press

1969a. 'Epistemology naturalized', in Quine 1969d, 69–90

1969b. 'Existence and Quantification', in Quine 1969d, 91–113

1969c. 'Speaking of Objects', in Quine 1969d, 1–25

1969d. *Ontological Relativity and Other Essays*. New York: Columbia University Press

Raven M. 2009. Ontology, From a Fundamentalist Point of View. Ph.D., New York University

forthcoming. 'In Defence of Ground', *Australasian Journal of Philosophy*

Rayo, A. 2008. 'On Specifying Truth-Conditions', *Philosophical Review* 117: 385–443

Read, S. 2000. 'Truthmakers and the Disjunction Thesis', *Mind* 109: 67–79

Restall, G. 1995. *What Truthmakers Can Do for You. Automated Reasoning Project.* Canberra: Australian National University

1996. 'Truthmakers, Entailment and Necessity', *Australasian Journal of Philosophy* 74: 331–40

Rodríguez-Pereyra, G. 2002. *Resemblance Nominalism: A Solution to the Problem of Universals.* Oxford: Clarendon Press

(ed.) 2003. *Real Metaphysics.* London and New York: Routledge

2003. 'Resemblance Nominalism and Counterparts: Reply to Bird', *Analysis* 63: 229–37

2005. 'Why Truthmakers', in Beebee and Dodd 2005, 17–31

2006a. 'Truthmakers', *Philosophy Compass* 1 and 2: 186–200

2006b. 'Truthmaking, Entailment, and the Conjunction Thesis', *Mind* 115: 957–82

Rosen, G. 1990. 'Modal Fictionalism', *Mind* 99: 327–54

2010. 'Metaphysical Dependence: Grounding and Reduction', in Hale and Hoffman 2010, 109–36

Ross, W. D. (ed.) 1954. *The Works of Aristotle*, vol. VIII: Metaphysica. Oxford: Clarendon Press

Ruben, D. 1990. *Explaining Explanation.* London and New York: Routledge

Russell, B. 1910. 'Some Explanations in Reply to Mr. Bradley', *Mind* 75: 373–8

1918. *The Philosophy of Logical Atomism.* Reprinted with an introduction by D. Pears 1985. La Salle: Open Court

1919. *Introduction to Mathematical Philosophy.* London: Allen and Unwin

1992. *A Critical Exposition of the Philosophy of Leibniz.* Rev. edn. London: Routledge

2003. 'Analytic Realism', in Mumford 2003, 91–6

Salmon, W. C. 1984. *Scientific Explanation and the Causal Structure of the World.* Princeton University Press

1989. *Four Decades of Scientific Explanation.* Minneapolis: University of Minnesota Press

Sartorio, C. 2006. 'On Causing Something to Happen in a Certain Way Without Causing it to Happen', *Philosophical Studies* 129: 119–36.

Schaffer, J. 2004. 'Quiddistic Knowledge', in Jackson and Priest 2004, 210–30

2005. 'Contrastive Causation', *Philosophical Review* 114: 327–58

2009a. 'Spacetime the One Substance', *Philosophical Studies* 145: 131–48

2009b. 'On What Grounds What', in Chalmers, Manley, and Wasserman 2009, 347–83

2010a. 'Monism: The Priority of the Whole', *Philosophical Review* 119, 1: 31–76

2010b. 'The Internal Relatedness of All Things', *Mind* 119: 341–76

2010c. 'Contrastive Causation in the Law', *Legal Theory* 16: 259–97

forthcoming. 'Causal Contextualisms: Contrast, Default, and Model', in M. Blaauw (ed.), *Contrastivism in Philosophy*. Routledge

manuscript. 'Structural Equation Models of Ground'

Schaffner, K. 1976. 'Reductionism in Biology: Prospects and Problems', in Cohen, Hooker, Michalos, and van Evra 1974, 613–32

Schnieder, B. 2006a. 'A Certain Kind of Trinity: Dependence, Substance, Explanation', *Philosophical Studies* 129: 393–419

2006b. 'Troubles with Truth-Making: Necessitation and Projection', *Erkenntnis* 64: 61–74

2006c. 'Truth-Making Without Truth-Makers', *Synthese* 152: 21–46

2010. 'A Puzzle about "Because"', *Logique & Analyse* 211: 317–43

2011. 'A Logic for "Because"', *The Review of Symbolic Logic* 4: 445–65

forthcoming. 'Bolzano on Causation and Grounding', *Journal of the History of Philosophy*

Schopenhauer, A. 1813. *Über die vierfache Wurzel das Satzes vom zureichenden Grunde*. Rudolstadt: Hof- Buch- und Kunsthandlung

Sharvy, R. 1972. 'Euthyphro 9d–11b: Analysis and Definition in Plato and Others', *Noûs* 6: 119–37

Shoemaker, S. 1998. 'Causal and Metaphysical Necessity', *Pacific Philosophical Quarterly* 79: 59–77

Sider, T. 2007. 'Against Monism', *Analysis* 67: 1–7

2008. 'Monism and Statespace Structure', *Royal Institute of Philosophy Supplements* 83: 129–50

2009. 'Ontological Realism', in Chalmers, Manley, and Wasserman 2009, 384–423

2011. *Writing the Book of the World*. Oxford University Press

Simons, P. 1982. 'Three Essays in Formal Ontology', in Smith 1982, 111–260

1987. *Parts: A Study in Ontology*. Oxford: Clarendon Press

2005. 'Negatives, Numbers and Necessity: Some Worries about Armstrong's Version of Truthmaking', *Australasian Journal of Philosophy* 83: 253–61

Sinnott-Armstrong, W., Raffman, D., and Asher, N. 1995. *Modality, Morality, and Belief: Essays in Honor of Ruth Barcan Marcus*. New York: Cambridge University Press

Skiles, A. manuscript. 'Getting Grounded'

Sklar, L. 1967. 'Types of Inter-Theoretic Reduction', *British Journal for the Philosophy of Science* 18: 109–24

Smith, B. (ed.) 1982. *Parts and Moments: Studies in Logic and Formal Ontology*. Munich: Philosophia Verlag

1999. 'Truthmaker Realism', *Australasian Journal of Philosophy* 77: 274–91

Smith, B. and Mulligan, K. 1982. 'Pieces of a Theory', in Smith 1982, 15–109

Sorensen, R. 2009. 'Nothingness', *Stanford Encyclopedia of Philosophy*. Online available at http://plato.stanford.edu/entries/nothingness/

Spinoza, B. *Spinoza Opera*. Ed. C. Gebhardt. Heidelberg: Carl Winter, 1925

Spinoza: The Letters. Trans. by S. Shirley. Indianapolis: Hackett, 1995

The Collected Works of Spinoza, vol. 1. Ed. and trans. E. Curley. Princeton University Press, 1985

Strevens, M. 2008. *Depth: An Account of Scientific Explanation.* Cambridge: Harvard University Press

Tahko, T. (ed.) 2012. *Contemporary Aristotelian Metaphysics.* Cambridge University Press.

Tatzel, A. 2002. 'Bolzano's Theory of Ground and Consequence', *Notre Dame Journal of Symbolic Logic* 43: 1–25

Taylor, R. 1955. 'Disputes about Synonymy', *The Philosophical Review* 63: 517–29

Terese. 2003. *Term Rewriting Systems.* Cambridge: Cambridge Tracts in Computer Science

Thomasson, A. L. 2006. 'Metaphysical Arguments Against Ordinary Objects', *Philosophical Quarterly* 56: 340–59

Trogdon, K. forthcoming. 'Grounding – An Overview', in Hoeltje, Schnieder, and Steinberg forthcoming

Van Fraassen, B. 1969. 'Facts and Tautological Entailments', *Journal of Philosophy* 66: 477–87

1980. *The Scientific Image.* Oxford University Press

Van Inwagen, P. 1990. *Material Beings.* Ithaca and London: Cornell University Press

2008. *Metaphysics.* 3rd edn. Boulder: Westview

Wedgwood, R. 2007. *The Nature of Normativity.* Oxford: Clarendon Press

Whitcomb, D. 2011. 'Grounding and Omniscience', in *Oxford Studies in Philosophy of Religion* 4

Williams, J. R. G. 2005. The Inscrutability of Reference. Ph.D., University of St Andrews

2007. 'Eligibility and Inscrutability', *Philosophical Review* 116, 3: 361–99

2008. 'The Price of Inscrutability', *Noûs* 42, 4: 600–41

2010. 'Fundamental and Derivative Truths', *Mind* 119: 103–41

Williamson, T. 1999. 'Truthmakers and the Converse Barcan Formula', *Dialectica* 53, 253–270

2000. *Knowledge and its Limits.* Oxford: Clarendon Press

Wilson, J. manuscript. 'The Multiplicity of Grounding'

Woodward, J. 2003. *Making Things Happen: A Theory of Causal Explanation.* Oxford University Press

Yablo, S. 2001. 'Go figure: A Path Through Fictionalism', *Midwest Studies in Philosophy* 25: 72–102

Name index

Subject index

CPSIA information can be obtained at www.ICGtesting.com
Printed in the USA
LVOW10s1124221014

409871LV00005B/10/P